The intellectual development of
Karl Mannheim

The intellectual development of
Karl Mannheim
Culture, politics, and planning

COLIN LOADER

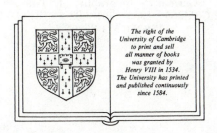

The right of the
University of Cambridge
to print and sell
all manner of books
was granted by
Henry VIII in 1534.
The University has printed
and published continuously
since 1584.

CAMBRIDGE UNIVERSITY PRESS

Cambridge

London   New York   New Rochelle

Melbourne   Sydney

For my parents,
Frederick and Dorothy Loader

Published by the Press Syndicate of the University of Cambridge
The Pitt Building, Trumpington Street, Cambridge CB2 1RP
32 East 57th Street, New York, NY 10022, USA
10 Stamford Road, Oakleigh, Melbourne 3166, Australia

First published 1985

Printed in the United States of America

Library of Congress Cataloging in Publication Data

Loader, Colin, 1941–

The intellectual development of Karl Mannheim.

Includes index.

1. Mannheim, Karl, 1893–1947.   2. Sociologists –
Germany – Biography.   I. Title.
HM22.G8M365   1985   301'.092'4   [B]   84-20040
ISBN 0 521 26567 3

Contents

Contents

Preface

As its title indicates, this is a study in intellectual history, an examination of Karl Mannheim not primarily as a person or as the producer of a consistent body of theory, but as an intellect developing through several sociocultural contexts. It occupies a position somewhere between the presentation of the experiential details of Mannheim's life and the evaluation of his work as a systematic body of theory. Of course, the latter two elements are present to some degree; however, they occupy a secondary position.

I have never gotten to "know" Mannheim as a person. He left little in the way of autobiographical writings, and the surviving correspondence presents him in a less-than-flattering light. Based on the limited number of letters available, one could say that he usually wrote when he needed something. Reminiscences of him are very contradictory and focus mainly on the later English period. The general picture is of a man who was rather traditional and stuffy in his personal bearing.

The difficulties of interpreting his theoretical work will be discussed in the Introduction. Here it suffices to note that most studies of his theory have failed to take into account the developmental nature of his work and therefore have been frustrated by what is seen as an inconsistent eclecticism.

In viewing Mannheim as an intellect, I have arrived at a much more positive picture of him – that of a man dedicated to intellectual growth. His thought experiments, attempts to incorporate a wide variety of ideas and subjects, capacity for self-criticism, and willingness to change, to move on without covering up his tracks – such qualities are worthy of emulation. Although I have not hesitated to criticize Mannheim, I have not been content simply to point out his "mistakes" but have tried to demonstrate their place in the dynamic totality of his thought. By presenting that thought as a dialectical process, by examining his individual

vii

works in the context of the whole, I hope I have provided a different perspective on his ideas.

Throughout this study, I have used shortened titles to refer to Mannheim's works. For example, "On the Interpretation of *'Weltanschauung'*" is referred to as *"Weltanschauung."* The full titles are given in the bibliography.

In the course of my work on Mannheim, I have accumulated a number of intellectual debts. Therefore, I would like to thank the following people and institutions.

The publishers of Mannheim's works have granted permission to quote from those works: Routledge and Kegan Paul for *Ideology and Utopia, Diagnosis of Our Time, Freedom, Power and Democratic Planning, Essays on the Sociology of Knowledge, Essays on Sociology and Social Psychology, Structures of Thinking,* and *Man and Society in an Age of Reconstruction;* Harcourt Brace Jovanovich for *Ideology and Utopia;* and Oxford University Press for *Freedom, Power and Democratic Planning, Essays on the Sociology of Knowledge,* and *Essays on Sociology and Social Psychology.*

The University of Keele Library, England, granted permission to quote from the unpublished papers of Mannheim and Lord A. D. Lindsay. Its archivist, Ian H. C. Fraser, greatly facilitated my work there.

Part of my research was made possible by a fellowship from the Deutscher Akademischer Austauschdienst (DAAD).

David Kettler, Nico Stehr, and especially Volker Meja very graciously shared with me materials by Mannheim as well as prepublication copies of their own work.

The following people provided helpful criticism and/or information: Adolf Lowe, Jean Floud, Jakob Marschak, David Kettler, Allan Megill, Sande Cohen, Peter von Bawey, Steven Seidman, Alois Hahn, John Horton, Hermann Beck, Robert Wohl, and the anonymous readers for the Press.

The following five people made very special contributions to the process that led to this book. Marvin Cox introduced me to intellectual history and gave me the confidence to pursue it. Hayden White introduced me to Mannheim and directed this study at the dissertation stage. Friedrich Tenbruck helped to refine many of my ideas about German culture in general and German sociology in particular. Jeffrey Alexander provided both a critical reading and unflagging support for this project at a time when both were sorely needed. Without his help, the book might never have appeared. My greatest debt is to my wife, Claire Loader, who has assisted in my work in every possible way, from research to editing to material and moral support. I am sure she feels a great sense of relief now that Mannheim, who has always been a part of our marriage, is finally out of the house.

Susan Allen-Mills and the editorial staff of Cambridge University Press have provided friendly and necessary guidance throughout the publication process.

Introduction
Mannheim's career as a dynamic totality

The name Karl Mannheim (1893–1947) is no stranger to most scholars; it appears in a wide variety of contexts, leading one to assume that Mannheim's works are very widely read. His name most often appears in discussions of the sociology of knowledge, which he is credited with co-founding.[1] He also figures prominently in examinations of the concepts of "ideology" and "utopia" and of the roles of intellectuals and elites.[2] His theory of generations has been called the most important contribution to that problem.[3] Intellectual historians have shown admiration for his essay on conservative thought,[4] whereas philosophers have questioned his epistemology and his historicism.[5] An important study in the sociology of literature has been dedicated to him.[6] His theories of planning and education have received attention.[7] His theories have been discussed by thinkers like Theodor Adorno, Karl Popper, and T. S. Eliot,[8] and he has been accorded an important place in the history of sociology and twentieth-century European thought.[9]

Yet, as A. P. Simonds has noted, very little of this literature does justice to Mannheim.[10] Examinations of his work are often superficial, and there is little attempt to make real use of it. Indeed, his work more often than not serves mainly as a straw man. Perhaps the best example of this treatment is the simplistic evaluation of his major work, *Ideology and Utopia,* by the man who translated it in a collection entitled "Twentieth-Century Classics Revisited."[11] Here we see the need to include Mannheim in a list of significant thinkers combined with a dismissal of his work as unrewarding. It's a nice book to visit, but we really wouldn't want to live there.

A large part of the problem is due to the nature of Mannheim's career and work. His theories were developed in three different milieus – Hungary during the first two decades of the twentieth century, Germany during the Weimar Republic (1919–33), and England during the 1930s and 1940s. He grew up in the Jewish commercial community of Budapest; however, part of his formal education was gained in the German university system. He associated with radical and reformist elements of

1

the Budapest intelligentsia and, despite his marginal and nonpolitical role in the unsuccessful Hungarian revolutions of 1918–19, went into exile in Germany when the repressive Horthy regime took power. His German career, which roughly coincided with the lifespan of the Weimar Republic, included stays at Heidelberg and Frankfurt. It was during this period that he formulated his sociology of knowledge, the contribution for which he is best known. In 1933, he was again forced into exile (this time by the Nazis) and took up residence in England. During his English period he was affiliated with the University of London, first with the London School of Economics and then with the Institute of Education. He died in England in 1947. This variety of settings has made his work less accessible to scholars in any one of them.

More important than the number of contexts was his flexible response to this variety of settings. He assumed what he called an "essayistic-experimental attitude," which he described as follows:

> This essayistic-experimental attitude in thought . . . explains why here and there repetitions have not been eliminated and contradictions resolved. The reason for not eliminating repetitions was that the same idea presented itself in a new context and was therefore disclosed in a new light. Contradictions have not been corrected because it is the author's conviction that a given theoretical sketch may often have latent in it varied possibilities which must be permitted to come to expression in order that the scope of the exposition may be truly appreciated. As long . . . as a connection between ideas is still in the process of growth and becoming, one should not hide the possibilities which are still latent in it but should submit it in all its variations to the judgement of the reader.[12]

Mannheim's works all reflect this unsystematic attitude. His prose form, the essay, was conducive to this wide-ranging approach.[13] Most of the essays were between fifty and one hundred pages long. Although they did not systematically exhaust a topic as larger works did, they were more general and complete than the essays one finds in journals catering strictly to specialists. He attempted to be neither definitive nor narrowly limited in his scope. This neither–nor style, which did not try to overwhelm opponents with a mass of data or to escape from them through specialization, invited controversy and challenge; and he found both. One of the main sources of challenge was Mannheim himself. He was constantly introducing new ideas and new terms, or modifying old ideas and old terms, and sometimes changing the ideas but not the terms that expressed them – or vice versa. Some of these competing concepts emerged victorious only to be challenged again, whereas others fell by the wayside. To a certain degree, this takes place with every thinker, but with Mannheim the process was more conscious and more drastic.

The consequences of this "dialectical" style for understanding Mannheim's work are apparent in the secondary literature about him. Most Mannheim scholars, being specialists, do not view this heterogeneity as a problem. Their interpretations, which primarily take the form of periodical literature, isolate and evaluate individual concepts (usually from *Ideology and Utopia*) and make no attempt to connect these to the rest of Mannheim's work.[14] Such an approach has provided insights into Mannheim's writings, but it has also led to some major misunderstandings. The longer studies that have appeared in recent years do not really challenge the pattern established by the periodical literature. Some interpreters divide his work into two periods, separated by his emigration from Germany to England, and then examine one of the periods in terms of one or more central concepts.[15] Others present his works as a chronological series with little attempt to relate one essay to another.[16] In short, these longer studies differ from the periodical literature only quantitatively (they encompass more material) and not qualitatively (they do not attempt to make some sense out of his eclecticism and dialectical style). Although there have been limited attempts to relate concepts in one part of his career with those of another,[17] no one has undertaken a comprehensive interpretation of Mannheim's entire career.[18]

The consequence of this collective piecemeal approach has been the tendency to overlook Mannheim's experimental attitude and to take the heterogeneity of his work simply as a weakness.[19] Even those who recognize Mannheim's experimental approach still generally view him as a confused thinker who has exhausted the patience of many commentators. Those who have tried to defend Mannheim without really taking this heterogeneity into account have actually done him more harm than good. No one, then, has successfully investigated the totality of Mannheim's career in a way that acknowledges its heterogeneity without succumbing to it.

I have attempted to meet this need by interpreting his writings neither as a series of heterogeneous, encapsulated essays nor as two static blocks, but rather as a "dynamic totality," one in which change can be systematically understood. Underlying this totality was a basic purpose that continued throughout his career – the orientation of the individual in the changing modern world. Mannheim's experimental approach, in which concepts for the discussion of this problem of orientation were continually changing, remained subordinate to the basic purpose of orientation, in whose service it comprised a vital element. The singular purpose and the heterogeneous methodology and conceptualization were complementary, not contradictory, for Mannheim. Therefore, presentation of only the heterogeneous experiments in a work that claims to be a comprehensive treatment of his work is a good example of an interpretation not seeing the forest for the trees.

I will undoubtedly be accused of imposing a structure on Mannheim's works and of not presenting them in all their variety. To this I plead "guilty," believing that one must steer perilously close to the Scylla of oversimplification to avoid the more dangerous Charybdis of confused and disorganized heterogeneity. In my interpretation, I have presented the heterogeneity of Mannheim's work, but I have also subordinated it to his single purpose and developmental structure.

To present this "dynamic totality," I have selected six methodological subconcepts derived from Mannheim's own works: (1) dynamic hierarchy, (2) center of construction, (3) analytical and valuative elements, (4) constellation, (5) perspectivism, and (6) the refugee strategy. I will merely introduce these concepts here and will discuss them further, in light of the body of the text, in the Conclusion. I also note that I have taken these concepts out of context, using only those elements of them that meet my own methodological needs; their complete description will be provided in the body of the study. By consciously taking some concepts out of context, I hope to present the dynamic totality of Mannheim's work in context.

A "dynamic hierarchy" consists of a series of temporal types, or stages, designed to demonstrate how ideas and experience interact in an intellectual development. Once, when Mannheim was accused of constructing types that were too "mechanistic," he replied: "If I want to grasp fundamental relationships in the spiritual realm, then I must formalize; if I only want to understand, then I can make do with historical, individual, graphic concepts."[20] In other words, to present more than a simple, straightforward description, to understand how ideas function in a person's intellectual development, it becomes necessary to create types and to relate those types to one another in a hierarchy that is not simply a linear progression. Concepts appear, disappear, and reappear, are modified, promoted, and demoted, but are not simply confined to one stage. Their changing relationship and the effort to make sense out of this kaleidoscopic development is the essence of a dynamic, hierarchical totality.

The "center of construction," which I have used to define the different stages of Mannheim's career, is a conceptual premise that serves as the organizational superior to other concepts. I have found three such centers, which have given this study its title. Accordingly, I have divided his development into three major stages. From the beginning of his career (1910) through the publication of the essay "Historicism" (1924), the center of construction was the concept of a cultural philosophy; in *Ideology and Utopia* (1929), the center was the theories of politics and political science; and from 1937 until his death in 1947, it was the concept of

4

"planning for democracy." I have also identified two transitional stages characterized by the weakening of one center of construction and the preparation for another. Each of these two stages gave a prominent place to an element that was antithetic to the concepts forming its center, creating a tension that contributed to the subordination of those concepts. In the first transitional period (1924–28), this antithetic element was the sociology of knowledge; in the second period (1930–36), it was the idea of "massification," a mass culture without sufficient orientation.

At different times in his career, Mannheim divided disciplines into analytical and valuative parts. The former related ideas to larger contexts of meaning to understand them in terms of the cultural or sociological "totality" of which they were a part. The valuative element attempted to decide which of those contexts was correct, to arrive at a standard for value judgments. I have taken this division as the main criterion for distinguishing the centers of construction from the concepts subordinate to them – the centers were valuative, the others analytical. Cultural philosophy, the theory of politics, and the theory of democratic planning were schemata for arriving at a standard of values, for deciding among competing positions. The analytical concepts, on the other hand, were "value-free," not in the sense of being perfectly "objective," but rather in the sense (articulated by Max Weber) that, although they could never escape valuative presuppositions, they were not designed to create value standards. This less-ambitious role made them subordinate, and sometimes antithetic, to the valuative centers of construction.

The failure to make this distinction has been most responsible for the misinterpretation of Mannheim's works. For reasons discussed in Chapter 4, many interpreters take the sociology of knowledge primarily as a valuative concept rather than as the analytical one it is; this causes them to slight the valuative political elements in *Ideology and Utopia*.[21] Then, finding similar analytical elements in "Historicism," they treat that work as an early version of the valuative system in *Ideology and Utopia*.[22] Thus, rather than being the culmination of his attempt at a cultural-philosophical synthesis, "Historicism" becomes simply the beginning of a methodological shift. In ignoring the division of analytical and valuative elements, these interpreters have raised an analytical discipline to the valuative level and have ignored Mannheim's own two valuative centers of construction. These failures, in turn, lead to a misunderstanding of his third valuative center, planning, which seems to be an abrupt departure from the sociology of knowledge. In making this contrast and not seeing planning's relationship to the earlier cultural and political centers, they accuse him of a shift in priorities and a lapse into a naive Comtean dogma, both of which are incorrect.[23]

5

Mannheim wrote that the next concept, the "constellation," was similar to the pattern of stars so important to astrology.[24] An astrologer seeking to read the stars does not examine the effects of one star upon another nor see the constellation as an unanalyzable whole. Rather, the astrologer interprets the pattern between the stars as a structural whole, as a constellation. In following Mannheim's lead, I have examined each of his five stages as a constellation characterized by a certain structure. Moreover, I have found that, although the centers of construction and the concepts they organized were constantly changing, the basic structure that organized them remained fairly constant due to the continuity of purpose behind the works. That structure was a trichotomy in which the elements of an organic–mechanistic dualism were synthesized by a structural world view. These three elements ordered different concepts and assumed different configurations in his development; however, they were always present. And it must be emphasized that they are relationships and not actual entities.

The first four concepts are purely intellectual, containing no attempt to tie Mannheim's conceptual development to his life and his place in the sociocultural contexts of Hungary, Germany, and England. This sociological element is contained in the final two concepts borrowed from him. I have attempted to relate the dynamic totality of his thought to the three sociocultural groups in which he participated – the response of the Budapest intelligentsia to the reactionary culture of Hungary and the revolutions against that hegemony; the response of the German academic community to the progressive elements of modern society in general and the Weimar Republic in particular; and the response of the refugee intellectuals to the English scene of the 1930s and 1940s. Because the connections between these two sets of wholes were not simple and direct, the challenge is not to present the contexts and his relationship to them in an overly reductive manner or in such a way that in avoiding a too simplistic and direct connection I end up with no connections at all or, at best, implied connections.[25]

The strategy I have used in making these connections is guided by Mannheim's theory of "perspectivism." He wrote:

> "Perspective" in this sense signifies the manner in which one views an object, what one perceives in it, and how one construes it in his thinking. . . . It is precisely these factors which are responsible for the fact that two persons, even if they apply the same formal-logical rules . . . in an identical manner, may judge the same object very differently.[26]

Thus, when Mannheim surveyed the pattern that composed the sociocultural context, he did so from a certain perspective. He did not respond to a "balanced" picture of his times but to one "distorted" by his viewpoint. Therefore, to strive for a balanced picture of the contexts in which he lived is to preclude an understanding of the relation of his thought to them.

We are left with one more methodological problem: Mannheim's perspective distorted not one but three sociocultural contexts; to retain the concept of dynamic totality, we must have a way of bridging his relationship to all three contexts. Simple temporal contiguity will not do; the dynamic totality is simply too complex to say: "New country, new Mannheim." Although we can locate him within each context, we also need a concept that will serve as an organizing element for the entire dynamic totality. Here I have chosen his concept of the "refugee."[27] To clarify the concept, one can compare it with a similar, and more famous, concept, Georg Simmel's "stranger."

Simmel's stranger is characterized by his ambivalent position as a member of a group – "he is near and far *at the same time; . . .* in spite of being organically appended to it, the stranger is yet an organic member of the group."[28] The function that the stranger performs, for example, trading, is an integral part of the group's activities. Yet at the same time his relationship to the members of the group is not the close personal one that they have among themselves. Held at a distance personally, he takes a more objective view of the group's culture. "He is freer, practically and theoretically; he surveys conditions with less prejudice; his criteria for them are more general and more objective ideals; he is not tied down in his action by habit, piety and precedent."[29] However, he does not represent an alternative to the group's culture; objectification does not mean challenge. And just as he offers no alternative to the group, there is no alternative to the group for him, for he is a part of the group; he does not come from a rival entity. His ambivalence, his inability to commit himself totally to any culture, his inability to move beyond an objective level – this is the tragedy of the stranger.

Like the stranger, Mannheim's refugee is a marginal man. However, his marginality is of a different nature. He is separated from one cultural tradition and not yet part of another. Unlike the stranger, his activities are not an integral part of those of his new group. His ties to his new culture are not as strong as those of the stranger, no matter how formal the latter might be. At the same time, he has ties to an alternative culture to his new one, namely, his old culture. Thus, whereas the stranger stands at the edge of one culture, the refugee stands between two cultures. This position makes the problem of orientation more difficult for the refugee than for the stranger, who must deal with only one culture. And yet, Mannheim believed that the refugee's position can be a rewarding one, for he

7

can transform his mediary position into a mediatory one. He can rely completely on neither his old nor his new culture for orientation, a position that can give him greater insight into both. Whereas the stranger can only objectify and formalize the elements of his culture, the refugee can move beyond that critical stage and aid in a synthesis of his old and new cultures. Whereas the stranger's role is analytical, the refugee's is potentially dialectical. Whereas the stranger is characterized by the tragedy of reification, the refugee is characterized by the comic possibility of synthesis, of reconstruction.

As a refugee, Mannheim's lifelong goal was synthesis – of his Hungarian and German experiences, of his German and English experiences. Once in Germany, his more radical Hungarian experience would serve as an antithetical element in his thought. While many of his university colleagues, who did not share this element, addressed the problems of German culture in dualistic terms that were essentially pessimistic, Mannheim's Hungarian experience led to his trichotomous formulation, which was essentially optimistic and which would propel him past his early cultural philosophy to the theories of politics and planning.

As I have stated above, I will plot this "dialectical" development in terms of five stages – three main stages, each characterized by a "synthesis," and two transitional stages, in which he challenged his earlier synthesis, in which his role as the refugee stood out. I have devoted a chapter to each of these stages. These five chapters will be preceded by one in which I describe his Hungarian and German experiences and place those experiences in larger sociocultural contexts.

Having indicated what this book will contain, I should note what it does not attempt. First, it is not basically biographical; it does not present in great detail his life and psychological makeup. Instead, I have treated him as a member of several groups, a strategy he used himself.[30] This is not to say that his writings were not highly individualistic, for they were. I have interpreted them as an individual's answers to group problems, or better, to a mixture of group problems.

Second, my work is more analytical than valuative. As a historian, I have left the question of "what is living and what is dead in Mannheim?" to other disciplines. Here, I believe, I am consistent with his own intentions regarding the sociology of knowledge, whose task he described as following the development of the dynamic totality by concentrating on the genesis of the various historical positions.[31] I feel that by providing a historical analysis of his career, I can add a perspective that will help to answer those valuative questions. To accomplish this task, I have devoted considerable attention to the many series of hierarchical typologies he constructed throughout his career. These series have been passed over

8

superficially by most scholars, because they appear to offer little to the methodological and epistemological discussion of the sociology of knowledge. However, I believe they provide an important key to the understanding of the basic presuppositions from which Mannheim developed his more famous theories. To understand what Mannheim means to us, it helps to understand what the world meant to him.

Of course, my work is not totally analytical. In borrowing the above seven concepts from Mannheim I hope to show the value of their application to intellectual history.[32] And I will claim that his final valuative position, the theory of democratic planning, deserves more positive attention than it has so far received.

1

The early sociocultural contexts

Mannheim's Hungarian years have drawn more attention recently.[1] However, efforts to relate the Hungarian and German sociocultural contexts to one another have been halfhearted or nonexistent. In this chapter I will make those connections, for they provide the necessary background to his refugee strategy. Also, it must be remembered that my description of these sociocultural contexts and their relation to one another is "distorted" to conform to Mannheim's perspective. I am not after a balanced survey.

Mannheim in Hungary

In 1893, Mannheim was born into the Jewish middle class of Budapest, the only large city in Hungary. The commercial Jews of Budapest, who formed a large proportion of the city's middle class,[2] were economically distinct from the traditional, anti-Semitic countryside, where almost 85 percent of the population and the base of the power structure were located.[3] However, this economic position was not accompanied by a corresponding political ideology. The Jewish middle classes were the "moral vassals" of the rural, aristocratic establishment; rather than challenging the old regime, the vanguard of Hungary's capitalist growth entered into its service. The intellectuals of Budapest shared the parochialism and conformity of the capitalists.[4]

However, the first decade of the twentieth century witnessed the emergence of a young, progressively oriented intelligentsia, who began to make some waves in the traditional calm. The reformers consisted mainly of the children of the Jewish middle classes. The young Jewish intelligentsia rebelled against the commercial success of their parents[5] (even though they continued to accept their parents' financial support) as well as against their parents' conformity. In this defiance, they emphasized the revolutionary role of the intellect and learning. Many of these young intellectuals had been educated abroad in less stifling societies and

10

seemed to have gained some of their inspiration there. Abroad, they found the philosophical and sociopolitical formations missing in Hungary.[6] Oscar Jászi, an important spokesman for the intelligentsia, summed up their program:

> On one side stood the feudal reaction, in alliance with the plutocracy, on the other side Socialism, and this was the only true issue, the only dynamic reality in Hungarian public life. . . . Although we were socialists, we soon recognized the short-comings of the Marxist orthodoxy. Our views, as opposed to those of social democracy . . . affirmed the decisive role of intellectual work in the society.[7]

The emphasis on the role of the intellect stemmed from the intelligentsia's socially free-floating position, to use Mannheim's term. As men and women of the city, they were very much aware of their isolation from the traditional culture of the countryside, and they considered the mainstays of that culture, the gentry and peasantry, to be their inferiors.[8] But, at the same time, there was no solidarity among the city dwellers. The conformist middle classes (from whom the intellectuals had come) and the traditionally minded academic hierarchy did not offer much support to the reform-minded intelligentsia. And the reformist spirit of the new intellectuals did not bring them closer connections to the labor movement, which was largely antiintellectual and anti-Semitic, or indeed to any other important segment of the Hungarian population.[9] As Lewis Coser writes: "They were men without firm attachment to any major strata and classes of their society. They were conscious of their marginality."[10]

Because of their isolation, the intellectuals did not preach a philosophy of social change from below. They did not see themselves as spokespeople for either of the two major groups in Hungary – the peasantry or the proletariat. Given the tremendous differences between city and country, they also did not see these two groups coming together on their own. So their answer was to place themselves above the two groups, to see themselves as the creators of a new "synthesis" that would win over both groups and bring them under the intelligentsia's leadership. Jászi wrote that the principles of social change had to be based on the sovereignty of the peasants and the proletariat "under the guidance of the genuinely creative intelligentsia."[11] He treated the intelligentsia as a group with an identity of their own rather than as merely an intellectual arm of the lower classes. The intellectuals were to be the creators of a new synthesis.

The Budapest intelligentsia represented a third distinct form of marginality. However, they came closer to Mannheim's refugee than they did to Simmel's stranger, for they saw their position as potentially comic, as the agent of synthesis, rather than of tragic resignation. The intelligentsia's self-proclaimed task was the synthesis of the new, progressive cultural forces of the West with the old Hungarian culture. Their role as the introducer of the new culture(s) into the old (rather than being forced to flee from the old to the new) meant a far greater degree of orientation than the refugee possessed and, hence, a greater optimism and activism.

In 1900, Jászi founded a group, the Society for the Social Sciences, and a journal, *Huszadik Század* (*The Twentieth Century*), which served as the early focal point for the activities of the reform movement. For the intellectuals, the journal was an expression of their desire for a new spiritual and moral synthesis. In 1906, Jászi's group created the Free School of the Social Sciences, in which progressive intellectuals held classes for some three thousand workers.[12] Here one sees the actualization of the concept of an intelligentsia leading and educating the proletariat, even though on a limited scale. Jászi wrote: "We intellectuals must work to transform that which lives half-consciously in the masses into an integral world view, and to undermine the existing society with the weapons of morality, science and the arts."[13]

The weapons that Jászi's group emphasized were positivistic; they strove for a rational politics based on a rational social science. Accordingly, their first publications were translations of works by Herbert Spencer, Benjamin Kidd, and Karl Kautsky. The group's reformist ideas reached the university in the form of the Galileo Club, a socialist undergraduate organization. The club was closely connected with Jászi's group and was politically active, opposing both the traditional establishment and the First World War.[14]

However, the reformist part of the Budapest intelligentsia was not free of internal divisions. Even before the war, opposition to the Society for the Social Sciences arose within the intelligentsia. This opposition movement, which was smaller than Jászi's group, took the form of a discussion group led by Georg Lukács. Lukács's differences with the Western-oriented intellectuals were exacerbated in 1908–9, when a new literary periodical, *Nyugat* (*West*),[15] rejected an article by him, according to István Mészáros, with "total incomprehension and hostility about his famous book *The Soul and its Forms* . . . [and attacked] his few literary comrades in arms. All this strongly contribute[d] to Lukács's decision to seek intellectual alliance and recognition in Germany."[16] Lukács went to Berlin in 1909 to study under Simmel and later would become a member of the Max Weber Circle in Heidelberg.[17] Never sympathetic to the "liberal-positivist eclecticism" of the Western-oriented intellectuals, he seems to have moved even further toward the traditional-romantic German cultural position during this period.[18]

From 1915 to 1918, Lukács's group held Sunday discussions, dominated by Lukács himself, which were mostly concerned with moral and literary problems and which concentrated on figures like Kierkegaard, Dostoyevsky, and the German mystics. The group opposed the positivistic and social emphases of Jászi's society. They believed that the solution to the breakup of the traditional culture was not a rational social science and politics, but rather a new cultural totality. They believed that the new synthesis should concentrate on the world of *Geist* rather than on social and political action. In fact, before the Hungarian revolutions broke out in 1918, Lukács's group refused to have political discussions. Lukács's later description of one of his early works also applied to his group – "a left ethic oriented towards radical revolution was coupled with a traditional-conventional exegesis of reality."[19] Although their commitment to change was even more radical than that of Jászi's group (as is shown by the fact that some of them became communists rather than support the Károlyi government), they expressed this commitment in idealist terms – in terms of creating a new culture rather than a new society. In this spirit, they formed the Free School of the Human Sciences to counteract the influence of Jászi's group.[20]

However, the doctrinal differences of the two groups were not such that there was unbridgeable hostility between them.[21] It should be stressed that both groups believed that the intellectuals were to be the leaders in the new era; both originally disassociated themselves from "party politics." Neither group identified with the traditional forces of Hungary, but rather considered themselves on the "left." Their disagreement centered on the nature of the goals that the intelligentsia would put before the people.

In accordance with the pattern just described, Mannheim chose an academic career and became a member of the new intelligentsia. As a student at the University of Budapest, he formed some attachment to the Jászi group. However, by 1910, he had come under the influence of Lukács, declaring to the latter: "I would like to thank you again for the kind reception which you have shown me and above all for the pointers wich helped me on the way. . . . Asking your further benevolence I am your respectful follower."[22] Undoubtedly due to Lukács's influence, Mannheim left Budapest in 1912 to study in Germany, a stay that lasted until just before the First World War. In Germany he was exposed to many of the same sources that Lukács had been, especially Georg Simmel. Lukács wrote that Simmel was his early philosophical guide,[23] and the same appears to have been true for Mannheim.[24]

When Mannheim returned from Germany, he became a leading member of the Lukács group and, in 1917, delivered the inaugural lecture in the Free School of the Human Sciences, defining the institution's aims.[25]

He taught classes in the school and concentrated on the discipline of philosophy. His interests were strictly intellectual, and he adopted the apolitical position of the Lukács group. Although sympathetic to social-reform movements, Mannheim believed them secondary to the creation of a new culture.

With the outbreak of the Hungarian revolutions of 1918–19, each group of intellectuals had its chance to inspire the people. The first revolution of October 1918 followed the Hungarian defeat in the First World War and a series of strikes and worker unrest in Budapest. After a relatively bloodless revolution, a bourgeois-socialist republic was set up under Michael Károlyi. The members of Jászi's Society for the Social Sciences became mainstays in the new government, while members of the Lukács group continued to occupy an apolitical position. However, in December 1918, this position was abandoned when Lukács announced that he was joining the Communist Party because he believed that a new culture could be achieved only after a new society had been created. He was followed by some members of his group, although most maintained their nonpolitical stance.[26]

In March 1919, a second revolution occurred in which the moderate Károlyi government was replaced by the communist Hungarian Soviet Republic under Béla Kun. Some of the newly-turned-communist members of the Lukács group now became the intellectual spokesmen for the new regime. Lukács himself was appointed deputy commissar of education. When the regime reorganized the University of Budapest, many of those who had not become communists received teaching positions.[27]

Mannheim maintained his apolitical stance throughout the revolutionary period and refused to follow Lukács into the Communist Party.[28] He attempted, with Anna Lezsnai, to continue the discussion group that Lukács had abandoned. However, he did become a professor of philosophy at the reorganized University of Budapest under the communists.[29]

Like its bourgeois predecessor, the communist regime was short-lived. In July 1919, it was replaced by the forces of Admiral Horthy, and the intellectuals were forced into exile. The collapse of both revolutionary governments resulted from their inability to gain any control over the rural countryside, to overcome the splits within Budapest society, and to reorganize the city. When the old ruling forces fell in behind Horthy, the revolutionaries could not resist them. The intelligentsia, some of whom had played active roles in both revolutions, had offered little help in overcoming the internal divisions within the revolutionary forces, much less within the whole of Hungarian society. The intellectuals had had no previous experience in politics and to the end remained divided in their goals and unable to implement them effectively.[30]

With the triumph of Horthy, Mannheim joined his fellow intellectuals in exile, bringing to a close his direct contact with the Hungarian sociocultural context. As we have seen, this context was one of social and political disorientation, which Mannheim, as a member of the intelligentsia, attempted to remedy. He identified the problem of orientation and change as cultural, rather than socioeconomic, in nature. His solution to these problems was to promote change rather than to hinder it. The terms by which he formulated this cultural position were taken from the German cultural tradition. Thus, there was a discrepancy between the ideology Mannheim formulated and the sociocultural context he was attempting to clarify.

In 1919, he took up residence in Germany,[31] first in Freiburg and then in Heidelberg, where he studied with Alfred Weber. In 1925, he became a *Privatdozent*, a lecturer, at Heidelberg and remained there until he accepted a position as professor of sociology at Frankfurt in 1929. We must remember that he did not go from being a Budapest intellectual to being a German academic. Rather, he became a refugee[32] and, although his refugee status was not nearly as traumatic as it would be in England, he still brought something of his old environment to help orient him in his new one. That something was the commitment to change and the optimistic aspiration toward a new synthesis. At the same time, his entrance into the German university system reinforced his commitment to intellectual rather than political activity[33] as well as his advocacy of a cultural synthesis over a social-scientific one.[34] In the absence of a substantial native philosophical tradition in Hungary, most of Mannheim's cultural concepts were already German ones. His residence in that country could only reinforce those concepts as well as efforts to seek a cultural solution to what for him was essentially a cultural problem. The will of the Budapest intellectual was combined with the formulation of the German academic, just as they had been in Budapest; the resulting tension between these two elements continued in his thought.

The German context

For us, the most important characteristic of the German social structure from 1890 to 1933 was its industrial-traditional character, to modify a term by Ralf Dahrendorf, who has constructed the best synthesis of this period.[35] This "faulted," that is, dichotomous, nature distinguished the German "cultural hegemony"[36] from both the essentially rural Hungarian society and the paradigm of European industrial development, England. In the late nineteenth century, the country had witnessed phenomenal industrial growth and demographic change. As one historian

15

has written: "All forces tending towards industrialism and urbanization had struck Germany at once."[37] The speed of German industrialization, along with its concentration and cartelization and the support it received from the traditional, authoritarian state, allowed the country's traditional power structure to remain relatively unchallenged by the new industrial elements. Thus, Germany became industrialized without the development of a corresponding cultural hegemony, leaving many Germans, who "tuned their instruments" to the tone set by the traditional elite, "unmodern men in a modern world."[38]

One social group in whom this traditional element was dominant was the *Bildungsbürgertum*,[39] which was defined by its possession of some form of academic training, be it at a university or simply at a *Gymnasium* (classical prep school). It enjoyed great prestige before the First World War due to its connections with the state bureaucracy and with the classical ideal of *Bildung*.[40] We are concerned with that part of the *Bildungsbürgertum* that Klaus Vondung calls the "socially-active core," those who were actively engaged in the process of *Bildung* "in the threefold sense of the development of interpretations of reality and classificatory schemes, the education of people and the cultivation of public opinion."[41] The relationship of this socially active core to the rest of the "intellectual and spiritual aristocracy" is analogous to the relationship between the greater and lesser nobility, that is, hierarchical rather than antinomic.

The socially active core can in turn be divided into two groups, those within the institutional framework of the state and those without. The former, as bureaucrats, were part of and hence defenders of, or at worst mild critics of, the cultural hegemony. Most of those outside the institutional pale were also supporters of the dominant culture. However, there were those who attacked the dualistic hegemony from either residual or emergent positions. The residual elements focused their attack on the modern elements of the dualistic hegemony.[42] Their difference with the institutional elements, who had an essentially traditional perspective, were largely over the degree to which the hegemony had been transformed from a hierarchical into a bipolar entity. In other words, there was not that much difference between them.

This basic agreement was not true for the emergent elements of the hegemony. The members of this group, which had been in existence since the early nineteenth century but had not achieved significant numbers until near the turn of the century, were university-educated but had become estranged from the university community. They tended to come from the middle classes (as opposed to the academics, whose origins were usually in the traditional middle ranks), and many of them were Jews. They favored an extreme individualism, which was experimental and

16

iconoclastic in spirit and shared none of the organic assumptions of the traditionalists. Wolfgang Sauer has appropriately labeled them "expressionist" in outlook.[43] Although these intellectuals were largely apolitical, most were in sympathy with the workers, and some actually worked for that cause. However, the ties between this latter group and the Social Democratic Party were at best tenuous.[44] Thus, in many ways they were like the Budapest intelligentsia, and their relationship to the rest of the *Bildungsbürgertum* was antithetic.

The institutional, socially active core of the *Bildungsbürgertum* can be subdivided into its elite, the university professors, and the rest, for example, *Gymnasium* teachers, ministers, etc., a relationship that was purely hierarchical. The professoriat could be seen (especially from within its ranks) as resting at the top of the traditional hierarchy of the *Bildungsbürgertum*, while at the same time facing the challenge of antithetic elements. Being a part of the hegemonic establishment, the university had a stake in the maintenance of stability and order within the nation. They saw the antithetic elements created by modernity as a source of potential chaos that had to be held in check. Before the First World War, they saw this check being provided by themselves, the cultural elite, as well as by the authoritarian state, the political elite. The two groups lived in a symbiotic relationship centered on the national spirit: The cultural elite were the interpreters of the *Volksgeist* and the values derived from it; the political elite were the defenders and servants of the *Volksgeist*. Fritz Ringer describes the relationship of these two groups as follows:

> The terms of the settlement [between the political and cultural elites] were that the bureaucratic monarchy would give unstinting support to learning without demanding immediately practical returns, and without exercising too strict a control over the world of learning and of *Geist*. In other respects also the state would acknowledge and serve the demands of culture. It would become a vehicle, a wordly agent or form for the preservation and dissemination of spiritual values. Indeed, it would seek its legitimacy in this function, and it would be rewarded by finding it there. The state would earn the support of the learned elite, who would serve it not only as trained officials but also as theoretical sponsors and defenders.[45]

The formulations of the professoriat reflected this participation in the German cultural hegemony, which it had enjoyed to different degrees since the late eighteenth century.[46] The formulations were based on the premise that the German nation was an organic entity, not only in its relationship to the historical process as a whole but, more importantly for us, also in its internal organization. The nation, which could be defined in either cultural or political terms or in a combination of the two, was viewed as an organic, indivisible whole rather than as the mere sum of

17

basic parts. In this belief, these traditions stood opposed to the mechanistic philosophy associated with the English and French Enlightenment, whose basic unit, epitomized by the contract theory, was the autonomous individual.

In contrast to this atomistic individualism, one current of German thought adopted a concept of the individual whose model was the Leibnizian monad. Although individual monads were self-contained entities, a preordained harmony existed among them. These unique individual units did not determine the whole by their interaction; rather, they reflected the organic order of the whole while maintaining their individuality. Individualism took place harmoniously within the organic whole and did not alter the nature of the organism. The thinkers who developed this type of individualism, men such as Schiller, Herder, Wilhelm von Humboldt, Eduard Spranger, Ernst Troeltsch, and Friedrich Meinecke, were associated with two related intellectual traditions, the monadic form of German historicism and the theory of *Bildung*, both of which emphasized the cultural character of the nation instead of its political side.

The basic concept of monadic historicism was the "individuality," whose essence was seen as spiritual rather than material.[47] Individualities were the "basic unities" of history, to use Troeltsch's term, characterized by their uniqueness (*Einmaligkeit*) and originality (*Urspünglichkeit*) and not susceptible to meaningful subdivision.[48] The essential nature of these spiritual entities could not be exactly, or causally, explained or quantified.[49] If individualities' essences could never be exactly explained, the same was true for their relationships with one another. The relationship of a person to a state or an epoch, all individualities, could not be grasped in any logical or exact way. In fact, the understanding of such a relationship was based largely on the faith of the historicist in the world's basic harmony and meaning. He believed that a spiritual unity, perceivable to some degree but not exactly demonstrable, existed behind the variety and finiteness of historical individualities.

Those individualities most important to the monadic historicists were culture and the culture-creating and -receiving personality. They assumed that culture was the primary objectification of the *Volksgeist* and that a basic harmony existed within the nation. In this, their views were organic; however, they believed that this harmony was achieved through individual activity.[50] In light of the assumption that the individual was a unique, self-contained entity and at the same time a participant in a larger spiritual totality, emphasis was placed not on the subordination of the individual to the organic whole (as it was in more corporate organic

18

theories), but rather on the development of the individual's spiritual potential, or soul (*Seele*), to the fullest.

The theory of *Bildung* shared these cultural and individualistic assumptions and, in fact, was the cornerstone of the German view of culture and education. This theory emphasized the development of the individual's cultural capabilities. One could think of the individual as a seed possessing a certain potential, whose development depended on the richness of the cultural soil in which it was planted. The individual exposed to the great genius of his or her cultural heritage had a better chance of realizing his or her potential than did the individual lacking exposure. The task of *Bildung* was to expose the individual to the rich cultural material of the past, which would enable him or her to develop his or her own "soul." In this sense, there was no utilitarian goal implied in the concept of *Bildung*. Its purpose was not to teach the individual to understand or manipulate external objects, but rather to develop himself or herself, the subject. According to Friedrich Meinecke, the individual "should accomplish something generally valid in which all that is instinctive is used on behalf of ethical and spiritual goals, and so establish the authority of the ideal realm in oneself."[51]

As Meinecke indicated, the concepts of culture and *Bildung* were ethical ones. Eduard Spranger wrote that the *Bildungsideal* was rooted in the attempt of an epoch to realize its meaning (*Sinn*), to establish an order of values.[52] This assumption of a monadic ethical harmony between the individual soul and the "objective spirit" of the organic national culture led to a certain disdain for any institution that would disrupt this harmony. The institution on which many of these thinkers focused such a hostility was the political party, especially in its proletarian form. They took great pride in being "unpolitical," in being above the fray of the materialistic parties, those divisive interest groups disrupting the organic unity of the nation. One observer has written:

> That many middle class Germans wanted and were able to lead a non-political life was not due to their lack of political power and education alone. Intellectually eminent people, in particular the "Goethe-Germans," lived under the exalted delusion that it was not becoming for them to meddle in politics, that the entire political tumult belonged to a lower level, that it was better to be concerned with what was "essential."[53]

The bearers of these intellectual traditions tended to view the relationship of society and the spiritually organic unity of the nation hierarchically.[54] However, with the development of the dualistic sociocultural hegemony due to the rapid growth of industrial-urban elements in Germany, many of these thinkers saw this hierarchical relationship being threatened. They feared that the societal elements were escaping their subordinate position and challenging the higher organic unity. As was the case with the perspectives of social structure, traditionally minded thinkers saw a hierarchical order being replaced by an antinomy. The ideological strategy most popular in expressing this transformation was Ferdinand Tönnies's *Gemeinschaft und Gesellschaft.*

Tönnies idealized elements of traditional society and culture into the organic unity of the *Gemeinschaft*, which he described as "a metaphysical union of bodies or blood which possesses by nature a will and force of life of its own."[55] The *Gemeinschaft* meant more than just social proximity, it meant unity of will. To analyze a social whole in terms of conflicting interests was to deny that it was a *Gemeinschaft*. The organic whole and not the part was the basic element. Objects, be they beings, land, or ideas,[56] had common value; that is, they had value in being shared.

This organic cohesiveness was lacking in the *Gesellschaft*, where the part and not the whole was the basic unit. The individual thought in terms of himself and his own interests, not in terms of the larger social unity. "What somebody has and enjoys," wrote Tönnies, "he has and enjoys to the exclusion of all others. So, in reality, something that has a common value does not exist."[57] Tönnies believed that the patriarchal relationship of the *Gemeinschaft* broke down when rational and materialistic individualism became dominant among the lower strata of the nation. When that happened, the followers also became motivated by consciousness and independence (previously restricted to the elite), and the essential content of the *Gemeinschaft* was replaced by the pure form of the *Gesellschaft*. This process, he felt, became inevitable with the growth of trade and capitalism. He wrote:

> To the extent that the common people, with its labor, is subjected to trade and capitalism, it discontinues being a [*Gemeinschaft*]. It adapts itself to foreign forces and conditions and becomes educated or cultivated (*gebildet*). Science, which in reality distinguishes the educated ranks (*Gebildeten*), is offered to them in many forms and shapes as a medicine for their rudeness. Thus, the common people become a "proletariat"; and much against the will of the educated rank, when this latter group is identified with capitalistic *Gesellschaft*, they learn to think and become conscious of the conditions under which they are chained to the labor market. From such knowledge, decisions and attempts to break these chains originate. They unite into unions and parties for social and political action.[58]

The power of the *Gemeinschaft–Gesellschaft* metaphor for traditionalists lay in its role as an apt analogy into which the complexities of modernization in Germany and the "faulted" sociocultural hegemony could be co-erced. The growth of the proletariat and the radicalization of its de-mands, the decreasing importance of traditional ranks and the increasing importance of modern classes, the growing role of political parties and the demand for parliamentary democracy, even the extension of positivism beyond the natural sciences – all these were interpreted as a negative thing, the *Gesellschaft*, which was nothing but the decay of the *Gemeinschaft*, that is, the dissolution of the organic totality.[59] And al-though Tönnies went on to become one of the more progressive members of the German academic community, his little book provided the leitmotif for traditionally minded people throughout the period.[60]

To sum up what has been said above, the traditionalists in the university postulated a divisive sphere of social-interest groups, represented by po-litical parties, which they hoped would be held in check and given order by the sphere of spirit and its interpreters (academia) and protectors (the authoritarian state). Some academics (those we are most interested in) emphasized the role of culture in preserving the organic order, and oth-ers emphasized the role of the state. But both emphases had the same traditional and idealist base.

This idealism can be seen in the divisions of the university curricula. One division produced two types of science, the philosophical and the specialized sciences. These categories were overshadowed by the second division of science into the human sciences and the natural sciences; nevertheless, they still deserve our attention. The philosophical sciences were concerned with the sphere of spirit. Their subdivisions included systematic philosophy (i.e., metaphysics, epistemology, logic), the philos-ophy of history, and the study of world views among others. In studying the spiritual realm, these sciences allegedly provided meaning (*Sinn*) for the cultural whole or, in other words, answered the questions of what one was and how the basis of one's existence could be contemplated in order to live and act correctly. Thus, the task of interpreting values belonged primarily to the philosophical sciences.[61]

The second group of sciences, the specialized sciences, did not have such a lofty role. They developed due to specific problems in the philo-sophical sciences. Their role was not to provide general meaning but rather to work out specific problems. Among the specialized sciences were such disciplines as history, law, economics, and the mathematical and natural sciences. Although it was admitted that the line between the philosophical and specialized sciences was not a hard and fast one, the latter clearly held an inferior status. They were also in a dependent posi-tion. Empiricism and specialization were condemned when they became autonomous from the sphere of spirit and meaning.[62] One should note

21

the parallel positions of the specialized sciences and the material interests (represented by political parties) – their autonomy from the ideal sphere was seen as a leveling of the hierarchy and thus as a state of degeneration.

The second dichotomy in the sciences – the human and natural sciences – overlapped with the first set of categories; however, whereas the first set was hierarchical, this set was antinomic. The human sciences included the philosophical sciences and many of the specialized sciences. The remaining specialized sciences fell under the rubric of natural sciences. Despite the differences among academics over exactly how these disciplines were to be constituted, the pattern was similar for all formulations.[63]

The natural sciences were allegedly modeled on the concepts and methods of the physical sciences, whose aim was the isolation of basic elements, for example, the Newtonian "particles," which were taken as universal and eternal. Larger entities were merely aggregates of the basic elements arranged according to universal causal laws. Because he or she dealt in universals rather than unique entities, the natural scientist sought to quantify the elements and the causal relationships between them. Newton's mathematical formulae for the laws of gravitation provide a good example. This approach was often described by the German academics as "mechanistic."

In congruity with the historicist tradition described above, the human sciences were not characterized by this nomothetic approach, but rather by an ideographic one. They were concerned with unique individualities, which were seen as essentially spiritual products not susceptible to exact causal explanations or quantification. Likewise, relationships among individualities resisted the methods of the natural sciences. Rather, the essence of the individualities and their relationships were grasped by inexact methods like sympathetic "understanding" (*Verstehen*) and "intuition" (*Ahnen*).[64]

Another important characteristic of the human sciences, not shared with the natural sciences, is demonstrated by Wilhelm Windelband's statement that the historical process had value only when it was unique.[65] In other words, only those sciences concerned with unique individualities were oriented toward values. Because each nation or culture was perceived as an organic unity of values, only those disciplines capable of an organic interpretation of the culture, that is, capable of seeing it as a unique historical entity, were in a position to interpret those values. Here the human sciences overlapped with the philosophical sciences of the other division in that both were concerned with interpreting culture as a meaningful whole and the source of the nation's values. This tie between the human-philosophical sciences and the interpretation of values for the nation was a crucial part of the German academic world view. It made discussions of the role of certain methods and disciplines more than simply academic discussions.

For most academics the dualism in the sciences paralleled the social dualism of *Gemeinschaft* and *Gesellschaft*. Just as the academic traditionalists saw the *Gesellschaft* encroaching upon the *Gemeinschaft*, they also saw the natural sciences encroaching upon the philosophical-human sciences. In fact, the division within the specialized sciences was articulated to prevent that kind of encroachment, to spell out just how far the natural sciences were allowed to go. The application of the "mechanistic" methods of the natural sciences to the cultural realm was seen by many traditionalists as the intellectual counterpart of the attack of the new industrial society upon the old organic order of ranks. In both cases, a force (the mechanistic methods and the priority of class orientation) had overstepped its ascribed position in the hierarchy at the expense of the existing elite, resulting in a defensive antinomic formulation by those threatened. In the nineteenth century, the main villain was Comte,[66] but during the first three decades of the twentieth century Marxism replaced French positivism and the main form of mechanistic thought to be combated. And although the characterization of Marxism as mechanistic was simplistic, there was a great deal of material among orthodox and revisionist Marxist writings to support such an argument.[67] Such a mechanistic philosophy of social science did not win this field many supporters among university traditionalists. In fact, the discipline of sociology was for most of the period we are studying considered an "oppositional science."[68] For many academic traditionalists, "society" came to be similar to Tönnies's typologized society, the *Gesellschaft*.

Most academics concurred with the view described above that this "society," the interrelationships of people in terms of fulfilling material interests, was simply the divisive element in human relationships, the potential conflict that had always to be subordinated to the unifying force of spirit, to the nation as a whole. Therefore, a discipline that treated society as a separate entity, as sociology proposed to do, was erroneous and potentially subversive.[69] In summary, one could say that the hostility toward the social and political changes that industrialism threatened to precipitate were reflected in the whole structure of learning in Imperial Germany.

The challenge of Weimar

Despite challenges to the traditionalist power and intellectual elites, their position remained predominant in Germany until the First World

23

War. In fact, at the beginning of the war it appeared that the attempt of men like Gustav Schmoller to bring the proletariat into the German community of values would be realized. With the unanimous support of the war credits by the *Reichstag*, the rift between the rebellious workers' movement and the rest of the nation appeared healed. The nation seemed to be once more spiritually united and capable of achieving its mission in the world. Kaiser Wilhelm II declared: "I know no more parties, I know only Germans." The economist Werner Sombart saw in the new war community, the Ideas of 1914, a new German herodom that combined Weimar (the home of Germany's cultural greatness) with Potsdam (the home of its political and military greatness).[70]

However, the Ideas of 1914 became the frustrations and divisions of 1917 and the revolutions of 1918. After the war, the establishment of the Weimar Republic, moderate though its leaders were, was a shattering psychological blow to the traditional elites and their world view. The republic meant the establishment of parliamentary democracy or, as the traditionalists put it, "party democracy" in Germany. The traditionalists feared this development because they believed it would allow the state to descend into the divisive turmoil of material-interest politics. The authoritarian elite, who allegedly stood above the social sphere, were now to be replaced by the representatives of that sphere. Government would be a matter of the compromise of interests rather than of their subordination to the sphere of spirit. For the traditionalists, this meant the rise of the realm of chaos at the expense of the realm of order. The national spirit, which had made Germany great, would wither and, to use Sombart's terms, a nation of heroes would be reduced to a nation of merchants.

The early years of the republic reinforced the belief of many traditionalists that industrialism, democracy, and increased social mobility brought only chaos. And the elite were not alone in these beliefs, for almost half the population thought in traditional terms.[71] They were perplexed by the strikes, revolution, coups, and economic dislocations (especially the inflation of 1923), which they often blamed on the leaders of the new republic.[72]

The disorientation of Weimar society provided a tremendous challenge to the German academics. The traditional role of the intellectuals as members of the cultural elite had been to prevent the occurrence of just such a disorientation. Although they were challenged by both Marxists and the "expressionist" intellectuals, many academics saw themselves continuing the traditional role of the cultural elite and took up the task of establishing norms for the divided nation. The fact that so many of the disoriented shared the traditional world view of the academics convinced the latter that they had a substantial audience for their ideas.

24

We must remember both the sense of chaos and the commitment to the idealist world view on the part of the academics who addressed themselves to these problems. Discussions over subjects such as the essence of culture and the role of values had a great deal more urgency than those questions have for us today. "Crisis" was a term that was used during this period and, accordingly, such discussions were often seen as critical. And we must remember that there remained a large traditionalist sector of society that looked to the academics as its spokesmen.

Many academics responded to the crises by hoping for a return to the days before the First World War.[73] But those in whom we are most interested, those associated with the traditions of monadic historicism and *Bildung*, accepted the new forces of Weimar, with the qualification that they must remain subservient to the sphere of spirit. They realized that the clock could not be turned back, that the old elites must somehow reconcile themselves to the new industrial and democratic forces, as well as to the new discipline of sociology. However, they continued to believe that this reconciliation could be accomplished "scientifically," that it was still possible to preserve the organic sphere of spirit as the source of the nation's values. They believed that a viable alliance of the old cultural elite and the new democratic forces was possible and called for the former to help develop a new democratic national spirit.[74] In this light, Friedrich Meinecke wrote: "Intellectual and spiritual aristocracy is by no means incompatible with political democracy. . . . The values of our spiritual aristocracy . . . have to be carried into political democracy, in order to refine it and protect it against degeneration."[75] In essence, this type attempted to maintain a traditional theory of culture and values based on a traditional social structure in the face of the sociopolitical reality. These academics maintained their insistence of the primacy of culture when the prevailing atmosphere was clearly "political." The result was an acute sense of "crisis" and "tragedy" on their part.[76]

One academic who did not accept this tragic position was Max Weber, the brother of Mannheim's mentor. He rejected both the political assumptions of those who placed primary emphasis on the old authoritarian state and the cultural assumptions of those who emphasized the ability of culture and *Bildung* to provide an organic unity of spirit and values for the nation. Weber made these pronouncements near the end of his life, at the juncture of the imperial and republican eras, in two speeches subsequently published as "Science as a Vocation" and "Politics as a Vocation." In the former, he denied that there was an organic unity of spirit, and he called on science to reconcile itself with this pluralism and give up its claim to the monopoly in valuation.[77] In the latter essay, he placed on the shoulders of the politician much of the ethical responsibility he had removed from the shoulders of the scientist. Accordingly, he rejected the idea that the party and the actions of the politician were motivated primarily by material interests. Instead, he believed the party should be a *"Weltanschauungspartei,"* dedicated to the realization of certain substantive political ideals.[78]

Weber put special emphasis on the politician who could provide leadership for the party. Although his speech did criticize contemporary politicians, it also expressed a hope that one day democratic politicians would be able to establish an ethical code by which they could direct the nation. At the center of this code was the individual responsibility of the politician, his dedication to a personal set of moral values. Weber's ideal politician was the charismatic leader, the party leader who, given the pluralism of competing world views and value systems, had firm standards of right and wrong and the will to live up to his code of ethics and struggle for its success. He wrote:

> Politics is a strong and slow boring of hard boards. It takes both passion and perspective. Certainly all historical experience confirms the truth – that man would not have attained the possible unless time and again he had reached out for the impossible. But to do that a man must be a leader, not only a leader but a hero as well, in a very sober sense of the word. And even those who are neither leaders nor heroes must arm themselves with that steadfastness of heart which can brave even the crumbling of all hopes. This is necessary right now, or else men will not be able to attain even that which is possible today. Only he has the calling for politics who is sure that he shall not crumble when the world from his point of view is too stupid or too base for what he wants to offer. Only he who in the face of all this can say "In spite of all!" has the calling for politics.[79]

In short, Weber advocated the cutting free of monadic individualism from its organic premises. At best, monadic organicism was there as a hope and not a certainty. Within the university, Weber's position was a "radical" one. However, despite the fact that he was somewhat of an outsider in the academic community, his stature was such that many members of academia, whether they agreed with him or not, felt that they had to come to grips with his position. (This was especially true for those who adhered to the monadic traditions of historicism and *Bildung*.) The confrontation with Weber's position was instrumental to the atmosphere of crisis that surrounded the human sciences at the beginning of the republic. It was this crisis that Mannheim tried to solve in most of his German writings.

Had the Budapest intellectuals and their programs been transferred directly into the German scene, they would have been part of the non-institutionalized sector of the socially active core of the *Bildungsbürgertum*, and their will to change would have made their relationship to the institutional sector antinomic. However, one sector of this modernist intelligentsia, Lukács's group prior to the revolutions, had developed a contradictory ideology. They were a radical group challenging the dominant culture and, yet, their program was not really in line with the emergent elements of Hungarian society, those who were in a position to take political action against the hegemony. Rather, it was couched in the terms of the German traditionalist culture, reflecting the group's apolitical stance at a time when the Hungarian sociopolitical context was becoming heavily politicized.

Mannheim's entrance into the university community upon arriving in Germany reversed this relationship – now it was the will to change rather than the traditionalist formulation that was anomalous. The institutional and ideological structures of the university system provided a buffer against the kinds of political demands that were prevalent in both Hungary and Germany. Mannheim was no longer in the midst of a group dedicated to furthering the cause of modernity against the forces of reaction, a group in which the will to change was dominant. Rather, most German academics saw change as something potentially dangerous to the organic unity of the nation. Their dualistic formulations, for example, *Gemeinschaft–Gesellschaft*, culture–civilization, human sciences–natural sciences, made sense in negative terms of the changes modernization was bringing to the German nation.[80]

As a refugee, Mannheim's first task was not the promotion of change, but orientation for himself in a new context. It is not surprising that he chose what was familiar to him, the "traditional-conventional exegesis of reality" that the Free School of the Human Sciences shared with the German academics. This cultural ideology was a bridge between his old and new cultures; it softened the culture shock and made orientation easier. The monadic organicism of men like Ernst Troeltsch and Alfred Weber was in some ways very much like his own formulations; and so, he addressed himself to the questions they had raised.

Gradually, he more thoroughly took up the task of relating his old culture to his new one. As he did, the bridge of cultural organicism proved inadequate. The conflict of two elements of his thought, the desire for some kind of organic unity and the will to change, would lead to attempts at a new synthesis, a combination that would do more than simply restore the hierarchical priorities of the German cultural hegemony. This was Mannheim's refugee strategy. It would lead him eventually to the issue raised by Max Weber, the relationship of science and politics.

2
The cultural-philosophical synthesis
(1910–1924)

Before the First World War, Mannheim wrote a series of letters to Lukács seconding the latter's choice of the idealist German world view over the positivist Western one. In 1911, the eighteen-year-old disciple wrote:

> We have to see through our own humanity that bond which ties us, and have to seek through this understanding the form which determines the way in which one man may approach another. Thus I wish to approach you through the possibilities ensured by culture.[1]

This idea of individuals relating to one another through culture was central to the traditionalist world view, especially that of the monadic historicists. Mannheim's statement here was similar to one by Alfred Weber, who would later replace Lukács as his mentor,[2] that the root of the question was the will to overcome the separation of the world into subject and object, to explode the limitations of egoistic individualism and create a synthesis for orientation. Culture, for Alfred Weber and all those who subscribed to the monadic theory of *Bildung*, was the synthesis of the personality with the world (which was made up of other personalities).[3] Culture, then, for Mannheim was the vehicle through which "one man may approach another." In 1912, he wrote to Lukács:

> To make conscious what is necessarily unknown to us at the beginning of things, to find ourselves while living; to get to know ourselves through others, and what is the same: others through ourselves and everything as if it were ourselves: this is the path of the soul from itself to itself. . . . I believe that we must seek the common root of all forms, I believe that it is in this that every true form professes community with every other: the drama, poetry, the novel, the [*sic*] philosophy.[4]

In this passage we see culture not only as a medium for interpersonal communication but also as an entity in itself. To use the traditional historicist terms, culture was an individuality that allowed the union of other individualities ("souls"). However, for Mannheim, this cultural unity was not automatic; it was something to be sought, to be achieved. Here we see

28

the activist (though not political) element that was so important to his position.[5]

His concern for culture in these early letters reflected other traditionalist concepts, if only in rudimentary form. One can find versions of the divisions of the sciences described in Chapter 1. The human sciences–natural sciences dichotomy was mirrored in his discussion of the relationship between literary criticism (Lukács's prime interest at this time) and philosophy. The two fields, he wrote, had in common their search "for interconnections[6] but not causes." Here he separated them from the causal approach of the natural sciences, the latter being inappropriate for the endeavors of the cultural community.[7]

One also finds a parallel to the hierarchical division of the philosophical and specialized sciences in Mannheim's discussion of the primary differences between philosophy and literary criticism – the former's emphasis on synthesis and the latter's on analysis. Criticism provided the specific material that philosophy needed for synthesis; it was a handmaiden to philosophy. "Philosophy – being synthetic – cannot feed itself, and can only occur as the integration of a certain degree of differentiation." On the other hand, philosophy provided the framework of meaning in which criticism operated. Philosophy was a form (cultural product) with the same origins as other cultural forms; however, by virtue of its synthesizing capabilities it stood above the others.[8] In other words, philosophy's task was valuation, whereas disciplines such as literary criticism (and sociology) were concerned with analysis.

Mannheim's letters reveal that he placed an emphasis on the monadic, organic qualities of culture and chose the traditionalist strategy for the interpretation of the culture even before he left to study in Germany. His German studies, of course, reinforced this position. In fact, at this early stage his traditionalist formulation appears to have been more fully developed than his cultural activism, which would grow with his increased prominence in Lukács's group.

The traditionalist emphasis on philosophy and culture continued into the mid-twenties and provided the unifying theme for the first period in his career, described in this chapter. All the works of this period, the Hungarian and the German, shared the preoccupation with the problems of culture expressed in the early letters, although the way in which the problems were formulated would differ considerably. His writings of this period can be divided into three parts, in which the thematic and chronological order roughly coincided.[9] First, there was the statement of the *problem* in his lecture to the Free School of the Human Sciences in 1917 – the crisis of culture in the modern world, the breakdown of the traditional synthesis of meaning and values in the modern world, resulting in the alienation of individuals from one another. Next came the *program*, a series of primarily methodological works designed to pave the way for the transcendence of the critical situation. These works, which explicated the logic of epistemology, the interpreation of world views and the sociology of culture, indicated an analytical development that was increasingly historical and sociological. Finally, in his 1924 essay, "Historicism," the *solution* was proposed – a new cultural philosophy able to provide orientation in light of the rapid changes accompanying modernization.[10]

The problem[11]

For Mannheim, the "tragedy" of culture began with the breakdown of the organic culture that characterized the traditional world, resulting in the delineation of three elements: (1) individuals, or "souls" (*Seelen*), who created and received meaning; (2) the "objective culture," or world view (*Weltanschauung*), the total context of meaning and values shared by the creators and receivers; and (3) the "cultural product" (*Kulturgebilde*), or "work," which was the vehicle or intersubjective meaning and communication within a culture.

Originally,[12] these three elements had no distinct identity of their own, but were part of an organic totality analogous to Tönnies's type, the *Gemeinschaft*.[13] Here, the subject did not think of himself or herself as an entity apart from the objective sphere of meaning; nor was the cultural product seen as anything but a part of existence. A static, concrete existence (*Sein*) was given meaning (*Sinn*) by an equally static transcendent realm (God). Meaning was not seen as something created by people, but rather as something bestowed upon them by the transcendent sphere. The concept of "culture" itself, therefore, did not exist, and cultural creation took place behind the back of the culture-creating and culture-receiving subjects. In this naive state, there was no division between meaning and existence; orientation and communication were automatic.[14] Mannheim wrote that "as long as this valuation was actually supported by the community consciousness, the other realities were attached to one another organically and the image of the world rounded itself out to a relatively stable completion."[15]

With the dissolution of this organic world, the relationship of the individual subject to the whole context became problematical. "Culture" came into being in order to designate one of the elements of this division – the "total objectification of spirit which had become part of the human legacy." The "soul" of the individual was then seen as something apart from this objective culture.[16]

Mannheim wrote that the individual soul had two possibilities for "realizing" itself, for overcoming its alienation from the larger context, the first being the rejection of the objective culture and the turning inward to itself. This solution, which involved the abandonment of existence, was possible only for a very limited number of people, for example Indian mystics.[17] The alternative to mysticism was "subjective culture," the indirect realization of the soul through the acceptance of objective culture. This was exactly what the traditionalist concept of *Bildung* advocated – the interaction of the individual personality with the surrounding culture.[18]

The basic unit of this reconciliation was the "work," or cultural product, the expression of the soul through a "foreign substance," the objectification of the individual psyche. Although the soul achieved historical form in the work, the two were not identical, for the latter could never completely capture the soul's "stream of lived experience" (*Erlebnisstrom*) and, therefore, was something less than the soul. However, the work had an existence of its own as a cultural object that it did not share with the soul and that made it something more than the soul – an element of the objective culture. This position made the work a bridge between the subjective culture of the soul and the objective culture.[19]

Yet the work itself was problematical, for there was the danger that it would become completely divorced from both its creator and from the larger objective sphere of meaning. Mannheim believed it possible to discover a type of meaning by examining the form of things (including works), but this discovery did not reveal true meaning, or essence. When this superficial meaning, or technique, was studied as a thing apart from essential meaning, the latter was lost. Works were viewed then as ends in themselves and not as means to more essential ends. Europe, he wrote, was in the era of "critical research," when "one was conscious of the subjection of the substance and its formation [work], which the creative instinct of previous generations unconsciously mastered, to laws."[20] Form had assumed its own laws and meaning independent of content. This reification resulted in a breakdown between individual meaning and objective cultural meaning, causing an "alienation process" in which individuals could find no orientation in the old cultural forms. Far from bridging the gap between the individual and the whole, the "critical" perception of the work widened the rift.

A third element of the crisis of culture was the fragmentation of the objective cultural whole, a process closely connected with the growing autonomy of cultural products. The examination of these products was most effective when they were isolated from one another in the hands of the specialist. With specialization, "the isolated products into which the whole of culture was split up were not viewed in the original totality of their atheoretical experience but were considered abstractly from points of view that differed from time to time."[21] It should be noted that Mannheim discussed the fragmentation of the cultural whole in methodological and philosophical, rather than sociopolitical, terms. His primary concern was with the competition among various cultural spheres and their methodologies to become the heir to the original pretheoretical religious unity. There was little attention, especially in the earliest writings, to class conflict.

So far we have seen Mannheim postulate two extremes, a pretheoretical world in which existence was intuitively grasped in its totality with no analytical powers being brought to bear, and a world in which that totality had been destroyed by a rational analytical specialization, giving rise to an alienated subject, a reified cultural product, and a pluralistic objective culture. This schema fit the traditionalist version typified by Tönnies's *Gemeinschaft–Gesellschaft* dualism with its tragic implications. However, Mannheim refused to accept the back-to-the-*Gemeinschaft* attitude that characterized the most traditional of his colleagues. He wrote that a return to a naive, intuitive approach was not possible in the modern world. Intuition did provide entrance to the atheoretical sphere of human existence, but it was incomplete without scientific consideration. Rational conceptualization was a necessary element in the interpretation and ordering of cultural products.[22]

This acceptance of rational concepts was not what set Mannheim apart from the tragic view of German historicism, for men like Tönnies and Simmel took a similar position. However, they believed that the modernization process did not stop short of the reified, pluralistic *Gesellschaft*, that culture did not stop at a golden mean but rather moved to the extreme, so that change brought eventual deterioration. Mannheim, as a member of the Budapest intelligentsia, rejected this dichotomy with its tragic view of change for a trichotomy that embraced modernization and change. The "critical stage" for him did not simply represent decay but prepared the way for a new synthesis and thus was a necessary occurrence that had to be exploited. It was not simply antinomic but was antithetic. He believed that the best way to prepare for the new culture was to push the critical stage to its extreme, to examine the forms of every individual culture field in the hope that these investigations would lead to a new unification of these various fields in one culture.

Mannheim believed that the pluralism resulting from the critical investigations of individual cultural fields would not hinder the Free School's attempts to find the way toward a new culture. It was more important to recognize the variety that the last decades had brought than to have peace of mind by accepting a false monism. Although admitting that the recognition of pluralism was necessary, he denied that it was the final answer. A school that promoted only specialization, that presented a great variety of knowledge without attempting to arrive at a context to make it meaningful, did more harm than good. Thus, the Free School, in spite of its research in individual fields, would always be unified by the belief that the various cultural fields that its members were studying were parts of a unified culture.[23] The end product of the school's efforts would be a new set of intrinsic values and a new comprehensive metaphysics.[24] Here, then, in his definition of the cultural problem and his call for a new solution, we see an outlook that embraced change formulated in a terminology originally used to express pessimism about change, the result being a tension between the structure of his thought and the concepts that structure organized.

In the years directly following Mannheim's emigration to Germany, we find variations on the themes of the Free School lecture with a marked difference in tone. In 1920, he wrote a one-act play (never published) entitled "The Lady from Biarritz," which portrayed the relationship between a painter, Döring, and his wife, Ruth.[25] Their marriage represented the alienation of two souls from one another; the failure of the form of marriage to give shape to a deeper content of meaning. Ruth sought this deeper relationship; she pleaded with Döring not to withdraw, to "hear my heart." But he reiterated his position that he was fond of her but did not love her, that what she thought was a growing love was really their growing accustomed to one another. He sought to capture her as she was through portraits, so that when her beauty had faded he would have an objective record of their relationship. However, such a work remained on the level of form; it represented reification, not some deeper interrelationship of souls.

At the root of the problem was his having given his soul previously to another woman, the lady from Biarritz. Once a year, on a certain date, he left for Biarritz to meet this mystery woman. Then he returned home to continue his faulted relationship with Ruth. The anticipation of this annual event, the fear of this unknown rival, caused Ruth to suffer greatly. Yet Döring apperared oblivious to her plight. After he was underway to Biarritz, she told a friend, Eis, that she wanted to bring this unknown "idea," her rival, into existence. She sent Eis to Biarritz to learn the woman's identity, then proceeded there herself. To her surprise, Eis had discovered that Döring was meeting no one, so she confronted her husband and made him explain these unusual circumstances.

The lady from Biarritz, explained Döring, was a creature of fantasy, conjured up in a state of ecstasy when he was eighteen. He described her as perhaps a dream, perhaps a possibility, bound to nothing in existence,

33

floating free from the world. "She is the other way that no one ever takes." Döring returned to Biarritz each year to relive this ecstatic experience, which dominated his soul. "Since this time, I have not been free; my soul is anchored there. I flee from everything that binds me, no longer a citizen of your world, only an uprooted stranger always prepared to move on."[26]

When Ruth accused him of living a lie, he replied that "she is truth for me, false truth for you." In other words, they did not share the same context of meaning. Eis then asked why Döring continued his incomplete relationship with Ruth. If he could not free himself from this apparition, why did he not remain with his truth and give Ruth her freedom. Döring's answer was that one could not reject the world; one should dare to face reality.

However, now that the lady from Biarritz had been revealed, the bridges between Döring and Ruth were destroyed. The gulf between their souls was laid bare; the conventional forms of marriage were exposed as inadequate. Ruth, too, realized that the relationship was over, that they belonged to different worlds. What did the future hold for Döring? Ruth was his last tie with the world. Now that that tie had been broken, he would attempt to separate himself from all conventional forms – house, wife, art. He would have to sweep away everything that "binds," "unmask" everything that obscured. He wanted to dismantle everything in himself, to go beyond himself, to seek the possibility that he was. The play ended, appropriately, with him sitting alone in his room engulfed by clouds of smoke from his pipe.

Great drama this is not. Yet we do see, in another form, some of the same issues touched upon in the Free School lecture, namely, the problem of intercommunication of souls and the reification of objective forms. For Döring, "subjective culture" had proven a failure; he was unable to establish a bond of meaning between himself and Ruth through the cultural forms of marriage and art. Instead, he chose the other alternative described in the Free School lecture, rejected all cultural objectifications, and turned inward to himself in a manner akin to mysticism. This "other way" was not for everyone, as was shown when Eis admitted that he had similar dreams but could not attach himself to them as Döring did. Rather, he remained solidly within the existing cultural and social forms.

It is significant that terms later to be used in *Ideology and Utopia* were contained in this work: "free-floating" (*freischwebend*), "to bind" (*binden:* the later forms would be *standortsgebunden* and *seinsgebunden*), and "to unmask" (*enthüllen*). "Free-floating" would be used consistently in Mannheim's work as an antonym of "bound." For example, the free-floating intelligentsia of *Ideology and Utopia* were not bound to the perspectives of the competing political parties. "Unmasking" pointed out one's "bonded-

34

ness" and, thus, prepared the way for transcending one's bonds. Later, Mannheim would present unmasking as a Marxist tactic by which bourgeois ideology was exposed, preparing the way for the victory of the proletariat. (He saw this tactic as successful only in its negative element, for it would be turned on the Marxists themselves by their rivals.) The last "bond" of Döring to objective forms was his marriage to Ruth. When this was unmasked as lacking any deep meaning, both realized its hollowness. Ruth's belief that the marriage could work was shattered. Döring would become free floating, bound only to the mystical lady from Biarritz. The energy of the apparition (in the later version it would be the utopian force) had destroyed the cultural forms between them.

This is not to say that the concepts as they appeared in the play were identical to the later versions, for they certainly were not. Later, free floating would not be identified with transcendence beyond wordly forms, but rather with a clarification that allowed one to interact culturally and politically. Unmasking would be seen as ultimately stultifying rather than liberating. And the entire relationship of these terms would be given sociopolitical connotations entirely absent here. One of the tasks of this study will be to examine how those terms changed in their conceptual content while retaining their structural relationship.

Right here, what is most important for us is the absence in this play of the central concept of the Free School lecture, subjective culture, on which Mannheim based his hope for synthesis. Döring saw his alternatives as participation in the reified objective cultural forms or mysticlike rejection of the world. He attempted the former but failed, unable to use the cultural work (his art) as a mediating force between souls. From the standpoint of intercultural communication, the play was a tragedy. Döring and Ruth were unable to establish a common context of meaning. Because Mannheim would quickly return to the theme of cultural intercommunication, this play can be seen as something of an anomaly, an experiment in personal philosophy using elements in accord with the interest of Lukács's Budapest group in thinkers such as Kierkegaard, Dostoyevsky, and the German mystics.

It is possible to speculate on the reasons for this experiment. When the play was written, Mannheim was in an unsettled state, having moved from Budapest to Vienna to Freiburg, before settling in Heidelberg. He had gone from being the spokesman for a culturally active group to being a minor itinerant intellectual. His attempt to reestablish lasting contact with Lukács and those around him had been rebuffed. One can see why he might, then, experiment with the free-floating character of Döring, who was unable to establish meaningful cultural ties.

By 1921, when he had gained entrance into Heidelberg intellectual circles, he had rejected the position of Döring. In an open letter intended mainly for Hungarian émigrés, he stressed the ability of culture to build bridges between people.[27] Culture, he wrote, "creates a new group of people cutting across the categories of economic and sociological classification." He saw the intellectuals as the main bearers of culture, as had been the case in Hungary, where their elimination (exile) resulted in the demise of Hungarian culture. In Germany, the intellectuals also had great cultural power, although it was much more decentralized than in Hungary.[28] He saw Heidelberg as an important center of cultural (but not political) power, and he wanted to study how the intellectuals there "relate to their contents," how they exerted cultural influence, the implication being that someday these observations might be applied to the Hungarian scene.

Mannheim saw the German cultural world as much more pluralistic, with many different prophets and their followers, each advocating a different cultural element as the cultural center. He saw the two poles of this cultural scene typified in the persons of Max Weber and Stefan George. Significantly, the circles of these two men had been the model for Lukács's Sunday Circle in Budapest.[29]

Mannheim's letter centered on George and his group, who represented the "boundless literary world." He defined the George Circle as a "charismatic" group in which souls related to one another not on the basis of "objective intellectual contents" but according to a "magical spiritual attraction." Such a charismatic community, he wrote, could be contrasted to everyday forms such as family, school, and politics. When founded on belief and religion, it was the deepest form of human existence, but, as with mysticism in the Free School lecture and Döring in the play, he believed that this was a rare occurrence, the "other way" open only to a few. In the case of the George Circle, who as moderns replaced profound religious belief with a dedication to the humanities, this charismatic relationship did not achieve great depth.[30] The circle preached a message of antiprogress – a return to the old classicism divorced from the current sociopolitical forces. Thus they became an intellectual, aristocratic community shut off from outside events, a group of lonely intellectuals whose ideal was self-centeredness.[31] When the charismatic seed disappeared, the contents of their movement, with no reference beyond itself, would fall apart. When compared with his later (1925) description of conservatism, which held similar anti-progressive sentiments but which gave them political expression, his account of the George Circle was very negative.

Although he wrote very little about the other pole, typified by Max Weber, one could surmise that this type won by default. Rather than

36

being "boundless," Weber had definite ties to the sociopolitical and sociocultural contents of his day. He should have become a politician, but the limited size of Heidelberg precluded this and forced him to settle on a career as a scientist. Weber, therefore, represented the university and sociology, which Mannheim equated with involvement in the issues of the world rather than escape from them.[32]

In these letters, we see Mannheim paying lip service to the kind of world rejection typified by Döring and George, only to reject it as a viable alternative for himself. This position represented a final parting from the mystical elements that were of concern to the Lukács group in Budapest. However, it did not mean the abandonment of his concern for culture and the communication of individuals through culture. Despite the redefinition of some of the central concepts, the basic purpose remained the same. Also, by remaining in Heidelberg, he continued to reject any role for himself in politics. Instead, he would devote himself to the questions of culture and its connections to the material world.

This did not mean that he believed the university was without its problems. In a 1922 newspaper article entitled "Science and Youth,"[33] he amended his optimistic comments on the university's connection with the sociocultural context. In doing so, he addressed some of the earlier issues from the Free School lecture, especially the problem of the alienation of the soul from a larger context of meaning due to the reified objectification of forms. The "souls" belonged to students, the "new generation," who came to the university with strong ties to life communities and to those communities' prescientific approaches to spiritual realities. At the university they encountered a realm of learning, typified by "historicism and scientific 'schools,'" which was complete unto itself, following its own laws. In participating in this scientific enterprise, which operated totally independent of their psychic (*seelisch*) needs, these students gained theoretical depth, insight, and clarity, but at the same time became estranged from their original life instincts, so that they "have forgotten their foundations." In transforming their total life energy, the objectified scientific world had extinguished their "fire."[34]

However, the situation was not as clear-cut as some critics of the university claimed. Some "life" communities from which students came could comprise a deteriorating form of things that had already been surpassed. (Here Mannheim seemed to refer to the George Circle, although this was not explicitly stated.) Rigorous scientific thought was of great value to such thinking by intensifying it through a concentration on certain points. This article, then, did not reject university science, but rather indicated the direction in which it had to move. Mannheim believed that university teachers had to recognize their pedagogical role as mediators between youth and the realm of science. They had to see themselves not simply as representatives of scientific traditions, but also as the stewards of the life contents streaming into the university in the form of the students. Science could not ignore these connections and attempt to make students into purely contemplative subjects, for to do so was to cut itself off from its own true foundations, to become alienated from life. Instead, teachers had to help students formulate the questions that arose from their vital concerns.[35] The teacher's primary duty was not to science but to the would-be scientist.

An element in this article, not present in the Free School lecture, was the collective context, the life community, from which the soul came. (As we shall see later in this chapter, this development also occurred in the primarily methodological writings.) In "Science and Youth," Mannheim identified that context as primarily generational in nature. The other life communities he described, the political group and the philosophical religious community, were supplementary to the generational entity. His position here was similar to that of Alfred Weber, who placed great faith in the youth movement – that youth infused new energy into the cultural scene and that the task of science was to guide, to help form, that energy without destroying it. During the course of Mannheim's German writings, this description of the community would change and the generation would become a supplementary concept to the political party. With this change came an increasing distance from Alfred Weber's position, which was evident to both men.

An element present in the Free School lecture but not in this newspaper article was the need for the creation of a new metaphysical synthesis. As a result of this absence, the role of intellectuals was much less clear in "Science and Youth" than it had been in the Free School lecture. In the lecture, he implied that the Free School represented both youth and the intelligentsia and, therefore, would provide both the form and the content of the new synthesis. In the newspaper article, the two functions appear to be separate, intellectuals being distinguished from youth. Also, he was not talking about the creation of a new syntheis but about the infusion of new blood into the already existing institutions. While the role of intellectuals (and his own, because he identified with the form-giving academic rather than the energy-giving youth) seemed to be less ambitious than it had been in the Free School lecture, the task of orientation of individuals in a meangful totality remained essentially the same.

To accomplish this task he would work in the seminar of Alfred Weber, signaling that he would resume where the Free School lecture left off. He would study various cultural fields to foster an effective subjective culture. Thus, whereas the optimism of the Budapest lecture had been tempered, probably due to Mannheim's more marginal position in his intellectual group, his central philosophical cultural purpose remained the same.

The program

The second and largest part of Mannheim's early writings was primarily analytic rather than valuative. One could take it as the critical stage of the early years, an examination of the makeup and relationship of various cultural fields in preparation for the synthetic solution of the third part. As with the definition of the problem, the elaboration of the program was an extension of the model found in the youthful letters to Lukács, and, hence, was in accordance with the monadic world view. This can be seen in the very first article he published in Germany, a review of Lukács's *Theory of the Novel*. Mannheim praised this work, which came from Lukács's precommunist period, for its willingness to subordinate specialized cultural disciplines, such as sociology, to a philosophy of history.[36] Such a position certainly did not put him at odds with monadic historicists such as Alfred Weber and Ernst Troeltsch. In addition, his investigation of cultural fields in other early works began with the dualistic formulations that characterized the German academic conceptualization of science. The dichotomies of philosophical – specialized sciences and natural – human sciences played a prominent role in his work.

He based one schema for the cultural fields on the objects they investigated. The main division was between those objects perceived as natural, which were devoid of meaning (*sinnfrei*, *sinnfremd*) and value, and those perceived as cultural, which were meaningful (*sinnvoll*, *sinnhaft*). The former objects were seen as impenetrable by the spiritual. They were not vehicles for the creation and communication of meaning and, hence, were autonomous from the subjects who created and received that meaning. For the natural sciences, there was no problem of intersubjective communication; it was assumed that natural objects would be perceived the same regardless of the subject. The subject was irrelevant.[37]

In contrast to the natural sciences, the cultural sciences were concerned with the creation, interpretation, and communication of meaning. They also were separated from other cultural forms, such as art, in seeking some kind of synthetic knowledge. Art, for Mannheim, was the expression of the atheoretical sphere. As long as art expressed the organic unity in which the individual partook, there was no problem of intersubjective meaning. But when this organic totality broke down, art became the work of the isolated soul, as one-sidedly subjective as the natural sciences were objective.[38]

39

The cultural sciences sought some form of both rationality and meaning and so offered a synthetic position in relation to natural science and art. Crucial to these sciences was the relationship between the sphere of meaning, or spirit, and that of existence, or the "context of lived experience" (*Erlebniszusammenhang*).[39] In fact, Mannheim believed that understanding this relationship was the fundamental cultural problem of modern times.[40] Accordingly, he divided the cultural sciences into those concerned primarily with meaning and those concerned primarily with human existence. Philosophy was the basic science of the former group, which separated the cultural products from thier historical contexts and sought objective meaning.[41]

The sciences of concrete human existence were concerned with those contexts, investigating the "functionality" of cultural products, their existential role. Although these sciences dealt with concrete existence, they were not akin to the natural sciences, since that existence was "connected" (*verbunden*) to the sphere of meaning. Mannheim wrote that cultural forms and society existed in a reciprocal relationship in which each was a function of the other. The two basic sciences of this sphere were psychology and sociology, which dealt with individual and collective concrete existence respectively.[42]

He did not see these two types of cultural science as equal. Rather, their relationship was hierarchical, with the philosophical sciences being the "higher" and the existential the "lower."[43] Because the cultural sciences were distinguished from the natural sciences by the element of meaning, those sciences that dealt exclusively with meaning were assigned the higher position. This schema represented a continuation of the stance taken in the letters to Lukács.

The other schema by which Mannheim divided the cultural fields was essentially methodological and was based on three pairs of categories.[44] The first pair consisted of "*immanent*" methods, which treated articulations of meanings as "ideas" in isolation from concrete existence, and "*extrinsic*" methods, which saw intellectual phenomena as "ideologies," as "functions" of concrete existence.[45] The second pair consisted of "*systematic*" and "*genetic*" approaches. The systematic approach assumed that intellectual phenomena could be given meaning in terms of a closed intellectual system.[46] Only immanent methods could be systematic, but not all were. Some immanent and all extrinsic methods were genetic. A genetic approach traced the origins of intellectual phenomena to some other element, from a logical system to a concrete object. "*Interpretation*" (*Interpretation, Deutung*) and "*explanation*" (*Erklärung, Klärung*) formed the third pair.[47] The former clarified phenomena in terms of a more inclusive totality for example, intellectual system, a world view, or a context

40

of lived experience. It interpreted the part in terms of the whole. The explanation clarified more elements through simpler elements, for example, the atomic theory. A part was explained in terms of another part, or a whole in terms of the parts of which it was composed. Explanation made use of the concept of causality,[48] whereas interpretations shunned it. Although explanations were always extrinsic and genetic, interpretations should be immanent or extrinsic, systematic or genetic. For Mannheim, these three pairs offered four possible combinations, diagrammed as follows:

1.	immanent	systematic	interpretation
2.	immanent	genetic	interpretation
3.	extrinsic	genetic	interpretation
4.	extrinsic	genetic	explanation

Mannheim wrote little about immanent systematic interpretations or extrinsic genetic explanations, for neither really grappled with the problem of the relationship between meaning and existence. During this early period, he examined two intrinsic genetic interpretations (in "Epistemology" and "*Weltanschauung*") and one extrinsic genetic interpretation (in "Cultural-Sociological Knowledge"). These three works, together with the essays on the sociology of knowledge, represent a movement from the second to the third combination. This movement should not be seen as unilinear, from one stage to the next, but rather as a movement between levels in which one level did not negate the other.

In "Epistemology," Mannheim's goal was the clarification of cultural products, in this case philosophical "systems," which were the creation of historical subjects (e.g., Kant's epistemology). As we have just seen, there were a number of ways in which this cultural analysis could be accomplished. An intrinsic systematic interpretation would confine itself to the system under investigation, to an examination of Kant's epistemology as an isolated system. A cultural-historical genetic interpretation, either immanent or extrinsic, traced the system to the historical context of its creator, for example, to Kant's participation in an "actual life-system at a given time." This was the method that was primary in Mannheim's approach to cultural products. However, in "Epistemology," he used an ahistorical "meaning-genetic" (*sinngenetisch*) interpretation, which sought to trace the components of a system to a basic "systematization," an a priori structure that transcended historical reality. Such systematizations were located only in the realm of meaning and not in historical existence; they were discernible only to the "transcendental-logical subject," the knower who stood above the flow of history.[49] The system, the cultural product, was seen as a manifestation and was to be analyzed logically,

41

stripped of its historical attributes to determine its systematic origins. Each system was seen as the attempt of an "individual reflecting subject" to approach the knowledge of the transcendental-logical subject, to "push to its logical conclusion a tendency already prescribed in the systematization."[50] Taking our example, one asked: What did Kant's epistemology share with all other epistemologies?

Here Mannheim made a clear methodological separation between meaning and existence and assigned the historical method to a subordinate role. He wrote that "historical factors determine only the actualization of the meaningful product in question"; when one remained on the temporally determined genetic level, one had to face the flux of history.[51] Essential meaning could be discovered only in the cultural product's "systematic origin in the transcendental systematization of the field to which it belongs."[52] Thus, in "Epistemology," he sought to deduce the logic and elements of the epistemological systematization shared by all epistemological systems. He decided that the problem inherent in that systematization was bipartite, consisting of (1) the attempt to identify the ultimate presuppositions of any possible knowledge and (2) the evaluation of those presuppositions.[53]

Most of the essay was devoted to the first, analytical, part. Concern with the presuppositions of knowledge, he believed, distinguished the epistemological systematization from others, which were concerned with the objects of knowledge.[54] Whereas the other sciences sought a knowledge of things, epistemology sought a knowledge of knowledge. This gave the latter a "free choice of reference" (*freie Blickwendung*) with regards to the usual objects of knowledge and an ability to reflect on knowing itself.[55] The specific problem of this science was the "subject–object correlation," the relationship of the subject to the object in the acquisition of knowledge. These three elements, the subject (knower), the object (to-be-known), and knowledge (known), were present in every epistemological system; however, as the constituent elements of the epistemological systematization, they did not refer to specific contents but to relationships. The actual contents of these elements (e.g., the nature of the subject and the object) were not determined by epistemology, but rather were left to the systematization that directly described existence.[56]

Thus, although epistemologies sought the ultimate presuppositions of knowledge, the epistemological systematization could only elaborate on the relationships of contents provided elsewhere. In other words, an epistemological system was dependent on a nonepistemological systematization to provide its contents; the relationship of these contents was then clarified by the epistemological systematization. The systematizations that provided the actual presuppositions of knowledge were labeled "primary" (*Ursystematisierungen*)[57] and were three in number – psychology, logic, and ontology.[58] Each primary systematization was "universal" in that it could incorporate anything, including the presuppositions of other primary systematizations, into its own context. Mannheim wrote that "under the aspect of psychology everything is 'lived experience' (*Erlebnis*), from the standpoint of logic all is 'meaning' (*Bedeutung*), and for ontology everything appears likewise as 'being' (*seiend*)."[59]

Because each of the primary systematizations was able to incorporate the others into its own structure, no epistemology based on one of them could win the "struggle for primacy" outright. Epistemology, as a "mixed, intersystematic systematization" which was dependent on the primary systematizations, could only clarify the contents provided for it, but could not mediate between the three sets of contents. For example, he wrote that Kant's epistemology assumed that the ultimate presuppositions of knowledge were logical and, as a logical epistemology, could mediate only logical categories, not psychological or ontological ones.[60]

The same relationship held for the second part of the epistemological problem, valuation. All epistemological systems shared a common value, truth, which was, then, inherent to the epistemological systematization. However, there was no common standard to determine what was true; those standards varied with the presuppositions of the primary systematizations. Still, the epistemological systematization had a raison d'être in that it imposed a common goal (value) on the primary systematizations. Its great worth was its intersystematic nature, which promoted a self-clarification among the holders of the primary systematizations. Mannheim wrote:

> Nothing can appear as valuable or normative as long as we remain within the context of psychological, ontological or logical systematizations. A context which in itself can be valuable, can have standards, only when viewed from another, alien systematization. . . . Epistemology is a systematization sui generis precisely because it enables us to place ourselves outside of the various universal systematizations, whereby it becomes possible to relate the purely descriptive contexts of the latter to its own characteristic value, and thereby to transform them into matters of value, into value standards. . . . Moving among the primary systematizations, its essential contribution is to provide a position from where it becomes possible to observe these regions in their full extent.[61]

"Epistemology" stood apart from Mannheim's other writings through its ahistorical, logical, meaning-genetic methodology. Yet in some ways the essay would anticipate problems that would arise in his cultural historicism; and it has some interesting structural parallels to the later *Ideology and Utopia*. In both, he postulated an unresolved struggle for primacy among different perspectives (primary systematizations in "Epistemology," political consciousnesses in *Ideology and Utopia*), which was missing from the other early cultural writings. An important role in this struggle for primacy was played by another element (epistemology, the intelligentsia), which had a distinct identity of its own. This element was separated from the conflict of perspectives in that it was somewhat removed from the existential connections of the other positions ("free choice of reference," "socially free-floating"); and yet its contents came from them. This semiautonomy gave it a more inclusive perspective that allowed it to clarify relationships, to help raise presuppositions to consciousness, and to serve as a vehicle for intersystematic communication. At the same time, it could not resolve the conflict, but simply clarify it. In the period between "Epistemology" and *Ideology and Utopia*, this element was pretty much set aside, only to be brought back in a new form when Mannheim had moved from the problem of cultural philosophy to that of political science.

The published article that was much more important to the development of this early period was "*Weltanschauung*," in which he moved from the suprahistorical level to the historical one. He described this move in terms of three levels of meaning – objective, expressive, and documentary. Objective meaning was concerned with the object and not with the subject, at least not with the historical one. Although the object was meaningful within the cultural sciences, its meaning at this level was interpreted by the transcendental-logical subject (to use the term from "Epistemology"), and it was presented as an objective structure of fixed forms (*Setzungen*).[62] Put another way, one could say that those sciences that dealt with the objective meaning of cultural products had suprahistorical systematizations. To move the other two levels of meaning meant to move away from systematized, or theoretical, knowledge to an atheoretical knowledge.

On the level of expressive meaning, this knowledge "cannot be divorced from the subject and his actual stream of lived experience and acquires its fully individualized meaning only with reference to this 'intimate universe' (*Innenweltbezug*)." One could have no theoretical knowledge of this expressive content; rather, it was grasped in a "pretheoretical manner." And because of the intimate ties to the real historical subject, expressive meaning, unlike objective meaning, had to be investigated as a unique historical fact.[63]

To illustrate the difference between these two types of meaning, Mannheim distinguished between "sign" and "formation" (*Gestaltung*), the former being pure form without any real emotional content, the latter giving form to emotional content from which it could not be separated. Objective meaning could be realized through the sign, for it concerned only the object itself, the form perceivable to everyone, the laws governing the sensual field. Expressive meaning, although it was embedded in the stratum of objective meaning in that it had form, also had a deeper level in which this form was connected to the contents of the soul. Sign language could convey only stereotyped psychic contents; however, at the expressive level of meaning "each individual pattern of movement conveys a specifically unique state of emotion."[64]

"Formation" conveyed a subjective feeling, which was understood by the receiver through a faculty such as understanding. An artist, wrote Mannheim, gave formation to his or her soul when he created an artwork, and in doing so produced a cultural object. Approaching the artwork on a purely objective level, viewing only its form was possible but incomplete, for it meant divorcing the work from the artist. However, limiting one's interpretation to the expressive meaning of a cultural product would uncover only a "cross-section of [the artist's] stream of lived experience," the "actualization of a psychic life."[65] In the terms of the Free School lecture, one would grasp the individual creative soul but not the general meaning of the culture itself and the soul's place in it. Because the organic link between soul and culture had broken down, interpretations limited to the expressive level of meaning were by themselves inadequate and had to be supplemented by the third level of meaning, the documentary one.

Documentary interpretation brought with it not only a new method, but also a new object, the world view (*Weltanschauung*). The latter, which could be considered synonymous with the concept of "culture" in the Free School lecture, was a nonrational totality (although it contained rational elements) that was pretheoretical; that is, it could not be presented in its totality in theoretical terms. This nonrationality could be contrasted with the systematization from "Epistemology," which was a logical structure and could be presented in its entirety in exact, theoretical terms. He wrote that as long as the world view was considered to be theoretical, entire areas of cultural life would remain inaccessible to interpretation.[66] However, he said, "we cannot accept the extreme form of irrationalism which holds that certain cultural facts are not merely atheoretical but are radically removed from any rational analysis." It was not that the world view was impervious to rational analysis, but simply that a theoretical system could not be imposed upon it. Although its form was qualitatively different from theoretical form, it was not without form. Although the world view was nonrational, it was not irrational, that is, resistant to "translation" into rational terms and hence communicable only through intuition.[67]

In addition to its pretheoretical character, the *Weltanschauung* differed from the systematization in its historicity. A world view was the cultural

45

totality of a specific epoch, a cross section of the historical flow of spirit. For example, Kant's epistemology, in having a certain structure and certain components, could be traced to the epistemological systematization. However, the historical elements that had to be stripped from Kant's system in order to interpret it meaning-genetically could be included in a historical-genetic interpretation as elements of the world view of the late eighteenth century.

Although the world view was temporally more limited than the systematization, culturally it was more inclusive. The systematization was restricted to a cultural field; the *Weltanschauung* incorporated all cultural products in a given era. At the same time, this totality was organic in nature; that is, it was greater than the sum of its parts and could never be objectified completely in them. Mannheim wrote:

> In themselves the cultural objectifications as they present themselves to us are meaningful products (*Sinngebilde*) and therefore belong to the rational (not the theoretical!) sphere; whereas the unity that is sought here is a whole that lies beyond the meaningful products, although it is somehow given through them. . . . Every cultural objectification, and also every self-contained and incomplete part of it, appears from this aspect as a fragment, and the corresponding totality cannot be supplied at the level of the objectifications.[68]

Not only was the *Weltanschauung* beyond the cultural product, it was also beyond the creator of the product, greater than the consciousness of any creative individual subject.[69] Documentary meaning, like expressive meaning, was concerned with a context and subject beyond the objective level of the work; however, it differed from expressive meaning in that the context and the subject were collective rather than individual and were purely spiritual rather than experiential. With regards to the latter, he warned against confusing documentary collective subjects[70] with the subjects of sociology and anthropology such as class and race, for documentary interpretation dealt not with the temporal actualization of the subject but with "a deeper meaningful unity."[71] Although he agreed that collective experiential subjects existed, he made no attempt in this essay to relate them to the collective cultural subject. This was not the case for the individual experiential subject, whom he saw as directly involved in the process of cultural creation. Thus, for Mannheim, the question of the relationship between existence (*Sein*) and meaning (*Sinn*) was that of the individual subject's experience and the collective subject's spiritual essence.[72]

Because the documentary interpreter sought a totality beyond the cultural product and the experiential subject, there was no need for him or her to respect the work as an integral whole. Although the interpreter of

46

expressive meaning had to treat the work as a whole, because it was the expression of the individual subject who created it, the documentary interpreter, not bound by objective form or experiential content, could make use of any fragment of the work to uncover the atheoretical totality behind it.[73] In addition, such a fragment (the "document") could give a complete characterization of the *Weltanschauung* and its collective subject. Relating parts to one another was not necessary, for additional documents did not add new meaning, but rather corroborated the same meaning "in homologous fashion." "This grasping of the homologous in various contexts of meaning belongs to a class apart that should not be confused with either addition or synthesis or a mere abstraction of common properties."[74] Accordingly, these monadic documents were not to be related to one another directly, as was the case with objects on which objective and expressive meaning was based, but rather indirectly through the organic whole.[75] This insistence on an indirect monadic approach was dominant throughout his early period,[76] and, as we shall see in the next chapter, carried over into his description of the sociology of knowledge.

The organic unity of the world view seemed to free this essay from the problem of pluralism in "Epistemology," where each systematization remained autonomous from the others, connected only relationally by the epistemological systematization, and where there was no conclusive resolution to the "struggle for primacy." The world view seemed to overcome this pluralism in that it incorporated all cultural fields, forming a totality of meaning not present in the other essay.[77]

However, this organic totality was not unproblematical, for its historical and pretheoretical nature presented Mannheim with the danger of relativism. Here we see that the formulation of the Free School lecture had been complicated by doubling the number of elements presented. There the problem was one of intersubjective meaning and communication of individual souls within the same objective culture; in "*Weltanschauung*," the same problem was extended to different objective cultures (world views). Because documentary interpretation was "closely interwoven with the spiritual historical position from which the interpreter attempts to approach the spirit of past epochs," it had to be performed anew in each epoch.[78] Again Mannheim was left with the problem of pluralism, but this time it was temporal – there was a competition between organic world views rather than between universal systematizations.

The nonrational nature of world views exacerbated the problem, for it meant relating qualitatively different entities to one another. The question, wrote Mannheim, was: "how can one form that unity that we sense [documentarily] in all cultural objectifications which belong together into

47

concepts and scientific terms capable of control and verification?"[79] He believed that certain epochs would be spiritually closer than others to the world view being interpreted and, therefore, the interpreters within those epochs would have a better grasp of the documentary meaning in question. It was not a matter of which image was more correct, for they all were, but which was most "adequate." The test of adequacy was comprehensibility; the most adequate interpretation was the one that could completely translate the others into its own language. However, Mannheim did not take into account the possibility raised for systematizations in "Epistemology" – that a number of world views would be able to completely translate the others into their own languages. If this were the case, then a more viable standard of "adequacy" would be necessary.

Mannheim's ambivalence to the problem of pluralism can be seen in his review of a book about the classification of the sciences.[80] He wrote that there were a number of ways one could classify sciences because there were a number of different viewpoints from which one could undertake this task. As these viewpoints were incommensurate, there was no way to resolve the resulting pluralism. Yet, one could not accept the relativistic implications of this pluralism. Again, his answer was to establish a hierarchy of adequacy. Here, he was unclear as to just how such a hierarchy was to be established.

At the end of the essay he suggested that perhaps the essence of a science could be determined through its total progress of historical development and the latter's "spirit."[81] Although he simply posed the question here, one gets a glimmer of his preference for the historical approach of *"Weltanschauung"* over the logical, ahistorical methodology of "Epistemology." Despite the differences between these two essays, they did have one very important factor in common – both were immanent genetic interpretations, operating under the assumption that "spirit can be understood only by spirit."[82] In this they differed from "Cultural-Sociological Knowledge," a two-hundred-page manuscript finished in 1922 but never published, which represented a shift to an extrinsic genetic interpretation.

The "extrinsic" element introduced by Mannheim in this manuscript was the collective "context of lived experience" (*Erlebniszusammenhang*). Although he previously had not denied the existence of collective experiential subjects, he had largely ignored them in the matter of cultural questions in favor of the lived experience of the individual, the soul. Now he emphasized that lived experience could be either individual or collective, the latter being not simply the sum of individual experiences but an entity in its own right. This "new" element, then, required that he address its relationship to the two elements already given in *"Weltanschauung,"* the

48

individual experiential subject (the soul) and the collective spiritual essence (the world view).

Mannheim wrote that, although both individual and communal lived experiences were real, there was no clear dividing line between them. Usually, the collective context shaped that of the individual to such an extent that any differentiation between the two was not problematical and the individual appeared as a microcosm of the collective macrocosm.[83] Even when individual opinions contradicted one another, both sides were usually based on the same common foundation of experience. Therefore, the task of distinguishing between the individual and collective contexts of lived experience required the imposition of artificial boundaries upon an organic continuum, a method he described as "imputation."[84]

Mannheim concerned himself more with the relationship between the collective spiritual and existential subjects, both of which he included in the context of lived experience. This context, which was described in such terms as "life system," "basic foundation," "basic substance," and "total person," was an atheoretical totality, an organic entity that could never be grasped conceptually in its entirety.[85] In this organic, nonrational nature, the context of lived experience resembled the world view described in "*Weltanschauung*." An important difference between the two essays was that in the earlier one the world view was considered a spiritual entity separate from empirical subjects,[86] whereas in the latter one it had definite ties to social reality through the context of lived experience.[87] In this context, cultural products and social relationships were "connected" with one another in a reciprocal relationship in which each was a function of the other.[88] How this basic entity was conceptualized depended on the attitude (*Einstellung*) of the interpreter and on which objectification of the context he focused.[89]

In his manuscript, Mannheim sought to locate the sociology of culture in relation to the various attitudes that could be taken. He began by postulating the two extremes, which concerned themselves only with meaning or social existence. The former viewed cultural products as forms transcending historical experience and forming a sphere of validity (*geltungsmässig*). Such disciplines could be described as immanent, systematic ones and took their lead from systematic philosophy.[90] Among those disciplines at the other pole, that of extrinsic genetic explanation, was the type of sociology that was strictly a science of social aggregates (*Gesellschaftslehre*).[91] These two basic sciences existed side by side but had no direct relationship to one another. Mannheim thus saw the necessity of building a bridge between them through a new discipline, one that would relate meaning to existence.[92]

As in "*Weltanschauung*," he saw Dilthey's human scientific psychology as a pioneering discipline in the construction of this bridge.[93] However, it was concerned with the individual subject, the soul, and, therefore, the connection of the collective subjects had to be left to a new form of sociology, cultural sociology. This discipline was different from philosophy in that the latter's immanent consideration of meaningful content and validity (*Sinngehalt, Geltungscharakter*) was not of concern to it, just as the origins and functionality of a "result" were irrelevant to the immanent question of validity. On the other hand, cultural-sociological interpretation was distinguished from positivistic explanation as a new, meaningful discipline; and he defined "interpretation," including its cultural-sociological form, as one meaning being made understandable by another.[94] What would seem to be a contradiction here can be resolved by differentiating the genetic clarification of meaning from the arbitration of values in meaning. The former was analytical, the latter valuative, but both were concerned with meaning. Thus, the functional interpretation of meaning gave cultural sociology its intermediary position between philosophy and sociology.[95]

Although cultural sociology acted as a bridge, it was not the synthesis that Mannheim had called for in his Free School lecture. This can be seen in the concept of "displacement" (*Verschiebung*), which he attributed to the discipline. Displacement meant the examination of conceptual content on a level foreign to it, the understanding of one level of conceptualization from another. Such a nonimmanent interpretation demonstrated the "intermeshing" and "interweaving" of these concepts in the totality of life and lived experience. It provided a "distance," a new perspective that further clarified cultural products, demonstrating their functionality and the collective context of lived experience in which they were produced.[96] However, social structure "penetrated" (*hineinragen*) only so far into cultural phenomena, and cultural sociology was limited to that penetration in its interpretation. This limitation, which provided the distance, also dictated that cultural sociology could not be the primary discipline for the interpretation of culture; that honor, as we have seen, fell to philosophy. The latter was the synthesizing discipline, the arbiter of values in the spiritual sphere.[97] Bridges to the existential realm offered clarity but not meaning.

Having laid out the basic task of cultural sociology in relation to other kinds of knowledge, Mannheim concluded his study with a discussion of the new discipline's methodology, which varied with the methodology of sociology itself. He listed three types of sociology, pure, general, and dynamic, each with a corresponding type of cultural sociology.

Pure sociology used a nonhistorical, noninductive method akin to that of the phenomenologists, wanting to dispense with the multiplicity of historical forms and to discover the essential human forms. The key concept here was "essence" (*Wesen*), an a priori entity, yet one that could not simply be deduced, but rather had to be extracted from lived experience. At the same time, essence had to be distinguished from fact; one did not reach the essence of a social form through a process of induction from facts. Rather, one "stripped" the factuality away from experience and put the factuality in "brackets" (what he called the "phenomenological reduction"), leaving the essence. For example, one experienced various kinds of communal relationships, tried to remove what was historically unique about them, and arrived at the essence of "*Gemeinschaft.*" This essence was not a generalization of spatiotemporal data; facts were not the building blocks for essences, nor were they proof for them, but simply served as examples.[98]

Pure cultural sociology sought to examine how cultural forms could become social factors and how far the social penetrated into their constitution.[99] In a world of continual historical change, pure cultural sociology sought essences stripped of historicity, a "sociological cogito ergo sum."[100]

In contrast to pure sociology, general sociology was a discipline of inductive factuality rather than essences. It sought to establish generalities drawn from and supported by facts. The basic element of general sociology was the "type," which helped to unravel causal contexts. This concern for causality took two different forms: a study of the susceptibility of these types to general laws and an applied helping science for history whose types helped clarify unique historical events without subordinating those events to general laws. However, even in the latter case, these types, like the essences of pure sociology, were nonhistorical. They simply stood side by side with no temporally "hierarchical" order, with no dynamic relationship of interaction.[101]

General cultural sociology sought to know and order the most general relationships between sociological formations and general cultural types. The latter, although expressed as world views, were not the historically unique entities that Mannheim defined as "world views," but rather were repeated and schematically demonstrable types inductively arrived at.[102] Thus, whereas general cultural sociology examined that area discarded by pure cultural sociology – inductively gathered facts – the types it formed based on these facts were still not historically ordered. These two kinds of cultural sociology would be adequate only if every social form was possible at every time. Because this was not the case, an historical approach, said Mannheim, was required.

Such a historical approach characterized dynamic sociology. Nevertheless, this discipline was sociological, and he felt it necessary to distinguish it from the disciplines of history and the philosophy of history. Dynamic sociology differed from historical studies in two ways: It placed primary emphasis on types rather than on historical individualities,[103] and it viewed time as primarily hierarchical rather than simply chronological. The historian saw history as a temporal contiguity, a chronological sequence of unique causal contexts; the dynamic sociologist, on the other hand, saw history as a series of distinct hierarchical stages.[104]

This hierarchical structure, in which the temporal sequence was seen as instilling meaning, was shared by both dynamic sociology and the philosophy of history. But, despite the common desire to create a hierarchy of meaning, the two differed in two ways. First, because dynamic sociology was concerned primarily with social formations rather than cultural ones, its types could not be immanently construed but had to be gathered from actual individual products. Second, it was not teleological. In doing away with the metaphysics of a basic plan and final goal that characterized the philosophy of history, dynamic sociology and its sociogenetic typologies were not "valuating" (*wertend*) entities. What came "later" was not seen as "higher" in the sense of having greater value, but simply as a condition in which the earlier was "transcended" (*aufgehoben*) by the later.[105] Mannheim's description here was consistent with his assignment of the task of valuation to the purely cultural science of philosophy rather than to the existentially oriented science of sociology.

The tasks of dynamic cultural sociology were threefold: (1) the arrangement of cultural products into cultural spheres and the charting of the development of those spheres; (2) the incorporation of those spheres into a world view, which was imputed to a certain context of lived experience; (3) the establishment of a hierarchical structure of world views, that is, tracing the change from one world view to another.[106] The third task distinguished dynamic cultural sociology from the pure and general types, whereas the second task distinguished it from his immanent genetic interpretations of "Epistemology" and "*Weltanschauung.*" Their combination meant that dynamic cultural sociology posited a series of totalities, which were characterized by their social aggregations rather than their cultural products and whose relationship to one another was seen as "discontinuous, 'dialectical.'"[107]

The dialectical element, although increasingly important during this early period, was not new; it was present in "*Weltanschauung*"[108] and so was compatible with an immanent, genetic interpretation. It was the sociological element, the context of lived experience, that was novel in this manuscript. However, mere appearance did not necessarily mean priority, and he subordinated the sociological element to the cultural one. First, he defined the totalities temporally rather than spatially, in terms of eras rather than social groups. He wrote that one must work with a relatively stable typology for a period derived from the "valuations and innermost tendencies" of an era.[109] And even in qualifying this statement by noting that such stable typologies were exaggerations, he wrote: "The men of an age do not all live in the same time. It is the time of philosophy of history which is of course intended at the end of that saying."[110] Second, he characterized social groups as "culture bearers" rather than as culture creators, with the cultural element seeming to have a degree of autonomy. For example, he wrote that, even though the nobility was replaced by the bourgeoisie as the main culture bearer, the world view imputed to the nobility continued to exist. It might lie dormant for some time or it might be taken over immediately by new culture bearers.[111] It is clear here that the main concern was with the world view and that the sociological element was supplementary.

Cultural sociology, then, served not as a new synthesis but as an agent of clarification. It was certainly useful in what Mannheim saw as the central task of the modern era, the establishment of rational connections between the existential realm of historical science and the sphere of meaning interpreted by philosophy. However, the primary task remained not clarification but synthesis,[112] the creation of the new philosophy he had called for in the Free School lecture. In "Cultural-Sociological Knowledge," with its methodological emphasis, this problem remained in the background.

The solution

Mannheim's 1924 essay "Historicism" did sketch out that new philosophy and, thus, represented the culmination of his early cultural writings. (This position continued into Part One of "Sociological Theory of Culture" (1924), which will also be discussed here.) Historicism, he wrote, "epitomizes our world view" in that it not only organized the human sciences but also permeated everyday thought. In short, it was the "basis on which we construct our observations of the socio-cultural reality" and, as such, was the successor to the universal world view of the Middle Ages, which was pictured as an unreflected, static, organic synthesis of meaning and existence. When this unity broke apart under the pressure of the universal rationalism of the Enlightenment, its irrational elements were raised to the level of reflection through the efforts of Romanticism and later by the phenomenologists. The result was a duality in which the modalities of subjective consciousness were examined in isolation from the logic of objective cultural forms. As such, these investigations remained simply specialized ones. For them to be raised to the level of a philosophical world view, they had to be "employed as parts of a striving for a totality to comprehend the world."[113]

What form would such a totality take? Mannheim believed that the days of the great systematizers were past, that his age was lacking in a substantive philosophy of its own. It was "questionable nowadays whether there exist any starting points in our consciousness which give promise of a positive affirmation (*Positivität*) of our own, able to give shape to the world."[114] This absence resulted in a pluralism that took place largely at the level of methodological inquiry, so that neo-Hegelians and neo-Kantians did not confront one another with the systems of their founders but with the methodological ramifications of the premises of those systems. However, he believed that being confined to this level allowed thinkers of his era to achieve a certain distance, a certain insight denied to more philosophically synthetic ages.[115] One can view this state as a restatement on Mannheim's part of the idea of the critical stage of cultural development.

He suggested possible reactions to this condition that bring to mind his letters from exile in 1922. One approach was that of the George Circle (not actually named here), which sought to "leap" from the current situation, to "strike a prophetic pose for some positive affirmation to transcend the present state." Mannheim's criticism of this approach was essentially the same one that earlier was leveled at George – it was "false" and "inauthentic," the "mere reassertion of obsolete positions." Another reaction, that of Max Weber, accepted as fate the state of suspension (*Schwebezustand*) in which "the intention towards positive affirmation is already present, without however, finding fulfillment."[116] Here one can note a change in the position attributed to Weber from that in 1922. Weber's position was now seen as more negative, a characterization that would continue until *Ideology and Utopia*.

Mannheim stated that one need not accept either of these two positions, for there was a way out – historicism, which accepted neither the fatalism of Weber nor the "leap" of George, but rather had the "confidence that the matter will in the end transcend itself on its own."[117] Historicism, he believed, earned a position of universality through its ability to make sense of the very forces that had caused the medieval world to disintegrate; it "is able to derive a principle of order from the manifold changes and is in a position to penetrate the innermost structure of this all-pervading change."[118]

The new philosophy had to make sense not only out of the temporal flux but also out of the fragmentation of cultural fields that accompanied that flux. It transcended individual cultural disciplines and the methodological specialization that accompanied them "with the help of the category of 'totality.'"[119] Here Mannheim, as in the Free School lecture, was not calling for the abandonment of specialization, but rather for its transcendence. Specialization was seen as a useful tool for examining different cultural fields, but a tool that should be subordinate to a higher synthetic level of meaning.[120]

The construction of the historicist totality required two separate operations: One had to examine (1) the historical development of the individual cultural fields and (2) the relation of the fields to one another within a temporal cross section. The synthesis of these two operations resulted in an interpretation of the relationship of the cross sections to one another.[121] It can be noted already that Mannheim's emphasis here was temporal and cultural rather than spatial and sociological.

In examining the historical development of different cultural fields, he divided them into three basic types: civilizational, psychic-cultural, and philosophical. The first two corresponded to the dualism expounded by his mentor Alfred Weber[122] – a variation of the standard traditional–modern dichotomy of the German academic community. Mannheim saw the third type as an incomplete synthesis of the other two.[123]

The civilizational type, which he associated with Enlightenment rationalism and the positivism of the natural sciences, was committed to an eternally valid set of mechanistic laws and/or a priori rational concepts, for example, cause and effect, and set as its goal the quantification of knowledge. "Quantification," he wrote, "the reduction of phenomena to a static system of measurement, assures us that the 'progress' of the findings of the natural sciences takes place within a 'static system.'" By static he did not mean the absence of change, but rather the absence of qualitative change. He believed that the conceptual change of the natural sciences, and for that matter the Enlightenment idea of progress, was merely the progressive articulation of "one and the same system which merely becomes more complete as time passes." Civilizational change, then, did not bring qualitatively new entities but simply quantitative additions to the same eternal system. The rationalists assumed that any new data were governed by the rational conceptual apparatus already in existence.[124]

What did Mannheim believe to be the assumptions of such a static system? First, it perceived the knowing subject as supratemporal or, using the terminology of "Epistemology," as a "transcendental-logical subject." Such a subject was purely rational and purely contemplative – he or she was divorced from the activity of the individual historical subject. This separation of knowledge and activity was most successfully applied to the world of rigid things; when it was applied to the dynamic world of human beings, it was incomplete.[125] The same was true for the second assumption of the civilizational sciences – that it was necessary to deal with forms and not with any "deeper" content of the objects to be studied. These forms, the rationalist believed, could be theoretized, classified, and analyzed without having to deal with the nature of the stuff being formed. As we saw in the preceding essays, Mannheim believed that the purely abstract formalism of civilization, divorced from the deeper meaning of life, was inadequate when applied to the human world.[126]

These assumptions by the civilizational sciences resulted in a "truth" that was one-dimensional. These sciences perceived knowledge as a "unilinear series of approximations toward the one and only possible form of truth, where the last assumption simply discounts as error all previous hypotheses about the same facts." Thus, the Ptolemaic and Copernican systems of astronomy could not both be correct; the latter negated the former.[127] Again, Mannheim believed this appropriate only when restricted to the natural sciences.

At the opposite pole from the civilizational type stood the psychic–cultural type, which saw development as an irrational flow resisting any formal systematization. The fields characterized by this type were essentially "psychic" (*seelenhaft*) in nature and were grasped less as systems than as elements of the unified psychological *Gestalt* of an epoch.[128] Such a perception was organic, intuitive, and irrational and could be identified with traditional historicism and its concept of individuality (which in fact Mannheim did). Its most extreme form, for him, seems to have been artistic creation.

The subject of this type was the "accidental, subjectively and empirically determined ego of the historian."[129] The cultural products perceived and created by the subject were connected with "expressible endowment of meaning" and "aspirations toward formation."[130] The products, therefore, could not be treated simply as forms but as formations of a deeper stuff connected with the soul.[131] This represented a marked contrast to the logical subject and purely formal object of the civilizational type.

Despite the "dimension of depth" into the historical material that the psychic-cultural type provided, it was not able to deal with change in a systematic manner. Whereas the civilizational elements could be organized in terms of one system, the psychic-cultural elements formed a number of qualitatively different *Gestalten* with no systematic conception of the change from one *Gestalt* to another. Change was viewed as simple contiguity, as "chronological," to use the term from "Cultural-Sociological Knowledge." Here the static system was opposed with pure flux.[132]

Because there was no universal system, or subject, the development of the psychic-cultural element could not be interpreted "progressively; each epoch must reinterpret it anew from its own psychic center."[133] This did not mean that past epochs were inaccessible to interpreters in the present; however, those past epochs had to be interpreted in their own terms, "on the basis of their own standards and values, . . . from their own centers, a comprehension called the immanent critique and description of the past."[134] But this kind of "truth" was incomplete, resulting in a series of "profiles" (*Abschattungen*) viewed from "local positions," much like Husserl proclaimed for spatial objects. "The different historical pictures," wrote Mannheim, "do not contradict one another in their interpretations, but encircle the same graphically identical given historical content from various positions and depths (*Tiefpunkte*)."[135] As he had written earlier: "No painting will ever contradict a picture by Giotto."[136] Such a truth would seem to involve the same temporal relativism that characterized traditional historicism.

Mannheim saw his third type, the philosophical, occupying a position between the other two. This type was characterized by the logical-dialectical construction of the philosophy of history represented by Hegel. It saw development as neither the unilinear progress of a single static system nor as a series of autonomous *Gestalten*, but rather as a continual reorganization of elements around new centers. One philosophical system did not vanquish the preceding one (as in civilizational development), nor did it have no impact at all (as in psychic-cultural development). Instead, a new world picture was organized around a more comprehensive center, and earlier insights were "transcended" in the new system.[137] Old centers remained but were hierarchically subordinate to the new center, although nothing precluded them from one day reassuming their central position. This dialectical conflict provided the basis of past and present systems and allowed for a historical rationality, a synthesis of the suprahistorical rationality of the civilizational type and the historical nonrationality of the psychic-cultural type.

Mannheim did not elaborate on the philosophical type as much as the other two, because it overlapped with his philosophy of "dynamic historicism," which was essentially the merger of the philosophical and psychic-cultural types. Dynamic historicism combined the dialectic with the *Gestalt*, so that the philosophical centers were "supra-theoretically based" and were dependent on new "life-situations" (*Lebenslage*).[138] This combination of the philosophy of history and history proper was also reflected in the knowing subject, who was neither transcendental nor purely empirical. Mannheim wrote: "The subject relevant to the philosophy of history is just that kernel of the person whose content and aspirations are consubstantial with the dominant tendencies of history."[139]

57

This is not to say that he excluded the civilizational type from cultural interpretation, for he did not.[140] However, there was much greater affinity of the philosophical and psychic-cultural with one another than with the civilizational, for the latter was ahistorical.[141] This relationship was similar to that in *"Weltanschauung,"* where the expressive and documentary levels of meaning were closer to one another than to the objective level of meaning. "Historicism" differed from the earlier essay in that documentary meaning was assigned to the psychic-cultural type rather than to the more synthetic dialectical type.[142] This switch was possible because of two developments in his thought, the first occurring in "Cultural-Sociological Knowledge," the second in "Historicism" itself. In the unpublished manuscript, he had extended the context of lived experience from the individual to the collectivity with the provision that there was no distinct dividing line between the two. As a result, the antinomy of "document" (collective, nonexperiential) and "formation" (individual, experiential) was resolved, and the two levels could be seen as one. Also, both the expressive and documentary levels were analytical rather than valuative; the emphasis on valuation came only in "Historicism," where the imputation of a context was secondary to the determination of "truth" among competing contexts. Accordingly, the analytical distinction between the formation and the document was of less importance than it had previously been, and the discussion of the dialectical shifting of centers, which played a secondary role in *"Weltanschauung,"*[143] became primary.

Mannheim believed his philosophy of dynamic historicism could solve the problem of valuation in the changing modern world. In the following passage, he described the essentials of this new world view.

> There is a utopia,[144] a logical postulate, underlying this historical conception of philosophic truth, namely, that the overall philosophic process does possess its truth. But we should not imagine the truth as one that can be grasped from a position (*Standort*) above the historical stream. Rather, we can grasp it as it is embodied in self-contained philosophical systems and their centers which grow out of that movement. That philosophy has its life means that it constantly projects new elements into a new totality and creates new positions for the collection and organization of both previously grasped and new elements. . . . It is, then, possible in principle to work out on the basis of this dialectical-dynamic utopia an historico-philosophical hierarchy of philosophical positions succeeding one another and one can do this in a rationally exact fashion. . . . This change from one type of system to another may be explained by the shift (*Verschiebung*) from one center of construction of these systems to another, and it always can be shown which of these opposed systems is more comprehensive. Such a presentation must

indeed concede that every systematization (even the highest available) is positionally bound (*standortsgebunden*) and in this sense is spiritually perspectivistic.[145]

The two terms at the end of this passage, "positionally bound" and "spiritually perspectivistic," were central to Mannheim's dynamic historicism. "Perspectivism,"[146] like his later concept "relationism," was designed to prevent any charge that his philosophy was relativistic. The concept meant that within any historical period only one systematic formulation of the totality could be correct; that, whereas truth was dynamic, it could be determined for any cross section of the historical flow.[147] Because there were competing centers of construction, there had to be a standard for deciding which was primary within a certain cross section. Mannheim believed that, for a philosophical system to be dialectically "true," it had to be more comprehensive than its competitors, including those that preceded it; it had to reorganize elements from the past with new elements on a higher level.[148] Such a hierarchy was made possible by ascertaining the "depth of penetration" (*Tiefdimension*) that each position possessed. Some interpretations would be able to penetrate an object more deeply than others and, hence, were more comprehensive.[149]

Mannheim wrote that this dialectical process revealed a kind of progress, although not the unilinear type of civilizational rationalism. Because the new systems had to compete with the old, they would become increasingly more comprehensive. However, this was not automatic; there was no preordained goal toward which the historical process was moving.[150] Despite his use of Hegel as an example, he rejected the teleological element of the latter's thought. We saw this same rejection of teleology in "Cultural-Sociological Knowledge"; however, there it was limited to cultural sociology and, in fact, was used to contrast that discipline with the philosophy of history. Now his philosophy of history was also nonteleological.

This convergence raises an important question: What role did sociology play in the process of valuation? We have seen that, although he concentrated on the role and methodology of cultural sociology in the unpublished manuscript, he left that discipline out of the process of valuation, assigning that role to the pure cultural sciences, especially philosophy. Did this division continue in "Historicism," or was sociology assigned a new and more important role? Did sociology form a major component of his dynamic historicism, or was it a supplementary discipline for the new metaphysics called for in the Free School lecture?

Although Mannheim believed that his dynamic historicism was supported by the fact that "our view of life has become thoroughly sociological,"[151] he continued to view sociology as a supplementary discipline. Here his use of the term "sociological" was much like that of the traditional historicists – as a designation for socioeconomic change and increasing politicization of events, which hindered attempts to establish a cultural unity for Germany. The term described a problem to be solved rather than a solution. The acceptance of sociological elements to be synthesized did not equal acceptance of sociology as the synthesizing discipline.

My contention is supported by an examination of the other term from the long passage quoted directly above – "positionally bound." "Position" was an inexact term and could have both a temporal and a spatial meaning; however, in "Historicism" it was essentially a temporal term.[152] Mannheim's historicism treated a philosophy as something that resulted from the subject's place in time, not his place in society. Each historical era was seen as potentially having a unified philosophical position, that is, as oriented around one center of construction. The competition between interpretations, between potential centers, was essentially one between historical eras rather than between social groups.[153]

Sociology was simply a useful supplementary science, one that provided genetic clarification but not standards for validation. It was as a supplementary science that the discipline had finally found its proper role. Previously, he wrote, sociology had been viewed as a static, mechanistic discipline, which made it of little help to historicism. This assignment to the civilizational sphere continued even though a number of different sociologies (such as those described in "Cultural-Sociological Knowledge") were being formulated that seemed to preclude its civilizational role. The result was that the discipline was given a solid place by historicism, which demonstrated that a differentiated sociology could serve a useful supplemental role. Thus, his emphasis was not on what sociology could do for historicism, but on what historicism could do for sociology.[154] He wrote:

> Positional bondedness of knowledge, and of the whole cultural creation and life-formation, may be seen in a sense different from that above [his discussion of dynamic historicism]: as a bondedness to and a connection with (*eine Gebundenheit an und eine Verbundenheit mit*) certain social strata and their particular dynamics. The philosophy of history which mostly treats historical periods only as units, overlooking their inner differentiation, must be supplemented by a socially differentiated view of the movement of the whole in which the distribution of social roles and their meaning for the dynamics of the whole must be taken into consideration. . . . The enrichment of the total picture of the philosophy of history through the problem of social differentiation of this totality and the social bondedness of the tendencies is another point of view, which can only be mentioned here.[155]

60

Further confirmation of the subordinate position of sociology comes from comparing "Historicism" with "Cultural-Sociological Knowledge." Dynamic historicism and dynamic cultural sociology shared many characteristics, including the attempt to establish hierarchies and to connect the realm of meaning with that of existence in a nonteleological, dialectical process. One could then ask: Why did he write about historicism rather than cultural sociology in his published essay? He provided the answer to this question when he wrote: "If one places primacy on the philosophy of history, this requires the discovery not only of a genetic but also a meaning-genetic sequence of formations which come into being."[156] Because sociology was simply a genetic method of analysis, it had to be downplayed in "Historicism" in favor of a meaning-genetic set of standards, provided by this philosophy of history.[157]

Although "Historicism" did continue the commitment to a philosophical synthesis from the earlier writings, it differed from them in perceiving that philosophy was dynamic rather than static. In "Epistemology," "meaning-genetic" had meant a logical development of a standard of values; in "Historicism" it meant a historical one. Historicism now took the place of epistemology by establishing "dynamic truth" as the standard to be met.[158]

Mannheim believed that, as the successor to epistemology, dynamic historicism could accomplish what its predecessor failed to do – not merely clarify but resolve the pluralism of philosophical positions. He was committed to the idea of a cultural synthesis of temporally bound positions, a perspectivistic truth. However, he never really offered a satisfactory set of standards for determining that truth other than his vague notion of "depth of penetration," in which he wrote of grasping such standards "instinctively" through participation in the "collective spirit."[159] In a lengthy footnote near the end of the essay, he seemed to realize these shortcomings, stating that historicism had not completed its task.[160]

In Part One of "Sociological Theory of Culture," he described the syntheses of historicism as "relative," because they could not overcome the limitation imposed by existence. He wrote:

> This limitation is twofold. It consists first of all in the circumstance that even synthesizing thought can only take into account the life-elements and currents which have become visible to the epoch, and it can manage these only with the methods of thinking, viewpoints, and concepts which have manifested themselves in thought up to then. Syntheses are furthermore relative, despite the most upright intention of doing justice to all currents, because they undertake their function (ascertaining the structure internal to world events in terms of the philosophy of history) only from a place where they themselves stand, a place which is historically determinate; and

this circumstance determines that their assignment of roles to meaningful formations within the depiction of history cannot overcome its "one-sidedness." Syntheses are ultimately relative because they will unavoidably be overcome by the process within which cognition itself is implicated.[161]

Mannheim stated that this self-relativization meant no self-denigration for the synthesizer, because his thinking was "connected with existence" (*mit der Existenz verbunden*). Yet, because his definition of "existence" was temporal (despite his use of Marxist class terms in this section[162]), the problem of historical relativism remained unsolved. He stated that this discussion was only a sketch, but he believed that one must "commit" oneself to working out such a theory of historical thinking rather than attempting to leap from history.[163] Mannheim never really resolved this problem. When it came to the issue of the philosophical consequence of the long methodological discussion of the sociology of culture that was supposed to lay the foundation for such historical thinking (and which will be discussed in the next chapter), he wrote that this had already been discussed in "Historicism."[164] Indeed, the fragmented and unfinished nature of "Sociological Theory of Culture" indicated that he would soon be forced to relinquish his hope for a philosophical synthesis and replace it with a political one.

I will summarize Mannheim's development during this early period by relating the valuative element in the first and last of these early writings, the Free School lecture and "Historicism," to the positions of other thinkers. He was widely read and borrowed concepts from many thinkers, among them Dilthey, Husserl, Riegl, Max Weber, and Alfred Weber. However, I am not as interested here in individual concepts as in basic positions, or centers of construction, and so there are three names that deserve our special attention: Simmel, Troeltsch, and Lukács.

The young Mannheim was very receptive to Simmel's ideas, especially those concerning the crisis of culture. The basic concepts of Simmel's 1911 essay "The Concept and Tragedy of Culture"[165] appeared in the Free School lecture in the argument that the tragedy of culture, the alienation of the individual soul from other souls and the objective spirit, stemmed from a reification of cultural forms. However, there was a difference between the two works, for, as David Kettler notes, Mannheim's lecture showed great optimism in contrast to Simmel's tone of resignation.[166] Simmel was a prime example of his own concept of the stranger, for, although he was a member of the university community, his position was marginal. Men who were his intellectual inferiors resented his ability and his being a Jew and prevented him from attaining the position his achievements merited.[167] The result was the "objective" attachment of the stranger, a commitment to the values of the German traditionalists accompanied by a skepticism about their continued viability. Mannheim saw Simmel as the idealistic seeker of truth restrained by his own skepticism, a man who "doubted when in fact he wanted to believe."[168] Simmel represented the epitome of the critical thinker, who sharpened perceptions of cultural forms but saw in these forms ultimately only reification and alienation and never strove for synthesis. Simmel's work, said Mannheim, "concealed a sense of involuntary resignation."[169]

Mannheim rejected this resignation. In contrast to Simmel the outsider, he was the spokesman for a group with a mission, the Budapest intelligentsia. The group's cultural militancy and optimism were evident when he spoke of a "program," a "task," of "striving," "promoting," and "directing," of the Free School as a "center of attraction." Whereas Simmel's view was that the reification of forms could only be overcome by a new, unformed life-energy, which in turn would become reified, Mannheim believed that the formal, critical stage was not the tragic fate of any historical development bur rather a necessary antithetic stage in the construction of a synthesis of which rational forms and nonrational contents would find a balance. Whereas Simmel confined himself to the brilliant critical analysis of individual forms, Mannheim constantly sought to break through such analysis to synthesis.

This optimism continued, even if somewhat modified, when Mannheim left Hungary and entered the German university system. As in Budapest, he was committed to synthesis and expressed this commitment in traditional, essentially cultural, terms. The difference was that he was no longer the spokesman for a group promoting change, but rather was a young scholar in an institution whose members in the majority abhorred change at a time when the process of change seemed to be out of control, when disorientation and chaos were prevalent. The result was what I have called his refugee strategy. He did not abandon the earlier commitment to change (a belief that change was a positive force and not a process of degeneration), which was antithetic to the traditionalist formulation of cultural synthesis. But he now wrote of understanding change, of coming to terms with it, rather than of promoting it. He now chose as his model Troeltsch, who had similar goals, was among the more optimistic of the German academics, and was one of those dedicated to reconciling the university with the new forces of the Weimar Republic. Mannheim wrote of Troeltsch:

> He has no yearning for the happy isle of academic seclusion where immured from life, unpolitical and inactive, he might lead out a partial existence in pursuing problems of detail in the apparent order of a fully-matured world. He prefers to be in the middle of things and to connect the lines of his theoretical interests with the suffering of an uprooted world. . . . He

63

desires, it would appear, to unite in his person the sociologically conditioned spiritual division in present-day German thought: on the one hand, the original and often profound non-academic scholar and connoisseur who, as a result of an absence of external and internal bonds (*Ungebundenheit*), frequently dissipates his energies; on the other hand, the academic who is bound to his teaching post, who is master of his subject but is remote from the living center of the present. Such a synthesis is in and of itself necessary.[170]

Troeltsch, as Mannheim described him, personified the young Hungarian's refugee strategy, combining the absence of bonds of the Budapest intellectual with the scientific form of the German academic to create a synthesis of aspiration and intellect. Both believed that a "cultural synthesis within the present" was possible, that the dynamic world could create a philosophical standard of values that matched its dynamic character. Both believed that the synthesis was tied to a historical context, rather than floating above it, and that this context contained both the contemplative subject and the "total" personality, the aspirations.[171] However, they also believed that, despite the existential connections, this synthesis could be achieved philosophically. In this belief, they remained within the context of the traditionalist academic world view, no matter how optimistic they might be about modernity.

These assumptions were challenged by Lukács after he became a communist. In a 1920 essay entitled "The Old Culture and the New Culture," he posed the same problem of cultural reification that Simmel and Mannheim had. He agreed with them that modern society had dissolved the continuous and organic aspects of the old culture, and, like Mannheim, he foresaw the establishment of a new culture as the solution. However, unlike Mannheim, he did not believe that the actual solution was cultural. A new culture could arise only after a new society had been established, and this new society had to be proletarian and communist.[172] Lukács maintained this position in his 1923 work *History and Class Consciousness*, with its emphasis on the political party as the prime agent of synthesis.[173] This stronger sociopolitical element separated his work from that of Mannheim, Simmel, and Troeltsch, as well as from his own earlier work.

In "Historicism," written after he had read *History and Class Consciousness*, Mannheim played down Lukács's political position, treating him more as a Hegelian than as a Marxist in order to contrast the rational dialectic with the "irrationalist intuitive" approach of the organicist historicists.[174] (He admired Troeltsch's historicism for synthesizing these two elements.) That he emphasized Lukács as a historicist rather than as a Marxist can be seen in the following passage.

The degree to which historicism governs our thought at present and, as we have demonstrated through Troeltsch, raises problems also could be corroborated through a comparison with [Lukács's] book. We could have shown the basic problems of historicism equally as well taking Lukács' book as an example. To compare these two books (Troeltsch's and Lukács') in order to examine the sociological differentiation of the same problems in authors of different social and political orientation would be a rewarding attempt and a contribution to the "sociology of thought" (*Soziologie des Denkens*). The different positions taken toward the irrational, the greater or lesser positiveness and decisiveness in the historical dialectic, etc. would be shown as determined by social and political position; but in the process, *one could not permit the important kinship in the ultimate point of departure to be overlooked.*[175]

In this passage, there was no indication on Mannheim's part that either Lukács's or Troeltsch's position, but not both, could be correct because they represented different sociopolitical positions. Rather, they provided different emphases of a basic philosophy, and the implication was that their differences could be overcome on a higher philosophical level.[176] Accordingly, the sociology of thought was seen as an interesting, but not crucial, approach, one that was subordinate to the basic philosophical concerns. Although Lukács's "activist-progressive" dialectic was fine for political activism, it was not the emphasis Mannheim chose,[177] hence his use of Troeltsch rather than Lukács in the explication of dynamic historicism. This is not to say that Lukács had no "influence" on him, but rather that he incorporated material from Lukács (as from so many other thinkers) into a structure more akin to that of Troeltsch. The latter's philosophical historicism, rather than Lukács's communism, became his center of construction. He had no urgent need to come to terms with *History and Class Consciousness*. This rejection of Lukács's political position represented a continuation of Mannheim's relationship to his ex-mentor in Budapest after 1918 and not any major intellectual turning point.

There were certainly changes in Mannheim's thought during this period: a tempering of his cultural activism, a greater appreciation of the complexities of cultural change, and a more important role for the collective experiential subject. As a result, the problems of cultural pluralism and historical development increasingly received more attention than that of individual alienation, which was reflected in the switch from Simmel to Troeltsch as the prime model. Before the soul could be reintegrated into a larger totality, one had to determine what the totality was, a task that appeared increasingly difficult to Mannheim. However, his center of construction remained that of cultural philosophy, unchanged by the increasing sophistication of the constellation around it.

3

Transition (1924–1928)

In 1929, replying to a critic of his recently published *Ideology and Utopia*, Mannheim wrote that sociology was a specialized science whose methodology could be of service to humankind if it were transcended in either of two directions. He saw Troeltsch (the model for his earlier dynamic historicism) as an example of someone who attempted to transcend sociology in the direction of philosophy. The other direction, a "politically active world orientation," that is, politics, was the one promoted in *Ideology and Utopia*, marking Mannheim's shift to a new valuative center of construction.[1] The period examined in this chapter fell between the most complete articulations of the old (philosophical) and the new (political) centers, hence its "transitional" label. These years also saw the development of his theory of the sociology of knowledge, the basic components of which first appeared in "Cultural-Sociological Knowledge" (1922) and found their most famous version in *Ideology and Utopia*. Because this analytical discipline was formulated within the context of both the philosophical and political valuative centers, this chapter will chart its development and its role in the shift from one center to the other. This shift was not an abrupt one, so that one cannot say, "in this essay Mannheim was switching centers of construction." Rather, one should say, "in *Ideology and Utopia* the shift in centers had been completed." Because the six major works to be examined here involved considerable overlapping and rewriting, they in no way should be seen as comprising a unilinear progression from one point to another. Also, because these essays were primarily (but not totally) analytical rather than valuative,[2] the problem of valuation remained largely in the background.

Given these qualifications, I offer the following scenario for this transitional period. It began in 1924 with Mannheim working on his second long unpublished manuscript, "Sociological Theory of Culture," the first part of which, as I have already noted, was very close to the position taken in "Historicism."[3] The long methodological section that is the heart of the work overlapped with two published essays, "Problem of Sociology of

66

Knowledge" (1925) and "Ideological and Sociological Interpretation" (1926). The three works can be seen as representing a development of the extrinsic genetic interpretation found in "Cultural-Sociological Knowledge."[4] Taken together, they contain the same three basic elements as the earlier manuscript: (1) a formal, phenomenological investigation of the place of cultural sociology and its components, (2) a dynamic historical interpretation of the discipline's development, and (3) a discussion of its methodology.

By the end of this series, Mannheim was no longer discussing "cultural sociology," but rather "the sociology of knowledge." The change in terminology represented not so much a change in the actual methodology used as it did an increasing uneasiness with the cultural-philosophical center of construction. Thus, he discarded a term that had more traditionalist implications for a term that did not carry the earlier implications and was, in a way, more neutral.[5] One could say that the change symbolized the process of transition from one center to another (although I do not claim this symbolization was intentional on Mannheim's part).

Soon after this first series of transitional works began, he started another with his unpublished *Habilitationsschrift*, written for entrance into the university teaching profession. The work, *Conservatism* (1925), was later published in abridged form as "Conservative Thought" (1927).[6] The latter essay was followed by ones on generational theory (1928) and cultural competition (1928). This later series can be seen as applications of and contributions to the sociology of knowledge developed in the other series,[7] with an emphasis on the definition of the experiential realm rather than on methodology. The exception is the first essay of *Conservatism*, which overlapped with the methodological discussion. (In fact, the two series should be seen as overlapping, the distinction between them being mine, not Mannheim's.) In the later works, one sees the growing presence of the political element, at first essentially as the object of his sociological investigations, but increasingly pointing toward being the primary standard of valuation, although not explicitly.

The sociology of knowledge

The methodological discussions, as one might expect from the first part of "Sociological Theory of Culture," began where the methodological element of the earlier writings left off – the dualism between the natural sciences and the human sciences.[8] This dichotomy appeared in "Sociological Theory of Culture" as the contrast between "communicative" and "conjunctive" knowledge. Disciplines based on the former, which was the equivalent of the "civilizational" sphere of his earlier writings, sought supratemporal, universal systems in which changes were quantitative and unilinear rather than qualitative. In such a static system, divorced from any sociohistorical context, meaning, like the thinglike objects and the logically constructed subject, remained changeless.[9] Conjunctive knowledge, on the other hand, was not universal, but limited to a given historical context. This historicity meant that the development of this type of knowledge was qualitative rather than quantitative.[10]

Mannheim, following the traditional academic pattern, associated this dichotomy in knowledge with the larger one of *Gemeinschaft–Gesellschaft*. He referred to the historical context as a *Gemeinschaft* of knowers and to the loosing of knowledge from the historically bound subject (the shift from conjunctive to communicative knowledge) as a process of *Vergesellschaftung*.[11] Thus, we see that in developing the sociology of knowledge, Mannheim did not abandon the traditionalist formulations of his earlier works.

In "Sociological Theory of Culture," he was primarily concerned with two varieties of conjunctive knowledge, understanding (*Verstehen*) and interpretation.[12] As in his treatment of dynamic historicism (which combined the psychiccultural *Gestalt* with the philosophical dialectic), he did not separate distinctly understanding and interpretation from one another. Understanding, which he defined as "the penetration into a communally bound experiential realm (*Erfahrungsraum*), into that realm's meaningful products (*Sinngebilde*) and their existential bases," was divided into two kinds, depending on whether its object was simple existence or a context of meaning. The former was basically a relation to another's psyche, an individual context of lived experience; the latter was the grasp of meaningful products having a significance beyong the individual experiential sphere (as *Bedeutsamkeiten*). Both were essentially pretheoretical operations, which distinguished them from interpretation, a theoretically reflective explication of that which was understood without exhausting the pretheoretical element.[13]

Despite its rational nature, interpretation was a form of conjunctive knowledge and, therefore, was "perspectivistic."[14] It was distinguished from communicative "conceptualizing" (*Begreifen*), which was suprahistorical and whose objects virtually disappeared as spiritual (cultural) products.[15] Interpretation, then, was both theoretically reflective and perspectivistically bound, sharing characteristics with both conceptualizing and understanding, although it was much closer to the latter, due to its historicity. In fact, Mannheim did not specify where the understanding of meaning ended and interpretation began; they were complementary approaches to cultural knowledge, much like the philosophical and psychiccultural spheres in "Historicism."[16]

Mannheim was primarily concerned with the interpretations, due to their rational nature and their concern with contexts of meaning. As noted above, the type of interpretation he emphasized during this period was the sociology of knowledge, which he saw as a part of the sociology of culture.[17] As in the earlier "Cultural-Sociological Knowledge," he saw the object of this discipline as a historical totality, now termed "experiential realm" (*Erfahrungsraum*),[18] in which meaning and existence were connected (*verbunden*). The discipline itself was a product of the changes in the experiential realm, which Mannheim portrayed in a series of dynamically related types.[19]

The first type, or stage, the "consensus" of the "life-community" (*Lebensgemeinschaft*), resulted from socially homogeneous strata or societies in which social relationships were static and egalitarian. Within this primitive community, there was no spatial and temporal delineation. Subjects were unaware of an individuality apart from the communal context; the community lived in the eternal present, with all past products being treated as if they were contemporary. All tension, that is, aspirations, was directed toward a common goal and was often formulated in a commandmentlike language (e.g., "It shall be so"). Knowledge at this stage was unreflective and dependent on the close bonds of its subjects; it could not be communicated to an individual who was not a member of the community.[20]

Mannheim termed the more complex types of experiential realm "cultural communities." Here the actual physical contact (*Kontagion*) of the consensus life-communities was unnecessary as long as the members possessed a common "origin" (*Keim*), from which sprung a common context of meaning, a cultural totality. (However, this origin must have been the product of a life-community.) At these levels, there was an increase in the delineation of component elements and a resulting increased consciousness on the part of their members.[21]

The first type of cultural community was the "monopoly," which retained many of the characteristics of the consensus life-community, most importantly the structural stasis of the social body and the unity of communal aspirations. It differed in its division of the *Gemeinschaft* into a spiritual elite and the laity, the former's monopoly in the determination of the context of meaning being gained by either intellectual or nonintellectual means. The spiritual uniformity maintained by the monopoly did not mean the absence of strife but rather the establishment of limits for that strife so that it did not challenge the basic presuppositions of the community. In the monopoly, knowledge was more reflective and rational; however, this rationality was integrated into a preordained order rather than challenging that order. Existence itself was not held up as a test for knowledge, the empirical spirit being absent. Instead, knowledge was gained from the interpretation of texts, whose clarification put them in harmony with the preordained order. Mannheim saw as the prime examples of this type the Middle Ages and their great spokesman, Thomas Aquinas.[22]

The social and spiritual stratification of the monopolistic level did create the potential for divisions in its unified world view. Here we see the same condition described by Tönnies in Chapter 1, where reflective knowledge ceased to be the monopoly of the elite and, as the lower groups became conscious of the difference of their aspirations from those of the elite, the organic conjunctive community began to disintegrate. Mannheim saw a number of different social groups participating in this process of "atomistic competition," which had three basic characteristics: There were (a) no universally accepted axioms and (b) no hierarchy of values, resulting in (c) a number of different epistemologies and ontologies. Doubt, which brooked no authority or dogma, became an important fact, as men like Descartes were no longer willing to fit facts into a preordained order. The result was the loosening of knowledge from the communally bound subject (what Mannheim referred to as the *Vergesellschaftung* of knowledge), so that "everything seems to fall apart, as though people did not live in the same world."[23]

Mannheim wrote that one of the prime forces in the disintegration of the monopolistic stage was the capitalistic bourgeoisie, which was also the bearer of a new kind of rationality, supraconjunctive communicative knowledge. Largely through its agency, cultural knowledge, which had been based mainly on religious presuppositions and social stasis, became atomized into a number of competing conjunctive aspirations, while an attempt was made to establish a new universality based on civilizational rationality, whose model was the natural sciences. One of the disciplines to develop out of this process was general sociology, which used the positivistic methods and sought to deal with experience in a supraconjunctive fashion.[24]

This three-stage structure was almost identical to that of Mannheim's earlier writings, especially the Free School lecture and "Cultural-Sociological Knowledge," and these, in turn, followed the traditional dichotomous pattern characterized by Tönnies's *Gemeinschaft und Gesellschaft*.[25] Atomistic competition (pluralism) and civilizational knowledge (reification) were seen as complementary elements of an essentially negative process. And as he had earlier, Mannheim saw the development of the sociology of culture/knowledge as part of this process.

He wrote that a specific confirmation of elements was necessary for these sociological disciplines to develop.[26] First, culture emerged as a problematical sphere leading to the "self-relativization of thought," the realization that thought was not an autonomous entity (and thus could not be interpreted simply immanently) but was somehow related to more comprehensive factors, "in which the systematizing subject actually and most intensively lives." Thought did not consist simply of immanent "ideas" but also of functional "ideologies." Second, the more comprehensive factor, in terms of which thought was relativized, was increasingly defined not by religion but by sociology, which was the product of an antimetaphysical positivism. In other words, such interpretations were not simply ideological but also sociological.[27]

The third element, which can itself be divided into two parts, was the appearance of new attitudes and methodologies vis-à-vis cultural products, the means by which thought was relativized in terms of a sociological totality. The first methodological element was the technique of "unmasking," a hallmark of all rising classes but given its first reflective formulation in Marxism. This technique aimed at the "extra-theoretical destruction of the efficacy of theoretical propositions" by demonstrating the sociopolitical function they served. As such, it was a political tool, coming from the existential struggle of classes. However, said Mannheim, there was a tendency for the technique to lose its political character as it became the property of all groups within the experiential realm and instead to become a scientific endeavor that served to contribute to conjunctive historical knowledge.

He listed four forms of his scientific sociology of knowledge, two of which were discounted as incomplete. One of these first two, positivism, looked for existential explanations of knowledge and was blind to meaning. The other, the formal philosophy of validity, sought an immanent approach ignoring existence; in making values supratemporal, it attempted to rescue them from their historical and social genesis.[28] Using Mannheim's methodological classification, one could say that positivism was an extrinsic genetic explanation and the formal philosophy of validity was an immanent systematic interpretation. He did not pursue either of these approaches further due to their inability to investigate the connections between existence and meaning. They seem to have been included to establish the extremes that the other two types, both genetic interpretations, tried to mediate. The latter were the phenomenological sociology of knowledge developed by Max Scheler and Mannheim's own dynamic sociology of knowledge.

Scheler postulated three realms of meaning, each with a corresponding type of knowledge. The first, the absolute spiritual realm of truth, could be grasped only by "knowledge for salvation," defined as partaking in the ultimate being, a divine knowledge. This type of knowledge was similar to that depicted by Mannheim in the Free School lecture as the mystic's inward turning of the soul. The second realm was the material world, whose human relationships arose from a structure of drives, for example, power, reproduction, nourishment. Scheler believed that these relationships were the objects of "knowledge for achievement," which used the mechanistic, causal explanations characteristic of the positivistic natural sciences. The third realm combined the other two into unique cultural complexes, whose meaning was interpreted in "knowledge for *Bildung*." As did the traditional concept of *Bildung*, this type of knowledge sought to mediate between the individual and the cultural whole. Scheler saw metaphysics as the most important discipline for the attainment of this knowledge. His sociology of knowledge consisted of a typology of the cultural complexes designed to aid the metaphysician's task; therefore, in his view as in Mannheim's, it was a specialized science subservient to philosophy.[29]

Scheler believed that the eternal, ideal realm determined the possibilities of culture, its essences, whereas the real, material realm of drives selected from the possibilities presented by spirit. The two realms were mediated by the cultural product of the elite in which the two sets of universal elements acquired unique historical configurations. Mannheim recognized the historicist element in Scheler's concept of culture but felt that the phenomenologist's sociology of knowledge could never do justice to historical knowledge, because it was depicted as simply the juncture of two nonhistorical spheres. He wrote:

> Scheler tries to incorporate historicist ideas into his theory of timelessness, and even adopts the idea of "perspectivistic" vision. But his static conception of eternity never gets reconciled with the alien "position" of historicism with which he tries to combine it.[30]

Mannheim's "dynamic" sociology of knowledge differed from Scheler's phenomenological one in its belief that meaning and existence formed a totality best illuminated by a "historico-philosophical, sociological" approach and that the two spheres were reciprocal "co-determinants" of one another.[31] As the terms "dynamic" and "historico-philosophical, sociological" indicate, Mannheim was reiterating here a position he had taken in "Historicism." He did not object to Scheler's subordination of sociology to philosophy, but to the characterization of that philosophy as a static metaphysics rather than as a philosophy of history. Scheler, he wrote, in subordinating sociology to static metaphysics, defined the spheres of meaning and existence in such a way that the methodological consequences were inadequate. The definitions that Mannheim proposed retained, with modifications, the elements introduced in the earlier writings, especially "Cultural-Sociological Knowledge": the context of lived experience, the world view, the soul, and the cultural product.

The most important of the elements was the cultural totality, now called the "experiential realm" in "Sociological Theory of Culture."[32] As before, this realm was defined by the concept of "aspiration" (*Wollen, Wollung*), which came from Riegl's "art aspiration" (*Kunstwollen*) and which Mannheim defined as an "unconscious latent tendency" that moved the subject in a certain direction. Most important was aspiration's ties to activity; it was the will to produce, the will to accomplish something. He classified aspirations by specific cultural fields, for example, art aspiration, economic aspiration, intellectual aspiration, or by the world view of the experiential realm as a whole, the "world aspiration" (*Weltwollung*).[33]

Both the cultural field and the world view fell under the general category of "collective mental image" (*Kollektivvorstellung*), which was the objectifiable element of the experiential realm. Mannheim emphasized the collective conjunctive character of these mental images, writing: "Their power to connect and symbolize is bound and connected with a group existence at a certain stage of historical time."[34] His definition of the world view remained consistent with that of the earlier writings – it was the objectifiable part of the experiential realm.[35] It was also a "functional" entity; its identity was dependent on the aspirations connected to it. But as the objectification of those aspirations, the world view actually named the conjunctive totality. The world aspiration was the will to realize the goals articulated by the world view. As in the earlier writings, Mannheim identified the pretheoretical totality with the part of it that could be objectified and considered reflectively.[36]

He continued to view the cultural product, which he now termed the "spiritual reality," as the bridge between meaning and existence and to shift his emphasis from the psychic origins of the "work" in the Free School lecture to its collective cultural character in "Cultural-Sociological Knowledge." The "work" was described now not as the expression of the creative individual soul, but of the collective mental image in which individuals shared. In addition, he added collective cultural products not included in the earlier writings: institutions in the Durkheimian sense, elements of the natural and psychic world that the conjunctive community endowed with meaning, and collective works such as language, customs, and self-regulating social relations.[37]

In the Free School lecture, the work was presented as the bridge between individual souls by allowing them to participate in the totality of meaning, the objective spirit; in "Sociological Theory of Culture" it was presented as the objectification of collective aspirations.[38] Although these two presentations were not necessarily contradictory, they represented a definite shift in the definition of the central problem. In the Free School lecture, the objective spirit was taken as a given; the overriding problem was the alienation of individuals from one another due to the disintegration of this given. From "Cultural-Sociological Knowledge" on, the objective spirit was no longer a given, and the relationship of the individual to it was no longer the central problem. Rather, the definition of the objective spirit itself became problematical; hence the emergence of the concept of the dialectic as a means of organizing this increasingly complex entity. The problem of alienation (of the individual) was subordinate to the problem of pluralism (within the relam of objective spirit). The central problem of historical knowledge was not to relate individuals to a context, but rather contexts to one another.

It is important to note here that Mannheim continued to view the subject as an imputed entity, a construction. He wrote:

> Things and the souls of individuals exist, as do, in a special way, significancies [collective mental images] and also contexts of significance (*Bedeutsamkeitszusammenhänge*) of the most varied kind. But subjects of knowledge – individual as well as collective subjects – are only constructions, expressions of one of the two members of the logical relation between subject and object.[39]

Mannheim envisioned three types of imputed subjects – the supratemporal, communicative one who knew thinglike objects (the logical-transcendental subject from "Epistemology"); the individual subject who knew the lived experience of the soul; and the conjunctive historical one who knew communal contexts of meaning. He believed the latter to be the most adequate construction for historical knowledge.

The collective subject presented difficulties that the other two subjects did not, namely, the identification of the experiential unit to which it corresponded. The communicative subject was not tied to any experiential entity and thus could know all things "objectively." The individual subject was imputed for the experiential unit of the soul. The collective historical subject, however, was neither free from all experience nor derived from an existing experiential unit; it was imputed for the conjunctive meaningful context. It was defined by meaning, not experience. This necessitated a second imputation, an experiential unit to correspond to the collective subject.[40] The construction of the *Gemeinschaft* was a basic factor in the task of relating the sphere of meaning to that of existence.

In "Problem of Sociology of Knowledge," Mannheim criticized Scheler's construction of the collective experiential unit, which was defined by the traditional historicist terms of nation and epoch rather than by social strata.[41] This criticism of Scheler was also a criticism of his own earlier writings, in which "nation" (i.e., cultural totality) and "epoch" predominated. The spatial term, the nation, was taken as an unproblematical organic whole, with attention being focused on the temporal development and the relation of epochs to one another. True, he did see dialectical conflict occurring within the whole, but this was largely conflict between cultural fields, not experiential totalities; and these fields were subordinated to the totality. They did not challenge the priority of the temporal unit, the national epoch characterized by its world view. Now, in this transitional period, Mannheim did challenge this organization, if only on the analytical level.

This rejection of a predominantly temporal organization in favor of a spatial one required a closer examination of Marxism, especially its concept of class, on Mannheim's part. He objected to the Marxists' use of economic aspiration, or "interests," to characterize the entire world aspiration of the experiential realm. Although a general sociology might manage by using the "one-sided" shallower concept of "interest," a cultural sociology could not.[42]

He proposed replacing economic interest with a more inclusive concept, "commitment" (*Engagiertsein*), thereby defining social groups by their commitment to world aspirations. He denied that this was merely a retreat into idealism, arguing that world aspirations could not exist independently from the social groups committed to them. Although the group was defined by a world view rather than an element of the existential realm, the world view was made functional by the commitment of the group, and this commitment shaped the world view in form and content. Whereas Scheler's sociology of knowledge was basically idealist (the existential realm only actualized the ideal essence) and Marx's was basically materialist (the ideal realm only reflected the material essence), Mannheim believed that the concept of commitment grasped the spatial unit in which meaning (articulated in the world view) and existence (the aspiration toward action) were indirectly connected in a reciprocal relationship.[43]

The methodology by which the sociology of knowledge uncovered world aspirations remained fairly consistent from this period on.[44] In "Problem of Sociology of Knowledge," he described a three-stage procedure. In his 1931 encyclopedia article on the discipline, he listed four levels of imputation which, with minor differences, reiterated his ideas for determining the adequacy of imputation in the unpublished *Conservatism*.[45] Here, I will combine these presentations into one composite discussion with an emphasis on "Problem of Sociology of Knowledge." In

75

placing my emphasis here rather than on the expositions of the discipline in the second transitional period, I am making a statement about where the sociology of knowledge played its most important role in Mannheim's intellectual development.

The first step of the methodology traced a particular cultural formulation, or "style of thought" (*Denkstil*) back to the world view of which it was a part. This operation, an immanent one along the lines of documentary interpretation described in *"Weltanschauung,"* identified a context of meaning and, in doing so, defined the primary unit to be investigated. For example, in *Conservatism* a methodological approach (a style of thought) was traced to the conservative world view, the meaningful entity.

At the next level, the sociologist of knowledge identified the "spiritual stratum," those people whose commitment to the world view made it functional, that is, made it a world aspiration. This level of imputation (which Mannheim called "factual" as opposed to the "meaningful" level) examined the world view as it appeared in the works of individual thinkers. In *Conservatism,* he concentrated on four thinkers – Justus Möser, Adam Müller, Gustav Hugo, and Friedrich von Savigny – who represented varieties of the conservative world aspiration. These two levels acted as reciprocal controls upon one another. Without examining individual thinkers, the construction of the meaningful context would become too removed from the historical world. But without the general construction, the discussion of individual thinkers would miss the meaningful totality, which is incorporated by the work of no one thinker alone.

With the third stage, the material interests of the members of the spiritual stratum were identified. In *Conservatism,* for example, Möser was identified with the provincial nobility, Hugo with the nonnoble bureaucracy, Savigny with those noble officials who had strong ties to the landed nobility, and Müller with the free-floating intellectuals of middle-rank origin who joined forces with the landed nobility. These "social strata" were identified as being among the bearers of the conservative world aspiration. Mannheim emphasized that the spiritual and social strata were not identical. As we have just seen, one spiritual stratum could consist of several social strata, and the reverse case could also exist by which one social stratum could contain members of different spiritual strata (e.g., the middle ranks also included the defenders of the rival of conservatism, Enlightenment rationalism).

Finally, by examining the changing situations in which the spiritual and social strata found themselves, a developmental element was added, preventing the interpretation of the world aspiration from becoming a static construction. Mannheim placed the four conservative thinkers in temporal relationship to one another and to historical events, such as the

French Revolution and the Battle of Jena, to demonstrate that the world aspiration, while maintaining its morphological configuration, displayed changing intellectual and aspirational contents.

Mannheim wrote that these different levels did not in fact have separate existences; they were simply heuristic devices. Accordingly, he did not attempt to assert a causal priority among them; they were simply connected. However, there was a hierarchical priority, for the world view corresponded exactly with the spiritual stratum it defined. The social strata added information by relating material interests to the world aspiration, but with no one-to-one correlation. Rather than deny the Marxian concept of class, Mannheim adopted it but relegated it to a supplementary position.[46]

For example, in *Conservatism* (as in "Sociological Theory of Culture") the basic pattern for Mannheim's investigation came from the traditional–modern dichotomy, which also found expression in Tönnies's categories. Manneim used class terms as elements of this dualism, so that "class society" became a synonym for "modern society," or *Gesellschaft*. Its most important characteristics, for Mannheim, were spiritual fragmentation and excessive rationalism. There was no real explanation of these terms using Marxist concepts; they were simply supplementary labels (as they had been for Tönnies as well). It is also important to note that his use of Marxist categories was much more prominent in these unpublished writings than in his published works of the same period.

One could speculate on the reason for the introduction of these economic categories at this time, remembering that it is undocumented speculation. I have noted that when Mannheim first appeared in Heidelberg, his entrance into intellectual circles was facilitated by his earlier association with Lukács. When the latter's *History and Class Consciousness* appeared in 1923, one would expect Mannheim to have something, indeed something positive, to say about the book. It would only be natural for him to experiment with Lukács's Marxist categories, especially in his unpublished works.[47] However, experimentation with these concepts did not mean commitment to them. In his published works, they more often than not served as examples of "one-sided" explanations.

This is not to say that Mannheim's thought had not changed. Although a new center of construction had not clearly established itself during this transitional period, the analytical element, with its emphasis on collective aspirations, operated on a more distant orbit around the center and became increasingly antithetic to it. This widening gyre continued in the studies of conservatism, generations, and cultural competition, in which he continued to develop the sociology of knowledge but more importantly gave increasing attention to the political element. Although the latter was primarily analytical in these articles, it would eventually form the basis for a new valuative center in *Ideology and Utopia*.

Defining the experiential realm

In his studies of conservatism (1925 and 1927), Mannheim examined the origins of that political doctrine "to determine the specific morphology of the style of thought, to reconstruct its historical and social roots, to trace the change in form of this style of thought in connection with the social fate of the groups that bore it."[48] He began by distinguishing conservatism from traditionalism, which was a universal psychological category to be found to some degree in most people at most times – the instinctive acceptance of past ways and the aversion to change. Traditional action was an act of pure will (*Wollen*); one could examine specific historical individuals to determine what aspects of their conduct could be attributed to this universal psychological category. Conservatism, on the other hand, was the articulation of a world aspiration that provided meaningful orientation in the world. It was intimately tied to traditionalism in that it was the traditional will operating in light of a specific historical constellation; conservative action was an act of will given conjunctive meaning by an objective context. It combined unreflective will with a spiritual context forming a world aspiration.[49]

Mannheim believed that the conservative world aspiration was a relatively modern phenomenon, appearing only in response to the eighteenth-century Enlightenment and French Revolution. Before those movements, traditional society was characterized by harmony between the individual will and the larger will of the organic whole. Traditionalism predominated, as relationships were intuitive and pre-theoretical. However, the challenge of the new forces was responsible for the emergence of conservatism, the traditional will raised to articulation and consciousness as a world aspiration. In a static, unchanging world, conservatism was unnecessary; it was needed only when the traditionalist had to locate himself or herself in a world of change to make sense of that world.[50]

In "Conservative Thought," Mannheim wrote that the genesis of conservatism was dependent on four factors (three of which coincided with his earlier description of the emergence of cultural sociology): (1) The historical social context became dynamic; (2) this dynamism increasingly took the form of social differentiation in which some groups furthered the process while others hindered it; (3) ideas and the aspirations connected to them were differentiated along lines parallel to those of social differentiation.[51] The fourth, and new, factor was the increasingly political character that social differentiation took. Politics became the center around which the spiritual currents agglomerated, so that a constellation of antagonistic world aspirations was formed. Conservatism, then, was traditionalism that had become not only historically conscious but also political. Politics, as part of the experiential realm, was still defined by the world views to which the political forces were committed.[52]

Mannheim made this same point in Part One of *Conservatism*, but there his discussion was longer and more qualified. He denied that the political element had any hierarchical primacy within the world aspirations of the nineteenth century. It was simply easier to characterize the intellectual cosmos in terms of its political currents, especially concerning the relationship of world aspirations to one another. One could view this explanation as an attempt to keep the discussion strictly analytical. Yet, there was an interesting indication of the direction in which he was heading. He wrote that the reason world aspirations were most easily characterized by their political elements in the nineteenth century was the increasing fragmentation of the intellectual cosmos, which allowed certain currents to be perceivable in an unequivocal manner. He contrasted this to the Middle Ages, when these currents were subordinate to the religious orientation and so were less clear-cut. During his first primary period, he had contrasted the cultural pluralism of the modern world with the religious unity of the Middle Ages. In this transitional period, he emphasized the pluralism as political rather than cultural, while limiting and qualifying that characterization.

The identification of the spiritual with the political continued in his essay on cultural competition (1928). Here he added a fourth stage of cultural development, "polarization," to the three above-described stages of consensus, monopoly, and atomistic competition.[53] This stage consisted of the concentration of the various social groups of the earlier stage around several positions, each characterized by a "spiritual current," that is, a world view. These positions corresponded to the cultural communities in "Sociological Theory of Culture" in that the spiritual currents originated in certain concrete groups (*Lebenskreise*) and then were expanded to incorporate other concrete groups in the polarization process. In other words, each of these positions represented the gathering of different concrete aspirations into one context of meaning. In absorbing these various groups, the spiritual current was itself modified somewhat, so that the relationship between the larger context and the concrete group was reciprocal and the latter did not lose its identity totally. "Thus, the spiritual currents made for uniformity, but also for a conservation of the peculiarities of local relationships."[54]

These polarized spiritual currents differed from the earlier cultural

79

communities in the importance of competition to their appearance. They were not formed simply independently but in competition with one another; as "poles," their relation to their opposites was an integral part of their existence. For example, conservatism could not be adequately defined without also defining its competitor, liberalism.[55] The goal of this competition was the domination of what Mannheim called the "public interpretation of existence." Each polar position tried to establish the kind of monopoly that had existed prior to atomistic competition. In other words, each attempted to overcome the pluralism of meaningful contexts (by which the public made sense of the world) through the establishment of its own interpretation as the sole one.[56] In keeping with the premises of his sociology of knowledge, Mannheim saw the spiritual polarization as part of the larger conflict of experiential realms, or "general social relationships."[57] To equate the competition with the ideal elements of these relationships was as one-sided as equating it with the economic elements. He wrote that the conflicting positions did not arise

> through the simple summation of the elements of thought, but rather in the meeting of basic aspirations, principles of formation and interpretations of the world. The merging of these elements is not achieved by the contemplative subject (insofar as one can separate rightfully the contemplative and the active), but by the active and ultimately – insofar as activity directed at changing the world is in the end political – the political one.[58]

Here again, we see the emphasis on the political element of the experiential realm, and we also see an experiential unit to correspond to the spiritual objectification – the political party. In "Problem of Sociology of Knowledge," Mannheim described the experiential unit as the spiritual stratum, that, simply in terms of its world view, with the social strata in a supplementary role. In "Competition," the spiritual element continued to define the experiential realm and the social strata continued to hold a supplementary position. Concrete local groups were also present, but they appear subordinate in that they were not as inclusive as the spiritual currents. The political party, on the other hand, corresponded directly with the political doctrine; it too was more inclusive than the social strata or concrete local groups. Mannheim's party, on the other hand, corresponded directly with the political doctrine; it too was more inclusive than the social strata or concrete local groups. Mannheim's party was essentially identical to Max Weber's "*Weltanschauungspartei*," defined by its members' commitment to a certain world view (e.g., the conservative, liberal, and socialist parties).[59] The relationship between the institution and the doctrine was reciprocal; one could not be separated from or reduced to the other. In short, by characterizing the experiential realm by its political elements, he emphasized a conflict not as evident in his earlier writings.

With the predominance of the political elements, Mannheim also shifted his emphasis away from the concept of "center of construction" to one of multipolar "selection." The former served as the organizing factor in an essentilay temporal schema, with each epoch having a hierarchy of cultural fields based on its center of construction. Centers came and went, but there was always a center and, hence, the possibility of a philosophical synthesis based upon that center. In "Competition," a multipolar conflict replaced the one organized about shifting centers, as his emphasis switches from a temporal to a spatial one, in which there was "no unified basis for thought." I shall have more to say about the valuative implications of this change later in this chapter and in the next one. For now, it is enough to note that he had gone from a temporal framework in which philosophical synthesis was possible to a spatial pluralism of limited political synthesis.

This shift also can be seen in "Generations" (1928), an essay that, ironically, has been hailed as a seminal contribution to that temporal concept. Here one finds basically the same potential schema found in "Competition," although dressed in a generational terminology consisting of five elements: (1) the biological generation, (2) the generational location (*Lagerung*), (3) the generational context, (4) the generational entelechy, and (5) the generational unity.

The biological generation was an ahistorical concept based on date of birth; all those born at a certain time were part of the same generation. Because generations were given a prescribed length, this biological element could be quantified.[60] Mannheim viewed it much as he viewed Scheler's concept of drives, as a positivistic element more akin to the natural sciences than to the historical-cultural sciences. He admitted that the fact of birth was essential to any generational theory, just as the fact of physical necessities of life was essential to any class theory. However, both generation and class went beyond the biological data; they were cultural formulations imposed on the physical data.

The most general of the generational cultural formations was the location, which limited the biological element to a specific cultural space.[61] Simple contemporaneousness, wrote Mannheim, did not define a generation; Chinese and Germans born in the same year did not belong to the same generational location, because of the difference in the cultures. Because Mannheim realized that generational theory was above all a way of interpreting change, he compared the generational location to the basic unit of another major theory of historical change, the Marxian concept of class. Both concepts defined limits, the potential range of lived

81

experience and thought. The change of generations, like the change of classes, involved new possibilities in sensibility and, therefore, a new approach to the world. In addition, the generational location had the same limitation as the economic class – its "one-sidedness." To explain change strictly in terms of generational locations or classes was too reductive; the historical process was not so simplistic. Location and class described a common condition, but not a communal aspiration or a communal consciousness. Neither could be equated with the central element of Mannheim's sociology of knowledge, the world aspiration, and without this equation they remained merely elements of a supplementary taxonomy.

The "generational context," he felt, sharpened the focus somewhat by indicating participation in a common fate and sensibility within the location.[62] Being a member of the same generational context meant, more than anything, having the same perception of change, resulting from exposure to or isolation from a process of social and spiritual destabilization. For example, peasant youth, whose world was pretty much routinized, therefore, with little awareness of historical change, belonged to a different context than urban youth, to whom that change was evident. Mannheim believed only the latter would perceive themselves as being members of a generation in conflict with other generations.[63]

Although members of a generational context shared a common awareness of historical change, not all reacted to that change in the same way. This divergence necessitated a definition of the different positions within the historical process. Mannheim chose as a foil for his own concept that of the art historian Wilhelm Pinder, the "generational entelechy," which was a modification of Riegl's "art aspiration."[64] For Pinder, the entelechy was a spiritual goal and an organic entity, but not for an entire epoch. People living in the same generational location did not all live "in the same time" and so formed different entelechies. (This "non-contemporaneity of the contemporaneous" was similar to what Mannheim had expressed in "Cultural-Sociological Knowledge.") The different generational entelechies were joined by other entelechies, such as those of art, language, individuals, nations, and even Europe. Such a theory, Mannheim recognized, was a version of the historicist concept of individuality, in which these entities had a monadic relationship to one another and were the transient products of some mysterious, vital force. Mannheim had two related objections to this romanticist, historicist position: First, it was totally immanent, with no reference to the social factor, the experiential realm; and second, the relationships of the entelechies to one another were inadequately presented, with the emphasis on organic "growth" rather than on a more rational structure. In short, Pinder did not even rely on a "center of construction" to organize his cultural fields (entelechies), believing that the postulation of a monadic harmony was sufficient.[65]

Obviously, it was not sufficient for Mannheim, who proposed another concept, the "generational unity," in which the members shared "contents of consciousness" (i.e., world view) and a "basic intention" and "principles of formation" (i.e., aspirations).[66] Like the earlier cultural community, the generational unity was characterized by a world aspiration, and its members did not have to be spatially connected as long as they shared in that aspiration, although the nucleus of the unity had to have originated in a concrete group. Unlike Pinder's entelechies, the unities did not exist as monadic individualities; rather, they were related to one another as competing positions. Within a generational context, a number of generational unities competed to establish their world aspiration as that of the "generation." Therefore, the generational unity was essentially a political concept and occupied the same position that parties did in "Competition." (He used the same examples – liberalism, conservatism, and socialism – in both essays.)[67]

An important difference between "Generations" and "Competition" was the use of the earlier concept of "center of construction" in the former. Mannheim wrote that one of the generational unities was dominant, reducing the others to the status of "diverted" or "suppressed."[68] In "Competition," this hierarchy was dropped in favor of an actual multipolarity. Thus, "Generations" might be termed the most transitional essay of this transitional stage of his career. It contained the political element that would become dominant in *Ideology and Utopia* and organized that element with a concept from the earlier works, especially "Historicism," whose emphasis was temporal rather than spatial. (In addition, it contained a transitional position regarding intellectuals, as will be described later in this chapter.)

As Robert Wohl has noted, many intellectuals of the period saw "generation" as an alternative to "class."[69] This was certainly true for many within the university as it was for many without. Mannheim's mentor, Alfred Weber, was an advocate of the youth movement, seeing it as a way to overcome the fissures in German society. Although many of the traditionalists[70] saw the youth more as apprentices than as rebels, they agreed that the new generation would provide a new energy, a vitality that seemed to have been lost. One can understand, therefore, why Mannheim would examine the concept of generation; but one could also ask, as Wohl does, why he did not carry the examination further, given the intellectual respectability of "generation" as a competitor of class. The answer would seem to be that, although he believed that generation offered an alternative to class, he did not think it offered an advantage over class. Both were essentially dualistic, pitting a favored, future-oriented group (youth, proletariat) against a stagnant, repressive (adult, bourgeois) structure. Whether the dualism was temporally or spatially perceived, it remained a dualism and, therefore, unfruitful for Mannheim. He rejected both formulations in favor of a pluralistic political one that held all positions open to examination.

The role of intellectuals

An important question for Mannheim, with his shift toward the political, was the role that intellectuals would play in that new schema. As long as he postulated the necessity of a philosophical synthesis, their role was central; but how did they fit into the multipolar political world? He answered this question in *Ideology and Utopia* with his theory of the socially free-floating intelligentsia. As did his interest in the political, that concept developed in stages during this transitional period.

In the first work of this period, "Sociological Theory of Culture," he introduced the concept of *"Bildungskultur,"* which he described as "the culture that has been rendered relatively independent from the particular, narrowly limited life-community and its existential connectedness."[71] It accompanied the appearance of atomistic competition and the mingling of various cultural contexts and social circles, especially in the cities. The cultivated stratum *(Gebildeten)* that participated in the *Bildungskultur* originated in these conjunctive cultural contexts and shared in their tensions and aspirations. The latter were introduced into the *Bildungskultur*, although not in their totality, for part of the aspirations always remained at the level of the life-community. Only the objectifiable element, the world view, was transferred to the level of *Bildung*, where it entered into competition with other world views and achieved a certain distance from the original context. In the dialectically constructed *Bildungskultur*, the intellectuals were exposed to the competing world views and the tensions (aspirations) they objectified.

Mannheim believed that this tension was to a certain extent free floating *(freischwebend)* because, although the intellectual tended toward the world view of his original *Gemeinschaft*, there was a certain amount of freedom of decision.[72] Cultivation meant mobility, extension of spiritual space, and increased sensibility, not found in the original cultural context, and these allowed the tendencies of that context to develop more freely and in a quicker and more direct way than if they had been dependent on the slow pace of communal existence. The intellectual, then, could move on ahead of the group that had produced him or her and the cultural position he or she brought to the *Bildungskultur*. And yet the latter was not completely free floating; whereas, as a collective entity, it was supracommunal, it remained conjunctive due to the origins of its members. It represented a level at which conjunctive aspirations gained a conscious, reflective perspective on themselves and their place in the dynamic whole of the historical process. It was at this level that the kind of cultural synthesis called for in "Historicism" took place.

This concept would appear to be as elitist as Scheler's "knowledge for *Bildung*," for both postulated a cultural elite as the synthetic agent for the nation. Despite Mannheim's use of some Marxist terminology, he continued to define the problem culturally and to seek a solution on the cultural-philosophical level. In this light, one can compare it to the concepts of epistemology and the free-floating intelligentsia discussed in the previous chapter – all three were bound to different contexts and yet attained a certain distance from those contexts that permitted them a perspective missing at the more basic level. However, the *Bildungskultur* was presented as more synthetic than either epistemology or the intelligentsia. Although the latter two were clearly subordinate to the basic totalities (primary systematizations, political parties) and offered only a perspective, not an inclusive synthesis, the *Bildungskultur* does not appear to have been subordinate to anything. Mannheim seems to have seen it accomplishing the dialectical, philosophical synthesis of "Historicism," and in fact he called it the highest level of conjunctive knowledge.[73] Perhaps the only aspect of this concept that did not strike a responsive chord with the academic traditionalists was his emphasis on the *Bildungskultur* as a promoter of spiritual change. This view was more in tune with the outlook of the Budapest intelligentsia. However, his interest here was clearly cultural and philosophical, not political.

In "Conservative Thought" and "Generations," one finds a politicization of the role of the intellectuals, but not yet an abandonment of the concept of "center of construction." In these essays, he also introduced the famous term "socially free-floating intelligentsia," which he attributed to Alfred Weber.[74] These two essentially analytical works focused on those German intellectuals during the late eighteenth and early nineteenth centuries whose origins were in the middle ranks, a group he described as themselves free-floating and vacillating due to their social and political immaturity. Having no clearly defined place in the social structure, the members of the middle ranks lacked a unified goal and a conscious aspiration and tended to be politically indifferent. The intellectuals who came from this group also had no binding commitment to any sociopolitical group.[75]

> These free-floating intellectuals are the typical intellectual legitimizers, "ideologues," who can find arguments in favor of any political aspirations

they serve. Their own position does not result in bondedness (*Gebun-denheit*), but they have an extraordinarily refined sense for the collective aspirations around them and the ability to detect them and feel at one with them. . . . The fate of the spiritual world is in the care of a stratum with no roots, or at least few roots, to which no position of class or rank can be precisely imputed, which does not create the bases for aspirations itself, but rather when it takes up something, takes up aspirations which are born by strata more intensively socially bound.[76]

In Enlightenment France, this group still had strong connections with their bourgeois origins, and their rationalistic theories had the support of the powerful bourgeois world aspiration. However, this philosophy had practically no effective social base in Germany, where the bourgeoisie were small and weak. There was not only no "world aspirational" support for the Enlightenment theories, but also no financial support for the material needs of intellectuals who would espouse them. The unstable economic position of the intellectuals, combined with their increased sensibility, turned them into intellectual mercenaries who sold their talents to the most powerful bidder, the traditional groups, especially the nobility.[77] This position represented a retreat from the role of intellectuals described in the Free School lecture, whose will made them the leaders. These intellectuals were merely the articulators of someone else's aspirations.

However, the intellectuals were not mere parasites who contributed nothing to the dynamic of the political process. They offered clarity and perspective by allowing political doctrines to be seen in their total context, thus enabling the aspirations of political groups to include not just specific causes but also the desire to monopolize the public interpretation of existence. The romantic intellectuals of the early nineteenth century provided a good example of this contribution. Romanticism, which had its social base in those elements of the middle ranks who were hostile to the modern world, did not respond to modernity politically, but rather launched an attack on the intellectual position of the Enlightenment. Although this world view had the potential to become either a revolutionary or counterrevolutionary world aspiration, in Germany the power structure encouraged romantic intellectuals to align themselves with the conservative political forces. In doing so, they increased the viability of conservatism, which, although it had already emerged from traditionalism, had not progressed beyond being a very restricted form of political consciousness.

Mannheim saw Justus Möser as an example of this "original conservatism." Möser's views had none of the reflectiveness of romanticism, but rather were political in the most restricted sense, that is, in a purely concrete and practical way. They were rational, but the rationality was that of a peasant farmer with limited sensibility. He advocated the diversity and particularism associated with the concept of individuality, but he formulated his aspirations according to the limited experience of practical politics, in this case as an attack on the rationalizing and centralizing bureaucracy of Prussia. The same limited practicality dominated Möser's view of the past. "He does not want to go back to the past; he lives in remnants of the past which still exist in the present." Rather than challenge the present, he was confined to that part of the present that had survived from the past. His attitude was defensive, trying to find a sensible reason for those remnants, based on the conviction that "our forefathers were not fools." Such a restricted attitude was inadequate for challenging the forces of modernity. One could not compete for the public interpretation of reality with a siege mentality.[78]

The union of conservatism with romanticism propelled it past this original stage into a more effective counterrevolutionary doctrine. Mannheim saw the work of Adam Müller as an example of this union; it was characterized by two elements missing in Möser's work: (1) a more inclusive view of himself and his opponents and (2) an aspiration to move beyond the limited concrete circumstances. Müller characterized the opposition not simply as an institution but as a world view, the natural-law doctrines of the revolutionary bourgeoisie. He portrayed bourgeois rationalism as inadequate, as a static, overly abstract system that could progress only unilinearly and hence could not effectively treat the complexity of historical development. He offered an opposing world view, romantic conservatism, as a more fruitful concept of historical change. In addition, he viewed the past as not simply a corner of the present, a remnant, but as a full-fledged alternative that represented the transcendence of the increasingly modernized present. Möser's ideological defense was replaced by a utopian leap. In short, Müller went beyond concrete individual experience and developed a philosophy of history to give meaning to the changing times. By combining the more general view and utopian fervor of romanticism, he helped make the latter an effective counterpole to Enlightenment liberalism.[79]

In a long section (Chapter Two of Part Three) of the then unpublished *Conservatism*, Mannheim added two more conservative thinkers, Gustav Hugo and Friedrich von Savigny, to the discussion. These four men typified, for him, not only the various spiritual and social strata of the conservative world aspiration, but also its developmental sequence. Möser (1720–94), as noted above, represented the earliest stage, when conservative thought had just emerged from traditionalism and was at its lowest level of reflection. Hugo (1764–1844) represented the next stage, which Mannheim termed "disillusioning realism." Müller (1779–1829) and Savigny (1779–1861) represented the final stage,[80] in which the conservative world aspiration assumed two different forms of positive affirmation (*Positivität*).

Mannheim wrote that Hugo, who came from a family of officials, represented "bureaucratic conservatism," whose cornerstone was "positive law," the code of the bureaucracy under the authoritarian Prussian state. As we shall see, Mannheim characterized bureaucratic conservatism by its lack of political aspiration, and the same held true for Hugo. The latter was content to disarm the theory of natural law (the cornerstone of the rival rationalist world view) by relativizing all positive affirmations, including his own. The result was a stalemate, a lack of *"Willensentscheidung,"* a state of suspension (*Schwebezustand*) in which aspirations toward the future were deflated through their exposure as limited and relative. This disillusioning realism, wrote Mannheim, represented the negative aspects of historicism (even though Hugo himself could not be considered a member of the Historical School). In "Sociological Theory of Culture," Mannheim had identified this negative aspect of historicism and the resulting state of suspension with Max Weber. He continued to do so in *Conservatism*, writing that bourgeois sociology, represented by Weber, had relativized the utopia of socialism.

Savigny also represented officialdom, but that branch of the bureaucracy that was bound to the position of the romantic nobility. Unlike Hugo, he saw positive law not as an end in itself but as the objectification of much deeper forces anchored in "existence," the *"Volksgeist."* Whereas Hugo's defense of positive law lay in the relativization of all positive affirmations, Savigny put forth the *Volksgeist* as the basis of a positive affirmation that could counter the theory of natural law (on which the world aspiration of the revolutionary bourgeoisie was based). Where the theory of natural law gave priority to the formal, rational norm, which molded existence, Savigny gave priority to the irrational existence of the *Volksgeist*. In establishing this counteraspiration to that of the Enlightenment, he joined Müller as part of the Romantic movement.[81]

However, Mannheim also drew important distinctions between the two thinkers. As a representative of the Historical School, Savigny believed that history would eventually validate his world aspiration over one based on empty, abstract forms. His thought, then, contained an evolutionary view of progress, although it was not the Enlightenment's rational, mechanistic idea of progress. Müller, on the other hand, resisted putting his faith in the progress of history; he was a reactionary who wanted to turn the clock back to the Middle Ages.

This difference in their conceptions of history corresponded to different theories of knowledge. The terminus for Savigny's view of knowledge was "clarification" (*Klärung*), a peaceful enveloping of oneself in the "living substances" that are in one. His approach represented a "quiet" opposition to the Enlightenment, an interpretation of cultural products, such as law, that continued into Mannheim's own day in the historical-cultural sciences. For Müller, history meant not the clarification of the *Volksgeist* but the struggle of ranks. His approach was a political radicalism in which the terminus for his theory of knowledge was "mediation" (*Vermittlung*). Whereas Savigny believed that knowledge would gradually reveal the truth of his world aspiration, Müller saw knowledge as a tool of political struggle. Thus one could say that the two men represented not only two varieties of Romantic conservatism but also the first two of Mannheim's centers of construction – culture and politics.

Another important difference between the two men was their relationship to the romantic nobility, whom they represented. Savigny had been born into noble circles and so had always been bound to the conservative world aspiration. Müller, on the other hand, was a free-floating intellectual who threw in his lot with the extreme wing of the conservative forces. Although Savigny identified with the long-existing forces of custom and tradition, Müller, with no real roots, evaluated the situation in terms of which political camp he should align himself with, and, after choosing the nobility, adopted its most radical expression.

One could divide these four intellectuals into two basic types, each with two subtypes. Möser and Savigny represented intellectuals who were bound to world aspirations, with Savigny representing an expansion, both spatially and temporally, over Möser. The latter was limited temporally to a corner of the present and spatially to the community of his rank. Savigny, on the other hand, expanded this limited, defensive attitude into a full-fledged theory of history that foresaw a conservative victory. He increased the spatial realm from the noble rank to the entire "*Volksgemeinschaft*" and maintained that the nobility were the spokesmen for this entity. Thus, he was not content with holding his own against the forces of Enlightenment rationalism; rather he claimed the superiority of his position. Later, in *Ideology and Utopia*, Mannheim would refer to this aspiration to move beyond one's bondedness as a potential utopian consciousness.

Hugo and Müller formed the other type, the intellectual who was not bound from the beginning to the conservative world aspiration. As a member of the state bureaucracy, Hugo never developed those ties to the landed nobility that Savigny had. Given this absence of ties to the nobility, he was content with the compromise between that group and the monarchy and was resigned to a stalemated present (*Schwebezustand*). Although his position was more sophisticated and intellectually radical than Möser's, it still represented a restricted, present-oriented defensiveness. Müller, the free-floating (*freischwebend*) intellectual, also began with no ties to the conservative world aspiration, but he chose to establish those ties. Like Savigny in the other type, his subtype represented a breaking forth from the restricted, defensive position of the earlier subtype to an actual challenge to the world aspiration of the Enlightenment. Like Hugo, his position was more radical than the corresponding "bound" type, but now this radicalism was primarily political rather than intellectual.

As I have noted, Mannheim did not structure the four stages in this way. He contrasted Möser to Müller as stages in the development of political Romanticism and Hugo to Savigny as stages in the development of historicism. (He also contrasted Müller to Savigny in *Conservatism.*) One should ask why he left out the latter comparisons when he prepared the work for publication. There could be any number of reasons for this, including the possibility that no publisher would accept the longer version. However, I believe that a comparison of the two versions offers a viable explanation. During this period, Mannheim was becoming increasingly doubtful about the possibility of a cultural solution to the problem of orientation in the modern world. In dropping the essay on the Historical School (Hugo and Savigny), he achieved two results: He avoided a discussion of the more cultural element of historicism, and he softened Müller's position by not contrasting him to the more politically passive Savigny. In the published version, Müller's mediation was presented as activistic and anticontemplative but not explicitly radical.[82] This allowed Mannheim to pass over the cultural implications of conservatism without directly challenging them.[83]

At the same time, this decision also modified Mannheim's depiction of intellectuals. In discussing just Möser and Müller, he presented the rooted intellectual as an early stage and the free-floating intellectual as a later stage. Once again, Savigny as an alternative type to Müller disappeared. This growing uncertainty on Mannheim's part can also be seen by comparing the intellectuals as they appeared in "Conservative Thought" with the concept of *Bildungskultur* from "Sociological Theory of Culture."

Despite the contributions of the romantic intellectuals (as represented by Müller) to conservatism, Mannheim did not assign them the same synthetic position that characterized the intellectuals of the *Bildungskultur*. The latter were less free floating than the intellectuals of "Conservative Thought" and "Generations"; they were not forced to abandon their original ties as the others did when they became intellectual mercenaries. The reason for this was that in the later essays there was no equivalent to the *Bildungskultur* itself – a medium in which conflicting aspirations could be reconciled, or organized around a center of construction, making an intellectual synthesis possible. Instead, one finds a number of competing, polar positions and a collection of vacillating intellectuals who were attracted to one position or another but were unable to synthesize the positions.[84] Thus the emphasis on politics was accompanied by a devaluation of the role of the intellectual.

Still, Mannheim was not willing to discard the possibility of synthesis or even the contribution of intellectuals to that synthesis. He frequently cited Hegel as an example of a synthesizer while pointing out the limitations of Hegel's spiritual and teleological approach. In "Competition," he wrote that a synthesis was impossible only if one took the one-sided view of those who "absolutize the theoretical differences as a class-bound irreconcilability based on interests."[85] True, a grand synthesis in the teleological sense would never come about, but a limited synthesis in the sense of a common fund of knowledge for political parties was possible. The agent of this synthesis would be cultural competition itself. Indeed, polarization meant partial synthesis of local concrete groups through competition; there was no reason that this process of consolidation could not continue using the vehicle of selection. "Selection means synthesis" – parties would select what worked for them as well as for their rivals while discarding the ineffective elements. "The stream of history sifts out in the long run those contents, paradigms, attitudes, etc. of experience that are most useful."[86] Gradually, a set of common holdings would accumulate that could be characterized as a limited synthesis.

However, this concept of synthesis through selection leaves some unanswered questions, the most important of which Mannheim posed himself: Can the politically pragmatic be equated with meaningful validity? Pragmatic selection was an inadequate replacement for the center of construction, for it did not offer the possibility of a hierarchy of positions as the earlier concept did and thus provided no alternative to pluralism. It rendered a judgment on techniques but not on the world aspirations themselves. In this analytical essay, Mannheim avoided this issue, saying that such a judgment was the task of epistemology, not the sociology of knowledge. At the same time, he repeated his contention in "Epistemology" that epistemological systematizations were only secondary constructions, only "advance posts in the struggle between styles of thought." All this left nothing settled.[87] If primary systematizations were defined politically, then some kind of political epistemology had to be developed. He attempted to do this with his concept of "relationsim" in *Ideology and Utopia*, although he never felt that he had been completely successful.[88]

91

The importance of the political

His transition toward a political center of construction can be summarized best by comparing his position to that of Alfred Weber, who in 1926 wrote an essay calling for a connection between aristocratic spirit and democratic politics.[89] Weber considered himself a democrat and put great stock in the German youth movement as a source of democratic energy and future political leadership. Yet he doubted the ability of the masses, and especially the youth, to provide the proper direction for their great energy, and he believed that the existing institutions, the party youth organizations, were inadequate for the task of formulating ideals. This void had to be filled by an intellectual aristocracy that would allow individual standards to develop independently of party opinion. Implicit in Weber's position was the possibility of an organic totality of spirit for the nation, which ideally subordinated the pluralistic political (democratic) level. One could describe this attitude as a desire for the "overcoming" (*Ueberwindung*) of the pluralistic forces through spirit, that is, the maintenance of the hierarchical priorities of the academic elite. Weber's was a classic statement of what I have described above as the monadic, tragic consciousness of those academics who tried to combine their traditionalist cultural ideals with a commitment to the Weimar Republic.

Mannheim's work at the beginning of this period did not contradict Weber's position, which was very close to that of Troeltsch. After all, "Sociological Theory of Culture" was written in conjunction with Weber's seminar, and its concept of *Bildungskultur* certainly implied the possibility of spiritual synthesis and the "overcoming" of political divisions. However, with the switch to a political emphasis, Mannheim began to move away from Weber on the crucial element of a spiritual synthesis to which politics was to be subordinated.

This growing rift can be seen in a discussion of "Competition" following its presentation at the Sixth German Sociological Convention in 1928, in which Weber accused Mannheim of promoting a Marxist materialism that negated the role of the creative individual.[90] Weber's objections were not directed at the methodology of the sociology of knowledge[91] but rather at the "political" description of the national context in which conflict permeated all spheres. Although he stated that he did not wish to discuss values, those were exactly his concerns. Implicit here was his argument from the earlier essay that values were to be arbitrated by the spiritual aristocracy (i.e., the creative individuals), who provided the necessary spiritual leadership for the aspirations of the political groups. Mannheim's inclusion of intellectuals and culture in the struggle for the "public interpretation of existence," rather than above it, seemed to

Weber a leveling process akin to that of the Marxists. At stake was not merely an analytical methodology but the shift to a new valuative center of construction.[92]

Mannheim, in his summation, avoided a direct response to Weber (other than to say that his position was basically that of those who had defended him against Weber).[93] He declared that his presentation had been directed mainly to sociological (analytical) questions rather than to metaphysical-valuative ones. However, he did respond indirectly to Weber's charge:

> I want to know why the person of today necessarily thinks in terms of these divided polarities, which somehow do not correspond essentially with one another. This question has brought me to the sociology of knowledge. This discipline, I expect, will point to that synthetic point from which the imposed alternatives will become transparent in thier imposition and their transitoriness. . . . What I have in mind is a synthetic analysis of the situation, which, . . . when viewed from the movement of spiritual and social powers, is at least just as possible and necessary as the polarization itself. I am trying, therefore, to put it briefly, to vivify once again the basic aspirations toward value-freedom (*Grundwille zur Wertfreiheit*), but not to realize in one blow scientific objectivity in the human and social sciences in this old, all-too-intellectual manner (which will not succeed). Rather, we must work out step by step the problems and methods of an exact scientific analysis in order to approach a solution gradually.[94]

In this passage, we can hear some echoes of the Free School lecture, but with important variations. In both, he declared his prime goal to be synthesis and saw the need to work through a pluralism of positions to achieve that synthesis rather than ignoring that pluralism for an imposed monism (which was what the competing poles did). However, in the earlier lecture, this pluralism was one of cultural disciplines, which did not challenge the premise of a cultural synthesis, a scientific solution. Now, he seemed to be saying that the most science could achieve was a "synthetic *analysis* of the situation." He believed the sociology of knowledge would contribute by establishing a common medium of analysis, a common language of intercontextual communication. However, the actual dynamic synthesis, the actual "making" of the world, would have to be accomplished in the sphere of politics, and any scientific contributions to that making would have to be in conjunction with the competing political aspirations.[95] This position was what offended Alfred Weber.

In taking it, Mannheim appeared to be moving toward the Marxist position that it was not enough passively to interpret the world, one must also actively change it. Such an activism would represent a strengthening of the inclinations of his Budapest days but in a different sphere, politics –

a step toward resolving the contradictory elements in his earlier writings. It would seem that he had finally followed Lukács and abandoned the monadic cultural premises of Simmel, Alfred Weber, and Troeltsch. To a certain extent, this was true. His work was becoming increasingly political but not partisan; that is, although he put more faith in politics and less in science, he could not follow Lukács and become a spokesman for one of the competing parties. He remained a scientist and tried to work out a role for himself and his colleagues. In doing so, he adopted a new model, Max Weber, whom he gave a new dimension beyond that of the earlier disillusioning realism. This choice and the new political center of construction were presented in his most famous work, *Ideology and Utopia*.[96]

4

The political synthesis (1929)

Ideology and Utopia, in which the political synthesis was described, has appeared in two different versions, the original edition of 1929 and the 1936 English translation. As Kurt Wolff has noted, the later edition, subtitled "An Introduction to the Sociology of Knowledge," is the one most scholars know.[1] Accordingly, most take the book to be a methodological treatise on the sociology of knowledge, and with justification, for the 1936 edition does offer Mannheim's most complete presentation of that discipline. However, such a portrayal cannot be applied accurately to the original work of 1929, for the 1936 edition is very different from its predecessor—partly due to the translation, but also to its two lengthy additions.[2] It lacks the focus, intensity, and spirit of crisis that dominated the original version.

The 1929 edition consisted of two semiautonomous essays and an introduction (now the middle three chapters of the translation). The first of the two main essays concerned the possibility of a political science, that is, the problem of theory and praxis, the issue of ideology.[3] The other main essay was about utopian consciousness. Each of the essays, then, contributed one half the book's (and the introduction's) title. Together, they went beyond the earlier and later explications of the sociology of knowledge and attempted to analyze the crises of political orientation and academic learning during the Weimar Republic. The book was an attempt to establish a new center of construction that defined the role of science and politics in the process of validation.

In treating *Ideology and Utopia* as essentially a treatise on the sociology of knowledge, most observers have given insufficient attention to the political element. Mannheim's theory of "utopia" has received considerably less attention than his theory of "ideology,"[4] a priority exactly the reverse of his own. This emphasis had led to the mistaken view that he tried to extend the Marxist theory of ideology to a totally relativist, that is, defeatist, conclusion. In fact, *Ideology and Utopia* was a call to action, an attempt to involve intellectuals in the political process. Under the old center of construction, Troeltsch had been the model for an involvement in the problems of the republic; now it was Max Weber.

Max Weber and Georg Lukács

Most interpretations of *Ideology and Utopia* have largely ignored this connection and, with their focus on the sociology of knowledge, have emphasized the ties to the work of Lukács. Even George Lichtheim, who has written that the book represented an "amalgam" of Max Weber and Lukács and who considers Mannheim's work an "epilogue" to that of Weber, devotes more space to a comparison of Mannheim and Lukács and seems to sympathize with the description of Mannheim as a "bourgeois Lukács."[5] The implication is that *Ideology and Utopia* was an attempt to come to terms with Lukács's *History and Class Consciousness* from a Weberian political stance. I will argue that, on the contrary, the book was an attempt to come to terms with the position Weber articulated at the end of his life and that the role of Lukács's book was secondary.[6]

As I indicated in Chapter 1, the works of Max Weber most important for understanding *Ideology and Utopia* are his two speeches on politics and science as "vocations." The speeches stood out as "radical" in relation to the monadic and idealist positions of German academics after the First World War in that they challenged the traditional beliefs that the academics were the arbiters of values for the nation and that the sphere of political activity should be subordinate to those of intellect and administration (officialdom).[7]

Weber contrasted the political activity of the demagogic politician who headed a *Weltanschauungspartei* (i.e., the striving for power) with administration (of power already attained).[8] The latter was the realm of the instrumentally rational. As a functionary, the administrator (bureaucrat) was not concerned with the establishment of values (ends); he took that as a given. His prime concern was with their application (means), carrying out value decisions rather than making them. It was the politician to whom the decision making fell; he was "value-oriented" and thus was the agent of political change. Wolfang Mommsen writes:

> Weber argued that it is the "value-oriented" actions of individuals, or, possibly, small groups of individuals, which bring social change about, and these actions are likely to be the more far reaching, the more the values, ideals, or normative principles in question stand out in contrast to social reality and the traditional patterns of social conduct given at the time. Or, to put this another way: it is the enormous tension between any given set of ultimate values on the one hand, and empirical reality on the other hand, which begets extraordinary social achievements.[9]

Weber saw three types of politician. The first of these, exemplified by the American machine politician, the "boss," was characterized by his essentially instrumentally rational conduct. He was indifferent to values, "without convictions" (*gesinnungslos*), in managing a spoils system in which ends and means were reduced to the common denominator of money.[10] Thus, the political machine approached the bureaucratic machine in its reified conduct.

The second type of politician was the revolutionary who held to his ends (values) and let them determine his means without any rational consideration. His conduct demonstrated the same indifference to practical means that the boss showed toward valuative ends. Weber labeled the ethic by which this politician operated the "ethic of ultimate ends"[11] or "ethic of conviction" (*Gesinnungsethik*). Although the boss succumbed to "reality" and operated in a purely functional (*sachlich*) way, the "revolutionary chiliast" resisted reality totally and, therefore, was unable to deal with the situation he faced. This "sterile excitation" often resulted in a retreat from that reality into mysticism.[12]

Obviously, neither of these types conformed with Weber's ideal politician, to whom he attributed three main characteristics: passion, a sense of proportion, and a feeling of responsibility.[13] Passion, for Weber, meant the commitment to a set of values, a willingness to suffer for them.[14] By a sense of proportion, he meant the ability to step back and see things from a distance, to see one's cause in perspective to the real world. Responsibility meant a combination of the two, "a hot passion and a cool sense of proportion." This third characteristic was clearly the more synthetic of the three and named the ethic that Weber associated with his ideal politician, the *Verantwortungsethik*.

The ethic of responsibility marked a new qualified optimism on Weber's part. It represented a shift in emphasis from reified administration to the active politician, the individual capable of implementing some kind of historical change. Weber did not minimize the difficulties facing Germany at the beginning of the republic. However, he seems to have believed that the new generation he was addressing could possibly effect significant political changes.[15]

Weber was at variance with most other German academics in that the synthesis he hoped for took place only on the level of the individual, not on that of the totality of society. He did not believe that pluralism could be overcome but that despite this the individual was capable of responsibile and effective action. Friedrick Meinecke, from the perspective of the mandarins, sought a way out of the "unending pluralism of individual values" toward cultural unity. He pleaded: "Everything is individuality following its own laws, everything has its own right to life, everything is

97

relative, everything is flux – give me a place where I can stand."[16] To this Weber quoted Martin Luther: "Here I stand; I can do no other."[17]

When Meinecke asked how did one arrive at a science of values,[18] Weber answered that one does not. In "Science as a Vocation," he wrote that science could not give answers to questions of values, to questions like "what shall we do and how shall we live?" As I have noted earlier, Weber attacked the ideological premise of the mandarins' position–the idea that they were the interpreters of values for the organic unity of the nation. The professoriat, like the bureaucracy and the army, had considered themselves unpolitical, or *"unparteiisch,"* and hence qualified to be the arbiters for the German totality. In Weber's pluralistic world, it was precisely the political arena where values were formulated, so that the scientists' unpolitical position excluded them from the value-making process. Like the rest of the bureaucracy, they were no longer leaders, but functionaries.[19] And for Weber, this was properly so. The scientist, he believed, was essentially the analytical specialist, the problem solver, the efficiency expert; he or she was not the cultural synthesizer. The growth of specialization in science could no more be overcome than the growth of industrialism or of other elements in the rationalization process. Science's role was to contribute to the technical progress of the modern world and to provide a rational method for analysis.

However, Wolfgang Schluchter is right when he states that "Science as a Vocation" was about political education,[20] for Weber indicated a contribution by which the scientist could aid the politician – clarity, which occurred on two levels. The scientist's advice on the first level was exactly like that of the technician in that it did not establish valuative ends. The scientist said:

> If you take such and such a stand, then according to scientific experience, you have to use such and such a means in order to carry out your conviction practically. Now, these means are perhaps such that you believe you must reject them. Then you must choose between the end and the inevitable means.[21]

However, on the second level, the scientist actually concerned himself or herself with the ends, not simply with the means for realizing given ends. Here science could help the politician achieve an "account of the ultimate meaning of his conduct."[22] The politician could act oblivious to the ends (*Weltanschauung*) implied by that action. The scientist's task was to impute the ends contained in the conduct and, in doing so, to help provide the sense of proportion necessary to the politician. But despite this second level, the scientist's position was still primarily instrumentally rational – that of weighing ends and means. Political responsibility, which involved decision making, was not his or her task. Although science could provide the meaning of action, it could not provide the "meaning of the world."[23] In other words, whereas the scientist could demonstrate how an action related to the various world views in this pluralistic world, he or she could not make a decision among them for the politician. Clarification was not truth. Only the political actor could make the decision, and it was valid only for himself or herself and his or her followers.

Despite a similarity of some concepts, for example, the dangers of specialization, the reification of the modern world, and imputation, Weber's position was fundamentally different from that of Lukács. One of the most important principles separating the two was Lukács's concept of "dialectical transcendence" (*Aufhebung*). Lukács wrote:

> It is the essence of dialectical method that concepts which are false in their abstract one-sidedness are later transcended. The process of transcendence makes it inevitable that we should operate with these one-sided, abstract and false categories. The concepts acquire their true meaning less by definition than by their methodological function as aspects that are then transcended in the totality.[24]

Lukács, like the monadic historicists, saw history as a dynamic totality, the comprehension of which was weakened by the reification of modern society and the specialization of positivistic science.[25] However, although the monadic historicists like Troeltsch hoped for the subordination (*Ueberwindung*) of the reifying, fragmenting forces and a reaffirmation of the organic unity of *Geist*, Lukács saw a transcendence of those elements, a propelling of them to their dialectical conclusion. Rather than preserving the old conception of totality, he wanted the creation of a new one by the proletariat. Whereas Troeltsch emphasized the "evil" of pluralism, which dissolved the order of the organic movement of history into flux, Lukács emphasized the "evil" of reification, which preserved the bourgeois order at the expense of the dialectical movement of history toward the triumph of the proletariat. Thus Lukács's position, unlike Troeltsch's, was trichotomous rather than dichotomous, comic rather than tragic.

Max Weber rejected the possibility of comprehending the totality of history and so rejected the hope for both *Ueberwindung* and *Aufhebung*. Instead, he believed one had to live with the pluralism of history and adopt a responsible course of action.

Another issue separating Lukács from Weber was the former's belief that one sector of society, the proletariat, was able to grasp the totality of history intellectually due to its unique position. But how did one understand the totality of the historical dialectic when one was only a part of that process? How could a part grasp the whole? That could happen, said

Lukács, when the essence of the part and the essence of the whole were the same. The subject could grasp the whole only when knowledge of the whole was essential to the achievement of its goals.[26] He wrote:

> Only when a historical situation has arisen in which a class must understand society if it is to assert itself; only when the fact that a class understands itself means that it understands society as a whole and when in consequence, the class becomes both subject and object; in short, only when these conditions are all satisfied will the unity of theory and practice, the precondition of the revolutionary function of theory, become possible.[27]

Lukács believed that only the proletariat met these conditions. The essence of the proletariat was the same as the essence of capitalistic society. In understanding this essence, it understood the evils and contradictions inherent in capitalistic society and the necessity to break through these contradictions to a new society. The proletariat's unique position of being at once subject and object allowed the transformation of a "theory of praxis" into a "practical theory."[28] Proletarian class consciousness was the true consciousness of society, whereas all other consciousness was false, that is, ideological. In achieving its true consciousness of the historical process, the proletariat "unmasked" the false consciousness of its rival, the bourgeoisie. In other words, theory not only informed proletarian praxis, it also verified it. The proletariat was in a position to grasp the true meaning of the totality of history. Class consciousness was true historical consciousness. Whereas the monadic historicists wanted the subordination of the pluralistic social realm to the unified sphere of *Geist*, where truth and values lay, Lukács reversed the priorities and then declared that only two positions (bourgeois and proletarian) were essential to that base and that only one of these had the potential to dialectically transcend its position and create an organic totality of history that could be theoretically verified.

Max Weber, in denying the possibility of comprehending the totality of history, rejected the premise that the proletariat was the agent of dialectical transcendence. In "Politics as a Vocation," he wrote: "The materialist interpretation of history is no cab to be taken at will; it does not stop short of the promoters of revolutions."[29] Accordingly, Weber rejected the notion that theory could verify praxis; the most if could do was clarify praxis. Weber rejected teleological conceptions of history, be they from the "aristocratic" premise of the unity of *Geist* or from the revolutionary premise of the dialectical transcendence of proletarian praxis.

If we can answer the following questions, we should be able to determine which of the three positions described above is closest to that taken by Mannheim in *Ideology and Utopia:* (1) Was Mannheim's view of history teleological, that is, did he believe that history could be grasped in its totality? (2) Did he believe that one sector of society, be it a spiritual aristocracy or the proletariat, had the ability to achieve this teleological comprehension? (3) Did he believe that theory could verify praxis, either from an aristocratic or a proletarian standpoint? (4) Did he view the relationship of science (theory) and politics as one of (a) subordination (*Ueberwindung*), (b) dialectical transcendence (*Aufhebung*), or (c) clarification for responsibility (*Verantwortung*)? As I have already indicated, I contend that the answer to all these questions, with the exception of 4c, is no and that, therefore, Mannheim was closest to the position of Max Weber. In addition, the concepts used in *Ideology and Utopia* corresponded most closely to those used in Weber's two speeches on science and politics as vocations.

Ideologies and utopias

Our examination of *Ideology and Utopia* must begin with an explication of some of its major concepts, starting with the two that give the book its title. Mannheim defined utopia as a will (*Wille, Wollen, Wollung*), or aspiration, to change, a drive that did not recognize any limitations. Utopias provided the nontheoretical basis for significant political conduct and, in fact, could not be separated from creative political activity. As we shall see, these utopian desires to break through the existing structure were, for Mannheim, the driving forces of history.[30] They were every bit as positive for him as the "essential will" of the *Gemeinschaft* was for Tönnies.

This was not the case for ideology, which had two different definitions in *Ideology and Utopia*. One of these was obviously negative – ideology was a failed would-be utopia. If a will to change did not break through the existing structure, it was ideological. One should note that Mannheim was not really concerned with ideology as a successful defense of the status quo. For him, ideology was not the successful resistance to change, but the failed attempt to bring it about.[31] This definition was clearly secondary to the second one, to which the title of the book refers.

The primary definition of ideology, upon which most interpretations of Mannheim have focused, was the extension of the Marxian tactic of "unmasking" the social base of the ideas of one's opponents. Here ideology was viewed as a defense of a certain position; however, it was only temporarily successful (because it was being unmasked), and it was not willful. The ideologist did not formulate his or her ideology intentionally to defend his or her position, even though that was exactly what the ideology did. His or her intention was to formulate some universally valid principle, a task thwarted by the exposure of the ideology.[32] Thus, where-

101

as utopia was a successful willful effort to break through the status quo, ideology was either an unsuccessful attempt at the same thing or an unwillful defense of the existing structure. In either case, ideology was perceived as a negative thing, especially when judged by the criterion of the promotion of historical change (which Mannheim had accepted since his Hungarian days).

Equally important was his conception of ideology (in the primary sense) as a product of the reflective subject, not the active subject. A utopia was the world as seen by the utopian actor; it was tied to praxis. An ideology, on the other hand, was the actor's world as seen by his or her opponents. It was not a part of the actor's praxis (it could be tied to his or her opponents' praxis); rather, it was designed to stymie that praxis. It sought to deprive the world aspiration of its will, of its subjective drive. To continue the parallel to Tönnies's dualism, like the rationality of the *Gesellschaft,* ideology represented the absence of the positive element, the utopia. Therefore, many of those scholars who have emphasized the connections between ideology and the sociology of knowledge in Mannheim's book have seen the work as negative and defeatist.[33] But to do so is to ignore the primary importance of the positive element, utopia.

One further point should be made about the two terms ideology and utopia. Mannheim was not concerned with individual elements, be they utopian or ideological, but rather with "totalities," the "utopian consciousness" and the "total conception of ideology."[34] This concern represented a continuation of his emphasis on world views and world aspirations. In fact, the utopian consciousness was very similar to the world aspiration, with the political element being emphasized.

A second division found in *Ideology and Utopia* ran parallel to Max Weber's division of authority into two basic spheres – that which was routinized and that which was not. The routinized sphere, according to Weber, was subdivided into traditional and legal-bureaucratic authority, whereas the sphere that resisted routinization was termed "charismatic." In "Politics as a Vocation," Weber called these two spheres "administration" and "politics." Mannheim adopted the same schema and terminology in *Ideology and Utopia,* writing:

The contrast between the "routine affairs of state" and "politics" offers a certain polarity which may serve as a fruitful point of departure. If the dichotomy is conceived more theoretically, we may say: every social process may be divided into a "rationalized sphere" consisting of settled and routinized procedures and an "irrational matrix" which surrounds the former. We are, therefore, distinguishing between the *"rationalized structure"* and *"irrational matrix."* A further observation presents itself at this point. The chief characterization of our world is the tendency to rationalize as much as

102

possible and to bring it under administrative control – and to allow the irrational matrix to disappear.[35]

Both men agreed that within the routinized sphere rationalization was replacing traditionalism and that this sphere was encroaching upon the irrational matrix of politics. Because the latter was perceived as the location of the will to transform society, to act as a historical agent, both interpreted this development as a process of reification. Administration involved no value decisions but rather the implementation of someone else's decisions. Mannheim described it as an essentially negative thing – the absence of conduct. Conduct, and the whole problem of the relation of theory to praxis, was located in the irrational sphere dominated by politics.[36] He wrote of this sphere:

> All those deeper irrational elements that fill our supra-economic life, our innermost sphere of lived experience, emanate from and shape themselves here. Viewed sociologically, this is the place where their collective displacement and transformation occurs and can be structurally grasped.[37]

Here Mannheim was announcing his replacement of the cultural with the political as representative of the pretheoretical sphere that occupied so prominent a part in his writings. This sphere was no longer seen as having (or potentially having) some kind of organic unity but rather as being an arena for pluralistic competition. He agreed with Weber that there was an irreconcilable conflict of world views (aspirations) represented by political parties.

In *Ideology and Utopia*, then, we have two dualisms that paralleled the *Gemeinschaft – Gesellschaft* pattern. Utopia and politics were both positive, "irrational" elements where the subjective decision-making process took place and where the world changed in a historically significant way. Ideology and administration were both negative, "objectified" elements that represented a process of reification. These two dualisms overlapped, because Mannheim identified the political with the utopian.[38] The relationship of ideology to administration was more complex; they were not equated but did represent the negation of the concepts that were equated.

When these two dualisms were combined, they formed the central elements of Mannheim's theory of history: First, the will (utopia) was the motor force of history. Second, the modern world was characterized not by a single will but by a pluralism of utopias represented by political parties. So we have a plurality of parties, each of which was committed to a different world aspiration and, refusing to accept the existing pluralism, sought to make that world aspiration universally valid. Mannheim felt that the will to determine the public interpretation of reality was stronger than any accrued material benefits that might serve to dampen that will. It

103

was this combination of pluralism and the utopian will to overcome that pluralism that provided the central dynamic of his theory of history and distinguished it from his earlier position.

However, if utopias represented wills that actually succeeded in bringing about change and in propelling the historical process, the utopian groups could never be completely successful. Although they could shatter the existing order, they could never establish a new order based on the total victory of their world aspirations. Because they formed only a part of the social spectrum, their world views were always limited perspectives and thus could not be valid for the entire social realm.[39] Success was always limited; new challengers would always arise; today's utopians would be tomorrow's ideologists. Will provided change, but not total change, so that the limited success of the utopian will did not threaten the dynamic of history but rather propelled it.

In *Ideology and Utopia*, Mannheim outlined the basic polarized positions in a series of types.[40] I will demonstrate how these types related to the ethics portrayed in Max Weber's vocation essays, namely those of instrumentally rational fatalism (Mannheim's term was "ethic of fatalism"), the ethic of ultimate ends, and the ethic of responsibility. Like Weber, he saw these types as the successors to the disintegrated organic unity of the traditional world. Two of Mannheim's types had their roots in the traditional schema. One of them, bureaucratic conservatism, represented the routinized sphere of administration, whereas the other, chiliasm, gave rise to the utopian consciousness and modern politics.

The bureaucratic conservative treated all action, political and administrative alike, as if it were purely administrative, that is, subject to systematic classification. He could not comprehend political action as something positive in itself – politics to him was simply the lack of administrative order.[41] All the limitations that Mannheim attributed to administration also applied to the bureaucratic conservative. In assuming that the status quo was "rational" and that everything could be adapted to and classified by this rational system, in implementing decisions rather than making them, in never recognizing the possibility of essential change in society, bureaucratic conservatism could not be utopian in either its traditional or modern form.[42] For Mannheim, therefore, it was a negative type.

This was not the case with chiliasm, which stood at the opposite end of his spectrum of types. There were two essential differences between the two types. First, whereas bureaucratic conservatism was entirely rational in approaching the world, chiliasm was completely irrational. Mannheim described the chiliast as being driven by "ecstatic-orgiastic energies" not by ideas.[43] The chiliast, then, was characterized by the absence of reflective consciousness.

104

Second, chiliasm was "existentially transcendent" (*seinstranszendent*). "Existence" for Mannheim meant a "concretely valid" order of life that included all forms of "human living together," lived existence, and thought. It was roughly equivalent to the concepts of "context of lived experience" and "experiential realm" from his earlier unpublished manuscripts on the sociology of culture. "Transcendent" meant those mental images that did not concur with the "operating order of life."[44] The transcendence of certain world aspirations provided a basic tension that was the core of all potential utopias. This anomalous position on the part of chiliasm (and other utopias) was willful and hence positive. If the bureaucratic conservative saw concrete existence as an order to which everything must be adapted, which rejected "unbound" sociopolitical forces, the chiliast saw that existence as something at odds with his or her world aspiration, as something that had to be defeated or abandoned. Chiliasm, with its unbound, transcendent posture, was for Mannheim the "driving" force in history.[45]

Mannheim qualified this statement by writing that chiliasm did not achieve such an important role until it became political. Prior to that, the chiliast was a religious figure, often a mystic, whose ends were totally otherworldly and hence free from concrete objectives. Mannheim, in his Free School lecture, had identified mysticism with the individual soul's rejection of objective culture and its turn inward. In *Ideology and Utopia,* he retained this belief and added the observation that at times this irrational mysticism emerged from its dormant state to take the form of chiliastic activity. Chiliasm was mysticism made concrete in the world, an "eruption [which] had its roots in much deeper-lying vital and elemental levels of the soul." In this active form, chiliasm was potentially revolutionary yet could always be defused by the authorities because it had no sociopolitical base. "From the point of view of our problem," wrote Mannheim, "the decisive turning-point in modern history was the movement in which 'chiliasm' joined forces (*Bündnis schliessen*) with the active aspirations of the oppressed strata." Hopes that had been "free-floating" were "experienced as realizable here and now and infused social conduct with a singular zeal."[46]

However, although political chiliasm provided movement, it did not envision historical change. The social groups with which it joined forces had an orientation toward neither the past nor the future but simply were reacting against the present. They were dislocated groups, for example, the peasantry, journeymen, the incipient *Lumpenproletariat,* etc., that had no real historical vision but simply mythic yearnings. Without any substantial ties to the past, present, or future objective culture, chiliasm (including its most modern form, fascism)[47] found meaning only in its adherents' own irrational actions, only in the deed of the immediate present. Like the bureaucratic conservative, the chiliast divorced the active, willing subject from the contemplative subject, but with exactly the opposite emphasis. If the world for the bureaucrat was an external static system to be accepted, for the fascist-chiliast it was an eternal struggle.

These two types, despite being at opposite ends of the administrative-political spectrum, did share an important characteristic (which was also shared by the traditional sphere) – they were ahistorical. Both isolated the present from the past and future, even though their conceptions of the present were very different (service and resistance). Neither was concerned with a systematic concept of historical change, the bureaucratic conservative because he or she detested change, the chiliastic fascist because he or she detested systems. Mannheim, with his emphasis on a historical world view, considered the pure form of bureaucratic conservatism and the pure will of chiliasm to be unacceptable types of consciousness, extremes to be avoided.

Bureaucratic conservatism corresponded to Max Weber's ethic of fatalism, whereas chiliasm corresponded to the ethic of ultimate ends. Like Weber, Mannheim opted for a third possibility that combined the two extremes to allow for historically understandable change – the ethic of responsibility.[48] He did not describe one ethic of responsibility but three, liberalism, conservatism, and socialism, forming a new triad within the original one. In describing these types, I will concentrate on two elements. The first is their view of history. If utopia was their will to change, then their view of history was an explanation of how that change occurred.[49] The second element is their philosophy of consciousness and action. If one wished to discredit his opponents' consciousness and actions as "false" (ideological), then one had to have a philosophy of the "true" relationship of consciousness and praxis.

Liberalism, the first of the "historical" types, resembled bureaucratic conservatism in that both had what they considered to be correct rational systems by which to evaluate concrete events. However, this similarity was overshadowed by an important difference between the two types. The bureaucrat saw no conflict between his or her universal system and concrete reality; he or she treated his system as if it had always existed and would always exist, as the eternal present. The liberal, on the other hand, believed that his or her universal system stood at odds with concrete existence, which was still burdened by traditional and irrational elements. The task of the liberal, as the representative of humankind, was to transform concrete existence to conform with his or her universal truths. In other words, liberalism was potentially utopian (depending on its success); the liberal did not ignore the realm of will and action as the bureau-

106

crat did but rather saw the necessity of change. Instead of rejecting chiliastic "ecstasy," liberalism transformed it into the "idea," which was no longer a negation of reality but a yardstick by which to measure the transformation of concrete events. Liberalism's program was not the all-or-nothing of the chiliastic deed; it saw its goals being implemented steadily and surely with the growth of reason. Thus, liberalism's view was historical – the world was characterized by a process of change that could be systematically comprehended. Historical movement for the liberal conformed to the "idea of progress," the gradual unilinear realization in historical life of an a priori, suprahistorical, rational system, the "idea."[50]

Mannheim believed that liberalism marked the first step toward a philosophy of consciousness. With the breakup of the traditional ontological unity, liberalism tried to replace it with the unity of "consciousness in general," the universal reflective subject, which was an ahistorical, unsociological, and hence ficticious entity. Historical subjects were evaluated by the degree to which they overcame traditional limitations and approached the "idea." Those individuals who remained bound by irrational forces such as tradition and superstition were incorrect, or "ideological," in their assumptions. He believed that the main fault of this type of consciousness was that it separated the active and contemplative subjects, the former being the historical, atomistic individual, the latter the suprahistorical, universal mind.[51]

The political conservative was the antithesis of the liberal. As we have seen in the preceding chapter, Mannheim viewed conservatism as a counterattack of the traditional forces against the liberal offensive of the Enlightenment; here he described it as a counterutopia. Whereas the liberal saw the universal idea and concrete existence as opposed to one another in the past and present, the conservative saw them as complementary. The idea could not be separated from the concrete content of the historical world, which Mannheim described as "the inner form of historical individuality existing at any given time . . . and the external conditions together with the past that lies behind it."[52] The conservative agreed with the liberal that the "here and now" was an essentially irrational collection of forces that resisted rational systematization, but he denied that this made it "evil." In fact, he said that the idea could only be realized through this historical development, for the universal idea was not accessible to people in an abstract, suprahistorical form, but only in its historical form. The rational idea was not the guide for history, but rather its product, or, in the words of Hegel, "the owl of Minerva spreads its wings only with the falling of dusk."[53]

For the liberal, who saw concrete existence as something to be transformed in accordance with the suprahistorical idea, history was the uni-

107

linear process by which the present was transformed into the more progressive future. The old present, the past, had no real value; it was the victim of progress. The conservative, on the other hand, who saw concrete existence as the embodiment of the idea, placed positive emphasis not on the transformation of the present (into the future) but on its coming into being (from the past). Accordingly, the past, for the conservative, was not something that merely preceded the present in a unilinear process, but something that continued to exist and have value in the present. The conservative's view of history, unlike the liberal's, was multidimensional.

Conservatism's philosophy of consciousness reflected its view of history. For the conservative, the "idea" was not accessible in a suprahistorical form but only through historical individualities. The idea in its historical form was not universal, nor was the reflective subject who perceived it. For the liberal concept of "consciousness in general," the conservative substituted the *Volksgeist,* the nationally differentiated subject. While restricting the reflective subject, the conservative extended the active subject beyond the atomistic individual to the participant in the national community. As a vehicle through which the *Volksgeist* developed, the individual's position was determined to a greater degree than was that of the individual envisioned by liberalism. However, at the same time, the gap between the reflective and active subjects was narrowed and both were tied more closely to concrete historical reality. That reality, rather than the transcendent idea, was the conservative's yardstick for separating "correct" from "ideological" positions, a standard just the opposite from that of the liberal.[54]

At this point, a summary of the relationship of the above-described types is in order. Mannheim divided the traditional, prepolitical world into two parts, both nonrational – routinized traditionalism and nonroutinized religious chiliasm. Bureaucratic conservatism represented the rationalism of the routinized sphere, whereas utopian chiliasm represented the politicization of the nonroutinized sphere. With the breakup of the traditional ontological unity, the need for a new synthesis of the subjective will and the objective sphere of meaning asserted itself. This "need" was simply the reformulation in political terms of his earlier schema: the need for a synthesis of the objective culture and the soul of the individual. Both bureaucratic conservatism and political chiliasm failed to attempt this synthesis, the former rejecting the subjective soul, the latter rejecting the objective culture. These two types were modern, but incomplete, forms of the earlier traditional world. The three types that I have characterized as versions of the ethic of responsibility – liberalism, conservatism, and socialism – represented the historicization of the nonroutinized sphere. All three were concerned with history and consciousness, with the comprehensibility of change and the relationship of theory and praxis in the process of change. All attempted to realize the unity of subjective will and objective culture, now seen as necessarily political.

Mannheim believed that liberalism and conservatism had failed to achieve that needed synthesis. As historical types, they were a great improvement upon the ahistorical types; however, they did not manage to overcome the divisions of bureaucratic conservatism and chiliasm. Liberalism was in one sense closer to bureaucratic conservatism (the routinized sphere) in its belief that concrete reality could be made to conform to a rational system, whereas conservatism was closer to chiliasm in denying this possibility. However, conservatism had even more in common with bureaucratic conservatism in its emphasis on the here and now of concrete reality; liberalism was closer to chiliasm in opposing concrete existence with a suprahistorical ideal. Mannheim admired the more sophisticated sense of history and consciousness that conservatism embraced; he clearly considered the liberal versions of those concepts more simplistic.[55] And yet the liberal demonstrated a stronger will to change, an orientation toward the "should" as opposed to the conservative's "is."[56] The utopian element, which was admired as the motor force of history, was clearly stronger in liberalism. Mannheim proclaimed neither liberalism nor conservatism as victorious over the other. The previous dualism had simply been raised to a higher, more sophisticated historical level.

With the final type, socialism, we would seem to have come to some kind of synthesis, especially if one takes Lukács's *History and Class Consciousness* as the point of departure for *Ideology and Utopia*. I do not, and I will show that socialism for Mannheim, rather than achieving a synthesis, extended the dualism of ideology and utopia to its most critical position. Here, Mannheim's critique of socialism was similar to Marx's critique of capitalism – its contribution lay not in resolving contradictions but in making them more evident. For Mannheim, socialism best explained the crises of pluralism and reification, but it did not "overcome" or "transcend" them.

He wrote that socialism did combine elements from both the conservative and liberal poles. Like the liberal world aspiration, socialism was future oriented; socialism emphasized the "should," the necessity of change, rather than the "is." The socialist also believed in the importance of making the irrational rational. However, he or she also adopted the conservative position that values were not abstract and supratemporal, but rather arose from history itself. History for the socialist was not the unilinear process it was for the liberal. His or her present, like the conservative's, also contained essential elements and values of another era, al-

109

though this era was the future rather than the past.[57] Mannheim wrote of the socialist idea: "It leads a life of interaction with 'real' events, not as a purely formal and transcendent regulator for events but as a 'tendency' that continually corrects itself with reference to this reality."[58]

This combination for Mannheim marked a noticeable change in the development of utopia. Until socialism, the revolutionary element, in both chiliasm and liberalism, emphasized the subjective element of will, which embraced a transcendent ideal in opposition to restrictions of concrete existence. The one utopia that embraced concrete existence existence was conservatism, the counterutopia. In socialism, a revolutionary utopia now embraced concrete existence and the element of the determination of the individual that that implied. The result of this combination, said Mannheim, was that

> the modern form of reciprocal conflict is . . . peculiar in that the destruction of one's adversary *does not take place on the utopian level,* a fact which is most clearly perceptible in the way the socialists have gone about unmasking the ideologies of their antagonists. . . . It is . . . inevitable that . . . the utopian element disappears the more this lived experience of determinateness grasps spheres of consciousness.[59]

A movement that furthered the development of ideology (unmasking opponents' world aspirations), as socialism did, weakened utopia (the core of those world aspirations). If socialism's prime contribution was to the development of ideology, then it was simply an exacerbation of the dualistic contradictions and not a synthesis of them. To combine was not necessarily to synthesize.

Mannheim wrote that socialism achieved the third step in the development of the philosophy of consciousness (which I have associated with ideology) by introducing the concept of class, or class consciousness,[60] an advancement that he termed the "total conception of ideology." Both liberalism and conservatism, using the older "particular conception of ideology," referred individual ideas to a universal criterion of validity. Each assumed that there was only one correct structure of meaning and values, its own, and that this structure was also shared by its opponent. The latter's values were assumed to be only perversions of the true structure resulting from faults of human nature or of particular individuals. The assumption was that if the opponent would just see the light, his or her ideological views could be corrected.[61]

Socialism, on the other hand, rejected this notion of a universal truth available to everyone. Rather than attempting to disprove his or her opponents' world aspirations, the socialist attempted to show that they were limited to the social position of their proponents. Rather than being "false," they were "bourgeois" or "feudal." They were neither universally right nor universally wrong. Neither liberalism nor conservatism challenged the other's universality, but simply its correctness. The socialist, on the other hand, did not say that "your" system was wrong because it did not coincide with "mine," but rather that your system could be shown to be sociologically determined. And once the social determinant (your class) had been swept away, your system would have no social base and would also disappear.[62] Pluralism supported this contention that the opponents' views were limited and could never be universal, switching the burden of proof from the challenger to the challenged.

The difficulty with the socialist's method was that it was incomplete, because he or she applied the total conception of ideology to all doctrines but his or her own. (Mannheim termed this the "special, total conception of ideology.") This exemption could not last long, as Max Weber (quoted by Mannheim) noted.[63] The unmasking technique was turned on the Marxists themselves; Marx too was shown to be looking at the whole from a particular point of view – as the spokesman for the nineteenth-century proletariat. The victory of the proletariat, the emergence of a classless society – these concepts were just as limited as any of the opponents' theories. Mannheim called this sociological examination, which included one's own position, the "general, total conception of ideology." With the shift from the special to the general, total conception of ideology, "the simple theory of ideology develops into the sociology of knowledge."[64] The latter made the technique of unmasking ideologies universal; it extended the analysis of pluralism to the extent that it endangered the utopian will to overcome that pluralism. By itself, the sociology of knowledge was essentially a negative, destructive discipline. Its position was analogous to the critical stage of culture in his Free School lecture.

Mannheim feared that if utopias were exposed as limited, the utopian will to make itself universal, to change the existing order, would give way to defeatism. The ethic of fatalism ("the complacent tendency to accept the present") would prevail, and society would become no more than a "thing." The end of utopia would mean "the decay of human will," the loss of desire to provide meaning for the world, which would mean the stagnation of the historical process.

> We would be faced then with the greatest paradox imaginable, namely, that man, who has achieved the most rational mastery of things, becomes a mere creature of impulses. Thus, after a long, tortuous, but heroic development, just at the highest stage of awareness, when history is ceasing to be blind fate, and is becoming more and more man's own creation, with the relinquishment of utopias, man would lose his will to shape history and therewith his ability to understand it.[65]

111

The intelligentsia and synthesis

The tone of the above passage, with which Mannheim ended his book, was much more anxious than that found in his earlier attempt at synthesis, "Historicism." It indicated the difference between the more optimistic philosophical orientation of the earlier essay and the more problematical political orientation of *Ideology and Utopia*. This shift is clarified by the terminology of these years, an element largely ignored by most Mannheim scholars. The terms I will examine are "positionally bound" (*standortsgebunden*), "existentially connected" (*seinsverbunden*), and "existentially bound" (*seinsgebunden*). They are often treated as synonymous, and the latter two are often considered identical for purposes of translation.[66] In fact, they do not even belong on the same plane. (To equate them would be like saying: It is as cold in the winter as it is in the mountains.) The confusion here results from the refusal to distinguish Mannheim's methodological writings from his synthetic writings and his syntheses from one another and, hence, to treat "Historicism," "Problem of Sociology of Knowledge," and *Ideology and Utopia* as progressive steps in the same process rather than as parts of a dialectical development. The terms should be designated as follows: "Positionally bound" belongs primarily to "Historicism"; "existentially connected" primarily to the methodological essays on the sociology of knowledge; and "existentially bound" primarily to *Ideology and Utopia*.[67]

"Positionally bound," as we have seen, when used in "Historicism" was basically a temporal term and implied the temporal relativism characteristic of traditional historicism, namely, that one's ideas were "bound" (limited) by one's place in time, that they were not eternally valid. This term has, if not an implication of causality, at least one of directness. One could postulate a direct relationship between a historical period (the "position") and its world view while also assigning an indirect relationship to that world view and the individual cultural products within the period. To say that a world view was the product of a certain period of time avoids the question of the relationship of that world view to the realm of material existence.

In the essays on the sociology of knowledge, Mannheim's concerns were analytical rather than valuative and, with this limited scope, the valuative problems of pluralism and relativism were not really addressed. He was concerned with the relationship of world aspirations to concrete existence but not with the relationship of world aspirations to one another. Hence, he opted for the indirect term, "existentially connected," which implied that knowledge was attached to concrete reality but assigned no causal priority. These two terms did not contradict one another because they were located on two different planes (e.g., winter and mountains) – "positionally bound" addressed the relationship of world views to one another, whereas "existentially connected" addressed the relationship of world views to concrete existence. The latter term retained its meaning in *Ideology and Utopia* but, being analytical, played a lesser role. The former term was replaced by "existentially bound."

In *Ideology and Utopia*, as in "Historicism," the question of a valuative synthesis was primary, but, in contrast to the earlier essay, he now divided the organic era, the temporal position, into a pluralism of social, or spatial, positions. To be bound to a social position ("existentially bound") implied limitations that were not there in being bound to a temporal position ("positionally bound"), for the former denied the possibility of achieving universality within the nation, whereas the latter did not.[68] To demonstrate that a position was existentially bound was to deny its utopian potential, for utopias sought universality. "Existentially bound" was a political term for Mannheim, and, further, a negative political term. It was tied to the perception of one's opponents' world aspirations as ideologies and, hence, could be seen as antithetical to the utopian term "existentially transcendent." In a pluralistic world, all competing world aspirations were existentially transcendent, for all claimed universal validity yet none achieved it. Those that were utopian would realize the potential of this transcendence by transforming existence to some degree (but never completely) in accordance with their aspirations. Those that were unmasked as ideologies by their opponents were also existentially transcendent, but at the same time existentially bound, so that they could not realize the utopian potential of that transcendence. They became ideologies in both the primary and secondary meanings of the term.[69] Existential bondedness, for Mannheim, meant relativization and reification, both of which were anathema to him; so he introduced a new concept, "relationism," as the solution to this problem.

Relationism offered a new standard of validity, which he contrasted to relativism. The latter held that it did not matter who the concrete subject solving a problem like "2 + 2 = 4" was; the correct answer was always "4." But if different concrete subjects arrived at different answers, and no one could determine what the universally correct answer was, then the different concrete answers had to be dismissed as "relative." Relativism did not deny the existence of universal truth; it simply denied that this truth could be grasped by any one concrete subject. In Mannheim's terms, the concrete subject was existentially bound (limited in his or her perspective), whereas truth itself was universal.

The other alternative, relationism, abandoned the older epistemological theory of an eternal truth in favor of a "truth" that con-

113

tinually changed. In giving up the concept of absolute truth in favor of relational truth, he sought "to discover in the totality of the historical complex the role, significance and meaning of each component element" to show that all elements have an interrelationship with one another, but that this totality of relationships was always changing.[70]

> It is not a self-contained and stable view. Totality means an intention toward the whole that assimilates particular views and then bursts them. It represents the continuous process of the expansion of knowledge, and has as its goal not achievement of a supra-temporally valid conclusion but the broadest possible extension of our horizon of vision.[71]

This concept of the dynamic theory of truth sounds similar to Mannheim's earlier theory of perspectivism found in "Historicism." However, the differences were more than just semantic and, like the above-discussed terminology, demonstrated the distance between the earlier work and *Ideology and Utopia*. The prime difference between relationism and perspectivism was the former's recognition that "truth" for an epoch could not be intellectually determined, that is, one theory could not conquer the others on the theoretical level. The truth value of a world view was not decided by its logical, or noological, qualities. The relational thinker assumed that a particular world aspiration had a place within the pluralistic system of meaning that could not be philosophically overturned. Rather, the judgment of validity was made on the sociopolitical level. The sociology of knowledge was not to be a neutral scholastic discipline, but rather one subservient to political concerns.[72]

Although validity could not be determined philosophically, Mannheim did believe that there was a political criterion. He wrote:

> A consciousness is ethically false when it is oriented by norms with which conduct at a given level of existence, even with the best of intentions (*Wille*), cannot comply. . . . A consciousness is false in its subjective inner interpretation when, through its acceptance of customary meanings (forms of life and lived experience, conceptions of the world and humanity), it generally obscures and hinders novel psychic reactions and the transformation of man. A consciousness is theoretically false when, in its orientation toward life, it thinks in categories whose consequence is one's complete inability to find his way at a given level of existence.[73]

The emphasis in this passage was on the ability to promote change. Mannheim was not concerned with who had captured reality, for reality was always changing, but with who had changed it, a position that was consistent with his emphasis on utopias. That world aspiration was valid that allowed one to change reality and to change oneself with it. How could one determine in advance which world aspiration best promoted orientation for change when to make such a decision was to look into the future? Mannheim's criterion was temporally multidimensional, in keeping with his view of historical time, and so could not be decided in the single dimension of the present. However, he wrote that the future was impenetrable from the present,[74] so the relational thinker could not judge the validity of present world aspirations in terms of the future but could only judge the success of past political positions. And this judgment was to be made concerning their promotion of change in accordance with their world aspirations.

Relationism, then, meant the postponement of certainty, the commitment to a future judgment of validity. One would struggle for one's convictions, knowing they could never be universal because there was no such thing as universal validity, but believing that when these convictions and their resulting conduct were examined by future generations they would be found to have had the best understanding of the pluralistic totality in that they had been best able to promote change in the desired direction and had contributed to the formulation of the programs of the future. Relationism was the result of, the confirmation of, and the solution to the end of existential transcendence (the utopian will) as well as to existential bondedness (the ideological perception). It provided the synthesis of ideology and utopia, theory and praxis, by moving to a new kind of historical dynamic. Existential transcendence, which had promoted the motor force of history, depended on two elements – the will to achieve universal validity and the existential connectedness that prevented this achievement. Consciousness of this inability resulted in existential bondedness, the state of relativism and reification that Mannheim wished to avoid. If universal truth were replaced by relational truth, one would have, in place of existential transcendence, "existentially congruent" conduct,[75] the product of a "sociologically fully clarified consciousness." Existential congruence also consisted of two elements – the will to achieve relational validity and existential connectedness, which now did not result in existential bondedness.[76] The old form of utopia would be gone. But, more importantly, the commitment to the promotion of historical change would be strengthened, and the negative force of ideological perception would be eliminated.

The question remains: How was relationism to be instituted? How were political activists to become relational thinkers? Mannheim's answer was probably his most controversial (and least understood) concept, the "socially free-floating intelligentsia."[77] Most scholars take this group to be Mannheim's alternative to Lukács's proletariat, that is, a group capable of achieving universal truth. As such, they are seen as a suspension of his own skepticism "parallel [to] Munchhausen's feat of extricating himself

115

from a swamp by pulling on his whiskers."[78] I will attempt to show that this criticism is unwarranted, that the free-floating intellectual was akin to Max Weber's scientist and that the existential congruence he or she helped the politician to achieve was similar to the ethic of responsibility that Weber's scientist helped his politician to achieve.

To help clarify Mannheim's concept, I will describe two contemporary critiques of it. I have chosen these two, not because they were the most brilliant, but because they illustrate the reaction of the two extremes of traditionally nonpolitical and radically political intellectuals.

The traditionalist attack was represented by Ernst Robert Curtius,[79] who was afraid that in modern times the principle of *Bildung* (the basis of the mandarin social and intellectual position) was disintegrating before the onslaught of a new irrational barbarism of the masses. Curtius believed that this irrationalism, which took the form of nationalism, had to be rejected in favor of a stricter cultivation of thought and learning, a higher attention to reason, and a greater respect for tradition.[80] The more a nation became a mass phenomenon, wrote Curtius, the more important was an elite to provide the necessary cultural leadership. He viewed the university as the center for this elite; it would provide the required spiritual synthesis and become a living *Gemeinschaft* of teachers and scholars where *Geist* became conscious. To preserve this community, he believed it was necessary to free the university from the hold of "party spirit," which fostered individual interests at the expense of the whole.[81]

Following the mandarin model, Curtius railed against "sociologism" – the intrusion of divisive interest politics in academic dress into the university. Curtius classified *Ideology and Utopia* as sociologism, for he believed the book made the claim that sociology, which was properly only a specialized science, should be the central or basic science in place of philosophy.[82] He believed that the same divisiveness that one found in interest politics could be found in the "relativism" of Mannheim, who did not realize that, when the historical and sociological aspects of man were removed, "we are not left with nothing but rather with a unique person, and this person is a spiritual essence."[83] By trying to reduce everything to its sociological determinants, sociologism and Mannheim had made "destruction" one of their prime categories, an emphasis that prevented the achievement of any real synthesis. *Geist,* said Curtius, had an autonomy, unrealized by Mannheim, which prevented it from being unattached and transitory as was the sociology of knowledge. Disciplines like sociology, which studied partial aspects of man, were only a preparation for a philosophical study of essence. Philosophy alone could provide a total orientation because of its preoccupation with *Geist;* it was the only truly synthetic discipline.[84]

Whereas Curtius attacked *Ideology and Utopia* for being too sociological, the Marxist Adalbert Fogarasi attacked it for being too philosophical.[85] He wrote that the great shortcomings of the sociology of knowledge were its "formal" philosophical approach and its belief that the crisis of bourgeois society was simply a spiritual crisis. Bourgeois sociologists, especially Mannheim, did not realize that the problem of relativism was a problem of the capitalist social structure and could not be overcome until that social structure was overcome. In seeking an intellectual solution to a socioeconomic problem, the sociology of knowledge was trying "to overcome ideology ideologically" and was ignoring the true dialectic of social classes and their parties. Mannheim's "partyless" approach was nothing but bourgeois false consciousness, an attempt to rescue bourgeois ideology from Marxist sociological analysis.[86]

Fogarasi declared that Mannheim's concept of the sociology of knowledge was misleading, for it implied that the Marxists themselves had not examined the sociological base of their own thought. The Marxists had always recognized that their view of society came from a proletarian position, but they also recognized that Marxism's proletarian origins did not invalidate it. Just because all knowledge was sociologically determined did not mean that it was ideological. The Marxist insistence that bourgeois knowledge was ideological was based not upon the fact that knowledge was socially determined but that the very social conditions themselves were contradictory and that bourgeois knowledge was not able to recognize this.[87] The class position of the proletariat, on the other hand, permitted a true knowledge of reality, because the proletariat's class interests were not limited but rather led to a dialectical "totality" (*Allseitigkeit*) and the victory over ideology. Mannheim did not understand that

> the political and party-affiliated character of Marxism is exactly the foundation of its scientific objectivity, for the revolutionary class standpoint of the proletariat enabled the most comprehensive, synthetic, total treatment of all social questions and therewith the only authentic objectivity.[88]

Although these two critiques of Mannheim differed greatly – Curtius accusing him of a sociological, party-affirming doctrine that undermined the sphere of *Geist* in favor of the materialistic realm of the masses, Fogarasi charging him with a philosophical, party-rejecting doctrine that undermined the dialectical materialism of the proletariat in favor of the elitist sphere of *Geist* – they did agree on the major point that his position undermined the possibility of a universality of values in favor of relativism.[89] And with the rejection of universality came the denial that any group held a privileged position vis-á-vis that universality. Mannheim denied Curtius's contention that a cultural elite could speak for the entire organic nation and Fogarasi's contention that the proletariat (and proletarian intellectuals) could achieve universality due to their socioeconomic position. He wrote that in a pluralism of world views, there would naturally be a pluralism of intellectual commitments, which eliminated the possibility of an organic intellectual elite. But he also rejected the Marxist view that ideas were determined by material interests and, therefore, that intellectuals were no more than spokespeople for the parties, that their chief role was simply to awaken and promote the consciousness of their class. Such a direct causal attachment of intellectuals to material interest groups was too simplistic. And so Mannheim's position earned from Curtius the charge that he was sociologizing intellectuals and from Fogarasi the charge that he was placing intellectuals above class conflict.[90]

Whereas Curtius's traditional intellectuals philosophically subordinated pluralism and Fogarasi's proletarian intellectuals (as part of the proletariat) dialectically transcended it, Mannheim's socially free-floating intelligentsia incorporated it. For Mannheim, pluralism was a fact of life that could not be overcome or transcended. Intellectuals represented a multiplicity of groups and commitments, and they were becoming increasingly aware of this due to their increasingly diverse social origins. At the same time, they were frustrated in their attempts to enter completely into any of the competing sociopolitical groups. They were becoming aware that their intellectualism made them outsiders. He wrote: "The repeated attempts to identify themselves with, as well as the continual rebuffs received from, other classes must lead eventually to a clearer conception on the part of the intellectuals of the meaning and value of their position in the social order."[91]

This position was derived from their common medium of intellectual pursuits, which permitted them to exchange perspectives with one another, to begin to understand the interrelationships of the different world views to which they were committed. Mannheim believed that this possibility of communication was limited to the intelligentsia, who, because of their heterogeneity, were in a position to be exposed to a greater variety of world aspirations than any other group in society. Being a microcosm of sociopolitical conflict at large, and not simply a part of it, the intelligentsia alone would be able to construct a pluralistic synthesis, to use a paradoxical term. This unique capacity gave the intelligentsia a social identity of their own.[92]

The question arises: How could the intelligentsia be termed "socially free-floating" when they had a definite social identity? The answer to this question is that "socially free-floating" was the antonym of "existentially bound" but not of "existentially connected." The intelligentsia did not float above social conflict but rather were directly connected to it; intellectuals had their origins in and maintained ties with the competing sociopolitical groups and their world aspirations. This existential connectedness resulted in the intelligentsia as a whole being heterogeneous; and their heterogeneity prevented them from becoming existentially bound, for they were not limited to any one perspective but incorporated them all. The intelligentsia's free-floating, that is, existentially unbound, position gave them the power of "synthesis."[93]

This position would seem to cast the intelligentsia into the role of political savior and bring Mannheim into conflict with Max Weber's views. Indeed, Mannheim stated that, despite the appearance of a lack of conviction (*Gesinnung*), the intelligentsia alone could really have conviction.[94] Because we have identified the ethic of conviction with the existential transcendence of the pure utopian will, it would seem that Mannheim saw the intelligentsia as a utopian force. He wrote that because intellectuals did not enter into an "unproblematical existential congruence," they attempted to "reach out beyond that tensionless situation."[95] Was he saying that while the rest of the world was becoming reified, the intelligentsia were capable of some kind of existential transcendence?

To a limited extent they were. Intellectuals could be existentially transcendent, but not in a political manner. The intelligentsia as a whole could not be politically committed and free-floating at the same time. Political change resulted from groups (parties) committed to certain world aspirations; the individual members of the group were committed to the same political changes. (This commitment was what characterized the group.) But members of the intelligentsia, characterized by heterogeneity, could not be committed to the same political changes. Their common will was not the political will to change the world but rather the intellectual will to clarify political positions. They were not politicians but political scientists. Because they did not have political responsibilities, they could have a pure "conviction" (for clarification), which the responsible politician could not. In short, Mannheim, like Max Weber, called on the intellectual to have a passion for science, to take science as his or her vocation, but at the same time to realize that science as a vocation was qualitatively different from politics as a vocation. His or her role was to help the politician realize his or her ethic of responsibility by renouncing that ethic for himself or herself.

The concept of the socially free-floating intelligentsia was presented in the first of the two main essays of *Ideology and Utopia*. In the second essay, he wrote that intellectuals had four possibilities vis-à-vis politics in the modern world.[96] One group of intellectuals sought a flight to the past, to the golden age of the traditional *Gemeinschaft*. They sought to revive old myths and symbols in the hope of spiritualizing the present. A second group, the radical wing of the socialist-communist intelligentsia, were still bound to the political utopia of the proletariat, a bondedness that relieved them from the problems (and the potential) of the free-floating intellectuals. The first two groups, which corresponded to the positions taken by Curtius and Fogarasi respectively, refused to give up the dream of universality, were existentially transcendent and existentially bound, and were, for Mannheim, unacceptable.

A third group shut themselves off from the historical world, demonstrating pure utopian radicalism but divorcing this will from any concrete political activity. The result was an ecstasy similar to that of the mystics and prepolitical chiliasts. It might have been considered free-floating; however, it was also socially unconnected and, therefore, its world rejection precluded any real contribution to the political process. Clearly, this escapist position was as unsatisfactory to Mannheim now as it had been throughout his career.

The final group, "which was cast up (*freigeben*) by the social process at the same time that its utopia was discarded, becomes skeptical and proceeds, in the name of authenticity to destroy the ideological elements of science . . . (M. Weber, Pareto)."[97] This is his complete description of this group, the shortest and least specific description of the four. Also, the tone, if not as negative as it was with the other three groups, was not as positive as his description of the free-floating intelligentsia.[98] Yet we are given no fifth alternative, so this fourth group must have been the one in which Mannheim placed his hopes. They did share with the free-floating intelligentsia a lack of utopian commitment and a critical spirit. However, their emphasis was on driving politics out of science rather than showing science how to contribute to politics. In "Science as a Vocation," Max Weber set limits for science but did not elaborate on how this restricted role could be of benefit to politics. In *Ideology and Utopia*, Mannheim was attempting just what Weber had omitted. His intelligentsia were an extension of Weber's scientists (group four); and his book was an attempt to describe the relationship between science and politics, to delineate the sphere of political science.

The task of the political scientist was to help the politician become a relational thinker, "to think out a problem that has resulted from self-orientation of the acting consciousness itself in the sphere . . . – understanding oneself and one's adversary in the matrix of the social process."[99] This task demanded the clarification of the constellation of sociopolitical forces, the analysis of political aspirations, the imputation of their sociopolitical correlations, and the connection of theory and praxis. "One must never sever the impulse of will, evaluation and world view from the product of thought, and must even, in case it has already been severed, establish the relationship anew."[100] Every political idea, aspiration, and group had to be related to each other and to other ideas, aspirations, and groups, a process Mannheim termed the "social equation."[101] The scientist said to the politician: "Whatever your aspirations, they are your aspirations as a political person, but when you aspire to this and that, you must do this and that, and this is your place in the total process."[102] The scientist showed the politician how his or her position related to those of others, how others viewed him or her, and thus helped him or her to realize the self-consciousness that came only with confrontation with the world.[103] The political scientist helped the politician to develop the tools for orientation in the changing world.

> This reorientation to an ever newly forming constellation is the basic practical capacity of the consciousness that is constantly seeking orientation for action. To awaken this capacity, to keep it alert and to make it effective with reference to the material at hand is the specific task of political education.[104]

However, there was one element of politics that political science could not teach – the actual decision making based on will (*Willensentscheidung*). All political scientists could do was show the interrelationship between decision and perspective.[105] One could think of them as cartographers who constructed a constantly changing social map for the political actors. A map helps one to make decisions; it clarifies the relation of one's position to others; but it cannot make the decision of where to go for one. "What is actually opted for lies ultimately with every individual. What has been described above can help him only to see the meaning of his option."[106] The actual decision making was left to the political actor.

Mannheim and Weber

Here we should turn to the question raised earlier in this chapter concerning the relation of Mannheim's position to those of Lukács and Max Weber. Lukács believed that one class, the proletariat, in achieving consciousness of itself also achieved true historical consciousness, that is, was able to grasp the universal truth of history. In achieving class consciousness, the proletariat could act knowing its conduct had been "scientifically"[107] verified. Weber denied that history could be teleologically comprehended or that political conduct could be scientifically verified. Mannheim, with his theory of relationism, sided with Weber. He denied that universal knowledge of history was compatible with the world aspirations of any class; such was the stuff of existential transcendence.[108] Accordingly, Mannheim agreed with Weber that theory could clarify conduct but could not verify it. Science helped the politician to develop an ethic of responsibility but it could not certify dialectical transcendence.

121

Science strengthened the rational element of responsible conduct but could not provide the actual values, nor could it provide certainty.

Mannheim did see differences between his position and Weber's, namely, that Weber presupposed too great a separation between theory and decision making.[109] When Weber talked about science he meant essentially a university discipline, the product of officials and, hence, a part of the realm of administration. He objected to professors using their administrative claims of authority and objectivity to validate their political preferences; hence his sharp delineation of the two spheres. Mannheim, with his background as a member of the Budapest intelligentsia, envisioned a political science that stretched beyond the walls of the university. Weber's reaction to the mandarins' aloofness from the sociopolitical sphere was to take them at their word and insist upon limits for their political activity. Mannheim tried to break down that aloofness and involve the university intellectuals with those outside of academia who were seen as their antithesis. The expansion of political science meant an increased heterogeneity of the political scientists and made them into a semipolitical, rather than administrative, institution. Part way between the "objectivity" of the university and the political engagement of the party schools, they sought to combine the perspective of the former with the decision making of the latter. In short, Mannheim was attempting to bring intellectuals into the political process without making them the pawns of political parties. They were to be a component of, rather than a superior or a subordinate of, political conflict. The gulf between university science and political activity was one that troubled Weber in his later years. Mannheim was attempting to bridge that gap, to spell out the contributions that intellectuals could make to the republic. His work should be seen as an extension of the basic premises he came to share with Weber. At the end of the essay on political science in *Ideology and Utopia*, he wrote:

> Max Weber has furnished the first acceptable formulation of this conception of politics. His ideas and research reflect the stage in ethics and politics in which blind fate seems to be at least partially in the course of disappearance in the social process, and the knowledge of everything knowable becomes the obligation of the acting person.[110]

Clearly, Mannheim had reevaluated the position of Weber since the beginning of the first transitional period, when Weber was described as the chief representative of disillusioning realism. Mannheim continued to assign this role to Weber in *Ideology and Utopia* but at the same time subordinated it to Weber's role as the spokesman for the ethic of responsibility. There is a plausible explanation for this change – Mannheim's explicit abandonment of the cultural center of construction for the political. In "Sociological Theory of Culture" and *Conservatism,* he had presented his cultural philosophy of historicism but at the same time was uneasy about its ability to really solve the cultural crisis. His defensive position toward Weber, who openly challenged the premise of "Historicism," that the problem of valuative pluralism could be resolved "scientifically," is understandable. In addition, his ambivalence toward Lukács's *History and Class Consciousness* also affected his view of Weber's work which he realized took a very different position. By 1929, he had come to accept most of Weber's restricted position for science and was now open to his political views, especially the ethic of responsibility. In this sense, *Ideology and Utopia* can be seen as the work on Weber that he had been promising to write.[111]

To further understand Mannheim's acceptance and extension of Weber's position, we must note the context in which he wrote *Ideology and Utopia.* The years following the publication of his first synthesis, "Historicism," were relatively calm. The political and economic crises of the early Republic had eased, and Germany was enjoying a great increase in prosperity. Accompanying this prosperity was the "rationalization" of business, the implementation of much-publicized organizational techniques from America. Extremism was on the wane, both the Communists and the Nazis having lost votes. The Social Democratic Party had demonstrated its place in the mainstream of moderate politics. Political parties seemed more than ever to be competing, not for *Weltanschauungen,* but simply for the material interests of their constituencies; and politics seemed to be sinking into the routine of daily life. The predictions of Weber, Lukács, and Michels of the routinization, bureaucratization, and reification of political life appeared to be correct. At the same time, this routinized political scene seemed to be without a sense of historical change.

The problem presented in "Historicism" was the understanding and synthesis of the tremendous changes taking place in Germany. In the chaos of the early years, the problem of routinization seemed less important, the task on hand being not to stimulate change but to understand it. In this setting, Mannheim was able to combine his will to change with a traditional formulation of the problem, although not without reservations. The latter moved him away from the traditional formulations to the sociology of knowledge, which he felt would provide a better understanding of historical change. In 1928 the problem was not simply to understand historical change but to promote it. In his new synthesis, Mannheim now saw sociology as a tool not of cultural philosophy but of politics. Such a position meant a reassertion of the commitment to change of his Budapest days, yet in a more radical formulation.

123

Ideology and Utopia was intended not as a description of the way things were but of the way they should be. It was a call to arms, a plea to intellectuals to open lines of communication with one another and to become more involved in the political process. His theories were based on the premise that utopias would be discredited "scientifically" (i.e., unmasked as existentially bound) and that the political scene would become increasingly reified and give way to administration. He believed that intellectuals could help to counter this trend, that if the gulf between science and politics was not bridged politics would suffer. Like Max Weber, his great fear was of ahistorical rationalization rather than the ahistorical chiliastic will. The ethic of responsibility was more in danger of lapsing into an ethic of fatalism than into an ethic of ultimate ends. Chiliastic energy, rather than becoming a successful utopia, would lapse into the escapist dream of the mystic where solutions were not forthcoming.

This scenario, of course, did not occur. Mannheim's call to the intellectuals went unheeded. In addition, the German setting once again changed dramatically. In the same year that *Ideology and Utopia* was published, the depression hit Germany and support for the radical activities of the Communists and Nazis increased greatly. These events demonstrated that Mannheim had overestimated the role that science and scientists could play in German society. The political actor refused to accept the scientific unmasking of his utopia, consciously and successfully opposing scientific criteria with the irrational myth. Instead of being exploded by the pressure of reality, the utopian dream of National Socialism became the conqueror of reality, "the dream that was no more a dream."[112] Instead of a loss of will, Germany was faced with the triumph of the will.

5

Transition (1930–1936)

After the publication of *Ideology and Utopia,* Mannheim's career took a number of turns for the better and worse, the most traumatic being his expulsion from Germany by the Nazis in 1933. There has been very little effort on the part of scholars to connect the German and English periods, as if Mannheim had undergone a complete metamorphosis. In opposition to this tendency, I shall treat his final years in Germany and early ones in England as a block forming a transitional period that displays not only change from but also continuity with his earlier years.[1]

Although Mannheim's emigration to England brought about an actual physical separation from the traditional German academic community, his appointment as professor of sociology at the University of Frankfurt[2] also marked an important step away from the traditional environment. Frankfurt, like Budapest and unlike Heidelberg, was a large cosmopolitan city with a sizable cultivated Jewish community. The university itself was relatively new and, being a city university, was less susceptible to the forces of traditionalism present in the older state universities and the bureaucracies that ran them. Lewis Coser describes it as "a harbor of liberal and even radical thought in the twenties and early thirties."[3]

Frankfurt was also the home of the Marxist-oriented Institute for Social Research. In 1934, the institute issued from exile the following statement of its philosophy that clearly repudiated the traditionalists' denigration of sociology's role in the universities:

> As social and economic crises recur and become more gripping, the social sciences are assuming greater importance for the reorganization of modern society in the sense of an adaptation of the social processes to the growing needs of humanity. . . . The economic and technical factors of social processes interact inextricably with cultural and psychological factors. . . . It is, therefore, necessary to combine economics, sociology, philosophy and psychology for a fruitful approach to the problems of the social sciences.[4]

Throughout his Frankfurt and English periods, Mannheim was in agreement with this statement of principle. Martin Jay's description of the institute in the early 1930s provides themes similar to those in Mannheim's work: the concentration on the cultural superstructure of society rather than on its socioeconomic substructure; a commitment to a "dialectical rather than a mechanical understanding of Marxism"; and a concern for the problems of mass society, such as the dominance of utilitarian values and specialization.[5]

Like other faculty members at the University of Frankfurt, Mannheim participated in seminars at the institute and shared office space there. He also participated in a regular discussion group with members of the institute, even though he disagreed with many of their Marxist ideas. His relationship has been described as a "friendly rivalry."[6]

In general, the men of the social sciences in Frankfurt were proud of their disagreement with the academic traditionalists. Like the Hungarian intellectuals two decades earlier, they believed that they were ahead of their time. Mannheim was no exception. His lectures were filled with enthusiastic students, and he greatly enjoyed this progressive academic environment, which offered both challenge and security at the same time.[7]

However, Mannheim's satisfaction with the intellectual conditions in Frankfurt did not dim his recognition of the fact that German society was in a period of crisis. He was concerned with the economic and social dislocation brought about the depression and with the growing political irrationalism that had invaded the university and would shortly force him out of the country.[8] And although he was once again a member of a self-proclaimed cultural vanguard in a time of great cultural change, his Frankfurt experience was quite different from that of Budapest. In Hungary, the progressive intelligentsia had opposed an establishment that could be considered truly feudal; their defeat was seen as a temporary victory for the forces of reaction. The Nazis, on the other hand, did not represent reactionary authoritarianism but an alternate form of revolution. On the whole, they were younger, more enthusiastic, and even more radical than the intellectuals at Frankfurt. And their success was not confined to spheres outside the university; they enjoyed great student support. Their irrational antiintellectualism did not take the form of a besieged fortress but of a marauding invader.

This very different competition forced Mannheim to rethink his entire position, to temper his optimism in the dialectical process of history. Although this reevaluation was begun in Frankfurt, it took place mostly in exile in England. If, in Frankfurt, he had been somewhat of an intellectual outsider, in England he was the outsider supreme – the refugee. Refugee status was nothing new for him; Germany was not his native land. However, the transition from Hungarian society and culture to those of Germany had been many times smoother than the move to England. Although there were many factors that hindered his acculturation in England, it is sufficient to note three.

The first factor was his difficulty with the English language.[9] Although there were Hungarian and German refugee communities in England, and although some of his English colleagues and students spoke German, his inability to really effectively communicate with these groups must have been extremely frustrating.

A second factor was the difference between holding an established position as a full professor in Frankfurt and filling a temporary position at the London School of Economics.[10] The uncertainty of this position was increased by the tension that developed between him and one of his original sponsors, Morris Ginsberg, who had held a position of power at the LSE.[11]

A third factor, overlapping the first two, was the fact that English social scientists had very different interests from his philosophical orientation. An example of the English reaction to his work was the historian G. M. Young's reference to one of Mannheim's projects as too grandiose. Young said that the project rejected the English approach to society ("academic realism") in favor of "a procedure which in every line betrays its continental inspiration, and is really a product of the political inexperience of the academic classes in Germany."[12] Although students were at first enthusiastic with Mannheim's "Marxism," they were not equipped to do the historical and macrosociological work that he favored, and so he did not have the student following he had had in Frankfurt.[13]

All three of these factors impressed upon Mannheim his position as an outsider in the English intellectual community and developed his refugee mentality. Because the classification "refugee" includes the entire spectrum of socioeconomic classes, it is dangerous to assume that he had more in common with a refugee laborer than with members of the English academic community. Still, there is one characteristic common to all these outsiders regardless of their position in society – the struggle to orient oneself in one's new surroundings.[14] As noted above, the refugee is a marginal person, separated from one cultural tradition and not yet part of another. He or she does not have an established pattern of orientation on which he or she can fall back automatically. He or she is more consciously aware of the questions: Who am I? Where do I fit in? What is there in my old culture that can be applied to my new one? It was to this last question that Mannheim primarily addressed himself in his early English writings.

In attempting to answer this question, he produced works that were usually shorter, more general, and more abstract than his previous ones.

A number of the works were actually programatic speeches similar in style to the Free School lecture.[15] The shorter published articles had two closely related basic themes: the place of sociology in relation to other disciplines[16] and the essentials of modern education, or *Bildung*. Using the terminology of Chapter 2, we can describe them as the "program." The "problem" to which the program was directed, the crisis of modern democratic culture, was outlined in two of his unpublished essays. In *Man and Society* (1934), he took all three of these themes – sociology, *Bildung*, and cultural crisis – and developed them into a theory of planning.

The problem

In outlining the cultural crisis of the times, Mannheim, as he had always done, devised a series of hierarchically ordered types. Perhaps due to the transitional nature of these writings, the types were more numerous and less coordinated than those of his earlier writings. However, I believe they can be understood in conjunction with one another and so have outlined a structure inherent in them.

The most basic of the various series of types consisted of the concepts of "substantial" irrationality and rationality and "functional" rationality. For Mannheim, substantial irrationality and rationality strove "to grasp objectively present objectives and situations and more or less [achieve] this goal." Whereas substantial rationality described "acts of thought," substantial irrationality described nonrational processes, "drives, impulses, wishes, feelings," which operated on both the conscious and unconscious levels.[17] The prime task of these substantial faculties was orientation and meaning, with the rational ones operating on a much more sophisticated level than the irrational ones.

It would appear that substantial irrationality referred to the naive organic stage Mannheim had described in his earlier writings.[18] Two other series of types, the stages of thought[19] and morality, began with a similar naive state. The first stage of thought, "chance discovery" (*Finden*), was a very primitive mental operation amounting to a trial-and-error approach whose primary vehicles for the transmission of knowledge were custom and tradition. Chance discovery demanded no "precise, reflecting knowledge of the environment," but simply an adherence to tradition. Any significant change meant that members could not subconsciously fall back upon a preordered group pattern but rather had to embark on a new trial-and-error process, with the new adaptations, if successful, becoming incorporated into the group's traditions.[20]

Mannheim also characterized the most primitive stage of morality, "horde solidarity," by the dominant role of tradition in the determination of the two essential elements of morality, range of vision and sense of responsibility. Horde solidarity was dependent on the enforcement of a "relatively homogeneous behavior" within the group through fear and tradition. The individual was not conscious of his or her own separate existence; responsibility was group responsibility, and the range of vision was determined by what the group had done in the past. In short, the individual "must stand or fall with his group."[21]

The antithesis of substantial irrationality was functional rationality, which Mannheim characterized as the organization of a series of actions in such a way that they lead to a previously defined goal. An action was functionally rational when it was calculable with relation to the goal from the standpoint of a third person seeking to adjust himself or herself to it.[22] Using Mannheim's earlier terminology, functional irrationality could be called "communicative" rather than "conjunctive," extending beyond the conjunctive community to a third party, an outside observer.[23] It was autonomous from the historical, conjunctive subject.

The stages of thought and morality corresponding to functional rationality were "invention" (*Erfinden*) and "individual competition." Invention replaced the role that tradition had played at the first stage with the establishment of a specific goal. At this stage, one did not have to orient oneself in terms of the total environment but simply in terms of the limited sphere in which one had to operate to achieve his or her goal. One's thought, unlike tradition-governed thought, which was past oriented, was future oriented, for one had to foresee the probable consequences of an event. However, this future-oriented thought was one-dimensional, or unilinear, for it was directed toward a single goal and so was incomplete.[24]

Mannheim wrote that this desire to solve specific problems led to the highest degree of abstractness, because people at the level of invention did not ask how an individual element was "embedded in the concrete environment." Rather they asked how one could solve a specific problem in terms of general laws and principles. Inventive thinkers sought to quantify atomistic parts so that they could be explained by abstract laws while ignoring the unique elements of the parts and the role they played in concrete historical contexts.[25]

The same abstract, atomistic approach occurred at the second level of moral development, "individual competition," where responsibility and range of vision were individual rather than group phenomena. Following the formula of classical economics, the individuals identified their own personal interests and then pursued those ends through calculation in terms of isolated causal sequences delineated by the ends. Although individuals were more aware of the immediate consequences of their actions, they were blind to the context in which those individual acts were interwoven with the concrete totality of events.[26] The result was a *Gesellschaft* in Tönnies's sense, in which conjunctive thought and values disappeared.

Clearly, in this series of dichotomies we have the traditionalist schema epitomized by Tönnies's dualism and dominant in Mannheim's early career. As he did earlier, Mannheim proposed a third type, which synthesized the strengths of the other two. He defined this third type, substantial rationality, as "the capacity to act judiciously in a given situation on the basis of one's own insight into the contexts involved."[27] Here, individual judgment (rationally making decisions for oneself rather than simply accepting those made by an organic group) was combined with the ability to think in terms of a larger context (rather than in terms of the simple causal series presented by one's immediate concerns), to think interdependently.

The corresponding types of thought and morality were "planning" and "group solidarity." In 1925, Mannheim had described a plan as a "context of essence" presented by history "whenever we put the seemingly most isolated individual fact into a context."[28] This basic definition continued over into *Man and Society*. The stage of planning occurred "when man and society advance from deliberate invention of single objects or institutions to the deliberate regulation and intelligent mastery of the relationships between these objects."[29] Planned thinking attempted to grasp society as a whole and so placed individual goals within context.

Here, Mannheim distinguished between "establishment" and "strategy." The former "proceeds from a fixed and finished scheme which exists in the minds of the founders before it is carried out" and thus was abstract, unhistorical, and alien to his concept of planning. It was simply a form of inventive thinking. Strategy, on the other hand, did not try to create a brand new whole, but rather to modify the existing structure, to reconstruct what was there, realizing that this reconstruction was a continuous process. This emphasis came from the strategist's recognition that one could not construct a perfect system from a blueprint, but rather one had to continually adjust and manipulate the structure to try to make the key position in understanding the structure one that would allow better control of it. Mannheim did not equate the attempt to understand the total structure of society with the necessity of changing society in its totality. The former was "a form of conduct still operating within the framework of history"; the latter tried to bring history to an end. This emphasis on understanding society as a constantly changing total structure combined the best features of the two earlier stages of thinking. Planning, like tradition, was able to grasp society as a whole and, like invention, was able to cope with social change.[30]

The third stage of human moral development was what Mannheim called "group solidarity." He believed that his contemporary society was in this third stage, where individual interests were suppressed in favor of the interests of larger social units. Big business, big labor, big organization had brought about a new feeling of group solidarity that differed from the horde solidarity of the first stage in that the group was not an organic whole as the traditional group had been. The modern group was not all-inclusive but rather had a high degree of interaction with other groups. An awareness of the interaction of these new groups developed a new sense of orientation in a larger context while retaining the rational approach that individual competition brought. Mannheim wrote:

> The individual, who here learns to subordinate himself, increasingly does so from better insight and more or less from his own well-considered aspirations. . . . People who previously were capable of seeing only parts of the social process, are becoming acquainted with the interdependence of events and are beginning to reflect on the whole. In short, the highest level of social reason and morality is awakened, if only in its germ, that of *planning*.[31]

It should be noted that Mannheim believed that group solidarity was only the "germ" of planning, that the individual had to develop the possibilities of interdependent thinking beyond their present state to fully reach the level of planning. This qualification, as we shall see, represented a change from the position taken in *Ideology and Utopia,* a partial reversal to an earlier orientation. This change was evidenced in several specific series of types describing the development of societies, elites, and their intermediary publics, through which Mannheim presented the crisis of democratic culture.

As he did earlier, Mannheim saw the cultural crisis beginning with the breakup of a consensus stage, where culture had been organic, homogeneous, egalitarian, and communal. Here one could imagine the types of substantial irrationality, chance discovery and horde solidarity being predominant. Increasing complexity divided such cultures into the spheres of meaning and existence and separated an elite from the rest of the community.

In one essay, Mannheim termed the sphere of existence "the continuum of everyday experience . . . in which the individual is forced to solve practical problems as they arise in his own life." The knowledge with which he or she solved these problems was acquired "without conscious method," being embodied in, among other things, "life experience." Separate from this sphere was that of cultural meaning, "the esoteric stream of transmission." "The esoteric world," he wrote, "is not a spontaneous acquisition, but the product of dedicated effort and cultivated tradi-

131

tion."[32] Elite groups were defined according to this dualism – on the one hand, the organizing (political, bureaucratic, economic) elite; on the other hand, the cultural (intellectual, artistic, religious) elite. The task of the former was the integration of a great number of wills; that of the latter was the sublimation of psychic energies that the daily struggle for existence did not exhaust.[33] The organizing elite would seem to preside over the continuum of everyday experience, the existential sphere, while the cultural elite presided over the esoteric stream of transmission, the sphere of cultural meaning.

Overlapping these two dichotomies was a third – regulated and unregulated conduct. By "regulated" Mannheim meant routinized, institutionalized conduct, in contrast to the unregulated type characterized by competition and conflict. This dualism, then, was basically identical to the political–administrative one in *Ideology and Utopia*.[34]

The interaction of these three postconsensus pairs resulted in three stages of societies, elites, and publics. In the first stage, society was traditional; the elite was organized along monopolistic, bureaucratic lines; and the public, which mediated between the elite and everyone else, was organic. In the second, society was liberal; the elite was selected according to individual achievement; and the public was disintegrated. In the third, the society was democratic; the elite was selected according to party activity; and the public was organized. These stages bring to mind those of monopoly, atomistic competition, and polarization in "Competition"; however, the divisions were not so neat, for the organic public survived into liberal society and the individualistic elite continued into the early stages of democratic society. (In fact, a pure middle type – liberal, individualistic, disintegrated – seems never to have existed.) To avoid confusion, I will identify the stages with the types of society (traditional, liberal, and democratic).

The traditional stage was almost identical to the monopolistic stage of "Competition." Despite the increased diversification of society and the emergence of an elite, a conjunctive, organic context remained that could be characterized as that of a *Gemeinschaft*. Both the continuum of everyday experience and the esoteric stream of transmission were presided over by a monopolistic elite, so that there was insignificant competition over basic meaning and values. Society was regulated, although in a traditional rather than legal-bureaucratic manner. The remaining unregulated sector was successfully sublimated by the cultural elite, especially in the realm of religion.[35]

Accompanying the cultural elite was an "organic public," which contained "certain social structures" (not described) providing for the existence of a somewhat exclusive audience for the cultural elite. This audience formed a buffer zone and filter between the creative elite and the masses and guaranteed that the esoteric stream of transmission would remain the monopoly of the former, separate from the continuum of everyday experience.[36] In doing so, the organic public enabled the elite and the masses to participate in the same organic context of meaning, the substantial irrationality of tradition, although with different degrees of sophistication.

The liberal and democratic stages brought about the destruction of this organic community as the divisions in status and power also became divisions in meaning and values. In this new *Gesellschaft,* organic unity was replaced by "a chance integration of many antagonistic activities," as individual judgment and adaptation increasingly replaced tradition. People acted in their own interests and remained blind to the interaction of these individual activities as a whole.[37]

As society became increasingly unregulated, that is, characterized by atomistic competition, functional rationality grew at the expense of substantial irrationality. This rationality, in conjunction with the increased mobility demanded by capitalistic society, resulted in an increasing abstractness in which human relations more and more lost the element of truly personal contact. "When knowledge must be communicated to many persons of different position and background, it must be couched in 'abstract' terms, for 'concrete' communications are intelligible only to those whose experiences and associations are very similar." One would no longer allow a force as rigid and concrete as tradition to govern one's decisions. Instead, the abstractness of society forced one to analyze these abstract and flexible relationships and then to make individual decisions based on his or her analysis of the situation.[38]

The liberal and democratic stages differed in the degree to which this individualism was spread throughout society. At the liberal stage, it was largely confined to the elite and their public. The elite were determined largely by "unregulated competition," in which the personal endowment of the individual became decisive. However, despite the new standards from the elite and the broadening of their base, they were able to maintain their monopoly over the esoteric stream of transmission due to the continuation of the organic public into the liberal stage. The cultural elite and the organic public fostered a belief that some kind of rational order stood behind the increasing functional rationality of society; they preached a faith in the solidity of national character and the "gradual progress of Reason in history."[39]

The democratic stage of society was marked by the spread of atomic individualism to the masses. Although the latter's lives had become increasingly functionally rational, their stage of morality remained at the

133

more primitive level of horde solidarity, individual responsibility being confined to the elite. As this changed, the masses demanded an increasing role in the responsibility of power. The demand for the equality of all people was, in fact, the death knell for the organic public and the hierarchical social order it promoted. Those groups whose roles had previously been limited to the realm of daily existence now claimed the right to interpret the esoteric realm of meaning, and the organic public gave way to the "disintegrated public," the absence of a cultural buffer group. Mannheim wrote: "The key to the new era lies in the fact that the educated no longer constitute a caste or compact rank, but an open stratum to which persons from an increasing variety of stations gain access."[40]

This disintegration hindered the formation of tastes and styles by the elite, because there was no opportunity for ideas to mature before being taken over by the masses. Now, instead of appealing to a selected audience that guaranteed some intellectual consistency, the cultural elite were forced to appeal directly to the mass public themselves, who were "inconstant, fluctuating" and "reassembled only through new sensations." In dealing with the masses directly, the cultural elite not only lost a great deal of their status but also became subject to the laws of mass psychology and adopted many irrational mass characteristics. In short, the cultural elite became unable to fulfill their function of sublimation, a situation Mannheim termed "massification" or "negative democratization."[41]

Massification was characterized by a disproportionate development of human faculties in which people's technological abilities (their functional rationality) outstripped their ability to orient themselves in the world (through substantial irrationality or rationality). Through its technological advances, modern society had become a finely tuned machine, flexible in some, functionally rational, ways but unable to deal with other elements in society, namely those irrational, nonroutinized factors that had always been sublimated by the cultural elite. By shifting matters that could not be rationalized into the private sphere and confining itself in public matters to universal rational standards, modern industrial society placed more responsibility on individuals and forced them to deal with the nonregulated sphere by themselves. Increasingly isolated, without the orientation that tradition had provided or that substantial rationality could provide, individuals were not able to direct their irrational impulses. Their failures to master the new responsibilities that had been forced upon them produced strong repercussions in society, like throwing a monkey wrench into a finely tuned machine. The breakdown of the functionally rational machine in turn disoriented individuals even more. "When the rationalized mechanism of social life collapses in times of crisis, the individual cannot repair it by his own insight. Instead, his own impotence reduces him to the state of terrified helplessness."[42]

Mannheim's argument here was simply a modification of Tönnies's contention that rational individualism was not disruptive when confined to the elite; the dissolution of the *Gemeinschaft* occurred when that individualism spread to the masses. However, Mannheim did not conclude his analysis here at the dualistic formulation of the German traditionalists, for, as we have seen, he postulated a third, synthetic, stage of substantial rationality, planning and group solidarity. This stage was structurally similar to that of polarization in "Competition," with the party forming a consolidating force, although it was not seen as an accomplished thing but simply as the "germ" of a substantial democratic society.

The group solidarity of the party became necessary when the liberal ideology of the invisible hand broke down. The party established a limited regulation of its members that was more flexible than traditional regulation and not as chaotic as atomic individualism. This regularity, determined by the strength of the group, replaced the personal endowments of the individual as the standard for elite selection. At the same time, the party began to shape a new public, the "organized public," as a defense against negative democratization. This public represented the transition to a society that was once again integrated, but this time "artificially" through conscious regulation. Thus, the organized public were really a number of organized publics in competition with one another. As earlier, Mannheim believed that such competition would stimulate people to think in terms of interdependence, which was the key to planning and substantial rationality.[43]

Despite the structural similarity of this pattern to the earlier one in "Competition," his position in these transitional writings, especially in *Man and Society*, had changed from that presented in the 1928 essay and in *Ideology and Utopia*, due to the Nazi political success in Germany. At the beginning of *Man and Soceity*, he stated that the central issue of the time was the tension between the principles of laissez-faire (i.e., unregulated competition) and regulation.[44] In *Ideology and Utopia*, he had taken a similar position with his political–administrative dichotomy. Then he saw the prime danger as a reifying rationalism, resulting in excessive administration, and he hoped for a strengthening of the nonrational element, the will. He believed that the free dialectical competition of the limited regulated positions of the parties would eventually lead to a new substantial rationality and the ability to act upon it. In the early 1930s, he shifted his emphasis away from competition toward regulation. However, this shift did not mean an abandonment of the commitment to the historical interpretation found in *Ideology and Utopia,* but rather a tempering of the optimistic belief in the ability of political activity to bring about dialectical progress.

In both *Ideology and Utopia* and *Man and Society,* Mannheim divided the world into three spheres: one of complete irrationality (chiliasm, negative democracy); one of complete regulation (bureaucracy, dictatorship); and one of historical change (historical consciousness, planning).[45] In both works, he advocated the middle course and the avoidance of the two extremes. Massification represented total irrationality combined with functional rationality, whereas dictatorship was the functionally rational exploitation of that irrationality, providing a false sense of orientation. Both were antithetical to the idea of the responsible citizen whose decisions and actions were based upon substantial rationality. In this sense, they were similar to chiliasm and bureaucracy in *Ideology and Utopia.*

However, there was a difference, namely that bureaucracy was simply ignorant of the irrational forces of chiliasm, whereas dictatorship exploited negative democracy. In *Ideology and Utopia,* chiliasm was the activistic element. In attempting to break through routinization and establish utopias, it pushed the historical process forward; when it occurred in combination with more sophisticated historical perspectives, it promoted the growth of historical consciousness. In *Man and Society,* the situation was reversed. Mass irrationality rather than rational routinization became the main threat to historical progress; and the rational form of dictatorial exploitation, rather than the irrational form of chiliastic will, became the activistic agent.[46] In *Ideology and Utopia,* the historical perspective meant the structural, interdependent clarification of the utopian will; in *Man and Society,* it meant clarification of dictatorial manipulation. In *Ideology and Utopia,* the historical solution was political, that is, unregulated (although not in the extreme form of chiliasm); in *Man and Society,* the historical solution (planning) was regulated (although not in the extreme form of dictatorship).[47] In short, he was no longer willing to trust the competition of the dialectical process. Change could no longer simply be promoted; it also had to be controlled (but not eliminated) as much as possible.

In *Man and Society,* Mannheim wrote that, prior to the stage of planning, the contexts of individual phenomena were "governed by a random causality and regulated by conflict, competition and the selection that followed."[48] In *Ideology and Utopia,* he had endorsed this process; in the 1930s, he considered it inadequate. Instead, he sought synthesis by identifying the "key position," around which the totality of events at a given time revolved. He wrote:

136

The mechanism of the social cycles can be mastered and guided only if the appropriate key positions are found and dealt with by a new method. Conduct oriented toward the center of the cycle has a principally new capability for action, for from this position not only immediate effects but also further ranging distant effects can be estimated, firmly mastered or newly created.[49]

The key position, for us, has two important characteristics. First, it occupied a position structurally similar to that of the "center of construction" in his earlier writings. This earlier concept had been abandoned when he adopted selection through competition; now he was returning to an earlier position. Second, he was not returning entirely to the earlier concept, for "key position" had an activist element that "center of construction" did not, an element that carried over from *Ideology and Utopia*. The key position was not the basis for interpreting a spiritual unity, but for directing social and cultural change. Thus, planning attempted to combine the major interpretive element from cultural philosophy with the activist element from politics. Mannheim outlined a program by which such a strategy could operate.

The program

An important part of this program involved the determination of the place of sociology – more specifically, the constitution of the discipline and its role in solving the existing social and cultural crises. In outlining sociology's structure and methodology, Mannheim presented a schema that resembled earlier programs (especially that of "Cultural-Sociological Knowledge") and yet contained significant differences from preceding works. In addition, the schema continued to change during this transitional period.[50]

He described three basic parts of sociology, each with a different function. The first, "general" or "systematic" sociology, was a specialized science concerned with the "processes of sociation (*Vergesellschaftungsprozesse*) that bring about the various forms of society at any given time." This axiomatic sphere was characterized by its abstractness, by its search for suprahistorical relationships.[51] He had acknowledged this type in his earlier writings, and its methodology remained pretty much unchanged from the description in "Cultural-Sociological Knowledge." However, during this period, he gave this sphere more attention than ever before. In addition to abstract social processes, he saw the need for a theoretical examination of human psychic equipment, restating his earlier assertion that the dividing line between psychology and sociology was determined more by the perspective of the observer than by the material observed. Psychology sought subjective intentions behind conduct, whereas sociology sought the social functions of the same conduct.[52]

Two possible explanations for Mannheim's new concern for abstract sociology and psychology must be discounted – the influences of the English environment and his wife (who was a psychologist). First, his increased appreciation for abstract sociology began in Germany;[53] and, even when he was in England, the majority of his citations for abstract sociology and psychology were German or American. Second, his wife probably did have an influence upon him, but why at this time? Why not earlier? Her "influence" was more an effect than a cause.

I believe the reason for his new interest lies not in the attractiveness of these abstract theories (due to the new "influences"), but rather in the failure of other alternatives. Mannheim had always subordinated such theories to the more inclusive and dynamic spheres of philosophy and politics, both of which had proven themselves, from his perspective, to be failures. His interest in abstract sociological and psychological theory indicated the vacuum in the realm to which they had been subordinate. However, it did not mean the elevation of those theories to that realm, but rather an experimentation with them in a transitional period. "General" sociology remained, ironically, specialized and ill-equipped to become a synthetic discipline.

This lack of synthetic capability was also true for the second part of sociology, the comparative, whose role was essentially negative, or "critical," to use the term from the Free School lecture. Comparative sociology's main task was the qualification of the abstractions of general sociology to prevent them from becoming too simplistic. Narrowly restricted to the field of sociology proper, comparative studies uncovered varieties of the abstract general concepts (e.g., different types of families). Despite the fact that history was the source of these types, comparative sociology was not historical because it lacked both the placement of its types in concrete historical contexts and an interpretation of historical development.[54] It did not represent an alternative to the specialized sphere of general sociology but simply a qualification of that sphere.

Mannheim did expand the comparative approach beyond sociology in *Present Tasks* by presenting a second comparative type, the sociology of individual disciplines (e.g., sociology of law, of art, etc.). Again, its role was basically negative, to demonstrate the restricted nature of these disciplines by connecting them to existential roots.[55] In effect, the sociology of individual disciplines did for those disciplines what the theory of ideology did for political doctrines – it unmasked them as restricted in perspective. As with its political version, the general form of this limiting approach was

138

the sociology of knowledge. By providing a framework for critically restricting the different perspectives, it played the same negative role it had played in *Ideology and Utopia*.[56] But, as in that book, it also served as a preparatory agent for a more inclusive view. While demonstrating "existential bondedness," it also pointed to the common quality of "existential connectedness," which was to provide the base for some kind of synthetic approach.

This position of accepting the perspective of the specialized disciplines as a necessary but limited component of modern society went back to the Free School lecture. He had always sought to transcend this compartmentalization through an "interconnectedness and interdependence of fields of specialization and particular interests, to achieve a more comprehensive perspective."[57] Although he had earlier assigned the synthetic task to philosophy, by 1932 he questioned that discipline's role. The sociology of knowledge had demonstrated philosophy's own existential connections and hence destroyed the latter's claim that its subject matter was an external, absolute sphere of *Geist*.[58] Any ontology would have to be based upon an approach that would connect the various specialized disciplines by demonstrating the interconnections of spirit and existence, of universal abstractions and the concrete individual. If these connections were not sought, if academics remained contented with an abstract philosophy and empirical specialized sciences that remained isolated from one another, the initiative for dealing with the crises of the times would be left to the dilettante, the outsider with no sense of responsibility to the facts.[59]

Mannheim believed such an approach to be the keystone of a new "*Bildungsplan*."[60] The goal of *Bildung* would remain the same – the development of orientation and responsibility in the individual – but the means for achieving this goal had to be changed considerably. The old concept of *Bildung*, he wrote, was based on the aristocratic, humanistic cultural ideal and separated itself "from everyday life and from the common man." Because this separation meant that it "could not be meaningful for the average man," the older cultural ideal could not survive in modern democratic society. The new democratic cultural ideal was quite different, stressing vocational specialization and "goal-oriented practice." Although the democratic ideal did reach beyond specialization, it maintained its connection with everyday occupation, so that "thought becomes congruent with life."

Mannheim reiterated this point even more strongly in a newspaper article written ten months after *Present Tasks* and a month before Hitler assumed power. He criticized those who saw the crisis in Germany simply as one of intellectual ideals. Such a limited, philosophical approach did not get at the heart of the problem, which involved the real lives of real people. A limited survey he had conducted indicated that people experienced a "crisis" only when dislocation occurred in their own life situation. Those whose circumstances remained secure experienced no crisis in values. Therefore, to simply complain about the dwindling of ideals was counterproductive. Instead, it was necessary to put oneself in the place of the real people who were undergoing radical changes in their situation. Academics had to understand how such changes they were experiencing were connected with the concrete changes taking place in Germany.[61]

Mannheim felt that the third part of sociology, "structural sociology," was best suited to demonstrate those interconnections. He wrote:

> Sociology . . . has a distinct prospect, due to the modern predicament, to move toward a solution to the problem of *Bildung* and to satisfy the traditional needs of knowledge for *Bildung* in a modern form.[62]
>
> Therefore I venture to assert that as long as in our research work and in our school and academic curricula we do not introduce sociology as a basic science, so long we shall not be good specialists – let alone be able to educate a generation of citizens on whose correct understanding of the functioning of the society in which they live it must depend whether the social process is in future to be guided by reason or by unreason.[63]

Before leaving Germany, Mannheim described structural sociology as cultural sociology, a description similar to that in "Cultural-Sociological Knowledge." However, there was an important difference from the earlier work – rather than being subordinate to philosophy, cultural sociology was a construction upon the base provided by the critical sociology of knowledge. In other words, it connected a pluralistic realm rather than clarifying an organic one.

Once Mannheim was in England, the term "cultural sociology" disappeared and was replaced by "structural sociology"; however, the discipline remained pretty much the same. Its task remained drawing connections between spirit and existence, the general and the individual. The prime methodological tool was the "principia media," which was a modified version of John Stuart Mill's "axiomata media," or "middle principles," described in the latter's *System of Logic*.[64]

For Mill, the "middle principles" distinguished "ethnology," the concrete science of character formation, from psychology, the abstract science of universal causal laws of the mind. In the formation of the middle principles, said Mill, the ethnologist mediated between the universal laws of psychology and empirical data, deducing from the former their operation "in complex combinations of circumstances." Although the middle principles organized empirical data, they were not rigid, unchanging concepts like the psychological laws from which they were deduced. Therefore, the middle principles had to be expressed in a more flexible form – as hypotheses, as "tendencies." The principles stated that, given a certain set of circumstances, the psychological laws should have operated in a certain way. But, wrote Mill, ethnology "must not assert that such and such will be the effect of a given cause, so far as it operates uncounteracted."[65]

Because of its hypothetical character, Mill wrote that ethnology could not be termed a "primary science" in the sense of being autonomous.[66] The primary position was reserved for psychology, which provided the universal premises from which the middle principles were deduced. In Mill's positivistic system, ethnology was limited to the role of handmaiden. "In other words, ethnology, the deductive science, is a system of corollaries from psychology, the experimental science."[67] Morris Ginsberg correctly labeled ethnology as "applied psychology." Ginsberg pointed out that the middle principles arose from a desire to discover how changes in one part of society were connected with changes in another part – they were principles of social interaction.[68] The middle principles were suppositions of the operation of the laws of psychology in the formation of an individual or group character when that character interacted with others. This social relatedness was what Mill meant by "complex combinations of circumstances."

Mannheim's principia media were very similar to Mill's middle principles. The former were described as

> universal forces in a concrete setting as they become integrated out of the various factors at work in a given place at a given time – a particular combination of circumstances which may never be repeated. They are, then, on the one hand, reducible to the general principles which are contained in them. . . . But on the other hand, they are to be dealt with in their concrete setting as they confront us at a certain stage of development and must be observed within their individual patterns, with certain characteristic subprinciples which are peculiar to them alone.[69]

Both Mannheim and Ginsberg agreed with Mill that the principia media were deduced from more general principles. However, they disagreed that these general principles necessarily took the form of inductive psychological laws. Ginsberg suggested that "there may exist sociological laws sui generis," and thus one might be able to deduce the principia media from "laws governing the life and evolution of human societies."[70] Mannheim, as we have seen, had reached a similar conclusion.

Most importantly, the concept of principia media contained a commitment to the structural whole. Mannheim emphasized that historical interaction could not be separated from that concept. He wrote:

> An epoch is dominated not merely by a single principium medium but by a whole series of them. A number of mutually related principia media, how-

ever, produce a structure, in which concrete patterns of factors are bound up with one another in a multidimensional way. In our frequent references to this multidimensionality, we have meant that while the economic, political, and ideological spheres (according to the cross-sections taken by different observers) each represent a single dimension of events as a whole, existing reality in fact consists in the mutual relationships between many such spheres and the concrete principia media at work in them.[71]

Mannheim warned against letting organic or mechanistic assumptions hinder the investigation of the structural interdependence of the principia media. He wrote that, although the structure of principia media should be considered as a "totality," it was not an organic totality. One had to work at uncovering the relationship between the principia media and not simply assume that they could be grasped in some metaphysical manner as a whole.[72] On the other hand, he wrote, although the process of uncovering the structure of principia media was not an organic one, neither was it mechanistic. The investigation of principia media should be a qualitative process, translating "the chaos of facts into a correct description of the complicated interplay of forces." The principia media, although representing general laws, were unique historical entities, and their interaction with other principia media was not quantifiable.

But even if one overcame the organic desire to intuit and the mechanistic desire to quantify, there were other dangers in determining the principia media. In static times, when the principia media were not in obvious transition, there would be a tendency to ignore their historical character and mistake them for general laws or types. In other times, such as Weimar Germany, when rapid change occurred, the concrete historical nature of the principia media became obvious. Here, one could witness old forms giving way to new ones as the social structure modified itself.[73]

Yet another danger in the investigation of the social structure was that of interpreting the total process of society by using only one or two principia media, an example being an exaggerated economic interpretation. Such a simplistic approach prevented the investigator from properly examining the interaction of principia media within the social structure. With this limited approach, factors were omitted or forced into categories where they did not belong.[74] The reduction of complex social processes to simpler relationships was too close to the mechanistic approach that he rejected.

However, there was also the opposite danger of assigning to all principia media an equal role within the structure and of making no attempt to relate them to each other. This led to all the dangers of relativism. Mannheim thought that there was probably a hierarchy (though not a

142

permanently fixed one) in which some principia media were more important than others.[75] It would seem to follow that this hierarchy was determined by the way in which the different principia media interacted with each other. This notion of a hierarchy fit in with the concept of the "key position," for when one determined the key position, he or she was simply determining the hierarchically most important principia media.

In *Man and Society*, Mannheim examined the attempts of the two major psychological theories, behaviorism and psychoanalysis, to order the principia media of human nature. Behaviorists, he wrote, attempted to manipulate a cross section of principia media to achieve certain types of behavior. They understood that conduct was affected by its social function, and so by manipulating the function one could manipulate the conduct. However, it never went beyond the control of pure action, of external behavior, ignoring inner motives and development. "Behaviorism is interested in the person only as a part of the social machine, not as an individuality but only as a dependable link in a chain of action." It made no attempt to transform the personality as a whole or to adapt it to a changed society, but rather it sought to achieve specific reactions to limited goals. In doing so, it did not develop the individual's consciousness about himself or herself and his or her place in society. Its goals were functionally rational ones, with no attempt to promote substantial rationality. "Once this essential feature of behaviorism has been perceived, its resemblance to fascism is unmistakable."[76]

Mannheim believed the goals of psychoanalysis to be more complete, for that approach sought to transform the whole personality (rather than simply an aspect of his or her behavior) and to increase the individual's own understanding of his or her conduct (rather than simply manipulating that conduct). "The individual was to be transformed within his own framework through a process of inner enlightenment and through the cathartic effects of a wisely guided analysis." But whereas psychoanalysis's goals were more complete, its means were less so, for it paid too little attention to the concrete social context of the individual. It tended to fall into two of the traps described above – reliance upon only the psychological principia media and treatment of those principia media as universal factors, ignoring their temporary nature. As a result, psychoanalysis was characterized by "the typical isolation of the individual when diagnosed, the obscuring of social interdependence and the oversimplification of the individual's relationship to his environment."[77]

Although both of these theories of human nature were incomplete, Mannheim clearly preferred the psychoanalytical to the behavioristic because of its goal – the self-conscious transformation of the individual.[78]

143

He believed that its limitation in means

> are being overcome step by step and revised in a new process of sociological orientation. . . . With this we enter the level of planning. The perception of the key positions which connect the psychic with the social mechanisms, the grasping of the "principia media," which characterize the psychic and social types in a given time and place, move more and more into the foreground.[79]

With the concepts of planning and key position, we have returned to where we left Mannheim's discussion of the crisis of his time. These concepts also reveal the major difference between his view of structural sociology in the early English writings and those of cultural sociology and political science in his first two syntheses. Cultural sociology took place within the framework of the university and presupposed a unified sphere of philosophical meaning that could be grasped by a cultural elite. The center of construction, on which the unity of this sphere of meaning was based, was given its position of priority due to its philosophical completeness, its ability to subordinate other potential centers intellectually. The role of cultural sociology was to aid in the clarification of the sphere of meaning and its center of construction through supplementary *interpretation.*

The political science of *Ideology and Utopia* moved beyond the universities to the political process and tried to establish a place for intellectuals within that process. It presupposed a dialectical conflict of parties in which meaning was established through pluralistic competition rather than through a hierarchy determined by a center of construction. The task of political science was to uncover the common medium in which the competitors could communicate with one another so that the selection process could progress. Interpretation of a unified sphere was replaced by *communication* within a pluralistic one.

Both cultural sociology and political science were subordinate disciplines, the former to a cultural philosophy, the latter to the political process. Both clarified by demonstrating the functionality of ideas and hence the connections between meaning and existence. The planning strategy, however, moved beyond interpretation and communication to *manipulation.* The planner did not simply clarify function but rather shaped it. Instead of coordinating conflicting world views, he or she manipulated the existence bound up with those world views. One did not simply transform ideas; one transformed people.[80]

Although the concepts of "center of construction" and "selection through competition" both placed a distance between the thinker and the actor, "key position" did not. The planner located the key position to use it. Yet, a void, accompanied this combination of thought and action, for

144

Mannheim pretty much ignored the question of valuation. In the early German writings, valuation came from the organic sphere of *Geist;* in *Ideology and Utopia,* it came from the political selection process. In *Man and Society,* values were instilled by the planner through manipulation, but where did he or she get the values he or she was to instill? Because planning was only a strategy, a means, to what ends was it to be subordinated? Or, to use Mannheim's own terms, "who plans the planner?"[81] In these writings, he offered no answer; and hence this chapter, unlike Chapter 2, does not have a section entitled "The solution," but instead:

The transition

Three factors sum up the transitional nature of this period in Mannheim's career. First, one sees a structural consistency, especially in his description of the crisis. The organic, communal stage disintegrated into mechanistic atomism,[82] which in turn was to be overcome in a structural synthesis –a tripartite schema that appeared in the earliest of his writings.[83] Although discarding earlier solutions, he would always retain the structure that organized his diagnoses. That he continued to interpret the crisis primarily as a cultural one rather than, say, an economic one was in part due to this structure and the cultural assumptions in which it had originated.

In addition to this consistent structure, one sees the continuation of a trend: the increasing confidence in sociology as the central discipline of a modern education. This importance appears even greater during this period because of the void above sociology; he had not decided to what it was subordinate. In both Germany and England, he saw it as the most synthetic of disciplines, but he made no sustained attempt to relate this institutional synthesis to the society and culture at large.

The third factor, that of discontinuity, was the discarding of the two previous spheres of meaning and valuation – the organic realm of *Geist* and the dialectical competition of politics – in the light of the Nazi triumph. In Frankfurt, he became aware that the invisible hand of political will was not leading to the extended mastery of the historical process, but rather to the abandonment of history. Accordingly, he attempted to move sociology away from the competition of political parties toward a more neutral position. Although he realized that knowledge would always be existentially connected, he believed that the attempt should be made to curb that bias as much as possible, that unmasking should mean conscious neutrality rather than conscious partisanship.[84] He attempted to separate, as much as possible, the scientific element from the utopian will, for that will was leading to disaster in Germany.

145

The first form this depoliticization took was a return to the cultural sociology of the earlier period, which was part of a discussion of the role of sociology within the university. In his published writings, especially *Present Tasks*, he did not attempt to relate the discipline, except in an indirect way, to the larger structure of society, the implication being that, if academic priorities were established, these priorities would filter down to the rest of society. To use the terminology of this chapter, his published discussions of sociology in Frankfurt presupposed the existence of an organic public, an educated stratum acting as an intermediary between the cultural elite and the larger public. However, he seemed to become increasingly aware that such a public no longer existed. Faced with the growing irrationalism of the 1930s, he realized that the people who had successfully dealt with the social and cultural disequilibrium in Germany were not the intellectuals in the classrooms but the Nazis in the streets. The public in Germany was not organic but disintegrated, and, therefore, discussions of university disciplines had a very limited area of impact.

This discrepancy between these two publics in Mannheim's writings indicates the very precarious position of his theories at this time. This position was accentuated by the move to England. The failure of the German university system and his marginal position in the English university system led to his rejection of the university as the prime institution for synthesis. Thus, in England he had rejected both the political agent (the party) and the intellectual agent (the university),[85] without naming their successor. The planner was not put in any institutional framework and, in this sense, was even more free-floating than the intelligentsia of *Ideology and Utopia*. This abstractness has drawn the fire of some of Mannheim's critics, who wanted more concrete formulations.[86] However, Mannheim was not concerned at this point with concrete solutions. His first step as a refugee was not to solve the problems of his host nation but to decide what could be salvaged from his old culture. He asked: What principles could be derived from the German experience? What lessons have been learned that go beyond the immediate tragedy of Weimar? To become less abstract would, in his terminology, be to confuse the principia media of Germany with more general principles. Therefore, the planning strategy was presented as a mode of thought rather than as a concrete program.[87]

This second transitional stage ended when Mannheim began to apply the lessons learned in his analysis of the German failures to his new English environment. This occurred sometime in the late 1930s. The opening lines of the 1940 English edition of *Man and Society*, nearly twice as long as the German edition, revealed that the period of transition was over.

146

The German edition of this book was dedicated to "My Masters and Pupils in Germany." Thus, it was originally dedicated to those who had experienced in their own lives the tremendous changes of an age of transformation. If the book appears in English, its function alters automatically. It is no longer an attempt at self-enlightenment, made for the benefit of those who have actually lived through these experiences; it attempts to explain the standpoint of these people to a world that has only hearsay knowledge of such changes and is still wrapped in an illusion of traditional stability.[88]

Mannheim gleaned three basic principles from his German experience – the ideal of *Bildung,* the historicist perspective, and the technique of manipulation. *Bildung,* as it always had for him, meant the development of an oriented and responsible personality. The individual had to be able to think synthetically and interdependently, which by 1930 meant sociologically. Faced with the irrationality and disorientation of the disintegrated public, Mannheim became even more adamant about this goal and especially its extension to all of society. He believed that the sociologically educated individual not only gained clarification about himself and his place in society,

> but also, after his pragmatic bonds become evident, he can attempt to regulate it. . . . His understanding still remains a product of this historical process which arose independently of him. But through his insight into these bonds, the individual for the first time transcends the historical process – he becomes more than ever before the master of his own destiny.[89]

This ideal, of the individual gaining control of the historical process through consciousness of his or her place in that process, was expressed in very similar terms at the end of *Ideology and Utopia.* This consciousness included not only the individual's social location but also the historical nature of the sphere of meaning upon which individual actions were to be based. If one understood that the world was constantly being transformed, then his or her decision was not whether to transform or not, but whether to participate in a transformational process that would occur whether or not he or she participated. However, in *Man and Society,* Mannheim questioned the automatic nature of the relationship between historical knowledge and historical action. Accessibility of knowledge did not mean acceptance of that knowledge – that was the mistaken assumption of *Ideology and Utopia.* Nor did membership in a single institution such as a political party guarantee acceptance, for this simply extended the automatic nature of the process to another level. The individual's life had to be manipulated in such a way that he or she would accept the knowledge accessible to him or her.[90] Accordingly, principia media, although a historical concept, were not simply a tool for the interpretation of historical forces but also for their manipulation.

147

This strategy of manipulation will be discussed further in the next chapter. Here it suffices to note that manipulation and exploitation were not in his mind synonymous; the former was a more inclusive category of which the latter was only a part (the part to be avoided). Exploitation required that the exploited be kept in the dark and, therefore, was contrary to the ideal of *Bildung,* which strove for orientation and self-responsibility. Manipulation, on the other hand, simply meant management, or direction; and the form Mannheim advocated (planning) was designed to promote rather than suppress self-enlightenment. In this sense, manipulation was an extension of the sociology of knowledge. That discipline uncovered the social role of thought and aspirations, showing both meaning and existence to be reciprocal agents in the historical process. Planning advanced from uncovering social functions to manipulating them. If it were successful, the functions would remain uncovered but cease to be random. To be consistent with the ideal of *Bildung,* planning had to provide that the manipulated, as much as possible, be a conscious and responsible participant in the process. But exactly how this rationality would work was something Mannheim was unable to describe during this transitional period. That would come only later when he applied his German lessons to the English environment.

6

The synthesis of democratic planning (1938–1947)

If the second transitional period provided an autopsy of the German sociocultural context, Mannheim's final synthetic period was characterized by a diagnosis of the English scene and a prescription for its continued health. The theory of planning was central to both periods; however, in his final years it was increasingly supplemented with theories of representative government and education. This shift was due to changes in both the English context and Mannheim's relation to it. I have designated September 1938, when he became a member of a group of intellectuals known as the Moot, as the beginning of the final period.[1]

The English context

Like Germany, England experienced widespread unemployment and economic dislocation during the thirties, which earned those years the title of "devil's decade."[2] In response to this situation, many intellectuals sought more radical alternatives.[3] A considerable number, especially those who might be termed "progressive," became increasingly political, demanding social change and guidelines for that change.[4] Some were revolutionaries, some opted for reform along Fabian lines, while others believed that reform and capitalism were not necessarily antithetical. What united all the progressive intellectuals was the belief that some kind of social reorganization was necessary.

The question of the reordering of society was certainly a burning one at the London School of Economics, where Mannheim taught during much of his English period. Perhaps nowhere within the university system was the new spirit of social change and involvement taken more seriously than at this institution. The LSE had been founded by Sidney and Beatrice Webb to increase the resources available for the scientific study of society and its institutions. Despite an ideal of political neutrality proclaimed by its leaders, the LSE had a reputation for being very modern, very radical, and very involved.[5] One might compare it with the social-science group at

149

the University of Frankfurt during the early 1930s. Both groups saw themselves as more progressive than the traditional academic establishment and were responsive to ideas about social change.

Yet this intellectual ferment had little effect before the Second World War. The British governments of the thirties were made up of unusually old men who looked back to the better prewar days. The labor movement offered little in the way of challenge, and there were few large-scale strikes during this period. The lower middle classes refused to support Oswald Mosely's fascist New Party, which went nowhere. Most people seemed to have an interest in stability and order.[6] Thus, England found itself in a contradictory position – on the one hand, there was a recognition of the need for change; on the other hand, there was a fear that this change might be for the worse and a feeling that stability was more important. The result, writes one historian, was an "inertia" in which "consciences were deeply stirred, but they could find no outlet in constructive action."[7]

This situation changed with Britain's entry into the Second World War in 1939, bringing a new sense of community and purpose. Although some hold that the "war community" was nothing but a myth, there was indeed a mood of national unity in sacrifice.[8] The presence of the Labour Party leaders in the national government indicated the kind of "civil peace" that Germany had experienced at the beginning of the First World War without the reactionary spirit of the latter. David Thomson described the mood of the country:

> Socially the war was a mighty crucible, melting many pre-war contrasts and softening (though not always removing) old rigidities. Experience of evacuation, of mutual aid in air-raids, of great collective sacrifice and service, of stringent rationing and controls in the cause of "equal shares," all helped to strengthen a tide of egalitarian sentiment that had been generated before the war began. Common humanity began to seem more important than distinctions of wealth or birth. Participation in so great a common effort made the pre-war years of insecurity and social hardship seem in retrospect grossly unjust. A new resolve was born to build, from the sacrifices of war, a better society wherein none should be deprived of the necessities of life, and where the opportunity to work and live in decent surroundings should be opened to all citizens.[9]

In the emergency of the war, the central government took a greater role in directing society than ever before. New departments sprang up to control areas of British life that had previously been unregulated or less regulated. In 1942, Lord Beveridge issued his famous report, which called for protection and security of all individuals "from the cradle to the grave" and which was met with overwhelming popular enthusiasm. *The*

Times commented: "Sir William Beveridge has succeeded in crystalizing the vague but keenly felt aspirations of millions of people."[10] From 1941 to 1948, the laissez-faire philosophy of government was abandoned as Britain actively embraced the welfare state,[11] a condition symbolized in the war hero Churchill's replacement by a Labour government more dedicated to planned social reform. The willingness of the English people to accept significant social change and some form of social planning encouraged Mannheim, for it indicated a potential audience for his theory of planning.

At the same time English society was moving toward a position more in accord with his ideas, Mannheim's personal career took a turn toward greater influence (at least from his viewpoint) than he ever before had enjoyed. The most important event in this change was his membership in the Moot, a group of influential Christian scholars that included T. S. Eliot, John Middleton Murry, Christopher Dawson, and Sir Fred Clarke.[12] The Moot was organized by the Anglican social reformer J. H. Oldham to discuss the questions raised by the 1937 international conference of the Universal Christian Council of Life and Work. It held quarterly weekend meetings for about ten years, beginning in April 1938, for the purpose of giving sympathetic intellectuals an opportunity to exchange ideas and exert some influence on the ecclesiastical hierarchy of England.[13] The founders of the Moot were impressed by the success of totalitarian regimes in articulating a basic faith that could win over public opinion. They felt that the Western democracies offered no alternative faith, so they proposed to articulate one tied to the basic principles of Christianity.

Mannheim's friend, Adolf Löwe, attended the original meeting, and he recruited Mannheim to attend the second meeting in September 1938. Mannheim became a regular member and in fact was considered by some to have been the central figure of the group. This is borne out by the fact that the group stopped meeting with his death in 1947.[14] The other members of the Moot were impressed by the experiences of Mannheim and Löwe in Weimar Germany; as Murry said, "These men have been through the hoop."[15] In addition, Mannheim's tripartite structure encompassed their basic position and gave it a systematic coherence.[16] His being a Jew never interfered with his relationship to the group, and he adopted as his own the Moot's goal of strengthening the role of Christianity in society.

In 1940, through his contact with Sir Fred Clarke in the Moot, Mannheim was invited to become a part-time lecturer at the University of London's Institute of Education.[17] In 1946, he left the LSE to accept the newly created Chair of Sociology and Education at the institute, where he was extremely popular. His lectures were packed, and he appeared to be making an impact on English pedagogical thinking.[18] This new popularity was cut short by his sudden death in early 1947.

When he first came to England, Mannheim's audience had been limited to his fellow intellectual refugees and some English academics. In the 1940s, his public had widened to sectors of the traditional elites (mainly through the Moot), and he saw the potential of expanding it even further to the country as a whole.[19] The use of the traditional elites as a medium to reach the larger audience is indicated in a 1940 letter to his friend, Lord A. D. Lindsay,[20] in which he stated that there were two main leadership groups in Britain – communists and potential communists (who were too radical) and the traditional elite (who were too inelastic). What England needed was a third group who would provide progressive leadership from the middle classes. He believed that there was a greater likelihood of changing the principles of the traditional elite than those of the communist leadership to what he had in mind. It was crucial, he wrote, to develop a sect within the old leadership to transform them into a new type of elite more responsive to the needs of modern democracy. He believed that it was better to transform groups already in power than to replace them with a new elite. In a paper circulated to members of the Moot in late 1940, he wrote: "There is no need for an organized new elite, but [rather a need] for the revitalization of the existing historical groups and the extension of the basis of selection of their membership."[21] Undoubtedly, this preference can be traced to his experiences in Germany as well as to the ties he was making in England.

Mannheim's view of the traditional elite was in accord with his view of English society as a whole. He wrote that the greatest effect that Britain had upon him was the renewal of his faith in democracy. In Germany, that form of government had been unable to survive economic and social dislocation; however, in Britain, "liberal democracy functions almost undisturbed."[22] This stability greatly impressed him and his fellow refugee Löwe. The latter wrote an open letter to their mutual friend Paul Tillich in which he expressed ideas that were very much in tune with Mannheim's own.[23]

Löwe's letter was largely a comparison of German and English societies. He saw Germany as the land of extremes – on the one hand, a complete individualism with no social consciousness; on the other hand, a repressive autocracy that suppressed all individualism. The result of this dualism, said Löwe, was that German society exhausted its strength by swinging between disintegration and repression. He felt that England had avoided both complete individualism and complete absorption of the individual, demonstrating what he called "spontaneous collectivism," a willing self-restraint and social conformity in which individualism existed but always in light of wider social ends. Because of this socialization, classes were not as divorced from one another as they were in Germany; there was more communication between above and below, and there was a greater predilection for the middle course. He concluded:

> The England and the Germany of the liberal age represent two extremes of social formation. On the one side a society which has grown up and is daily maintained by the spontaneous conformity of its members – on the other side a social chaos which from time to time produces wonderful flowers of individual development and then relapses into the dullness of the herd, held together by the mechanical forces of the state.[24]

Mannheim concurred with Löwe's analysis but also noted that the spontaneous collectivism of England was not guaranteed in perpetuity. There was no assurance that Britain would not follow the rest of European culture (of which it was the last remnant) into totalitarianism.[25] Although the elite were an important feature of spontaneous collectivism, individual citizens were more important, for the state in which the initiative came solely from above could never be truly democratic, and Mannheim believed that democracy was the only hope for Western culture. In short, there would have to be a transformation of the citizenry to accompany that elite. Although the elite would continue to guide society, their followers would be motivated not, as previously, simply by faith or deference but by enlightened insight. He proposed a transformation in which the spontaneous collectivism produced by the English tradition would be augmented by substantially rational and responsible collectivism able to deal with the complexity of industrial society. He called the program for this transformation "democratic planning" or "planning for democracy."[26]

Democratic consensus

The reciprocal relationship of these two terms, "planning" and "democracy," was the key to his last synthetic period – British democracy provided the planning techniques with the orientation (meaning, values) missing in the second transitional period, whereas planning allowed those values to adjust to modern society in a substantially rational and responsible manner. He postulated a relationship structurally similar to the one of the Free School lecture with its three elements: (1) a consensus of democratic values (an objective culture), which provided the degree of conformity necessary to hold society together; (2) the individual (the soul), who provided the qualities of freedom and spontaneity; and (3) an institutional structure (the work), whose manipulation through planning was a means of mediation for the first two.

This tripartite structure distinguished the final synthetic period from the second transitional period, where the element of consensus was missing.[27] We have seen Mannheim in the transitional period moving away from the pluralistic competition that characterized the political synthesis of *Ideology and Utopia* and seeking a more stable structure in planning. But planning was a means, not an end; it did not provide a consensus of values. Only when Mannheim weighed the positive elements of British democracy against the negative elements of German democracy could he add this additional factor. The positive element resulted in his association of the democratic consensus with elements such as "paradigmatic Christianity"; the negative in his advocacy of "militant democracy."

Militant democracy meant standing up for democratic values and not taking them for granted. Laissez-faire democracy had adopted an indifference toward values, Mannheim believed, a spirit of "neutrality," with the result that "we ceased to believe, out of mere fairness, in our own objectives."[28] Such neglect led to a loss of standards, especially in times when standards were changing, with the resulting *anomie* being a great danger to democracy and an invitation to dictatorship. He wrote:

> Only those who have seen the result of complete non-interference with valuations and deliberate avoidance of any discussion of common aims in our neutralized democracies, such as Republican Germany, will understand that this absolute neglect leads to drifting and prepares the ground for submission and dictatorship. Nobody can expect a human being to live in complete uncertainty and with unlimited choice. Neither the human body nor the human mind can bear endless variety. There must be a sphere where basic conformity and continuity prevail.[29]

The values that Mannheim wanted democracy to clearly establish consisted of basic rules and "virtues" and a faith in the viability of democratic institutions. It is important to note that these were not values he wished to introduce into English society; he felt they were already there. He wanted Britons to articulate and be militant about what they appeared to take for granted. Among the virtues he listed were brotherly help and decency, fair play, community spirit, justice, incentive to work, and, above all, cooperation.[30] He realized that a consensus on these values would not eliminate conflict in democratic society, for they could be interpreted differently; modern society would always have a strong pluralistic element. However, differences were positive elements, providing they took place in the spirit of cooperation and within the guidelines of democratic institutions. He wrote:

The essential thing about true democracy is that differences in opinion do not kill solidarity as long as there is fundamental agreement on the method of agreement, i.e. that peaceful settlement of differences is better than one by violence. Democracy is essentially a method of social change, the institutionalization of the belief that adjustment to changing reality and the reconciliation of divers interests can be brought about by conciliatory means, with the help of discussion, bargaining and integral consensus.[31]

Mannheim termed such a position "creative tolerance" and "integrative behavior," which he contrasted to "compromise." The latter was simply a matter of expedience, a "rational adjustment" between people who felt no sense of community, a form of functional rationality in which one gave up a little to preserve what one had. The result was "a type of emasculated mentality . . . that cares neither for principles nor a deeper understanding of life." Compromise for Mannheim was simply a form of relativism, promoting the notion that in a democracy there could be no agreement on fundamental ideals and that the best policy was one of neutrality. Integrative behavior, on the contrary, was characterized by a combination of toleration and commitment to democratic values.[32]

The idea of commitment was not a new one in his writings, having played, along with its companion term "aspiration," an important role in his German works. Yet there was an important difference in the use of the concept in this last period. Militant democracy was very different from the earlier "utopia."

In "Competition" and *Ideology and Utopia*, commitment was claimed by political parties that struggled to determine the public interpretation of reality. The possibility of an organic consensus was denied, and so this competition and the selection process that resulted from it were the only alternative to the atomistic competition of individuals in the *Gesellschaft*. But now Mannheim wrote that "unrestrained economic and political struggles may destroy the community" and that group egoism was more dangerous than that of the individual.[33] The competition of potentially utopian parties was now seen as an extension of chaotic, atomistic competition rather than as a viable alternative to it. He doubted that British parties, or classes, would be willing to pay the price of disorientation and dictatorship to gain a monopoly for their "interests." Rather than being basic units of will, parties became subordinate interest groups.[34] He still advocated will or striving, but now that striving would take the form of cooperation rather than competition.

At first glance, this would appear to be a retreat to the earlier monadic organicism of the German mandarins. This conclusion is reinforced by Mannheim's discussion of youth, which demonstrated a movement away

155

from his own generational theory of 1928 toward that formulated by Alfred Weber. In "Generations," Mannheim had introduced the concept of "generational unities," which were conflicting groups, the equivalent parties, competing with one another. Alfred Weber, on the contrary, had seen a basic organic consensus with youth providing a new input of energy for that consensus. Energy for consensus was exactly what Mannheim emphasized in his English writings.[35]

Youth, he wrote, were a force not totally involved in the social order; being young meant having a certain amount of rebelliousness, a certain amount of marginality. Such a position gave youth the potential to be a pioneering force for democracy. Past ages had sought to restrict this force, which was seen as a threat to the status quo, that is, as utopian. The revolutionary totalitarian parties, on the other hand, because they were dynamic movements, concentrated on winning over the young and using them as a means to shatter democracy, which was identified with the status quo. Militant democracy, said Mannheim, had to learn from its totalitarian rivals and mobilize the young to further the democratic consensus. Rather than neutralizing youth, democracy had to promote them as a source of reform and revitalization. Direction, rather than restriction, was the answer.[36]

Mannheim's prime concern, therefore, was how to keep youth from becoming indifferent toward democracy. This source of energy had to be made more dynamic rather than less, for if this dynamism was given direction it became a source of will for democracy. However, it was not utopian in that it would not attempt to shatter the existing order of values but rather to improve it through reform and new commitment.

Although the concept of militant democracy was a response to the negative situation in Germany, the inability of the neutralized Weimar Republic to resist the more dynamic forces of Nazism, "paradigmatic Christianity" accentuated the positive element of his English experience, the ability to maintain some continuity in values, a consensus of meaning, in light of great social change. As earlier in this chapter, the major factor was Mannheim's membership in the Moot, for the relationship was not one-sided. He received as much from that group as he contributed to it.[37] To understand the group's importance for him, a review of its basic position is useful.

The first concern of the members of the Moot was the survival of Christianity in the modern world in the face of an advancing paganism and secularism. T. S. Eliot wrote:

> I believe that the choice before us is between the formation of a new Christian culture, and the acceptance of a pagan one. Both involve radical changes; but I believe that the majority of us, if we could be faced immedi-

156

ately with all changes which will only be accomplished in several generations, would prefer Christianity.[38]

What was it that made Christianity so preferable to secularism? First,
the Moot believed that it was the true way to human salvation. But a
second argument, more important for us, was that Christianity provided
a necessary sense of community. Eliot wrote that the community's conscious mind and conscience were formed through culture, which he saw
as the expression of the collective communal unity of spirit. But culture
could not develop without religion, which provided a framework for
culture and gave meaning to life. Without religion, there would be no real
culture; and without culture, there would be no real community. There
would be only "boredom and despair."[39]

John Middleton Murry echoed this feeling in writing of the virtues of
the English countryside with its sense of community, which was thoroughly integrated with its religion. Religion for the members of the rural
community was something "that belongs to the continuity of their lives" –
it gave their lives meaning. This was in contrast to the lifestyle of the city,
where daily activities and religion were separated. In the city, going to
church was like going to the theater, an act that could be discontinued
without any real change in one's lifestyle. In the city church, one consciously separated oneself from the rest of the congregation – the audience was atomistic, not communal. Murry wrote that he felt a great
sense of isolation in the city, an isolation that was relieved only by a return
to the countryside. "Very gradually, in the country a sense of community
returned to me. I now had real neighbors. And slowly, my religious faith,
which had been real, but private and ecstatic, passed out of my consciousness into my being."[40] Only Christianity could provide the sense of
community and promote the development of the individual's whole personality, both of which were necessary to prevent society from falling into
administrative conformity or mass irrationalism. Murry expressed the
sentiments of the Moot when he wrote:

> The choice before democracy is simple: either the individual must learn to
> conquer his lower self and attain his true personality, as a citizen of a Chris-
> tian society; or the democratic state, abandoned to be the instrument of the
> lower selves of its members, will enforce upon them a uniformity which is
> destructive of the whole personality.[41]

However, it was not simply a case of democracy becoming Christian,
but also of Christianity becoming democratic. The members of the Moot
realized that preserving the traditional Christian spirit was different from
preserving the traditional forms of religion. Those forms had been
largely dissolved by the modern industrial nation. New forms would have

to appear based on some understanding of the changes in the social structure. There had to be a closer analysis of social forces to discover how Christianity and democracy could be made more responsive to one another.[42] For example, Alec Vidler emphasized the importance of the welfare state as a community based on mutual love and responsibility – here was a new kind of machinery that could successfully replace traditional customs and still foster basic Christian values.[43] Even the more conservative members of the group realized that institutions such as the church and university would have to change to continue playing a positive role.[44] And this change had to be democratic.[45]

The willingness of the Moot to combine Christian values with a commitment to democracy and social reform, its receptivity toward his theories of planning and social education, convinced Mannheim that Christianity could play an important role in shaping the communal consensus necessary for the survival of democratic society.[46] He wrote that this consensus was dependent on Christians' realization that their religion consisted of two different parts, a "paradigmatic basic experience" and the application of that experience in the social world. The paradigmatic experience was a religious view of the world, "a way of interpreting life" but not a way of regimenting behavior. It said "this is what life means" but not "this is how that meaning should be realized." The shared meaning of the paradigmatic experience united individuals into a communal group. It gave them a feeling of togetherness, a we-feeling, a value consensus, which provided orientation for those who shared in it.[47] Mannheim believed that, without a paradigmatic experience, the only type of human coexistence and cooperation that was possible was a purely functionally rational one.[48]

> If these paradigmatic experiences evaporate, as in secularized European history, it is obvious that the problem of values contains nothing but the adjustment character of human conduct. Right or wrong only means efficiency, and there is no answer to the question: efficiency for what?[49]

The paradigmatic experience was itself flexible; there were a variety of ways in which it could be adjusted to daily life. It would be a mistake, he said, to assume that, because the religious paradigmatic experience remained basically the same, the social interpretation of it must also remain the same. The archetypes of Christian attitudes were not given as abstract commands but rather as parables of Christ's life, concrete images of a certain historical and social setting. Because the historical and social setting had changed, a strict constructionism, an insistence that the form as well as the content of Christian principles be continued, was doomed to failure. Instead, wrote Mannheim, "the Christian is compelled to transfer the intention of Christ into varying situations."[50] In short, the duty of the Christian, and especially the member of the Christian elite, was to interpret the meaning of the paradigmatic experience in the parables and then to reinterpret it in light of his or her own social setting.

Quite clearly, then, Mannheim felt that the paradigmatic experience did not have much positive value without its continual reinterpretation in light of the changing environment. Therefore, it was the duty of the religious thinker to consult the sociologist, for society had become so complex that the application of the paradigmatic experience to society demanded an expert's knowledge of social structure. As he noted, it was hard to love your neighbor if you did not even know your neighbor.[51]

On the other hand, the sociologist also needed the religious thinker, for social science by itself was essentially neutral. "To the sociologist the social conditions which produce a gangster are as relevant as the social conditions which make for the development of a good citizen." This neutral method was beneficial for research, but as a measure of conduct it became a disintegrative force in society. Only the deeper values of conscience, developed by religion, could sustain people in crises of disorientation. Mannheim emphasized that "it is more than ever a matter of conscience for the Churches to test the basic principle of social organization in light of Christian values."[52]

As with militant democracy, Mannheim's emphasis on religious conscience reintroduced the irrational element in a positive role, something lacking in the second transitional period. In those late German and early English writings, he had emphasized the need for substantial rationality in the modern world and the chaotic, destructive effects of modern mass irrationality. Now irrationality, or better nonrationality, once again was described as an orienting force in the modern world, and he called for the "refinement of passion" through more socially aware religious and cultural institutions.[53] He now saw a degree of compatibility between religion and scientific rationality in the realization that both faced a much greater enemy. In spite of the tension between them, they could make a common cause and supplement one another in the struggle against the "Mechanized Barbarism" that threatened the world.[54]

This union was also crucial to the second element of democracy, the responsible citizen. Mannheim's views on the latter represented a continuation of the concept of *Bildung* discussed in the previous chapter. In the spirit of that earlier ideal, he advocated "democratic personalism," a balance between "overconventionalization and overindividualization." He wrote:

159

The interests of the individual, as these develop out of his individuality and specific place in the social system, should promote his understanding of the needs of the community. On the other hand the demands of the community should never become so powerful as to stifle all resistance, for a trend towards conformity is liable to suppress the call of the "I," that dynamic source of continuous creativeness.[55]

This description differed from that of the second transitional stage in its emphasis on the creativeness of the individual and his or her positive nonrational qualities. Of course, Mannheim still feared the irrationality of "unorganized masses" with "no social aim or function,"[56] and he continued to believe that the major contributor to such an irrational contagion was the fear and *anomie* of social mobility and rapid transition.[57] An insecure person, clinging to a precarious sense of individual identity and status, could not be a successful democratic citizen. Such a person preferred an authoritarian, or dominative, relationship in which there was no question about his or her position; therefore, he or she was ripe for totalitarianism.[58] The ideal democratic personality, on the other hand, felt secure, was open to change, was tolerant of others, and had a sense of responsibility. He or she was "unafraid of losing status or individuality by having his probity exposed to the testing powers of cooperation and exchange of ideas."[59]

The negative form of irrationality was weakened in part by the positive form, which stemmed from the value consensus described above. He believed that this consensus could aid in the development of the democratic personality by providing the necessary security of valuation. For example, his ideal for youth was "a pioneering and militant type which is not fanatical, an emotional type whose emotions are more than displaced fears, . . . [with an] obedience which is not blind, but a devotion to spontaneously believed ideals."[60]

At the same time, this commitment to a value consensus had to be accompanied by an ability to judge, an "awareness," which Mannheim defined as a "comprehensive sociological orientation."[61] He distinguished awareness from class consciousness, stating that the latter was a "partial awareness" that prepared a class to fight against another class at the expense of "covering up all other aspects of the whole situation." Class consciousness was "the social world seen in the perspective of a fighting group." Awareness, on the other hand, was a "synthesis that emerges after the different aspects of partial group experiences have been confronted and integrated."[62]

In his German writings, Mannheim credited the Marxist doctrine of class consciousness with uncovering, or unmasking, ideologies; now he accused it of covering up the whole situation. Also, he now attributed to the ordinary citizen the synthesis from partial group experiences that was characteristic of the free-floating intelligentsia in *Ideology and Utopia*. These changes are both explained by the larger switch, already discussed, from a pluralistic competition of world aspirations to the basic consensus of militant democracy. With no basic consensus, each group or individual had only a partial perspective of the pluralistic constellation, that is, each was existentially bound, a position uncovered by the Marxists. Likewise, "synthesis" could be performed only by the group that incorporated the pluralism and hence was not existentially bound, the intelligentsia. With a basic consensus, those who uncovered partial perspectives based on class interests did so at the expense of covering up the larger consensus shared by the citizenry. And because the citizenry shared in the consensus, there was no need for a free-floating intelligentsia to clarify it. The basic consensus eliminated existential bondedness (but not existential connectedness, which remained the object of sociological investigation).[63]

The two basic elements of shared consensus and sociological awareness reinforced one another and promoted spontaneity in the individual, who in turn added vitality to them. This reciprocal relationship was the basis of democratic society. A crucial factor in this relationship, one in which values and social existence were connected, was the concrete groups to which the individual belonged. In discussing these, Mannheim used the format he had used throughout his career, based on Tönnies's *Gemeinschaft–Gesellschaft* dichotomy, and called his two types "communal" and "functional."[64]

The main purpose of communal groups, which ranged in size from the family to the nation, was orientation. They "serve primarily the need to belong somewhere." Thus the most important characteristic of communal groups was the feeling of togetherness, the feeling of unity within the group, which Mannheim called the "we-feeling." He wrote that "the we-feeling emanating from communities of whatever origin contributes greatly to defining man's place in the world." This feeling, of course, was irrationally felt rather than rationally calculated. Communal group produced values that "appeal to elements in the human mind which remain untouched by abstract reasoning and can only be brought into play by a direct appeal to the unconscious." Such groups were characterized by traditions and symbols that bound members not only spatially to each other but also temporally to past generations. In short, communal groups gave people roots, to use an appropriate organic metaphor.[65]

The largest, most inclusive community, which in modern times was the nation and which Mannheim labeled the "frame group,"[66] coincided with the *general* consensus in his ideal democracy. Its relationship to lesser communal groups within its boundaries was ideally harmonious in a way

161

that brings to mind the historicist concept of individuality. But ideal and reality had not coincided in the history of the modern nation.[67] Modern society was so complex that any monadic organic relationship among the communal groups within the frame group was impossible. The result was a weakening of those agencies that were to instill values in the individual.

A major reason for the deterioration of communal groups was the increasing importance of functional groups, which were organized essentially upon the egoistic calculation that characterized the atomistic individual of the *Gesellschaft*. These groups were concerned with functionally rational problem solving, not with substantial orientation. In functional groups, one "remains at a distance from one's partner," maintaining a separate identity with no feeling of togetherness.[68]

Yet, when this "uprooting" was only "partial," it resulted in an emancipation necessary for a stable democracy.[69] Although membership in communal groups provided a source of values, emancipation from those groups allowed the individual spontaneity and a sense of perspective. Participation in functional groups, however, while promoting individualism, did not necessarily provide the sense of perspective Mannheim expected from emancipation and in fact often led to the instrumental rationality that prevented an adequate perspective. In short, the problem of substantial rationality and responsibility could not be effectively considered in terms of the dualistic typology of concrete groups, which led either to the naive optimism of laissez-faire or to the tragic view akin to monadic historicism.

Education and planning

As he had done throughout his career, Mannheim went beyond this dichotomy to a third, structural, alternative. The two most important elements of this final structural approach were those introduced in the second transitional period – education and planning. In that period, these two elements were by and large unconnected, with education being emphasized in the Frankfurt years, planning in the early English ones. They stood side by side with no real connecting element because each could be traced to a different synthetic position – his view of education was a sociological qualification of his first, cultural, synthesis; the theory of planning was a qualification of his second, political, synthesis. In the final English period, he found a common denominator to accompany his third valuative synthesis – the concept of "power." Both education and planning were viewed as both conflicting and complementary forms of power whose balance in democratic society was crucial to the consensual and individual potential of the concrete groups.

Mannheim defined power as the presence of "social pressures operating on the individual to induce desired conduct."[70] The means by which power was exerted were termed – "social techniques."[71] They were two basic types of power and techniques, direct and indirect. The types are self-explanatory, although it should be noted that with direct power the wishes of the power holder were expressly stated, whereas with indirect power they were not. The latter was the equivalent of the term "manipulation," defined in Chapter 5.[72] Mannheim believed that power had always been and would always be present. He denied that the doctrine of laissez-faire expressed freedom from power, but rather that the more obvious direct form of power had been increasingly replaced by the less visible indirect form.

As did society in general, power became increasingly indirect, complex, and centralized, which, Mannheim felt, was unavoidable and not necessarily harmful. Like the case of technology applied to nature, where properly directed by sound values and reason, it was a great boon to humankind. The social technology of power as a whole was neither good nor bad; that judgment could only be applied to the uses made of it.[73] To try to resist this trend was to take a position analogous to that of the Luddites, an attempt to return to the handicraft stage of social technology. Instead, one had to make sure that power was used intelligently and in keeping with the democratic consensus.[74] Mannheim's theories of planning and education were addressed to just such issues.

Mannheim certainly considered education a form of power, and its techniques increasingly received his attention, as is evidenced by his appointment to the Institute of Education.[75] His association with the institute coincided with a flood of literature about the nature of education and its place in English society. H. C. Dent writes: "From approximately the end of 1940 educational reform, the planning of a new order in English education, was to become a main preoccupation of English educationalists."[76] Dent maintains that the main reason for this new interest was the dislocation that English education underwent during the war. The evacuation of children from the cities to the countryside during the war broke up families and, at the same time, exposed people who had never imagined that such things existed to the degradation of life in the urban slums. The traditional distinction between town and country was sharpened by this revelation. Many people looked to education to patch up these cracks in family and society, but education was unable to respond. This sense of failure, together with the new spirit of reconstruction and

163

planning that emerged during the war, sparked a spirit of reform. Many, but certainly not all, educators began to reexamine the bases of English education in the hope of finding there tools with which to solve some of the existing social problems.[77]

George Kneller's *Higher Learning in Britain* provides a good survey of the wide range of arguments offered in the education debate. For this study, it suffices to note that the ideas varied from something resembling the traditional German university position to something Marxist and positivistic. The main issue in the debate was the degree to which the university should be involved with the rest of society. The conservative position held that there should be a basic separation between the university and the rest of society. Conservatives like F. R. Leavis maintained that the main role of the university was to preserve tradition and that, therefore, it must remain separate from a society becoming increasingly dominated by material interests.[78] The opposite view was taken by men like J. D. Bernal, who wrote that science should follow the lead of Marxism and become involved in society. "The relevance of Marxism to science is that it removes it from its imagined position of complete detachment and shows it as a part, but a critically important part, of economic and social development.[79] Men like Bernal felt that education's main task was not to preserve tradition but to help initiate change.

These two poles (traditional values and social change) are the same that we encountered in Mannheim's discussion of religion. As was the case there, he felt that the proper approach was an attempt to synthesize the two extremes, although his approach was closer to Bernal's than to Leavis's. His position found support in the Moot, especially with Sir Fred Clarke, who called for a synthesis of the literary and scientific approaches to learning. Clarke attacked the traditional educational system as too isolated from the mainstream of society and too static. Educators had to avoid the danger of a "dogmatic and overly-academic orthodoxy, occasionally so ingrown as to be quite incorrigible." They had to realize that English education was a function of English society.[80] He added that one must not only recognize the interdependence of educational and social institutions, but one must plan the role that education was to play as a social force. The old easygoing attitude of "muddling through" could no longer be successful because society was changing too fast for an unorganized approach.[81] Educators would have

> to estimate the degree to which the existing order is capable of adaptation to the demands that have to be faced, the demands of a régime consciously planned and directed towards the guaranteeing of freedom and diversity of personality in a social order much more thoroughly collectivist in its working than any of which we have yet had experience.[82]

In this spirit, Clarke stressed the importance of a sociological approach to education, which, he insisted, did not mean a positivistic approach. Science should not be dominant in education at the expense of the humanities, for culture, which Clarke identified with the latter, was essential to the process of valuation, providing the continuity and consensus necessary to counterbalance the utilitarian demands of science. So, although he saw the need for education to keep pace with change, he also believed that it could provide stability in the light of change. The main task of education was to provide orientation for people in modern society, which necessitated that culture be democratic rather than elitist. Therefore, Clarke placed emphasis on a common culture that reached all elements of society.[83]

Clarke's position was similar to that of Mannheim, who sought the same balance between traditional orientation and social science.[84] In his discussion of education, Mannheim made use of the three-stage structure that had characterized his earlier writings. He postulated an organic, traditional stage, when education took place mainly in the primary social groups such as the family,[85] and a liberal stage, when the educational role of the primary groups was weakened as society became more diversified and part of that role was assumed by formal institutions such as schools.

To adapt to this increasingly complex society, the educational process developed three new characteristics in the liberal stage – it became specialized, neutralized, and compartmentalized. We have seen that Mannheim regarded the first two as incomplete and potentially dangerous elements. Both provided a great deal of flexibility, allowing people to solve new problems that were beyond the older organic approach. However, they provided no interpretation of the world as a whole, no orientation outside a very limited sphere.[86]

The third characteristic of liberal education, compartmentalization, established a basic division between the school and the world. "Education was a compartment because the school and the world had become two categories not complementary but rather opposed to each other." This division between school and society was combined with a static, traditional theory of education, which held that "the basic values and the aims of education were eternal, and the final and exclusive purpose of education was the fostering of the free development of the personality through the unhampered unfolding of innate qualities." Such a theory, said Mannheim, did not admit the relevance of society to education; it was "society blind." It held that the interaction between individuals and groups in society did not affect the essential knowledge and values that education was supposed to engender in its students. Of course, the theory did not claim that the school was the sole dispenser of value orientation in society

165

– it recognized that the home also played a major role. But it made no attempt to provide any coordination between home and school. It simply assumed that a basic coordination existed.[87] Mannheim wrote:

> Liberal education, with its lack of insight into the social background, works fairly well when, as in times of prosperity and general expansion, everyone with any strength of character has a good chance of making his way in life. It fails, however, when the general expansion and prosperity cease and the various groups are thrown back upon their own resources. . . . Ignoring the sociological point of view does not abolish social problems, but leads to complete chaos, marked by the rising influence of those who try to establish order in society, not be scientific guidance, but by dictatorial decree.[88]

These first two stages of education were a reiteration of Mannheim's concepts of substantial irrationality and functional rationality. His third stage, structural education, was charged with the task of developing substantial rationality, by which democratic values were sociologically clarified. Only if the individual understood the social forces working upon him or her could he or she attain the type of orientation necessary for modern society. Unconscious tradition and functional compartmentalization had to be enhanced by a sociological perspective so that the educated could be transformed into his or her own educator. This role for sociology was basically in accord with Mannheim's writings in the second transitional period and need not be discussed further.[89]

Newly emphasized in this period was the sociological examination of the educational process itself. The school was a social institution that interacted with other social institutions; its members did not meet in isolation from the rest of society.[90] In addition, teachers had to be trained to recognize that the classroom was itself a group and that one had to consider the interaction of the various members of that group.

> The subject that is taught in school is not simply data which the learner has to acquire. From the learner's point of view it is also a symbol which relates him to his teacher. It carries with it strong emotional associations with other teachers and with the family. It is a truism to say that teaching is very different from learning but it is of the greatest importance that we should recognize that the teacher and the learner carry with them their own lifestyles and that the subject matter which passes from one to the other is more than acts linking intellect to intellect.[91]

This view of education paralleled the sociology of knowledge, in which sociological analysis was not simply applied to others but also to oneself. The teacher not only enlightened the child concerning its sociological existence but also examined his or her own position. Only when the existential connectedness of the school and its members was investigated could their compartmentalization be overcome.

166

Mannheim believed that such sociological clarification would result in the reexamination of teacher–student relationships, including the methodology of teaching. Teaching methods would have to vary, not only according to the subject taught but also "according to the learning situations, according to the depth of understanding that has to be achieved." Mannheim indicated that this sociological view would reveal the inapplicability of older authoritarian methods to modern society. If the student was to be an active participant in society, he or she also had to be an active participant in the educational process. The authoritarian methods were not very efficient in an age when knowledge was so rapidly expanding and the ways of acquiring it becoming so varied. This variety demanded that education foster the role of experimentation and spontaneity, and this was exactly what the older methods failed to do.[92]

But the methods could not be based on the concept that the student was a totally spontaneous and innovative creature. The student also needed a degree of stability and continuity. Teachers, for example, had to realize that when a child entered school he or she was entering a new social group with new norms and patterns. Upon entering a very flexible educational institution, a child raised in a very authoritarian family might suffer from a disorientation that would affect his or her ability to learn. The chance for spontaneity might actually prove to be a hindrance rather than a boon. Only if there was some communication between the home and school could the transitional problems be solved and the learning process be made easier for the child.[93] In short, Mannheim advocated a balance of spontaneity and continuity in education, as he did for society in general, according to the educational and sociological needs of the child.

Another aspect of education that Mannheim stressed was that the student was not always a child, that learning did not halt with the end of adolescence but continued informally throughout a person's life. Therefore, Mannheim saw no reason why it should not also continue formally. He was a strong advocate of adult education programs as an important element of educating a democratic citizenry.[94]

Despite Mannheim's belief that formal education should continue throughout a person's life, he felt it equally important that the person understand that education was by no means limited to formal institutions, but rather was acquired primarily from society. "The main educative agent is the community, the group of people in which the child lives and the objects which these people have created, their relationships, their culture, and their connections with a still larger society beyond." Although Mannheim saw the school becoming a more communal group and an agent for social change, its chief role was that of mediator between the primary communal groups and society at large. It accomplished this task in several ways: It complemented the communal groups by helping to instill values and encourage attitudes; and it served as a functional group by teaching both general and specific skills to the student. However, its most important task as mediator was the development of substantial rationality in the student by focusing, intensifying, and systemizing social experiences beyond the domain of any one communal group.[95]

Mannheim realized that, despite the mediating position of the school, it was a concrete group whose power was essentially direct and therefore was dependent on more inclusive forms of power, which in modern society were indirect. Control of these wider indirect powers, of the overall organization of society, was the task of democratic planning. Mannheim felt that this control was properly exerted not on groups and individuals themselves but on the space in which those units were located. The power of this space was characterized by the fact that it was not centered in concrete groups and thus was outside the sphere of influence of most groups in which the individual participated.[96]

The relationships of this space – which Mannheim divided into three types, "social mechanisms," "field structures," and "situations" – appear to be similar to the principia media of the second transitional period. In fact, most of the qualifications he made about principia media he also made about these forces: One should not see them as independent but as interdependent; one should not treat them all as equal but rather should realize that they have some sort of hierarchy; on the other hand, one should not assume that those presently dominant would always be dominant or that they were unaffected by lesser relationships.

Mannheim defined "social mechanisms" as abstract forces, such as competition, that were basically identical to the objects of general sociology in the second transitional period.[97] "Field structures" were specific patterns of organization that incorporated one or more of these abstract forces. The field structure, like the field of physics, affected concrete units (groups) and was in turn affected by them, but it could not be defined solely in terms of the unit. He cited commerce as an example of a field structure. Elements of commerce, such as economic exchange, transport, correspondence, and speculation, involved an interaction of different groups with different functional aims and possibly different systems of orientation. These elements "formed a sector of coherent activities and new forms of behavior cutting clean across the world of concrete groups." A field structure had a form, but this form was not as rigid as that of a concrete group. It could determine the "rules of the game," that is, supply and demand, or even property laws and laws of contract, but it did not determine individual moves in the game. One could again compare it to the field of physics, which determined certain

168

"rules," (e.g., the law of gravity), but this did not determine individual moves (e.g., the use and types of air travel).[98]

Mannheim defined the "situation" as "a unique configuration formed in the process of interaction between certain people." Situations, like field structures, did not coincide with concrete groups yet did influence individuals within those groups. But whereas the field structure provided the general rules of the game, the situations were the unique encounters of the players within the game. To continue with Mannheim's commercial example, a situation would be the encounter (competition) between two rival commercial firms. This situation could be peaceful if both parties seemed to prosper from the competition and abided by the rules of the game. In this case, the situation was not that noticeable, and so did not receive the attention that the field structure did. However, competition could become an open conflict in which the competitors were antagonistic toward each other even to the point of breaking the game rules to win the conflict. In this case, the situation was of prime importance, not the field structure. Thus, situations were more explosive, more unpredictable, and less susceptible to a general formula than were field structures and, as a result, "more easily escape the vigilance of centralized group control."[99]

Mannheim emphasized that the three types were not mutually exclusive and that their boundaries overlapped. He wrote:

> Competition in itself for instance is a mechanism but if it produces trade and the trade of one country becomes dependent on the markets of another, a homogeneous sphere is formed which conditions the reactions of the individuals concerned, so that we should speak, as we have seen, of a field structure. On the other hand, competition may give rise to situations. Out of the process of competition, competitive situations emerge. It is purely a question of emphasis whether we turn our attention to a single cross-section of the process and some particular combination of factors involved, that is to say, to situations, or whether we study the whole process of competition as a mechanism with all its cumulative effects.[100]

Mannheim appears to have thought of social mechanisms as elements of diagnosis, whereas field structures were the primary elements of manipulation. Situations held a position somewhat akin to concrete groups in that they occurred within field structures. In other words, when he talked of social techniques he was thinking primarily, although not exclusively, in terms of field structures.[101]

His own treatment of competition provides an example of how the planner diagnosed social mechanisms. He wrote that competition as a mechanism promoted individualism at the expense of communal ties. Therefore, were competition to be a primary organizing principle of democratic society, it would run counter to the very values of brotherhood, fair play, and a sense of community upon which democracy was founded. He believed that competition, as long as it remained subordinate to forces such as cooperation, that were more conducive to democratic values, played a positive role in encouraging self-reliance and independence. However, when allowed to operate unchecked (e.g., in a monopoly), it could actually weaken those same qualities. Therefore, competition had to be restricted to controlled spheres.[102]

> Controlled competition means that competition is first allowed to develop the will to self-adjustment and spontaneity in the participants, setting free, in its turn, those forces which have an individualizing influence on personality. But this process if checked as soon as it threatens the community and tends to undermine integrative behavior.[103]

The diagnosis of mechanisms such as competition guided the planner in his or her manipulation of field structures. This interference took place in light of the realization that field structures were dynamic entities with a reciprocal relationship to the groups and individuals within them. The latter were continually adapting to changes in the field structure and to the situations that occurred within it with varying degrees of success. The central authority, the planner, allowed this spontaneous adaptation and change to occur as long as it was in accord with democratic principles and did not threaten to bring about chaos or regimentation. When that threat appeared, he or she interfered with the rules of the game at certain "strategic points," that is, key positions, to move the field structure in the direction he or she wished. Mannheim was especially concerned with those field structures that made up the capitalist economy. He had seen the disorientation and irrationalism created by economic dislocation in Germany and was most insistent that this not be allowed to occur in England. In taking this position, he would appear to have been in accord with Keynesian theory, which was becoming so important at the time.[104]

His view of capitalistic economic institutions was in keeping with his view of competition in general – within limits, it promoted the individualism and spontaneity necessary to democracy; uncontrolled, it could lead to chaos, as it had in 1929. He wanted measures that would control the tendencies toward monopoly and destabilization in capitalism, which were harmful to democracy. Such techniques included "compensatory public investment, manipulation of the rate of interest, gradual redistribution of wealth and income, or even the building up of a Mixed System." In times of economic crisis, more direct interference, such as wage, price, and investment controls, might be necessary, but such movement toward centralization was never to go so far that it endangered democratic institutions.

170

As noted above, situations were less susceptible to planning than were field structures; however, this degree of autonomy did not mean that situations were independent social controls able to resist any attempt to plan them. In fact, Mannheim wrote, "the social process is continually moving between two extremes: producing situations which are controls in themselves or controlling them from the outside." One way of controlling them was by fitting them into established patterns to limit their variability. This was more difficult to do in times of social change, when new situations were occurring for which there were no adequate established patterns. One could be authoritarian, deny that there actually were new situations, and demand that they be treated according to old patterns. Or one could try to sublimate the conflict of dangerous situations into less harmful, or even beneficial, areas, for example, parliamentary debates instead of violent social conflicts. Or finally, one could try to influence the elements that would generate dangerous situations in such a way that the situations never appeared. Mannheim seems to have favored this preventative approach over strictly curative ones. However, he wrote, it was not necessary to control all situations. The fact that many situations escaped central control was not a bad thing, for a society that was overorganized, that eliminated unique situations altogether, would stifle its creative forces and could not be a democracy. As was the case with field structures, his treatment of situations emphasized the need for a balance between control and spontaneity.[105]

This balance, which we have seen as a central thread running through his English writings, was labeled "coordination." He wrote that "in the long run no society can survive unless there is some coordination between the network of institutions, educational devices, and basic valuations."[106] And no democratic society could survive in the long run unless this coordination occupied a place between "chaos and cage," between laissez-faire liberalism, "which has no theory of coordination," and totalitarian dictatorship, with its sinister form of total coordination, *Gleichschaltung*.[107]

The metaphor Mannheim used to describe this "Third Way" was that of orchestral harmony, with the planner as conductor.[108] This imagery was directly in tune with the monadic philosophy of *Bildung*, which advocated the harmony of creative individual personalities and which was clearly present in his early writings, especially the Free School lecture. The concept of the work in the latter occupied a role structurally similar to that of the social interrelationships ("the network of institutions") in the later English writings. The work served as a mediating element between the individual soul and the objective culture. Previously, this mediation had occurred in an organic, unreflective manner but, with the threats of specialization, reification, and pluralism (the critical stage), this spon-

171

taneous relationship had to give way to a new structural one. But, despite this new postcritical, structural approach, the goal of the human sciences (which interpreted works) remained the same – to foster the development of the creative individual (the producer of the work) and to ensure his or her harmony with the larger objective culture.

The goals of the planner were similar to those of the human scientist – to foster the development of the democratic citizen and to ensure his or her harmony with the democratic consensus. He or she, too, accomplished these goals through his or her attention to that sphere that had appeared previously to work automatically. Mannheim wrote:

> The essence of planning is control over those functional achievements which formerly grew up spontaneously and worked together without being consciously correlated. In planned society their mutual adjustment will not be left to chance but will be guaranteed through consciously planned institutions.[109]

In both cases, the aim was not to control the spontaneity of the individual but to promote it and its communication to other individuals within the same context. In place of the pluralism of utopian wills in *Ideology and Utopia,* he now opted for two contemporary wills – that of the democratic consensus and that of the planner.[110]

His introduction of these two wills raises again an earlier question from the second transitional period: Who plans the planner? His answer was "the planned." The relationship of the two wills was reciprocal – the planner acted in accordance with the will of the planned (the democratic consensus), which he or she, in turn, indirectly influenced to maintain the consensus in a changing society. But how did the popular will, which was not an entity in itself but the consensus of many individual wills, make itself known to the planner; and what guaranteed that the planner would be responsive to this consensus? Mannheim's answer was parliamentary institutions. He believed that each parliamentary representative refined, humanized, and individualized the wills of his or her constituents, and his or her interaction with his or her fellow representatives created a consensus in policy making.[111] He wrote of Parliament:

> Speeches and debates bring divergent issues and values to public attention, challenging and clarifying them by focusing on the legislation under consideration. The pressure for action and the need for agreement continuously produce interest and value adjustments. The parliamentary struggle serves to sublimate and transform hostile or antagonistic impulses into critical attitudes. Antagonisms of selfish interest and sheer impulse, as found in the life of the community, are subjected to adjustment; and constructive compromise may be reached in every phase of the debate. Whereas the antagonistic currents of workaday life may remain disturbing and unresolved,

under the pressing need for common policy policy-makers capitalize on them for constructively integrating will and thought.[112]

Mannheim and his critics

Mannheim's faith in the ability of parliamentary institutions to play this important role was reflected in his use of two terms, "planning for democracy" and "democratic planning," as synonyms. In reviewing the posthumously published work, *Freedom, Power and Democratic Planning*, one of his colleagues, Lord A. D. Lindsay, questioned whether this synonymity was actually the case. Lindsay implied that Mannheim was more concerned with "planning for democracy" (the role of the planning elite) than he was with "democratic planning" (the control of that elite by the citizenry).[113] Lindsay's reservations have been taken up and extended by Mannheim's critics, who have leveled three main charges against him: (1) He was an elitist; (2) he raised sociology to almost the status of a religion; and (3) he was concerned primarily with preserving stasis rather than promoting change. These three charges are the basis of the general view that he had become a twentieth-century Saint-Simon or Comte.[114]

Mannheim did believe, correctly, that complex societies could not function without an elite, a position that has never been refuted by experience. However, the important issue was not whether there was an elite but the manner in which individuals became members of it and to whom they were responsible. The charge that Mannheim was an elitist, that he saw the elite as an exclusive group answerable primarily to itself, is false.[115] When T. S. Eliot asked him if his theory of planning were not undemocratic, he replied that democracy involved the availability of leading positions, which were determined by certain principles not identifiable with wealth, to the general populace.[116] Indeed, the whole thrust of his theories of education was the shaping of the individual to be an enlightened, responsible citizen, on whose active participation in the affairs of the nation he placed a premium.[117] Responsibility could not be limited to Parliament, the representative of the people; it had to reach the entire population and be an extension of earlier, spontaneous collectivism. Democracy was not just for the people, but also by the people. In this spirit, he wrote: "The times are past when small minorities could base the perpetuation of their rule on the ignorance of the bulk of the population."[118]

Mannheim's faith in a democratic culture can be seen in his use of the term "popularization," which was the other side of the coin of "massification." The latter term, from the second transitional period, was essentially negative, expressing the fear that the irrationality and disorientation of the "masses" would spread to the cultural elite. "Popularization," on the other hand, expressed Mannheim's confidence that communication between the creative elite and the general populace need not involve dilution. In fact, he wrote, cultural creativity should not be thought of as the exclusive domain of "higher" thinkers, but rather occurred on all levels of society.[119]

> What we have to avoid at all costs is the academic aloofness which finds life sublime only in a kind of stratosphere where our minds are kept safely at a distance from suffering and vulgarity, and from the world of daily contacts in which people are jealous and hate one another and things really hurt.[120]

Mannheim's position, if presented in the terminology of the second transitional period, was that the esoteric stream of transmission should not be separated from the continuum of everyday experience in a democracy as it had been since the monopolistic stage. Democracy, like the premonopolistic type, had to be based on consensus, but not the naive organic one of that earlier stage. In place of unreflective traditionalism, he advocated substantial rationality and responsibility developed by the teacher and the planner.

The second charge against Mannheim is summed up by Jean Floud's statement that he "stopped trying to understand specific situations better and concentrated instead on preaching at large the gospel of salvation through sociology."[121] This accusation implies two things: that Mannheim's sociology was too speculative, that is, too far removed from empirical studies, and that he placed sociology in a position once held by religion as the primary source of values. His work was certainly more speculative than empirical, but no more so than it had been in Germany. There were reasons why he continued this approach. First, he believed English sociology was too empirical and tried to counter this characteristic by emphasizing the theoretical element.[122] Second, and more importantly, he had become an activist, an enthusiastic lobbyist trying to put across a program. Gaining a commitment from others for general principles came first; working out the detailed ramifications of those principles could follow.[123] He undoubtedly overstated his case, appearing to some like a true believer,[124] but he felt this was not the time for caution.

Despite Mannheim's faith in sociology as a crucial part of modern education, he did not make that discipline into a religion. As he did throughout his career, he viewed sociology not as a source of values but as a clarifying discipline. Sociology ideally informed the politician, the planner, the teacher, and the citizen, indicating the ramifications of their values in complex modern society. However, it did not provide those values, which came from sources such as primary groups, religious beliefs, and the viability of the democratic process.

174

Perhaps the most important charge against Mannheim was that he was a "utopian of the right," whose real preoccupation was with social statics, that he never welcomed change but instead sought a planned, dynamic equilibrium.[125] The adjective "dynamic" is important to the criticism, which does not claim that he resisted all change but that he wanted change controlled so it did not upset the existing political stability. Certainly one finds calls for both change and equilibrium, or balance, in these later writings; the issue is which element was primary and which adjectival. I believe that his priorities were the reverse of those presented by his critics, that he sought balanced change rather than dynamic equilibrium.

Mannheim believed that the sociocultural context continually underwent change, a position he had held since his earliest writings. Although he viewed his position as a synthesis of past and present contradictions, he did not depict it as the final synthesis. He never projected a future world in which history accomplished its goal and came to an end. As John Friedmann writes,

> Mannheim's utopias were immersed in the stream of historical change. They were not models of ideal society but instances of a continuously moving intelligence, its bearing set upon the future. Mannheim refused to fall into the trap of objectifying states of social order whose time has not yet come.[126]

When Mannheim advocated stability or change, he was not offering a universal prescription but one for a limited time and space, in this case postwar Britain. Within this restricted context, he adopted two ends, one from each side of the traditional–liberal dualism. Like the traditionalists, he wanted to maintain a stable consensus, an objective culture, although these values were democratic ones centered upon brotherhood and faith in representative democracy. Like the liberals, he wished the individual to be rational and self-responsible, capable of growth and not afraid of change. Yet he realized that these two contradictory elements were alone inadequate, the former due to its complete but outmoded substantial irrationality, the latter due to its modern but incomplete functional rationality. And he rejected the unproblematical, automatic assumptions by which the two envisioned the connection between the individual and the larger sociological context – the monadic harmony of the individual soul, the mechanistic progress of the invisible hand – in favor of a more activistic approach. It is the latter, the structural, substantially rational element expressed in the theories of planning and education, the means for reconciling the two contradictory ends, upon which a judgment about the static or dynamic nature of his views can be made.

He viewed the process of change as he viewed social mechanisms and techniques – as a means not an end. Change was valued not as a thing in

175

itself but as a process in which the two ends of democratic consensus and individual spontaneity were achieved and reconciled. In *Ideology and Utopia,* he implied that change was always for the best, that it propelled people forward to a better world. His final years in Germany convinced him that this was not true. However, they did not take him to the opposite position that change was harmful. Rather, the rate of change had to be judged according to the desired ends. He believed that, in a modern industrial society such as England, reform was more effective than revolution.[127] When change was too rapid, it could lead to disorientation and insecurity; to irrationality rather than to increased consciousness; and to a movement such as fascism, which exploited this uncertainty to achieve an undemocratic, antiindividualistic society. Such change, then, could actually lead to ends exactly the opposite of what one desired. In these circumstances, to insist on rapid, unlimited change was to advocate an ethic of ultimate ends, not one of responsibility.

Nevertheless, he knew that change had to occur, and to simply resist the new forces introduced by modern society was as dangerous and unrealistic as to call for unlimited change. Also, he was not so naive as to trust the direction of change to the existing elite. Democratic pressure, made increasingly effective with improvements in the educational system, was to be constantly applied, so that the barriers between the elite and the general populace could be gradually broken down.[128] Thus, although Mannheim's view of society was not revolutionary, it was certainly not static.

Nor did he give his ideals the aura of teleological certainty. He wrote that "setting up an ideal does not mean we shall ever attain it completely, but rather lends direction to education and mutual controls."[129] He realized that the world was much too complex to achieve the kind of scientific utopia envisaged by Saint-Simon and Comte. However, just because goals were not completely attainable did not mean one could not work toward them as best one could. He saw this version of the ethic of responsibility as a middle way between the poles of muddling through and revolutionary utopia. He wrote:

> In our age we are passing from a stage of tacit adjustment and tacit integration to deliberate reconstruction; we believe in the purposeful guidance of human affairs. This does not mean we can hope to master the whole turmoil of facts and the onslaught of an entirely changing world system. But social intelligence has reached a stage where we can be satisfied only if we have done our best to disentangle the causes and to master the course of events from the strategic points available to us.[130]

Perhaps the most valid criticism of Mannheim was his misunderstanding of the impact of his own personality. He correctly saw that the war offered an opportunity for ideas such as his to gain a wider acceptance, and he realized that he had considerable influence on some members of the cultural elite. However, in his zeal to make the most of this situation, he misjudged the influence of intellectuals like those in the Moot upon the cultural elite as a whole. His ideas were nowhere near as popular as his perspective gave him to believe. In fact, his theories were less appealing to his immediate following than he believed. His success there was due perhaps more to the dynamism of his personality than to the ideas themselves. His colleague Lord Lindsay wrote that Mannheim's "talk was so illuminating, so able and stimulating, that he was difficult to resist, and we gave up argument, silent but not convinced, and then went away to ask ourselves hard why we did not really agree."[131]

During this final period, then, Mannheim can be seen as a quixotic figure, embarked on a "mission" to preserve democracy, with qualified support from some and hostility or ridicule from others. Despite his hopes of influencing the traditional elite, and despite the encouragement he received from some quarters, he was certainly out of place within the English academic establishment. Perhaps the most apt symbolism of his situation lies in Peter Laslett's description of the setting (the Strand Palace Hotel in 1939) in which he, as a student rebelling against the traditional establishment, met with Mannheim.

> The meeting-place was itself an indication of how little Karl Mannheim seemed to be as yet at home in his English institution. The Strand Palace was a large, cosmopolitan establishment, not of the highest reputation; rather dingily garish, with a noisy lobby; low, dusty, uncomfortable chairs. We must also have met elsewhere, but my memory is of lengthy, complicated conversations in undertone, taking place amidst the waiters and the suitcases, with the boy-friends and girl-friends waiting for their partners at the surrounding tables.[132]

Conclusion
Mannheim's legacy

Mannheim's career, a series of attempts to provide orientation in the rapidly changing twentieth century, is certainly of interest to the intellectual historian. His experimental attitude and his refugee strategy led to a continual reexamination of his own work and the different contexts in which that work took place. The intellectual development that resulted made him an outstanding representative of his chaotic age and deserving of our attention. But can he escape the confines of history? Was he simply brilliant but wrong and, therefore, better consigned to the past?

Although this study has not attempted to answer those questions directly, some suggestions toward answering them are in order. To begin with, I will elaborate on those methodological concepts that I, as an intellectual historian, have found most useful – the six concepts used in presenting Mannheim's intellectual development as a "dynamic totality."

Through the concept of "perspectivism," I have defined Mannheim's relationship to a larger sociocultural context. Of course, such a context could be defined in any number of ways: as a collection of individual thinkers; as a large, inclusive category such as "*Zeitgeist*" or "generation"; as the kind of socioeconomic group defined by Marxism; or as a school of thought, for example, phenomenology or neo-Hegelianism – to cite some common ways. And in fact Mannheim was a part of all these contexts. In my interpretation, I have made all these, as well as other contexts, subordinate to that of the sociocultural group defined by its world aspiration, by its commitment to a certain world view. I do not deny that Mannheim was influenced by certain thinkers, that he faced problems common to his entire generation, that he was a bourgeois thinker, or that some of his ideas could be defined as Hegelian or phenomenological; and on occasion I have noted these connections. However, I believe that these definitions are less adequate than the one I have chosen for the purpose of understanding Mannheim's career as a whole.

The three sociocultural groups I have chosen to make up the context of Mannheim's career differ greatly in their constitution. The Budapest

178

intelligentsia are portrayed as a rather small, concrete group dominated by certain members, especially Jászi and Lukács. Here one sees Mannheim engaging in face-to-face relationships with the other members, sharing in their mission, and actually becoming their spokesman. He demonstrated a much greater commitment to the goals defined by this group than to those of the other groups, in which he played a less central role. Accordingly, I have imputed the aspirational element in Mannheim's dynamic totality, the will to change, to this group.

The refugees in England represent more of a category than a concrete sociocultural group, sharing only the most abstract qualities, especially the need for orientation in a new culture. For this reason, and because England was the last of Mannheim's three cultures, I have attributed a lesser role in the development of his career to this group (even though I have claimed that his English synthesis is his most important).

The German university community falls somewhere in between the other two groups. Unlike the category of the refugee, it was an actual sociocultural institution; however, its membership was much more heterogeneous than that of the Budapest intelligentsia. The latter certainly had a more unified aspiration, a shared sense of commitment. Yet the German university community was the most important of the three groups with regard to the conceptual apparatus of Mannheim's thought. His definition of his central task, the world-view element of the world aspiration, used the terminology of this group even before he became an actual member of it.

In presenting all these groups, but especially the German academic community, I have used ideal-typical constructions, the most important being that of "monadic historicism." My ideal types, like Max Weber's, are one-sided exaggerations and not balanced hypotheses. However, unlike the types in Weber's *Economy and Society,* they do not combine to form a comprehensive analytical set, and, unlike those in Weber's *Protestant Ethic and the Spirit of Capitalism,* they do not illuminate a certain historical factor for its own sake. Rather, they are simply means for interpreting Mannheim's development and are not intended to stand alone.

Here one sees a reciprocity in the relationship I have drawn between Mannheim and his sociocultural contexts. His position, or perspective, has "distorted" the presentation of the group, which in turn is used to define his position. This circularity and the ideal-typical construction in the presentation of the contexts do not permit direct causal explanations of his thought. Accordingly, I have not said that because he belonged to a certain group he had to have the ideas of that group. Rather, I have said that certain elements of his thought, an aspiration toward change, a conceptualization of cultural crisis, and the problem of orientation in a new sociocultural context, can be imputed to ideal-typical groups to which he can be said to belong.

Not only does Mannheim's position within a sociocultural group distort my presentation of that group and require the use of ideal types, but also that group distorts the presentation of other possible sociocultural contexts with which it overlaps. For example, I have omitted any substantial discussion of the very rich cultural forces that have become synonymous with the Weimar period but operated apart from the university community. This is not to say that Mannheim did not have contacts with these intellectuals, for he certainly did. However, it was not they but the academics who posed the questions to which he addressed himself. Thus, the Weimar Germany I portray is quite different from that portrayed by someone like Walter Laqueur, who is after a more balanced and inclusive picture.

If the sociocultural group distorts the larger picture of the cultural generation, it also distorts the other extreme, the individual thinker. For example, my description of Max Weber should not be viewed as a summary of his work; many important elements are omitted, and other aspects are greatly emphasized, so a comprehensive and balanced view of his career is missing. Weber himself, then, appears here as an ideal type, as a position within the university community, an alternative to the ideal types of monadic historicism and Lukács's Marxism through which I have located Mannheim's changing position.

The imputation of certain sociocultural contexts to Mannheim's thought in order to clarify it in no way denies the individuality of that thought. Although he addressed certain group questions, his answers were his own. This uniqueness is apparent in the next of my methodological concepts, the "refugee," which was devised to deal with the problem that Mannheim was not part of one sociocultural context but three. "Refugee" is conceived of as an intellectual strategy, one that attempts to evaluate both an old and a new culture and then to arrive at a synthesis of them. Under this strategy, the old culture provides an antithetical element to the new one. In other words, the refugee has learned lessons from the old culture despite its failure, or even because of it, which are then applied to the new culture. Although the weighing of two cultures continued throughout Mannheim's career, it was strongest during the transitional periods before and after the publication of *Ideology and Utopia*.

It is important to note that refugee is an intellectual strategy and not a psychological concept. The psychological condition of being a refugee also plays an important role in Mannheim's career, but the two are not identical. The intellectual strategy was one way, but, as Mannheim himself pointed out, not the only way of facing the psychological state, which involved an intense feeling of being an outsider and a need for orientation in one's new surroundings. Using this distinction, we can see an important difference between the first and second transitional periods: Although the refugee strategy was important to both, the psychological condition was far more important in the English phase of the second transitional period. In fact, in England we see the intellectual strategy for transition on the part of the individual actually coinciding with the sociocultural group, which in this case was largely defined by its psychological characteristics. In the middle twenties, on the other hand, Mannheim, although he continued to identify with the Hungarian cause, was very much at home in Germany.

Of course, Mannheim could not pursue a refugee strategy in his native Hungary, so in its place I have used a similar strategy that corresponds to his sociocultural group, the Budapest intelligentsia. Using the refugee strategy, one sought to introduce elements of one's native culture into the new one, making the old culture the qualifying element. With the Budapest intelligentsia, the situation was reversed as these thinkers sought to change the Hungarian culture in light of their experiences abroad, making the new cultures the qualifying element. Nevertheless, the two strategies were closer to one another than either was to Simmel's stranger, who could merely objectivize and not synthesize. Mannheim's Hungarian and German periods can be seen as a continuous attempt to synthesize the two elements, the Hungarian will to change and the German traditionalist conceptualization. I do not claim that this was a conscious effort on his part, that he was aware of his intellectual experiments as a refugee strategy.

During the English period, this synthesis, or better the collapse of this synthesis, became the qualifying element to his new English culture. With the coincidence of the intellectual strategy and the sociocultural group, Mannheim became more conscious of the former. This increased consciousness of the actual "function of the refugee" as a synthesizer is demonstrated by his essay with that title. In contrast his letters from exile to Hungary in the twenties discuss the German culture and the Hungarian culture but not the function of the refugee.

An important aspect of the refugee strategy is that it allows the sociocultural contexts to be connected to Mannheim's thought without simply organizing that thought directly in terms of the contexts, that is, dividing his intellectual development into distinct Hungarian, German, and English parts. The importance of the German sociocultural context for Mannheim's thought before he emigrated to Germany has been established. The survival of elements of the Hungarian and German periods

181

into succeeding periods also precludes the possibility of simple lines of division. In fact, I have stated that the "Hungarian element" in Mann- heim's development, the will to change, actually grew stronger during the German period. The boundary between the English and German writ- ings is more easily established, but even here the issues are not clear-cut.

To meet the problem of periodization, I have devised the five-stage "dynamic hierarchy." These stages are defined by their intellectual ele- ments but are also connected with the changes in sociocultural context. I do not claim that this typological structure, which has been imposed upon the heterogeneity of Mannheim's thought, operated in some kind of mechanistic fashion propelling Mannheim's thought forward. To do so would be to deny the importance of the sociocultural contexts in his development as well as the experimental nature of his writings.

The stages have been arranged in a dialectical pattern in which each transitional stage is characterized by elements antithetical to the preced- ing primary stage, preparing the way for the new synthesis of the succeed- ing primary stage. As one would expect, the transitional stages display greater heterogeneity of concepts and a more dramatic change of ideas than do the primary stages.

I have defined each of the three primary stages by its "center of con- struction," a concept or theory that attained organizational superiority over other intellectual elements. The center of construction was not an a priori concept from which the other concepts followed; Mannheim's ex- perimental approach was not conducive to such a formal system. Rather, the center of construction was one of a number of competing concepts that, because of its ability to incorporate the others, became their organi- zational superior. Therefore, concepts' positions as centers of construc- tion were not necessarily their only role. For example, I have shown that his first center of construction was the idea of a cultural philosophy, which then gave way to a new center, his theory of politics. This did not mean that the idea of cultural philosophy disappeared, or even that he ceased to speak positively about it, but rather that the concept no longer held center stage, that it was now subordinate to the new center, which in turn had previously been its subordinate. The concepts of culture and politics are present in each of the first two primary stages, but their roles are reversed in the second. In short, the stages are not identified by the presence of certain concepts but rather by the function and relationship of those concepts.

Such an approach precludes the possibility of establishing clear bound- aries between the stages. I have not said that in a certain essay Mannheim's thought underwent a switch in centers of construction, but rather that in a certain essay one can clearly observe that a switch in centers has occurred. That work defines the apogee of a primary period but not its boundaries. The latter are determined in a less specific way by the transitional periods. During the transitional period, the switch in the centers of construction occurs, although only implicitly. When that switch is explicated in its most complete form, the transitional period is over and the boundary has been crossed.

The importance assigned to the centers of construction affects the amount of attention given to each of Mannheim's works. The more an essay challenges, articulates, or anticipates a center, the more consideration it has received. For example, I have devoted little attention to the two essays of the second transitional period that usually receive considerable attention from Mannheim scholars, the first and last sections of *Ideology and Utopia*. This is not to say that they have no importance to discussions of the sociology of knowledge; indeed, the final essay is perhaps Mannheim's most complete description of the discipline's methodology. However, these essays play a minor role in the development of his career. In the first transitional period, the sociology of knowledge is introduced, becomes the most important antithetic element to the synthesis of the first stage, and prepares the way for the synthesis of *Ideology and Utopia*. Mannheim's move toward the theory of democratic planning and education in the second transitional period contains some basic premises from the sociology of knowledge; however, the recapitulation of the discipline itself is of secondary importance. The most important antithetic element in this second transitional period was the problem of "massification," that is, of orientation for responsibility in mass democratic society. Accordingly, *Man and Society* and the final essay in *Essays on the Sociology of Culture* receive the bulk of the attention.

Not all concepts had the potential to become centers of construction. I have used the criteria of "valuative" and "analytical" to distinguish potential centers from concepts destined to be subordinate, claiming that the potential centers addressed themselves to the valuative element. I am in no way suggesting that Mannheim was ever indifferent to the problem of valuation in those essays in which a new valuative center was not articulated. On the contrary, valuation was always a major concern of his. From the beginning of his career, Mannheim recognized that a value-free objectivity was impossible. Therefore, analytical is not a synonym for value-free objectivity or for an indifference to values.

Analytical works clarify values, impute them to certain sociocultural contexts, and examine the methodological possibilities of interpreting them; however, they do not attempt to set up a standard by which values can be judged, a criterion for "truth." To examine the logical structure of a discipline, to impute ideas to a certain social group, to elaborate on the world view of an eighteenth-century thinker – these were exercises that did not try to establish the truth of those ideas vis-à-vis the ideas of other groups or thinkers. The reason that many of Mannheim's works could be so experimental was that they were operating on this analytical level rather than on the valuative one. And the reason that some critics are frustrated by the inconsistency of this experimental approach is their assignment of a valuative element to it. This is especially the case with *Ideology and Utopia,* where they have not distinguished between the valuative element (the theory of politics) and the subordinate analytical element (the sociology of knowledge). Again, this is not to say that these analytical concepts are not value-laden, for they certainly are. But to say that they have an implicit values system in them is simply to say that they are subordinate to centers of construction, which are valuative.

Mannheim's most significant analytical concepts and theories have come almost exclusively from the German periods of his career. When they have been perceived as analytical, they have been received more favorably than those theories that have been perceived as valuative. For example, the concept of the intelligentsia in its analytical form in "Conservative Thought" is generally admired, whereas its role in the valuative synthesis of *Ideology and Utopia* has been attacked unmercifully. The same could be said for the sociology of knowledge – its critics generally view it was a failed epistemological discipline, a valuative lapse into relativism. However, Mannheim never envisioned it as such, seeing its role as a subordinate analysis of the sociopolitical implications of thought, not its truth. Even the sections of *Ideology and Utopia* that spoke of an evaluative theory of ideology or sociology of knowledge referred to a demonstration of valuations implicit in ideas and a clarification of those valuations, but not a judgment of their truth. The sociology of knowledge remained subordinate to the valuative theory of politics, just as his earlier sociology had been subordinate to a cultural philosophy. My hope is that the intellectual utility of many of his analytical concepts will be recognized when they are relieved of the valuative burdens often cast upon them.

The first five methodological concepts have emphasized the discontinuity in Mannheim's career – the change in sociocultural contexts, the shift in centers of construction, the continual experimentation with analytical concepts. However, there are important elements of continuity as well, which allow one to describe his career as a dynamic totality. The most important of these elements is the basic purpose of all his writings – the communication of individuals with one another in terms of a larger totality of meaning, resulting in orientation in the changing modern world. From the early letters to Lukács to the final works on education and democratic planning, this communication and orientation remained his overriding goal.

Although Mannheim's works continually probed the problems and variations of knowledge, these questions were seen as a means to the more important end of orientation. He did not concern himself greatly with an objective knowledge by which data were increasingly added to a treasury of information. Rather, he saw knowledge as the means by which individuals communicated and oriented themselves, by which they gained meaning for their actions. Knowledge was an element of culture. In this sense, we can see Mannheim as closer to the classical tradition of *Bildung,* which was subject-oriented, than he was to the positivist movement, which was object-oriented. Yet, although he subscribed to the basic goal established by the tradition of *Bildung,* he challenged the components of traditionalist knowledge, seeing them as outmoded in the modern world. His attempts to modernize and eventually politicize this traditional project resulted in his changing centers of construction and his experimental attitude. Still, however much one admires this commitment to change, one must not allow it to obscure Mannheim's singular purpose. To do so results in viewing his later works on democratic planning, where this purpose is made very explicit, as a lapse into Comtean fanaticism – which is not the case.

Tied to Mannheim's basic purpose was a structural consistency, an unchanging "constellation," by which the changing conceptual material was organized. I have imputed this structure to the tension between the Hungarian and German sociocultural contexts in his early work. He adopted the tragic dualism of the German monadic historicists – in which an organic totality (a *Gemeinschaft*) dissolved into an atomistic, mechanistic collection of individuals (a *Gesellschaft*) – to portray what he saw as the cultural crisis: the alienation of the individual due to the absence of a meaningful cultural context. The optimism and cultural activism that he possessed as a member of the Budapest intelligentsia would not allow this tragic dualism to stand. He turned the mechanistic state of reification into one of antithesis, making the dichotomy a trichotomy, which remained throughout his writings. An organic thesis, which provided meaningful orientation for its members but was unable to deal effectively with change, was faced with a mechanistic antithesis, which provided little meaningful orientation but was very adaptable to change. These were succeeded by a structural synthesis, which provided both meaningful orientation and the ability to adjust to change. The sophistication and complexity of the structure varied, but the basic relational components remained the same. They are present even in the primarily methodological works.

The concept of constellation, as opposed to that of center of construction, describes relationships only, not actual contents. When, for example, a set of types from *Ideology and Utopia* is compared with a set from *Man and Society*, there is no claim that the contents themselves are identical, or even that they operate on the same level of interpretation, but simply that they are arranged in the same basic structural relationship. This is not to say that this structure played no role in the actual content of Mannheim's thought. Because he continually felt the need to define the specific problem he was addressing by means of a series of types and because he organized these types in the same structural trichotomy, these definitions delineated the nature of the solution as well as the scope of the various intellectual experiments.

As I have indicated, the philosophy that underlies these six concepts could best be described as an intellectual pragmatism. My methodology makes no claim to universal applicability, simply to have presented Mannheim's entire career in its most complete form. "Complete" is not meant here as the exhaustive treatment of every aspect of his work. Rather, I have made sense of his intellectual development as a whole while respecting his experimental approach and its resulting heterogeneity. My purpose in devising this series of types, stages, and categories is not to offer a definitive explanation of everything Mannheim wrote, but rather to cast a new light upon his work, to present him as more than a clever intellectual dabbler and convenient straw man. The very "arbitrary" nature of my methodology should help to convince the reader of the task of this study – not to eliminate the need to read Mannheim himself but to return and consider these texts.

Further suggestions on the usefulness of Mannheim's work can be gained by a summary of his intellectual development, emphasizing its valuative aspects and the thrust of the lessons to be learned from them. Here we are approaching his works at the valuative level.

During the first, and longest, primary stage, covering Mannheim's Hungarian and early German years, the "will to change" (the experimental attitude and the search for a new structural synthesis for individual orientation) of Mannheim's Budapest context and the traditional conceptual framework of the German university system coexisted in uneasy tension. The philosophical synthesis of culture anticipated in the Free School lecture was realized, after a series of primarily methodological works, in "Historicism" (1924). Although the philosophy of history played a much more important role in "Historicism" than in the Free

186

School lecture, this increasing historicity did not alter the essentially idealist nature of the cultural synthesis.

Yet, even while presenting this synthesis, Mannheim was uneasy with it; "Historicism" was certainly not a smug work. This was especially true in describing the sociological element, which had been introduced as early as 1920 in his review of Lukács's *Theory of the Novel*. In these early works, sociological knowledge was seen as subordinate and complementary to the larger philosophical synthesis, even if this was with some misgiving in "Historicism." After that essay, during the first transitional period, sociology came to play an increasingly antithetic role. However, as an analytical discipline, the newly developed sociology of knowledge did not form a new valuative synthesis. It helped to dislodge the old cultural-philosophical center of construction and to prepare for a new political one, which became central in *Ideology and Utopia*. This single work formed the second primary period with the theory of politics as its valuative center. Sociology was once again viewed as complementary, rather than antithetic, to the valuative center, but that center had changed and its relationship to sociology was much less tenuous.

In the new synthesis, one finds what I have labeled the Hungarian element, the will to change, at its strongest. Politics, previously peripheral to Mannheim's concerns, now emerged as central, whereas intellectuals, who had played the central role as synthesizers, were now subordinate in the valuative process. Mannheim had moved to a position close to that typified by Max Weber's vocation essays. The synthesis itself was seen as highly pluralistic and unstable, as the German conceptual element was far less important than it had been in the earlier synthesis. Accordingly, the tripartite structure was at its weakest here, taking a much more complex form than in earlier and later writings. In general, the tone of *Ideology and Utopia* is much less certain than it had been in his other syntheses, which was appropriate in view of the second synthesis's rapid disintegration.

The antithetic force in this disintegration was "massification," the advent of the "disintegrated public" of mass democratic society. The Nazi triumph demonstrated the failure of the two institutions that formed the basis of his earlier work, the progressive cultural intelligentsia and the traditional German university community. The acceptance of this condition characterized the second transitional period, which prepared the way for the third and final synthesis.

One can view the third primary stage as the synthesis of syntheses. Mannheim had returned to the idea of a larger shared meaningful context, which had characterized the first primary period. One also finds elements of the traditional theory of *Bildung* in the need to orient the individual in terms of this larger context. However, due to the second

187

primary stage, these theories had been stripped of their idealist foundations, politicized, and tied to social-psychological theories. The late English period, then, represents the culmination of the valuative level of his intellectual development.

Judgment of this valuative element should, therefore, center on the last synthesis; simply to attack the earlier syntheses is to beat a dead horse (killed by Mannheim himself) and serves only to obscure the analytical element of those periods. To evaluate the English synthesis, its subdivision into two elements is useful: (a) the diagnosis, in which he identified the prime values of English democratic society and the barriers to their realization; and (b) the prescription, in which he outlined the means by which the desired ends could be achieved.

His diagnosis came from "the point of view of a man for whom freedom and personal responsibility were the highest of all values."[1] In this sense, he considered himself a liberal. However, he also insisted that the social and political implications of this liberalism be examined. Here he differed from most other liberals, which can be seen in an exchange of letters with Oscar Jászi concerning *Man and Society*. Jászi wrote that the main difference between them was his belief in Natural Law and the corresponding view that human nature contained a basic layer that could not be altered by political and social forces. He believed that the individual had an original strength that could resist the currents of the time. In short, Jászi did not believe in human transformation, whereas Mannheim did.[2]

Mannheim basically agreed with this assessment of their differences, writing that Jászi's position represented a "noble defiance" of the times. He, on the other hand, wanted to learn the secret of the new times, even if it was infernal.[3] Unlike Jászi, he did not believe that the individual was automatically a responsible citizen. This responsibility was something that developed through the individual's interaction with society; and it could be lost through the same kinds of forces. The strength of English institutions had allowed the English to maintain views similar to those of Jászi. By providing a buffer against the social and political forces that promoted mass irrationality, they allowed this "naive" individualism to escape being put to the test. However, he did not believe this would always be so.

Whereas most liberals of the time were concerned about the development of the central government into a totalitarian tyranny to which the Lockean individual would be subjected, Mannheim feared just the opposite, the breakdown of democratic institutions and the consensus they embodied, leaving the individual on his or her own. The totalitarian regimes of the interwar period had resulted not from an extension of existing democratic institutions but from political opportunists taking advantage of an institutional void and a disoriented citizenry. He believed, then, that the main threat arose from an individualism with no sense of direction and responsibility in which an "attitude of believing in nothing" was combined with "an endless craving for new sensations."[4] The valuative void that resulted was the breeding ground for anti-democratic movements.

Mannheim's prescription for the continued development of a democratic citizenry was the combination of sociological education (to develop in the citizenry the range of vision necessary to meet their responsibilities) and democratic planning (the application of that understanding to preserve the democratic consensus). A sense of purpose and the range of vision to enact that purpose in a responsible manner – these were Max Weber's ideals for the politician. Mannheim's theories were designed to extend those qualities to the citizenry to which the politicians were answerable. Had he lived beyond the war years, his views undoubtedly would have changed, as they always had. One could surmise that the anticipation of an immanent crisis would have subsided. Yet, I believe the basic ideal of the responsible individual would have remained central to his work, as it had (although in continually changing forms) since the Free School lecture.

Mannheim recognized the complexities and difficulties of this task and realized that it could never be completely successful. Accordingly, he did not attempt to set forth a detailed program but rather to "lay down principles to convey the general vision of the kind of society we want to build."[5] Throughout his career, his main purpose was to raise issues rather than provide definitive answers. If many of his answers can be rejected, the questions he raised about civic responsibility cannot.

Abbreviations for Mannheim's major works

D   *Diagnosis of Our Time; Wartime Essays of a Sociologist.* London: Routledge and Kegan Paul, 1943.

ESC   *Essays on the Sociology of Culture,* ed. and trans. Ernest Manheim and Paul Kecskemeti. London: Routledge and Kegan Paul, 1956.

ESK   *Essays on the Sociology of Knowledge,* ed. and trans. Paul Kecskemeti. London: Routledge and Kegan Paul, 1952.

ESSP   *Essays on Sociology and Social Psychology,* ed. and trans. Paul Kecskemeti. London: Routledge and Kegan Paul, 1953.

FKM   *From Karl Mannheim,* ed. Kurt H. Wolff. New York: Oxford University Press, 1971.

FPD   *Freedom, Power and Democratic Planning,* ed. Hans Gerth and Ernest K. Bramstedt. London: Routledge and Kegan Paul, 1951.

IUE   *Ideology and Utopia; An Introduction to the Sociology of Knowledge,* trans. Louis Wirth and Edward Shils. New York: Harcourt Brace Jovanovich, n.d. London: Routledge and Kegan Paul, 1936.

IUG   *Ideologie und Utopie,* 5th ed. Frankfurt am Main: G. Schulte-Bulmke, 1969.

MG   *Mensch und Gesellschaft im Zeitalter des Umbaus.* Leiden: A. W. Sijthoff, 1935.

MS   *Man and Society in an Age of Reconstruction,* trans. Edward Shils. New York: Harcourt Brace Jovanovich, n.d. London: Routledge and Kegan Paul, 1940.

SD   *Strukturen des Denkens,* ed. David Kettler, Volker Meja, and Nico Stehr. Frankfurt am Main: Suhrkamp, 1980.

ST   *Structures of Thinking,* ed. David Kettler, Volker Meja, and Nico Stehr; trans. Jeremy J. Shapiro and Shierry Weber Nicholsen. London: Routledge and Kegan Paul, 1982.

W   *Wissenssoziologie,* ed. Kurt H. Wolff. Neuwied: Luchterhand, 1970.

Notes

Where English translations of Mannheim's works exist, I have cited them and, where possible, have used those translations for the quotations that I have selected. However, a translation is itself an interpretation, so I have often made modifications. I do not claim that these make the translations better, but rather that they make them more consistent with my interpretations while remaining true to the original works. Modifications are indicated in the notes by asterisks (*). For those readers wishing to go directly to the German versions, I have cited the page numbers in those editions in brackets following the English citations. Mannheim's major works are referred to by abbreviations given in the Abbreviations for Mannheim's Major Works.

Introduction: Mannheim's career as a dynamic totality

1 See, for example, James E. Curtis and John W. Petras (eds.), *The Sociology of Knowledge: A Reader* (New York, 1970); Hans-Joachim Lieber (ed.), *Ideologienlehre und Wissenssoziologie* (Darmstadt, 1974).

2 See Kurt Lenk, "Problemgeschichliche Einleitung," in Lenk (ed.), *Ideologie: Ideologiekritik und Wissenssoziologie* (Neuwied, 1967), pp. 52–9; Erich Hahn, "Ideologie," in Lieber (ed.), *Ideologie, Wissenschaft, Gesellschaft; Neuere Beiträge zur Diskussion* (Darmstadt, 1976), pp. 440–8; Judith Shklar, "The Political Theory of Utopia: From Melancholy to Nostalgia," *Daedalus*, vol. 94 (1965), pp. 361–87; S. N. Eisenstadt, "Intellectuals and Tradition," *Daedalus*, vol. 101 (1972), pp. 1–19; Urs Jaeggi, *Die gesellschaftliche Elite* (Berne, 1960), pp. 73–80.

3 Alan B. Spitzer, "The Historical Problem of Generations," *American Historical Review*, vol. 78 (1973), p. 1354; see also Robert Wohl, *The Generation of 1914* (Cambridge, Mass., 1979), pp. 73–84.

4 See Klaus Epstein, *The Genesis of German Conservatism* (Princeton, N.J., 1966), p. 65; Mannheim's typologies have been used in a formal way by Hayden White, *Metahistory: The Historical Imagination in the Nineteenth Century* (Baltimore, 1973), pp. 22–9.

5 See Virgil G. Hinshaw, Jr., "The Epistemological Relevance of Mannheim's Sociology of Knowledge," in Gunter W. Remmling (ed.), *Towards the Sociology of Knowledge* (London, 1973), pp. 229–44; Gregory Baum, *Truth Beyond Relativism: Karl Mannheim's Sociology of Knowledge* (Milwaukee, 1977); Maurice

Mandelbaum, *The Problem of Historical Knowledge* (New York, 1938), pp. 67–82.

6 Ernest K. Bramstedt, *Aristocracy and the Middle-Classes in Germany: Social Types in German Literature, 1830–1900* (Chicago, 1964), especially p. xxi.

7 See John Friedmann, *Retracking America: A Theory of Transactive Planning* (Garden City, N.Y., 1973), pp. 22–48; Ivor Morrish, "Die Soziologie der Erziehung," in Bernd Götz and Jochem Kaltschmid (eds.), *Erziehungswissenschaft und Soziologie* (Darmstadt, 1977), pp. 200–15.

8 Theodor Adorno, *Prisms*, trans. Samuel and Shierry Weber (London, 1967), pp. 35–49; Karl Popper, *The Poverty of Historicism* (New York, 1961), pp. 67–83; T. S. Eliot, *Notes towards the Definition of Culture* (New York, 1949), pp. 33–48.

9 See Lewis Coser, *Masters of Sociological Thought* (New York, 1971), pp. 429–63; Helmut Schoeck, *Die Soziologie und die Gesellschaften*, 2d ed. (Munich, 1964), pp. 317–24; H. Stuart Hughes, *Consciousness and Society* (New York, 1961), pp. 418–27.

10 See Simonds, *Karl Mannheim's Sociology of Knowledge* (Oxford, 1978), pp. 7–22. Simonds's book is a notable exception to the rule.

11 Edward Shils, "*Ideology and Utopia,* by Karl Mannheim," *Daedalus*, vol. 103 (1974), pp. 83–9.

12 *IUE*, pp. 52–3. Also see his letter in Kurt H. Wolff, "The Sociology of Knowledge and Sociological Theory," in Llewellyn Gross (ed.), *Symposium on Sociological Theory* (New York, 1959), pp. 571–72.

13 Even Mannheim's longer works, such as *Ideology and Utopia*, are collections of essays rather than unitary, systematic studies.

14 The best example is Robert Merton, "Karl Mannheim and the Sociology of Knowledge," in *Social Theory and Social Structure*, rev. ed. (Glencoe, Ill., 1962), pp. 489–508. Merton notes Mannheim's eclecticism and says that it should be treated but that it is not his intention to do so (pp. 491–2).

15 For the German period, see Arnhelm Neusüss, *Die Theorien des utopischen Bewusstseins und der "freischwebenden Intelligenz" in der Wissenssoziologie Karl Mannheims* (Marburg, 1966); for the English period, see Dieter Boris, *Krise und Planung; Die politische Soziologie im Spätwerk Karl Mannheims* (Stuttgart, 1971).

16 See, for example, Kurt Wolff's introductions to *FKM* and *W;* also see Irving M. Zeitlin, *Ideology and the Development of Sociological Theory* (Englewood Cliffs, N.J., 1968), pp. 281–319.

17 See, for example, John Heeren, "Karl Mannheim and the Intellectual Elite," *British Journal of Sociology*, vol. 22 (1971), pp. 1–15, which examines the changing concept of the intelligentsia throughout Mannheim's career.

18 The exception to the rule, although with a very different approach from mine, is David Kettler, Volker Meja, and Nico Stehr, *Karl Mannheim* (London and Chichester, 1984). Less successful is the work of Gunter Remmling, who simply combines the two above-described approaches in his *Wissenssoziologie und Gesellschaftsplanung; Das Werk Karl Mannheims* (Dortmund, 1968). A revised but not substantially improved version appeared in English as *The Sociology of Karl Mannheim* (London, 1975).

19 For a discussion of Mannheim's reaction to this reception, see the introduction of Kettler, Meja, and Stehr to *Konservatismus*. This work will appear while this study is in press. Also see their "Karl Mannheim and Conservatism: The Ancestry of Historical Thinking," *American Sociological Review* vol. 49 (1984), pp. 71–85.

20 *Verhandlungen des Sechsten Deutschen Soziologentages vom 17. bis 19. September 1928 in Zürich* (Tübingen, 1929), p. 123.

21 See, for example, Alexander von Schelting, *Max Webers Wissenschaftslehre* (Tübingen, 1934), pp. 65–177.

22 See, for example, Ernst Grünwald, *Das Problem der Soziologie des Wissens* (Vienna and Leipzig, 1934), pp. 184–218.

23 See, for example, Jean Floud, "Karl Mannheim," in A. V. Judges (ed.), *The Function of Teaching* (London, 1959), pp. 40–66.

24 "Problem of Sociology of Knowledge," *ESK*, p. 134. [*W*, p. 308.] Also see "Epistemology," *ESSP*, p. 31 [*W*, p. 188]; "*Weltanschauung*," *ESK*, p. 80 [*W*, p. 149]; "Cultural-sociological Knowledge," *ST*, p. 96 [*SD*, pp. 106–7]; "Klassification der Wissenschaften," *W*. p. 157.

25 These kinds of implied connections, i.e., general descriptions of the times preceding analyses of Mannheim's works, constitute the main additions to Remmling's English revision of his German edition.

26 *IUE*, p. 272. [*IUG*, p. 234.]

27 "The Function of the Refugee," *New English Weekly*, vol. 27, no. 1 (April 19, 1945), pp. 5–6.

28 Simmel, *The Sociology of Georg Simmel*, trans. and ed. Kurt H. Wolff (New York, 1967), pp. 407–8.

29 Ibid., p. 405.

30 See, for example, "Conservative Thought," *ESSP*, pp. 74–164. [*W*, pp. 408–508.]

31 "Problem of Sociology of Knowledge," *ESK*, p. 169. [*W*, p. 353.]

32 Here I disagree with Simonds, who feels that the sociology of knowledge is not predominantly a method of the history of ideas. Simonds, "Mannheim's Sociology of Knowledge as a Hermeneutic Method," *Cultural Hermeneutics*, vol. 3 (1975), p. 99.

1. The early sociocultural contexts

1 Most important is the work of David Kettler and Lee Congdon. See Kettler, *Marxismus und Kultur*, trans. Erich Weck and Tobias Rülcker (Neuwied and Berlin, 1967); Kettler, "Culture and Revolution: Lukács in the Hungarian Revolutions of 1918/19," *Telos*, no. 10 (1971), pp. 35–92; Kettler, "Sociology of Knowledge and Moral Philosophy," *Political Science Quarterly*, vol. 82 (1967), pp. 399–426; Congdon, "Beyond the 'Hungarian Wasteland,'" Ph.D. dissertation (DeKalb, Ill., 1973); Congdon, *The Young Lukács* (Chapel Hill, N.C., 1983); Congdon, "Karl Mannheim as Philosopher," *Journal of European Studies*, vol. 7 (1977), pp. 1–18; Eva Gábor, "Mannheim in Hungary and in Weimar Germany," *International Society for the Sociology of Knowledge Newsletter*, vol. 9 (1983), pp. 7–14; Coser, *Masters*, pp. 429–63.

2 William M. Johnston, *The Austrian Mind* (Berkeley and Los Angeles, 1972), p. 344.

3 Congdon, "'Hungarian Wasteland,'" pp. 5–10; Zoltán Horváth, *Die Jahrhundertwende in Ungarn*, trans. Geza Engl (Neuwied, 1966), pp. 39–40; Coser, *Masters*, p. 442; Johnston, *Austrian Mind*, pp. 337–8.

4 William O. McCagg, Jr., attributes this "feudalization" to the ennoblement of the new economic elite in Hungary. The Jewish nobility, with its enthusiasm for social climbing, seemed to set the tone for the Jewish middle classes. Three of the most important colleagues of Mannheim, Oscar Jászi, Anna Lesznai, and Georg Lukács, were the offspring of Jewish nobles. McCagg, *Jewish Nobles and Geniuses in Modern Hungary* (Boulder, Colo., 1972), pp. 16, 31–44, 98, 103.

5 Lukács was an example of this reaction. The son of a successful banking family, he rebelled against the crass materialism of the middle classes, which he associated with Magyar culture. Congdon, *Young Lukács*, pp. 3–6; McCagg, *Jewish Nobles*, p. 106.

6 Victor Zitta writes that Hungary did not have a viable philosophical tradition, and so Hungarian intellectuals turned to outside sources. Zitta, *Georg Lukács' Marxism: Alienation, Dialectics, Revolution* (The Hague, 1964), p. 23. This assertion echoes Lukács's own statement that Hungary lacked a philosophical culture. See Congdon, *Young Lukács*, p. 82.

7 Oscar Jászi, *Revolution and Counter-Revolution in Hungary*, trans. E. W. Dicks (London, 1924), p. 24; Jászi, quoted in Rudolf L. Tökés, *Béla Kun and the Hungarian Soviet Republic* (New York, 1967), p. 18.

8 Jászi, *Revolution*, p. 136.

9 Horváth, *Jahrhundertwende*, pp. 64, 133.

10 Coser, *Masters*, p. 442.

11 Jászi, *Revolution*, p. 36. Jászi also believed that the middle classes had to be informed about their false path in serving the traditional culture. McCagg, *Jewish Nobles*, p. 104.

12 Congdon, "'Hungarian Wasteland,'" pp. 81–4; Tökés, *Béla Kun*, pp. 17–19.

13 Quoted in Tökés, *Béla Kun*, p. 19.

14 Ibid., pp. 20–39; Congdon, "'Hungarian Wasteland,'" pp. 84–7; Coser, *Masters*, p. 443; Kettler, *Marxismus*, pp. 9–10.

15 This journal, whose aim was a literary revival, promoted a pro-western modernism. Like Jászi's journal, it was an important forum for the new counter culture; but unlike Jászi's publication, its interests were strictly literary, not social scientific. Whereas Jászi received inspiration from the Western positivists, the *Nyugat* group looked to artistic movements such as impressionism. See Congdon, "'Hungarian Wasteland,'" pp. 13, 21, 56; Andrew Arato and Paul Breines, *The Young Lukács and the Origins of Western Marxism* (New York, 1979), p. 11.

16 István Mészáros, *Lukács' Concept of Dialectic* (London, 1972), pp. 118–19; Congdon, *Young Lukács*, pp. 53–5.

17 Mészáros, *Lukács' Concept*, pp. 121–2. See Paul Honigsheim, "Der Max-Weber-Kreis in Heidelberg," *Kölner Vierteljahrshefte für Soziologie*, vol. 5 (1926), pp. 270–87; Arato and Breines, *Young Lukács*, pp. 50–1.

18 In 1911, Lukács founded a short-lived journal called *Szellem*, which is the Hungarian equivalent of the German term *"Geist"* (spirit). He also published articles, with the aristocratic "von" added to his name, in *Logos* and the *Archiv für Sozialwissenschaften und Sozialpolitik*, the two journals in which Simmel and Weber were publishing much of their material. In the introduction to the first two chapters of his sociology of the drama (orig. pub. in Hungarian, 1908; pub. in *Archiv*, vol. 38 (1914), pp. 303–4), he apologized for the emphasis on sociology and stated that he had moved away from that position.

19 Lukács, *Theory of the Novel*, trans. Anna Bostock (London, 1971), p. 21. A work important to him in this exegesis was Ferdinand Tönnies's *Gemeinschaft und Gesellschaft*, which, as we shall see, became a model for traditionalist German academic thought. See Congdon, *Young Lukács*, pp. 10–11.

20 Kettler, *Marxismus*, pp. 18–20; Congdon, " 'Hungarian Wasteland,' " pp. 163–4; Congdon, *Young Lukács*, pp. 118–19; Arnold Hauser and Lukács, "On Youth, Art and Philosophy; A 1969 Radio Meeting," *New Hungarian Quarterly*, vol. 16, no. 58 (1975), p. 98.

21 This is shown by the fact that Jászi's wife, Anna Lesznai, was one of the leading members of Lukács's group. Lukács continued to publish in both *Huszadik Század* and *Nyugat*.

22 "Letters to Lukács," p. 95.

23 Ferenc Tökei, "Lukács and Hungarian Culture," *New Hungarian Quarterly*, vol. 13, no. 47 (1972), p. 110. Also see Arato and Breines, *Young Lukács*, pp. 13–18; Congdon, *Young Lukács*, pp. 24–5.

24 Mannheim published two favorable pieces on Simmel in Jászi's journal. The first was a review of Simmel's book, *Der Krieg und die geistigen Entscheidungen;* the second was an obituary: *Huszadik Század*, vol. 36 (1917), pp. 416–18; vol. 38 (1918), pp. 194–6. See Congdon, *Young Lukács*, p. 121. In Hungary, Mannheim studied under the neo-Kantian philosophers Bernát Alexander and Béla Zalai. Gábor, "Mannheim in Hungary," pp. 7, 12–13.

25 Jászi reviewed the lecture favorably in *Huszadik Század*, vol. 37 (1918), p. 192. It was also reviewed by Julia Lang, who would become Mannheim's wife; *Athenaeum*, vol. 4 (1918), pp. 159–60.

26 Coser, *Masters*, p. 445; Kettler, *Marxismus*, pp. 44–8; Mészáros, *Lukács' Concept*, pp. 126–8.

27 Coser, *Masters*, p. 445.

28 Eva Gábor notes that for some reason the close relationship between Mannheim and Lukács had been disturbed in 1916; Introduction to "Letters to Lukács," p. 94.

29 Congdon reports that Mannheim lectured on the philosophy of culture; *Young Lukács*, p. 157. Also see W. A. C. Stewart, *Karl Mannheim on Education and Social Thought* (London, 1967), pp. 10–11.

30 Coser, *Masters*, p. 445; Jászi, *Revolution*, p. 20.

31 Before arriving in Germany, Mannheim spent some time in a refugee camp in Vienna, where he tried, without success, to reestablish ties with some of the members of the Budapest intelligentsia, including Lukács, who were also in Vienna. See Gábor, "Mannheim in Hungary," p. 8.

32 In two sets of "letters from exile," written in the early twenties, Mannheim established his role as a refugee. He told how his fate was connected to the failed Hungarian revolution and how he would never be able to build bridges to the Horthy regime. At the same time, he saw a gulf between his old Hungarian culture as it was manifested in cosmopolitan Budapest and the German culture that thrived in the more provincial university towns like Heidelberg. Nevertheless, he set as his task understanding and making ties with the German intellectuals. "Heidelbergi levél," *Tüz* (Nov.–Dec. 1921), pp. 46–50. "Heidelbergi levelek," *Tüz* (April–May 1922), pp. 91–5. "Levelek az emigrációból," *Diogenes*, no. 1 (1924), pp. 13–15; no. 2 (1924), pp. 20–3.

33 Mannheim's efforts were confined to intellectual matters within the university; the closest he ever came to joining an active political party was his membership in the Galileo Club in Hungary; even that membership has been disputed by Congdon. See Gábor, "Mannheim in Hungary," pp. 7, 12; Congdon, "Karl Mannheim," p. 2.

34 Although his mentor at Heidelberg, Alfred Weber, was certainly not a reactionary, his work was not basically at odds with the traditional outlook of the university system. His attempts to develop a "cultural sociology" definitely put more emphasis on culture than on sociology. See, for example, Weber, "Der soziologische Kulturbegriff," in *Ideen zur Staats- und Kultursoziologie* (Karlsruhe, 1927), especially p. 43. Even before he became a Marxist, Lukács criticized this article (which was first published in 1913) as too vague. "Zum Wesen und zur Methode der Kultursoziologie," *Archiv für Sozialwissenschaft und Sozialpolitik*, vol. 39 (1915), pp. 217–19.

35 Ralf Dahrendorf, *Society and Democracy in Germany* (Garden City, N.Y., 1969), p. 58.

36 Raymond Williams, following Antonio Gramsci, defines cultural hegemony as the interlocking of political, social, and cultural forces to ensure the dominance of a certain social class. This hegemony does not achieve its dominance merely through the strength of its symbols. Its patterns of meaning and values must be combined with successful practices to ensure its superiority. The cultural symbols, in turn, provide the practices, and the groups and institutions within which the latter occur, with legitimization, so that the relationship of all the elements is "reciprocally confirming." The hegemony contains a variety of ideas, traditions, institutions, and groups, which its defenders attempt to control, transform, neutralize, or even incorporate, with varying degrees of success. Because of the constant transformation taking place within the hegemony, the delineation of hegemonic from counterhegemonic elements is always tenuous. Williams divides these counterhegemonic elements into two types, "residual" and "emergent." Such elements contain experiences that resist incorporation into the dominant culture. The residual elements find their basis in some previous social or cultural institution or formation, whereas the emergent elements find their basis in a new class. Williams, *Marxism and Literature* (Oxford, 1977), pp. 110–27.

37 J. H. Clapham, *The Economic Development of France and Germany, 1815–1914* (Cambridge, 1966), p. 279.

38 Dahrendorf, *Society and Democracy*, pp. 49–51, 58–9, 100. This situation was somewhat similar to that in Hungary. In fact, McCagg based his model of the feudalization of the Jewish bourgeoisie on the descriptions of the German scene by historians such as Hans Rosenberg and Eckart Kehr. See McCagg, *Jewish Nobles*, p. 17. However, there was a difference. Despite the rapid growth of a modern economy in Budapest, Hungary as a whole remained a rural nation and its cultural hegemony traditional. In Germany, on the other hand, the process of industrialization and urbanization was much more widespread, so that the hegemony must be described as dualistic.

39 I have chosen to use the German term because neither of its elements is adequately rendered into English. "*Bildung*," which is usually translated as "education" or "cultivation," will be discussed shortly. "*Bürgertum*," which is usually translated as "bourgeoisie," does not have the Marxist class connotations of the French term. I also object to the term "petit bourgeoisie"; many members of this group, especially those we are most interested in, had an exalted status in society not shared by small artisans, shopkeepers, and white-collar workers, who are usually designated by this term. In short, the Marxist terminology underplays the role of traditionalist groups and mentalities in German society. For accounts of the *Bildungsbürgertum*, see Hansjoachim Henning, *Das westdeutsche Bürgertum in der Epoche der Hochindustrialisierung, 1860–1914* (Wiesbaden, 1972), especially pp. 483–91; Klaus Vondung, "Zur Lage der Gebildeten in der wilhelminische Zeit," in Vondung (ed.), *Das wilhelminische Bildungsbürgertum: Zur Sozialgeschichte seiner Ideen* (Göttingen, 1976), pp. 20–33.

40 Friedrich Paulsen, a member of the highest echelons of this group, made the following observation at the turn of the century: "The academically educated constitute a kind of intellectual and spiritual aristocracy in Germany. . . . Conversely, anyone in Germany who has no academic education lacks something which wealth and high birth cannot fully replace. The merchant, the banker, the rich manufacturer, or even the great landowner, no matter how well he stands in other respects, will occasionally be harmed by his lack of academic training. As a consequence, the acquisition of a university education has become a sort of social necessity with us, or at least the acquisition of the *Abitur* [upon graduation from the *Gymnasium*], the potential right of academic citizenship." Quoted in Fritz Ringer, *The Decline of the German Mandarins* (Cambridge, Mass., 1969), p. 35. Also see Leonore O'Boyle, "Klassische Bildung und soziale Struktur in Deutschland zwischen 1800 und 1848," *Historische Zeitschrift*, vol. 207 (1968), pp. 584–608.

41 Vondung, "Lage der Gebildeten," p. 27. Vondung includes in this group university professors, *Gymnasium* teachers, clergy, writers and artists, and journalists and editors.

42 See, for example, Fritz Stern, *The Politics of Cultural Despair* (Garden City, N.Y., 1965); Klemens von Klemperer, *Germany's New Conservatism* (Princeton, N.J., 1968).

43 Wolfgang Sauer, "Weimar Culture: Experiments in Modernism," *Social Research*, vol. 39 (1972), pp. 254–84. Also see Jenö Kurucz, *Struktur und Funktion der Intelligenz während der Weimarer Republik* (Köln, 1967).

44 See, for example, Istvan Deak's account of the *Weltbühne* circle in *Weimar Germany's Left-wing Intellectuals* (Berkeley and Los Angeles, 1968).

45 Ringer, *German Mandarins*, p. 116.

46 See my article, "German Historicism and Its Crisis," *Journal of Modern History*, vol. 48 (1976), on-demand supplement, pp. 85–119; Hajo Holborn, "German Idealism in Light of Social History," in *Germany and Europe* (Garden City, N.Y., 1971), pp. 1–31.

47 By "historicism," I mean the world view of the mainstream of German historical thought in the nineteenth and twentieth centuries, which has been described by Meinecke, Troeltsch, and, more recently, Georg Iggers. In addition to the monadic type, there was also a corporate type of historicism that saw the authoritarian state as the prime form of individuality. See my "German Historicism," pp. 95–6.

48 Troeltsch, *Der Historismus und seine Probleme*, vol. 3 of *Gesammelte Schriften* (Tübingen, 1922), p. 38.

49 This did not mean that the historicists shunned causal analyses, but simply that they qualified the latter's effectiveness. Causal analyses, they felt, could not penetrate all the way to the essence of an individuality and thus were subordinated to a more superficial level. See, for example, Eduard Spranger, "Allgemeine Kulturgeschichte und Methodenlehre: Eröffnungsbericht," *Archiv für Kulturgeschichte*, vol. 9 (1911), p. 366.

50 Helmut Schelsky, *Einsamkeit und Freiheit: Idee und Gestalt der deutschen Universität und ihrer Reformen*, 2d ed. (Düsseldorf, 1971), p. 64.

51 Friedrich Meinecke, *Schaffender Spiegel* (Stuttgart, 1948), p. 20.

52 Spranger, *Die deutsche Bildungsideal der Gegenwart in geschichtsphilosophischer Beleuchtung* (Leipzig, 1928), p. 3. "*Sinn*" was a very important concept that concerned what a person was and how the basis of his or her existence could be reflected upon in order to act and live. In other words, "meaning" was tied together with valuation. This information comes from a standard encyclopedia of the time, *Der Grosse Brockhaus*, vol. 17, p. 434.

53 Arnold Brecht, *The Political Education of Arnold Brecht* (Princton, N.J., 1970), p. 40. For a general account of this phenomenon, see Fritz Stern, "The Political Consequences of the Unpolitical German," in *History 3* (New York, 1960), pp. 104–34. For a specific example of the Protestant minister, see Karl Wilhelm Dahm, *Pfarrer und Politik* (Köln and Opladen, 1965), pp. 78–134.

54 In contrast to the corporate historicists, who saw the organic, spiritual unity embodied in the state, monadic thinkers were apt to substitute culture as the organic unity that stood "above" society.

55 Tönnies, *Community and Society*, trans. Charles P. Loomis (New York, 1963), p. 177.* [*Gemeinschaft und Gesellschaft* (Leipzig, 1887), p. 207.]

56 Tönnies formulated three basic types of *Gemeinschaft* – family, locality, and spirit. They represented a progression of increasing size and rationality at the expense of more intimate and emotional relationships. Ibid., pp. 43–62.

57 Ibid., p. 65.

58 Ibid., p. 169.* [Pp. 192–3.] I have replaced Tönnies's repetition of the word

"people" with *"Gemeinschaft,"* for this was exactly what he meant. See ibid., p. 225. [P. 280.]

59 René König makes this interpretation of Tönnies's work in "Die Begriffe Gemeinschaft und Gesellschaft bei Ferdinand Tönnies," *Kölner Zeitschrift für Soziologie und Sozialpsychologie,* vol. 7 (1955), p. 407. König realizes that this is not the only possible interpretation of the dualism, but feels that it was the one that dominated in Tönnies's book. I agree. For a good analysis of the changes the concepts underwent in the development of Tönnies's thought, see Arthur Mitzman, "Tönnies and German Society, 1887–1914," *Journal of the History of Ideas,* vol. 32 (1971), pp. 507–24.

60 Tönnies's book reached the height of its popularity during the Weimar period, when *"Gemeinschaft"* became a "magic word" among conservatives. Kurt Sontheimer, *Antidemokratisches Denken in der Weimarer Republik* (Munich, 1968), p. 251. Also see René König, "Zur Soziologie der zwanziger Jahre," in Leonard Reinisch (ed.), *Die Zeit ohne Eigenschaften* (Stuttgart, 1961), p. 68.

61 *Der Grosse Brockhaus,* 15th ed., vol. 17, p. 434; vol. 20, pp. 400–1.

62 See Georg von Below, "Zur Beurteilung Heinrich Leos," *Archiv für Kulturgeschichte,* vol. 9 (1911), p. 205; Below, *Deutsche Geschichtschreibung von den Befreiungskriegen bis zu unseren Tagen* (Leipzig, 1916), p. 66.

63 The basic difference was between members of the Baden School (Windelband, Rickert) and Wilhelm Dilthey. The former believed the division was determined by the method employed, the latter by the objects studied. See Windelband, "Geschichte und Naturwissenschaft," in *Präludien* (Tübingen, 1924), vol. 2, pp. 136–60; Heinrich Rickert, *Science and History,* ed. Arthur Goddard, trans. George Reisman (Princeton, N.J., 1962); Wilhelm Dilthey, *Einleitung in die Geisteswissenschaften,* vol. 1 of *Gesammelte Schriften* (Stuttgart, 1966). For a good summary, see Georg G. Iggers, *The German Conception of History* (Middletown, Conn., 1968), ch. 6.

64 See Troeltsch, *Historismus,* pp. 45–50. These academics did not deny that the human sciences had a rational, systematic element, but rather that this element could be taken from the natural sciences. See Erich Rothacker, *Logik und Systematik der Geisteswissenschaften* (Darmstadt, 1970), pp. 16–36.

65 Windelband, *Präludien,* vol. 2, p. 156.

66 Ringer, *German Mandarins,* p. 298.

67 Of course, the material had to be selectively chosen. For example, Hendrik de Man, a moderate and at one time a dedicated Marxist, offered the following analysis of Marxism in his popular book, *The Psychology of Socialism,* trans. Eden and Cedar Paul (London, 1928), pp. 340, 338, 346, 348: "Why does the dialectical causality which Marxism establishes between its categories do violence to historical reality? The answer is that Marxism assumes the existence of a kind of causal determinism which corresponds to *mechanism* and not to *will.* . . . The mechanical reaction consists of phenomena which can be weighed and measured. The aim of exact science is to abstract from the phenomena of matter and motion that are measurable in space and time.

"For the Marxists, the social revolution . . . very closely resembles the movement of mechanical forces such as results from the collision of two bodies moving in opposite directions. . . . The victory [of the proletariat] is not a gradual transition, but . . . a gradual increase in the tension of the [economic] forces, until a sudden disturbance of equilibrium [the crises of capitalism] pushes one of the two bodies [the bourgeoisie] back."

De Man's popular description of the mechanistic nature of Marxism can be supported by a selective reading of the leading theorist of Marxist orthodoxy in Germany at that time, Karl Kautsky. Kautsky assumed that society could be analyzed in much the same way as nature was analyzed, because like nature society operated according to universal laws of causation. He compared social laws to natural laws, such as the laws of falling bodies. See Kautsky, *The Social Revolution*, trans. A. M. and May Wood Simons (Chicago, 1916), p. 106. For a discussion of the problems that mechanistic thought raised within the ranks of the Marxists, see ch. 1 of David Joravsky, *Soviet Marxism and Natural Science, 1917–1932* (London, 1961). I am in no way claiming to present a balanced portrayal of radical thought at this time, but rather the stereotype of Marxism held by most conservatives, many moderates, and some Marxists.

68 The term is Carl Brinkmann's. See Brinkmann, *Versuch einer Gesellschaftswissenschaft* (Munich and Leipzig, 1919), pp. 15–21. Mannheim also made this point in "Problems of Sociology in Germany," *FKM*, p. 262 [*W*, p. 614], and in "Problem of Sociology of Knowledge," *ESK*, p. 139. [*W*, p. 314.]

69 The most outspoken critic of sociology, the historian Georg von Below, argued that it was really nothing more than a method, a way of looking at human relationships, which had always been incorporated into the established disciplines along with other methods. Because the method had already found a place within traditional disciplines, where it was properly subordinated to a more organic perspective, there was no need to create a new discipline to accommodate it. In fact, said Below, admitting sociology into the university as an autonomous discipline would be to allow the divisive social forces into the university without the necessary check by the established traditional disciplines. Below, *Soziologie als Lehrfach* (Munich and Leipzig, 1920), p. 55. Below represented the extreme and not the mean. However, although not all traditionalists demanded a total ban of sociology from the university, almost all believed that the discipline should not play a dominant role in the institutions of learning.

70 Werner Sombart, *Händler und Helden* (Munich, 1915), p. 85.

71 Theodor Geiger, *Die soziale Schichtung des deutschen Volkes* (Darmstadt, 1967), pp. 84–100.

72 Undoubtedly the severest blow to the republic was the inflation of 1923, which was especially devastating to groups in the middle ranks. Alfred Weber pointed out that in 1913 higher officials earned 7 times what unskilled workers earned, but that in 1923 the amount was reduced to 1.8 times as much. This meant that higher officials had to reduce their standard of living in relation to that of the worker by almost 75%. Weber, *Die Not der geistigen Arbeiter* (Munich and Leipzig, 1923), pp. 42, 45. For a group as status conscious as the *Bildungs-*

bürgertum, this was a severe blow, not only to their economic welfare but also to their social status.

73 Below showed himself to be a good example of this type in his autobiographical sketch in Sigfrid Steinberg (ed.), *Die Geschichtswissenschaft der Gegenwart in Selbstdarstellungen* (Leipzig, 1925–6), vol. 1, pp. 1–48. For an account of two more academics who fit this type, see Hans-Heinz Krill, *Die Rankerenaissance: Max Lenz und Erich Marcks* (Berlin, 1962).

74 See, for example, Alfred Weber, "Die Bedeutung der geistigen Führer in Deutschland," in A. Weber, *Ideen*, pp. 102–21.

75 Quoted in Ringer, *German Mandarins*, p. 212.

76 I have dealt with this type at greater length in "German Historicism." Also see ch. 1 of Kurt Lenk, *Marx in der Wissenssoziologie* (Neuwied, 1972).

77 Weber wrote: " 'Scientific' pleading is meaningless in principle because the various value spheres of the world stand in irreconcilable conflict with each other." Weber, "Science as a Vocation," in *From Max Weber*, ed. and trans. H. H. Gerth and C. Wright Mills (New York, 1958), p. 147.

78 Max Weber, *Economy and Society*, ed. Guenther Roth and Claus Wittich, trans. Ephraim Fischoff et al. (Berkeley and Los Angeles, 1978), p. 1398.

79 Max Weber, "Politics as a Vocation," in *From Max Weber*, p. 128.

80 Mannheim noted that, while Heidelberg had not fallen into the "whirlpool" of conservatism, the influence of the petit bourgeoisie presented a danger to the university. "Heidelbergi levél," p. 49.

2. The cultural–philosophical synthesis (1910–1924)

1 "Letters to Lukács," p. 95.

2 The relationship between Mannheim and Weber was not as intense as that with Lukács had been. Mannheim could never be considered Weber's "disciple." In a 1938 letter to Weber, on the occasion of the latter's seventieth birthday, Mannheim wrote of his appreciation for Weber's guidance. He especially praised Weber's refusal to use his authority to suppress the originality of his students. The result, he wrote, was spiritually independent students who felt no need to form a sectlike "school." Letter to Alfred Weber, July 25, 1938 (in the Deutsche Bundesarchiv, Koblenz). Mannheim actually had a closer relationship to Emil Lederer, whose wife was Hungarian and who was very instrumental in easing Mannheim's way into the Heidelberg academic community. Nevertheless, Mannheim developed his theory of the sociology of culture in the context of Weber's seminar. The basic questions he asked in the early German years were those of Weber, even if the answers were not the same.

3 A. Weber, "Soziologische Kulturbegriff," pp. 41–2.

4 "Letters to Lukács," p. 96.

5 Lukács expressed similar concerns in *Soul and Form*, trans. Anna Bostock (Cambridge, Mass., 1974), pp. 7–8. Mannheim had read this book in its German edition. "Letters to Lukács," p. 100.

6 Seeing "connections" rather than "causes" played a very important role in Mannheim's German analytic writings, especially in his expositions of the sociology of knowledge. The German term he would use was *"verbunden,"* about which I will have more to say in Chapters 3 and 4.

7 "Letters to Lukács," pp. 97–8.

8 Ibid.

9 In addition to the letters to Lukács, this chapter is based on five major works: the Free School lecture, "Epistemology," *"Weltanschauung,"* "Cultural-Sociological Knowledge," and "Historicism," and a number of minor articles. Because many themes were continued or modified only slightly, the references are not strictly chronological, but rather "hierarchical." The most prblematical work chronologically is "Epistemology," which was first published in a shorter form (chs. 1–5 of section 2 of the current German and English versions) in 1918. The early version, which was his dissertation at the University of Budapest, was published as "Az ismeretelmélet szerkezeti elemzése," *Athenaeum*, vol. 4 (1918), pp. 233–47, 315–30. The later version appeared in 1922, after *"Weltanschauung,"*

10 This chronology, which places the turning point in Mannheim's career after, instead of before, "Historicism," conflicts with most other interpretations of his work. See, for example, the introductions of Kurt H. Wolff and Paul Kecskemeti to *FKM*, pp. xxviii–xxx, and *ESK*, pp. 13–14, respectively, and Simonds, *Mannheim's Sociology*, p. 84. This chronology also calls into question the role of Lukács in the development of Mannheim's thought, as we shall see in Chapters 3 and 4.

11 Although this discussion was central to the Free School lecture, the first section of "Cultural-Sociological Knowledge" elaborated considerably on the earlier schema.

12 Mannheim did not attempt to locate this original stage (designated by the prefix *"ur"*) precisely in history. At one point he did associate it with the Middle Ages. "Cultural-Sociological Knowledge," *ST*, p. 39. [*SD*, p. 41.]

13 Mannheim distinguished here between *"Gemeinschaftskultur"* and *"Gesellschaftskultur"* and cited Tönnies. Ibid., p. 44. [P. 47.]

14 This unity is illustrated by the fact that he referred to this naive state as both "existential culture" (Ibid., p. 45* [p. 48]) and as "religious culture" (Ibid., p. 49 [p. 52]; "Seele und Kultur," *W*. p. 76).

15 "Cultural-Sociological Knowledge," *ST*, p. 39.* [*SD*, p. 41.]

16 "Seele und Kultur," *W*, p. 69.

17 Ibid. This inappropriateness of mysticism was a theme continued in *Ideology and Utopia*, but with different ramifications.

18 Mannheim used the term *Bildungserlebnis* to describe this relationship. "Cultural-Sociological Knowledge," *ST*, p. 44. [*SD*, p. 47.]

19 "Seele und Kultur," *W*, pp. 70–4. In "Cultural-Sociological Knowledge," he termed this objective existence the "result" (*Resultat*), which could be distinguished from the "meaning" that accompanied it (p. 68 [p. 74]).

20 "Seele und Kultur," *W*, p. 76.

21 *"Weltanschauung,"* *ESK*, p. 34.* [*W*, pp. 92–3.]

22 "Cultural-Sociological Knowledge," *ST*, pp. 85, 59. [*SD*, pp. 94, 63.]
23 Also see his review of Ernst Cassirer's *Freiheit und Form: Studien zur deutschen Geistesgeschichte* in *Athenaeum*. vol. 3 (1917), pp. 409–13, where he asked if interpretations of culture could do justice to two facets – the plurality of cultural objectifications and temporal diversity. This ambivalence toward pluralism continued in his early German writings.
24 "Seele und Kultur," *W*, pp. 68, 75, 77, 83–4.
25 "Die Dame aus Biarritz" (1920).
26 Ibid., p. 25.
27 "Heidelbergi levél"; "Heidelbergi levelek."
28 Mannheim believed that such a decentralized position served to protect German culture. The centralization of the Budapest intelligentsia had allowed the new regime to easily dissolve Hungarian culture by removing that single group. On the other hand, there were dangers in this decentralization, mainly the influence of the provincial petit bourgeoisie.
29 See Gábor, "Mannheim in Hungary," p. 12.
30 Not long before leaving Budapest, he had made a similar, although not as negative, criticism of Ernst Bloch's radical mysticism. Whereas the mystic conducted a restless search for God and himself or herself, he wrote, the philosophical specialist made due with the questions of the cognition of the world and its objects. Mysticism, therefore, was the conscience of philosophy, because it was a reminder of ultimate queries. Bloch, however, represented a decadent type of mysticism that simply put aesthetic substitutes in the place of logical categories. One found "magic force" mixed with empty and aimless cleverness. Although Bloch's work hinted at the road to a new metaphysics, it did not mean its arrival. Review of Bloch's *Geist der Utopie* in *Athenaeum*, vol. 4 (1918), pp. 207–11. Mannheim demonstrated more sympathy for the world rejection of Bloch in 1919 than for that of George in 1922. One obvious reason was that the former was forward looking and the latter backward looking. Also, in the earlier essay, Mannheim demonstrated a greater willingness to admit the viability of this anticonceptual approach in the modern world, while noting that it was the way of the very few.
31 He contrasted George here with the hero of the Budapest intellectuals, Endre Ady, who turned his charisma toward significant cultural change. For a discussion of Ady, see Congdon, "'Hungarian Wasteland,'" ch. 1.
32 As one can note from my introduction, presenting Max Weber as the symbol of the university gave a skewed view of that institution, whose mainstream still demonstrated a hosility toward sociology.
33 "Wissenschaft und Jugend," *Frankfurter Zeitung*, evening ed., higher education section (Nov. 30, 1922).
34 Mannheim provided individual examples. One student had been a journalist for a political party in a large city. At first, he resisted the contemplative life of the provincial university; however, after a year, he came to reject his prior political activities, which his studies had "unmasked." A second student, who belonged to a metaphysical-religious community, lived according to a totally philosophical orientation. After studying philosophy at the university for

two semesters, his spiritual intensity was weakened, and an essence-seeking unrest gave way to self-estrangement, perplexity, and indifference. A third student preferred to major in the history of art rather than in the history of literature, where he was more knowledgeable. When asked why, he replied that he did not want to spoil his enjoyment of literature.

35 Mannheim described maturation (which the university was to aid) as a process of "displacement" (*Verschiebung*) in which essential things came to be seen in a different perspective. This concept also appeared in "cultural-Sociological Knowledge," where it was attributed to the discipline of cultural sociology.

36 "Lukács' *Theory of the Novel*," *FKM*, pp. 3–7. [*W*, pp. 85–90.] This review of Lukács's book was very appropriate in view of Mannheim's position in Heidelberg. Gábor writes that his access to intellectual circles there was eased by his earlier connection with Lukács, who had made a strong impression during his time there. "Mannheim in Hungary," p. 9. Mannheim reinforced this connection by giving a year-long siminar of Lukács. This review would appear to do the same thing. It also served to underline that his connections had been with the precommunist Lukács, the one known by the Heidelberg intellectuals. The review appears to have had an earlier Hungarian version; see "Letters to Lukács," pp. 103, 105.

37 "Cultural-Sociological Knowledge," *ST*, pp. 45–6. [*SD*, pp. 48–9.]

38 "Epistemology," *ESSP*, p. 21. [*W*, p. 174.] In the Free School lecture, Mannheim saw impressionism as the height of isolated art; *W*, p. 76.

39 This term comes from "Cultural-Sociological Knowledge" and was missing in those works that preceded it.

40 "Epistemology," *ESSP*, p. 39 [*W*, p. 199]; "Weltanschauung," *ESK*, p. 39 [*W*, pp. 98–9]; "Cultural-Sociological Knowledge," *ST*, p. 90. [*SD*, p. 100.] Mannheim formulated this problem in different ways, e.g., the relationship of historicity to timeless validity and that of theory to the atheoretical; however, it was essentially the same issue, of *Sinn* and *Sein*, that was later central to the sociology of knowledge. See, for example, "Ideological and Sociological Interpretation," *FKM*, pp. 124–5. [*W*, pp. 398–400.] Also see Neusüss, *Utopischen Bewusstseins*, pp. 53–8.

41 "Cultural-Sociological Knowledge," *ST*, p. 57. [*SD*, p. 61.]

42 Ibid., pp. 55–7, 65–7. [Pp. 59–61, 70–2.]

43 "Lukács' *Theory of the Novel*," *FKM*, pp. 4–5. [*W*, p. 87.]

44 This schema comes from "Cultural-Sociological Knowledge," *ST*, pp. 77–80. [*SD*, pp. 85–8.] In 1926, this section was finally published in somewhat modified form as part of "Ideological and Sociological Interpretation," *FKM*, pp. 126–31. [*W*, pp. 400–7.] In this discussion, I will refer to both places.

45 Mannheim defined functionalization as "the uncovering of all existentially conditioned contexts that first make possible the emergence and establishment of a spiritual product." "Ideological and Sociological Interpretation," *FKM*, p. 121.* [*W*, p. 395.] Also see "Cultural-Sociological Knowledge," *ST*, pp. 65–7, 83. [*SD*, pp. 70–2, 91.] In the earlier work, he also connected the concepts of "functionality" and "ideology."

46 Mannheim gave three examples of systematic interpretations: (1) those that examined a work solely in terms of what the author was presumed to have intended, (2) those that started from the author's premises and drew conclusions from them ("to understand Kant better than he understood himself"), (3) those that interpreted a work solely in terms of another system (e.g., the interpretation of Plato on the basis of a modern philosophical system). "Ideological and Sociological Interpretation," *FKM*, pp. 126–8 [*W*, pp 400–1]; "Cultural-Sociological Knowledge," *ST*, pp. 77–8 [*SD*, p. 85].

47 "Cultural-Sociological Knowledge," *ST*, p. 49. [*SD*, pp. 52–3.]

48 Explanations were basic to the natural sciences and to those positivistic sciences based on the latter. See *"Weltanschauung," ESK*, pp. 80–1. [*W*, pp. 150–1.]

49 "Epistemology," *ESSP*, p. 24. [*W*, p. 179.] Here we must heed Paul Kecskemeti's note on Mannheim's use of the term "logic." Mannheim "follows the usage of the neo-Kantian school in defining logic: logic is the science which deals with concepts, judgements, and systems, and, above all, with their 'validity' or logical worth. This 'logic,' of course, has nothing to do with rigorous formal logic as it is understood by present-day logicians. . . . To him, the central problem of logic was, and remained, 'validity' rather than consistency." Introduction to *ESK*, pp. 9–10.

50 "Epistemology," *ESSP*, p. 25.* [*W*, p. 180.]

51 Ibid., pp. 37–39.* [Pp. 196–9.] Mannheim wrote: "The historical explanation of a meaningful product is a possible and necessary task, but all too often the mistake is made of trying to explain the meaning itself from the temporal determination of the product, from the empirical, real factors. If we seek to validate or invalidate meanings through such factors, we shall inescapably fall into relativism. The temporal as such contains only the possibilities for the actualization of the meanings, but not the meanings themselves; they can only be represented by means of structural analysis." Ibid., p. 37.* [Pp. 196–7.]

52 In "Klassifikation der Wissenschaften," also published in 1922, Mannheim wrote that the methodologically most adequate approach for viewing the essence of a science's theoretical achievement was through its systematization. He criticized Erich Becher for ignoring this approach. *W*, p. 158.

53 "Epistemology," *ESSP*, pp. 42, 47–8, 56–60. [*W*, pp. 203, 210–12, 222–7.]

54 Mannheim wrote: "All other sciences reply to the question: what is this? by fitting the designated element into a context, into an 'order,' without bothering to make a special study of the context as a whole. In contrast, epistemology would determine the nature and value of its object, i.e. knowledge, by looking into the contexts that are presupposed in every cognition without being discussed." Ibid., p. 44.* [P. 205.]

55 Ibid., p. 45. [P. 207.]

56 Ibid., pp. 54, 58. [Pp. 219–20, 225.]

57 Ibid., p. 72, [P. 244.]

58 In a 1916 review of Arthur Liebert's *Das Problem der Geltung*, Mannheim noted that Liebert postulated two basic types of validity – the psychological

and the logical. Mannheim then discussed the independence of these from one another. *Athenaeum*, vol. 2 (1916), pp. 489–93. By the time he first published his dissertation (1918), he had extended these categories to the entire realm of epistemology and had added the more inclusive category of ontology.

59 "Epistemology," *ESSP*, p. 48.* [Pp. 211–12.] The following diagram by Mannheim showed the possibilities of the epistemological systematization:

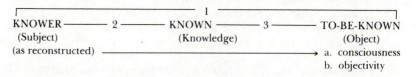

Both the psychological and the logical epistemologies placed the emphasis on relationship number 3 above, between the object and knowledge, and then proceeded to relationships numbers 1 and 2. By emphasizing the third relationship, they were "objective systems," i.e., they "de-subjectivize the actual experiences and produce neutral 'meanings' (*Bedeutungen*)." Even in psychology, which seemed to be dealing with concrete subjects, experience was "desubjectivized and transformed into an objective 'phenomenon' through the intervention of general categories of thought." The subject was then reconstructed as a universal concept as "consciousness" by psychology and as "objectivity" by logic (p. 56.) [P. 222.] Ontology, on the other hand, took relationship number 1, between subject and object, as its starting point. Mannheim wrote: "It is tacitly taken for granted, even before the epistemological problem is raised, that this connection is ontological. Even before the problem of epistemology is raised, we know, implicitly or explicitly, that the knowing subject as well as the object to be known are of the same 'stuff of Being.'. . . Since on this showing the ontological relation must be taken as unproblematical, the only question to be dealt with is how the relation between the knower and the known (2), and that of the known and the to-be-known (3) are to be conceived" (pp. 59–60.) [P. 227.] The ontological epistemology was clearly favored by Mannheim, because its primary interest was the connection of the subject and the object, the problem he saw as crucial in the Free School lecture. However, he admitted that the ontological system could not conquer the other two systems.

60 Ibid., pp. 72, 47, 63–4. [Pp. 244, 209–10, 232–3.]
61 Ibid., p. 71.* [Pp. 242–3.]
62 *"Weltanschauung,"* ESK, p. 46. [W, p. 107.] Mannheim wrote that objective meaning was also possible for the naive perceiving subject in a field like art, where such meaning involved that which was "purely visible."
63 Ibid., pp. 46–7. [P. 107.]
64 As an example, Mannheim postulated an encounter with a beggar: "If I tell the beggar 'I am sorry for you,' or if I give him a coin as a 'sign' of my sympathy, with a gesture that is purely superfluous and in no way claims any

particular attention, then I do not, properly speaking, express feeling – I merely name it or refer to it. But when the gesture shows that my soul has been moved, then the contents of my soul find real expression through the 'formation' of the gesture." Ibid., p. 52.* [P. 115.] Note that expressive meaning was not simply an irrational, emotive state, but could be communicated. Objective meaning, rather than being absent, was taken to a "deeper" level beyond the object itself.

65 Ibid., pp. 53–6. [Pp. 116–19.]

66 Mannheim wrote that cultural investigators who did not accept the limitations of the theoretical would have "the feeling that through this approach we are going much deeper into the essential, unintentional spontaneous unity, than when we rely on a purely theoretical consciousness, which can at best grasp the content in refracted form." Ibid., p. 39.* [P. 98.]

67 Ibid., pp. 38–9. [Pp. 98–9.] Mannheim did not use the terms "nonrational" and "irrational," but rather spoke of two forms of irrationality.

68 Ibid., pp. 41–2.* [Pp. 101–2.]

69 Regarding the example of the beggar, Mannheim wrote: "Analyzing all the implications of what I see, I may suddenly discover that the 'act of charity' was, in fact, one of hypocrisy. And then it can no longer matter to me in the slightest what the friend has objectively done, nor yet what he 'wanted' or 'meant' to express by his action – all that concerns me is what is documented about him, albeit unintentionally, by that act of his." Ibid., p. 47. [P. 108.] Documentary interpretation, then, can be seen as a kind of unpolitical unmasking.

70 The collective subject would appear to be a spiritual entity defined by its world view. It is hard to say where one ends and the other begins.

71 *"Weltanschauung," ESK,* pp. 58–60. [*W,* pp. 123–5.] Mannheim gave as examples of deeper unity, Sombart's "economic ethos," Dilthey's *"Weltanschauung,"* Max Weber's "spirit," and most importantly, Riegl's "art aspiration" *(Kunstwollen).* Mannheim would continue to use the term *"Wollen"* (aspiration, will) in his sociology of knowledge and political science; however, it would be defined differently.

72 Mannheim wrote: "Expressive meaning has to do with a cross-section of the individual's stream of lived experience, in order to gain an insight into the process of consciousness taking place; documentary meaning, on the other hand, is a matter, not of the actualization of the psychic life that takes place over time, but of the *Gestalt,* the character, the substantial essence of the creative subject that only appears in the work." Ibid., p. 55.* [P. 119.] He saw something along the lines of Dilthey's "human-scientific psychology" as the discipline that would be able to mediate these two elements. Ibid., p. 60. [P. 125.]

73 For example, Mannheim wrote, rather than an entire artwork one could take a characteristic treatment of line or color composition as a document. Ibid., p. 56. [P. 120.]

74 Ibid., p. 57.* [P. 121.]

75 Ibid., p. 81. [P. 151.]

76 In "Epistemology," he noted that the ontological approach, which he favored, used an indirect method as opposed to the direct methods of the logical and psychological epistemologies. *ESSP*, p. 49. [*W*, pp. 212–13.] And in "Lukács' *Theory of the Novel*," he wrote that the conceptualization of spirit could never be directly documented and that one of Lukács's important qualities was his capacity for indirect interpretation. *FKM*, pp. 6–7. [*W*, pp. 89–90.]

77 "*Weltanschauung*," *ESK*, pp. 36–7. [*W*, pp. 94–5.]

78 Ibid., p. 61.* [*P*. 126.]

79 Ibid., p. 74.* [*P*. 142.]

80 "Klassifikation der Wissenschaften," *W*. pp. 155–65. This essay, written in 1922, presented one qualification after another.

81 Ibid., p. 165.

82 "*Weltanschauung*," *ESK*, p. 61.* [*W*, p. 126.]

83 Mannheim wrote that the individual, once his attitudes were shaped by a collective context of lived experience, could have only "relatively" new experiences. When an individual left a group and experienced new forms of external existence (*Dasein*), he or she did so to a great extent "typically," i.e., as a continuation of those situations, constellations, perspectives, and attitudes that were characteristic of the common experience he or she was leaving. Mannheim saw this as an often unconscious process on the part of the individual, who did not distinguish between his or her experiences as a unique individual and his or her experiences as a member of a group.

84 "Cultural-Sociological Knowledge," *ST*, pp. 70–4. [*SD*, pp. 77–81.]

85 Ibid., pp. 50, 65, 77, 91–2, 97. [Pp. 54, 70, 84, 102, 108.]

86 In "*Weltanschauung*," Mannheim wrote: "The cultural object [as an objec-tification of the world view] is always a meaningful product (*Sinnge-bilde*) . . . and does not reside in either the spatio-temporal world (which at most aids in its realization) or in the psychic acts of the individuals who created or experienced it (these acts being at most necessary for the actualiza-tion of the meanings)." *ESK*, p. 44.* [*W*, p. 105.]

87 In this manuscript, the relationship between the world view and the context of lived experience is unclear. Mannheim wrote: "The factor which [is insert-ed] between these two extreme poles [the spiritual and the social] is the 'world view.' The world view (of an era, a group, etc.) is a structurally connected set of contexts of lived experience, which at the same time forms the common basis of the experience of life and the penetration of life for a multiplicity of individuals. The world view is, then, neither the totality of spiritual products present in an age, nor the sum of the individuals then present, but the totality of those sets of structural contexts of lived experience which can be deter-mined as much from the side of the products as from the side of the social group formations. . . . The world view, then, is by no means a quantity which can be known in itself and on its own, but rather something which can only be formulated in particular cross-sections, so to speak, referring to particular problems. . . . What distinguishes the world view (as a 'system' of mutually coherent lived experiences), however, is that it can be comprehended from

any variety of the most diverse spheres of objectification and from the problems connected with these spheres." "Cultural-Sociological Knowledge," *ST*, pp. 91–2.* [*SD*, pp. 101–2.] It appears, then, that the world view was that element of the context of lived experience that could be conceptualized. I will treat them as if they were synonymous.

88 Ibid., pp. 53–6. [Pp. 58–60.] At one point, Mannheim described the context as having "communal consciousness" and "communal lived experience" and being a "communal stream" (pp. 71–2* [p. 78]), which indicated the organic nature of the entity.

89 Ibid., pp. 66, 68, 77–8, 84. [Pp. 71, 74, 85, 93.]

90 Ibid., p. 57. [P. 61.] It should be remembered that the methodological typology I described earlier in this chapter came from this manuscript.

91 Ibid., pp. 47, 56, 89. [Pp. 51, 61, 98.]

92 Ibid., p. 90. [P. 100.]

93 Ibid., pp. 94–6. [Pp. 105–7.]

94 Ibid., pp. 48–9, 81, 84. [Pp. 52–3, 89, 93.]

95 Actually, Mannheim believed that cultural sociology formed a bridge not between the two extremes but between more moderate intrinsic and extrinsic disciplines, the philosophy of history and nonpositivistic sociology. In contrast to "Epistemology," where the classical philosopher discussed was Kant, here it was Hegel. Also, he wrote that cultural sociology was not possible until a concept of society was developed that was autonomous from the economic concepts of Marxism. He cited Simmel and Max Weber as leaders of this development. Ibid., p. 48. [Pp. 51–2.]

96 Ibid., pp. 63–4, 81, 88–90. [Pp. 68–9, 89, 99–100.] Mannheim used the example of law. In the original, lived experience of law (the naive organic stage), the element of validity was fulfilled but not known, grasped but not considered. Distance allowed for consideration. Philosophy and jurisprudence conducted this consideration immanently, in a theoretical manner abstracted from the experiential realm. Thus, the juristic position asked: What can be valued as ideal law? It sought normative meaning that could be determined in a logically correct way. The sociological position tried to place the concept of law into a context of lived experience. It asked: What occurs within a *"Gemeinschaft"* so that the chance exists that members see a certain order as valid and orient their conduct toward it? It demonstrated the functionality of law in the pretheoretical totality and, in so doing, added a perspective lost in the juristic abstraction. The naive original view was an immanent, existential "grasping" (*Erfassung*); the juristic view was an immanent, theoretical "consideration" (*Betrachtung*); the cultural-sociological view was an extrinsic consideration. Pp. 60–1, 64. [Pp. 64–6, 68–9.]

97 Ibid., pp. 81–4. [Pp. 89–93.] This limitation of cultural sociology had been suggested earlier in "Lukács' *Theory of the Novel*," *FKM*, pp. 4–5. [*W*, pp. 86–7.] Also see "Klassifikation der Wissenschaften," *W*, p. 160.

98 "Cultural-Sociological Knowledge," *ST*, pp. 101–10. [*SD*, pp. 114–25.] Mannheim listed Tönnies and Simmel as the outstanding practitioners of pure sociology. Unlike Tönnies, Simmel sought not large-scale forms, but

molecular ones, which he realized could not be combined into larger forms. But then, asked Mannheim, how did one arrive at the necessary larger forms? If this problem were not solved, the molecular elements might be subsumed under other nonsociological forms, or one might succumb to the belief that they could be combined in an inductive fashion. Pp. 103–5. [Pp. 117–19.]

99 Ibid., pp. 120–2. [Pp. 136–8.] Among the principal questions asked by pure cultural sociology were: "How is it possible that the individual human consciousness gives rise to products out of itself which do not by any means remain shut up within the monadic closedness of the individual consciousness, but become the common property of a *Gemeinschaft,* the individual members of which join into a union among themselves and with the generations that go before and after? . . . What sorts of act of consciousness posit culture as a social phenomenon? Are there spheres within fully human consciousness which are inaccessible to culture (as, for example, pure sensuousness)?" Pp. 120–1.* [Pp. 136–7.]

100 Ibid., p. 122. [P. 138.]

101 Ibid., pp. 111–13. [Pp. 125–8.]

102 Ibid., pp. 122–3. [Pp. 138–40.] Just as Mannheim saw Max Weber's *Economy and Society* as an example of general sociology, he saw Weber's "The Social Psychology of World Religions" as a prime example of general cultural sociology. That essay sought to show what generalizing contexts belonged to world religions as objective products. Pp. 112, 123. [Pp. 127, 139–40.]

103 Mannheim saw a circular relationship in which the dynamic type was taken from the individual products and was then used to interpret those products. Dynamic sociology's types, then, were empirical. Ibid., pp. 116–17. [Pp. 132–3.]

104 Ibid., p. 116. [P. 132.] Mannheim listed Comte and Marx as creators of incomplete dynamic sociologies. Pp. 115, 118. [Pp. 131, 134.]

105 Ibid., pp. 113–18. [Pp. 128–34.]

106 Ibid., pp. 123–9. [Pp. 140–6.]

107 Mannheim wrote that the totalities had an antithetic relationship to one another, but not in the logical, Hegelian sense. Rather, they represented competing "aspirations." Here, as in *"Weltanschauung,"* he cited Riegl's concept of *"Kunstwollen."* Ibid., p. 127. [P. 144.]

108 *"Weltanschauung," ESK,* p. 62. [*W,* p. 128.]

109 "Cultural-Sociological Knowledge," *ST,* p. 128.* [*SD,* p. 145.]

110 Ibid., p. 129. [P. 147.] Mannheim wrote that such a conception of time saw a certain spiritual direction as representative for each epoch.

111 Ibid., pp. 129–30. [Pp. 147–8.]

112 This subordinate role for cultural sociology can be seen in a passage near the end of the manuscript: "Poorer in metaphysics, more richly provided with differentiations and structural insights, the dynamic [cultural] sociology assumes the legacy of the philosophy of history. It is an attempt to illuminate once again an existence already ordered according to historical causality from a more sweeping perspective and to complement the purely causal

historical inquiry with an investigation of the presuppositions upon which the effectiveness of causes depends." Ibid., p. 129. [P. 146.] Here the dynamic sociology of culture was portrayed as a bridge, whose task was clarification but not synthesis.

113 "Sociological Theory of Culture," *ST*, pp. 167–9. [*SD*, pp. 184–6.]

114 Ibid., p. 169. [P. 187.]

115 Ibid., p. 168. [P. 185.]

116 Ibid., pp. 170–1. [Pp. 187–8.]

117 Ibid., p. 171. [P. 189.]

118 "Historicism," *ESK*, pp. 84–6.* [*W*, pp. 246–9.]

119 Ibid., p. 127. [P. 299.] Also see "Sociological Theory of Culture," *ST*, pp. 171–2. [*SD*, pp. 189–90.]

120 In the following passage, one hears echoes from the Free School lecture: "To work out the structure or the *Gestalt* of this totality on the basis of a thorough examination of its separate elements is the final aim of historicism." "Historicism," *ESK*, p. 87.* [*W*, pp. 249–50.]

121 Ibid., p. 87. [P. 249.]

122 See Alfred Weber, "Prinzipells zur Kultursoziologie: Gesellschaftsprozess, Zivilisationsprozess und Kulturbewegung," *Archiv für Sozialwissenschaft und Sozialpolitik*, vol. 47 (1920–21), pp. 1–49.

123 This was the same kind of tripartite relationship that he described in his earlier essays, i.e., art–science–philosophy in "Epistemology" and expressive–objective–documentary meaning in "Weltanschauung."

124 "Historicism," *ESK*, pp. 114–15. [*W*, pp. 282–3.]

125 Ibid., pp. 101–2. [Pp. 266–8.]

126 Ibid., p. 91. [Pp. 254–5.]

127 "Epistemology," *ESSP*, pp. 20–1. [*W*, pp. 173–4.]

128 "Historicism," *ESK*, p. 111. [*W*, p. 279.]

129 Ibid., p. 102. [P. 268.]

130 Ibid., p. 116.* [P. 284.] These terms are variations of those connected with the expressive level of meaning in "Weltanschauung."

131 Ibid., pp. 130, 122. [Pp. 303, 293.]

132 Mannheim wrote: "The irrationalist – e.g. the followers of the historical school – much as they are able to present graphically the hidden organic context of the individual life-spheres within the same epoch, can do no more than outline individual portraits of various periods (*Volksgeistern*). However, they never perceive the need to combine these isolated portraits into the dynamic unity of one developmental process. We saw, however, that it is a question of life and death for historicism to be able to connect the various epochs together in a meaningfully graduated totality of development in spite of their appearance as distinct individual totalities." Ibid., p. 107.* [Pp. 274–5.]

133 Ibid., p. 122. [P. 292.]

134 Ibid., p. 105.* [P. 271.] Mannheim believed this was possible through the intuitive faculty of understanding (*Verstehen*), which allowed a "penetration" into the object by the historian.

211

135 Ibid.* [P. 272.]
136 "Epistemology," *ESSP*, p. 20. [*W*, p. 173.]
137 "Historicism," *ESK*, p. 117. [*W*, p. 287.] Mannheim wrote: "A developmental sequence is dialectical in which successive rational products replace one another in such a way that the following product transcends the earlier in the form of a new system with a new systematizing center." P. 115.* [P. 283.] Earlier, Mannheim had written that the dialectical conflict in philosophy found its basic unit in the "problem." "Epistemology," *ESSP*, p. 35. [*W*, pp. 193–4.]
138 "Historicism," *ESK*, p. 117. [*W*, p. 287.]
139 Ibid., pp. 102–3.* [P. 268–9.]
140 Mannheim believed that there was no sharp delineation of the spheres within the entire cultural-historical domain, because "every concrete product contains, more or less, a stratum of civilizational, psychic and dialectical elements; and the range of each of these methods could be more or less extended to all fields." Ibid., p. 123.* [P. 294.] This idea that a cultural object could be interpreted on different levels was a carry-over from *"Weltanschauung."*
141 In fact, Mannheim's strategy was to first separate the ahistorical (civilizational) from the historical and then to divide the latter into its psychic-cultural and dialectical parts.
142 In "Historicism," Mannheim used the compound term "psychic-cultural," wheras in *"Weltanschauung"* each of these terms was separate. In "Historicism," he distinguished "the psychic 'expression,' 'document'" from the "spiritual and rational." *ESK*, pp. 111–12. [*W*, pp. 279–80.]
143 *"Weltanschauung,"* *ESK*, p. 62. [*W*, p. 128.]
144 Mannheim used "utopia" in a different sense from that in *Ideology and Utopia*. He wrote: "These utopias, these postulates of logic, are in no way arbitrarily contrived speculations; nor are they sudden visions imparted, as it were, by revelation; what they express is, rather, a concrete structural insight, thought through to the last consequences, for which the impetus is given by the concrete pattern of the historical movement itself." "Historicism," *ESK*, pp. 119–20. [*W*, pp. 289–90.]
145 Ibid.* [Pp. 288–90.] One can see a change from "Epistemology" in the use of the concept of "systematization." In the earlier essay, a systematization was an eternal rational structure that various historical systems tried to match. Now, in "Historicism," systematizations themselves were seen as historical, being bound by the position of the subject.
146 Actually, Mannheim did not turn the adjective "perspectivistic" into a noun until "Sociological Theory of Culture," later in 1924.
147 "Historicism," *ESK*, p. 130. [*W*, p. 303.]
148 Ibid., p. 118. [P. 288.]
149 Mannheim wrote: "A cultural-historical knowledge, as a matter of fact, must not only be correct (in the sense that it satisfies critically ascertained historical material and is immanently consistent) but must also grasp its object *adequately* at the depth that corresponds to it. . . . We can rank the various histor-

ical periods in terms of the depth of the interpretations they have furnished only by invoking 'qualitative' evidence 'coming from the content' of the object interpreted. That this solution of the problem really overcomes relativism will be doubted only by those whose orientation is an exclusively rational-formalistic one, who eschew the problem of material evidence as much as possible and believe that all appeal to non-formal, material evidence oversteps the boundaries of science." Ibid., pp. 122–3.* [Pp. 293–4.]

150 Ibid., pp. 90, 118. [Pp. 253, 288.] Mannheim used the example of nineteenth-century materialism not being "higher" than Kant's philosophy.

151 Ibid., p. 84. [P. 246.]

152 See my "German Historicism," pp. 88–9.

153 Mannheim was more concerned with identifying the concepts of conservative organicism, liberal rationalism, and progressive-dialectical historicism with the far past, near past, and present-future, respectively, than with any social classes. (There was more emphasis on rationalism as an Enlightenment concept than as a bourgeois concept.) His defense of dynamic historicism as the most adequate world view for his time did not claim that it was connected with any social group, such as the proletariat, but rather that it was "the only solution of the general problem of how to find material and concretely exemplified standards and norms for a world outlook which has become dynamic." "Historicism," *ESK*, p. 132. [*W*, p. 306.]

154 See the two-page section entitled "Historicism and Sociology" in ibid., pp. 124–6. [Pp. 295–8.]

155 Ibid., p. 125.* [Pp. 296–7.]

156 Ibid., p. 106.* [P. 273.]

157 Mannheim wrote: "As we integrate the element that is grasped (the historical fact) into a totality, indeed a dynamic totality, and thence assess its meaning, our question becomes philosophical and the specialized science of history as well as the consideration of life again becomes philosophical." Ibid., pp. 87–8* [P. 250.]

158 Ibid., pp. 97, 119. [Pp. 261–2, 289.] Mannheim wrote that historicism "means a philosophy and world view that does not attempt to do violence to that new element which moves us – the dynamic – by making it a relativized residue of the old center, but rather places it right in the center and makes it the Archimedean lever by which our whole world view is revolutionized." Ibid., p. 133. [P. 307.]

159 Ibid., p. 131. [P. 305.]

160 Mannheim wrote: "Our thinking is still to such an extent confined within partial systems that the dynamic is only visible for us in this dualistic contrast [of the positivistic sciences and the historical-cultural sciences] and in the set of problems which are thereby determined. This provisional position alone explains why we maintain a pluralism of progressive-rational, dialectical-rational and cultural-soulful (monadically-unconnected) structures. Only when one overcomes this position, which is based upon the specialization of sciences and methodological pluralism, and takes the dynamic drawn from the special science of history as a basis for philosophical construction, when

213

therefore, a dynamic totality is taken as the point of departure, can one ask oneself, what the static 'part-systems' mean within that totality. . . . That historicism has not yet solved this task must be emphasized rather than concealed." Ibid., p. 131.* [P. 305.]

161 "Sociological Theory of Culture," *ST*, p. 180.* [*SD*, p. 199.]
162 Ibid. His use of Marxist terminology will be discussed in the next chapter.
163 Ibid. [P. 200.]
164 Ibid., p. 272. [P. 304.]
165 Simmel, *The Conflict in Modern Culture and other Essays*, trans. K. Peter Etzkorn (New York, 1968), pp. 27–46.
166 Kettler, 'Sociology of Knowledge," p. 412.
167 Coser (ed.), *Georg Simmel* (Englewood Cliffs, N.J., 1965), pp. 29–39.
168 "Georg Simmel, mint filozófus," p. 194.
169 "A háboru böleseletéhez," p. 418.
170 "Historicism," *ESK*, p. 98.* [*W*, p. 263.]
171 Ibid., pp. 101–3. [Pp. 266–9.]
172 Lukács, "The Old Culture and the New Culture," in *Marxism and Human Liberation*, ed. E. San Juan, Jr., (New York, 1973), pp. 3–18. For two contrasting views on whether Lukács's ideas were primarily political or cultural, see Congdon, "The Unexpected Revolutionary: Lukács' Road to Marx," *Survey*, vol. 20 (1974), pp. 176–205, and Kettler, "Culture and Revolution."
173 This book will be discussed in more detail in Chapter 4.
174 "Historicism," *ESK*, pp. 106–7. [*W*, pp. 273–4.]
175 "Historismus," *W*, p. 296 note. My emphases. This passage is omitted from the English translation.
176 Mannheim lumped Lukács and Troeltsch together as late as 1925. See "Problem of Sociology of Knowledge," *ESK*, p. 150. [*W*, p. 328.]
177 "Historicism," *ESK*, p. 124. [*W*, p. 296.]

3. Transition (1924–1928)

1 "Problems of Sociology in Germany," *FKM*, p. 263. [*W*, p. 615.]
2 See, for example, "Ideological and Sociological Interpretation," *FKM*, p. 125 [*W*, pp. 399–400]; "Problem of Sociology of Knowledge," *ESK*, p. 136 [*W*, pp. 310–11]; "Competition," *ESK*, pp. 192, 226–7 [*W*, pp. 567, 610–11]; "Sociological Theory of Culture," *ST*, p. 272. [*SD*, p. 304.] In part 1 of *Konservatismus*, he emphasized that the sociology of knowledge was an empirical, specialized science and that he was not going to deal with the larger philosophical questions. When he did contrast the sociology of knowledge to another discipline, it was the history of ideas, which was also a specialized science.
3 The dating of this manuscript is more problematical than that of the earlier "Cultural-Sociological Knowledge," The facts that the pagination begins anew several times and that the page format changes in the middle of the manuscript indicate that Mannheim did not work continuously on it. See the Introduction of Kettler, Meja, and Stehr to *ST*. I believe that Part One was written before the publication of "Historicism," and that most of Part Two and the

fragment that was to be Part Three were written after the publication of that article.

4 This can be seen in the fact that "Ideological and Sociological Interpretation" was a reformulation of part of "Cultural-Sociological Knowledge," See Chapter 2, note 44. For another interpretation that emphasizes the difference between the two unpublished manuscripts, see Kettler, "Sociology of Knowledge," and the Introduction of Kettler, Meja, and Stehr to *ST*.

5 For Example, Paul Eppstein used Mannheim's works from this period as a basis for the acceptance of historical materialism as an acceptable methodology when taken in conjunction with other methodologies and given less political emphasis. Eppstein, "Die Fragestellung nach der Wirklichkeit im historischen Materialismus," *Archiv für Sozialwissenschaft und Sozialpolitik*, vol. 60 (1928), pp. 449–507.

6 This work now appears in three versions, the two mentioned in the text and the posthumously published English version. Where the three are identical, I will cite the versions of "Conservative Thought." Because my prepublication copy of *Konservatismus* (which will appear while this book is in press) is not paginated, I will cite it (referring to sections) only when the material is unique to it.

7 See "Competition," *ESK*, p. 193. [*W*, p. 569.]

8 "Sociological Theory of Culture," *ST*, pp. 151, 182. [*SD*, pp. 165, 201.] See Chapter 2, note 160.

9 Ibid., pp. 212–13, 219. [Pp. 236, 244.]

10 Mannheim made this same point earlier in "Cultural-Sociological Knowledge," *ST*, pp. 98–9. [*SD*, pp. 110–11.]

11 "Sociological Theory of Culture," *ST*, pp. 154, 203–4. [*SD*, pp. 169, 226.] Here he cited the typologies of Tönnies and Alfred Weber as examples.

12 He acknowledged that these two types were not the only forms of cultural-historical knowledge, simply the ones relevant to his topic. Ibid., p. 184. [P. 204.]

13 Ibid., pp. 242–4. [Pp. 270–3.]

14 Here we see a change in emphasis in the use of this term, which in "Historicism" included both the postulate that all historical positions had a limited sphere of vision and the belief that a historical standard of truth could be found to judge these different positions. In "Sociological Theory of Culture" and the other essays of this period, the second element remained in the background, due to the primarily analytical nature of the works. Eventually, the postulate of limited vision would be signified by the term *"Aspektstruktur"* (which has been translated as "perspective"), and the belief in a standard of values would be signified by the term "relationism."

15 "Sociological Theory of Culture," *ST*, pp. 241, 243. [*SD*, pp. 270, 272.]

16 In "Ideological and Sociological Interpretation," Mannheim used "understanding" as an adjective for the noun "interpretation" (*Deutung*). *FKM*, p. 130. [*W*, p. 406.]

17 See "Problem of Sociology of Knowledge," *ESK*, pp. 176, 184. [*W*, pp. 367, 379.] Mannheim often treated the two terms as identical. In the discussion

following "Competition" Alfred Weber distinguished between the procedural concept of "cognition" (*Erkennen*), the formal concept of "style of thought" (*Denkstil*), and the ontological concept of "knowledge" (*Wissen*). *Verhandlungen des Sechsten Deutschen Soziologentages* (Tübingen, 1929), p. 90. Mannheim did not make such distinctions, using "*Soziologie des Denkens*," "*Soziologie der Erkenntnis*," "*Soziologie des Wissens*," and "*Wissenssoziologie*" synonymously.

18 This term was essentially limited to "Sociological Theory of Culture"; however, he did use it in "Competition," *ESK*, p. 199. [*W*, p. 576.]

19 This series came from both "Sociological Theory of Culture" and "Competition," the first and last works of this period. In the latter, he wrote that these types could be taken as either "pure" or "dynamic" sociological types. (For example, the most primitive type, "consensus," could be exemplified historically as the "clan" or in its pure form as "common sense.") *ESK*, p. 199. [*W*, p. 576.] In accordance with his orientation, I will concentrate on the dynamic types.

20 "Sociological Theory of Culture," *ST*, pp. 206–7, 234–5, 248–9, 255–6 [*SD*, pp. 229–30, 262, 277, 285]; Competition," *ESK*, pp. 199–200 [*W*, pp. 576–8].

21 "Sociological Theory of Culture," *ST*, pp. 235–6. [*SD*, p. 263.] The size of the *Kulturgemeinschaften* was variable. The example he cited was the "European-American cultural community."

22 Ibid., pp. 255–6 [Pp. 285–6]; "Competition," *ESK*, pp. 201–3. [*W*, pp. 578–81.]

23 "Competition," *ESK*, pp. 203–7. [*W*, pp. 581–6.]

24 "Sociological Theory of Culture," *ST*, pp. 154–6, 259–60. [*SD*, pp. 169–71, 290–1.]

25 The stage parallel to "monopoly" in the Free School lecture was the "artistic stage," in which there was concern for shaping material, but form had not yet assumed its own laws independent of content. *W*, p. 76.

26 "Sociological Theory of Culture," *ST*, pp. 277–8 [*SD*, pp. 310–11]; "Problem of Sociology of Knowledge," *ESK*, pp. 136–44 [*W*, pp. 311–20].

27 "Ideological and Sociological Interpretation," *FKM*, pp. 119–20. [*W*, pp. 391–2.]

28 "Problem of Sociology of Knowledge," *ESK*, pp. 150–3. [*W*, pp. 328–32.]

29 Scheler, *Die Wissenformen und die Gesellschaft* (Bern, 1960), pp. 21–2, 25–6, 37–8, 61, 68, 86, 132, 149–50, 158; Scheler, "Die Formen des Wissens und die Bildung," in *Philosophische Weltanschauung* (Bern and Munich, 1968), pp. 41–2. Also see Frederic Lilge, *The Abuse of Learning* (New York, 1948), p. 152.

30 "Problem of Sociology of Knowledge," *ESK*, p. 169.* [*W*, p. 353.]

31 Mannheim listed eight points where his sociology of knowledge differed from Scheler's: (1) Essences and spiritual content were not preexistent and were not separable from history; (2) essence could not be grasped by a leap outside history; (3) essences were themselves dynamic, their fate being connected to the historical process; (4) one could not gradually cross over from a generalizing sociology to a historico-philosophical, individualizing one; (5) the dualism between meaning and existence was only a phenomenological one, so their context could be best illuminated by a historico-philosophical, sociological

construction of the totality; (6) the grasping of the meaning of history could only be accomplished perspectivistically; (7) metaphysics developed in and with the specialized historical sciences and, thus, the divisions of the specialized sciences were only "technical"; and (8) because thought was not totally immanent, a new epistemology was necessary. "Problem einer Soziologie des Wissens," *W*, p. 363.

32 "Sociological Theory of Culture," *ST*, pp. 192–3. [*SD*, pp. 213–14.] Mannheim gave no explanation of his change in terminology; however, one could guess that it was done to put more distance between his dynamic sociology of culture and Dilthey's individual psychology.

33 Ibid., p. 233 [P. 260]; "Problem of Sociology of Knowledge," *ESK*, p. 186. [*W*, p. 381.] "*Weltwollen*" and "*Weltwollung*" were synonyms, and, although he distinguished between "*Weltwollen*" and "*Denkwollen*," he tended to treat them as synonymous. See *Konservatismus*, part 1; "Conservative Thought," *ESSP*, p. 102 [*W*, p. 424]; "Competiton," *ESK*, p. 193. [*W*, p. 569.] The terms first appeared in "Sociological Theory of Culture," *ST*, p. 152. [*SD*, p. 166.]

34 "Sociological Theory of Culture," *ST*, p. 212.* [*SD*, p. 236.] My translation is of the original manuscript, which differs somewhat from the edited German version.

35 He wrote that the world view had both "expressive character" and "documentary significance." Ibid., p. 213. [P. 237.]

36 He wrote that the world aspiration was "the deepest unity of style belonging to the consciousness of the community in all its objectifications, conscious or unconscious." Ibid., p. 233. [P. 260.] Later, in *Ideology and Utopia*, he would replace the term "world aspiration" with "consciousness."

37 Ibid., pp. 231–2. [Pp. 258–9.]

38 Like the "work" in the Free School lecture, the "spiritual reality" had a semi-autonomous character. It contained a number of potential tendencies that could be objectified. What was important to Mannheim was its functionality, the objectification of those tendencies connected with collective aspirations. Ibid., pp. 234–5, 271. [Pp. 262, 303.]

39 Ibid., p. 218.* [P. 243.]

40 Ibid., pp. 208–9, 214–15, 223–5. [Pp. 232, 239–40, 249–51.]

41 "Problem of Sociology of Knowledge," *ESK*, p. 181. [*W*, pp. 374, 366.]

42 He wrote: "If the category of 'interest' is recognized as the only 'existential relation' involving ideas, then one will be forced either to restrict sociological analysis to those parts of the superstructure which manifestly show ideological 'cloaking' of interests, or, if it is nevertheless desired to analyze the entire superstructure in terms of its dependence upon social reality, to define the term 'interest' so broadly that it will lose its original meaning." Ibid., p. 183. [P. 277.] Also see "Sociological Theory of Culture," *ST*, p. 273. [*SD*, p. 305.]

43 "Problem of Sociology of Knowledge," *ESK*, pp. 185–6 [*W*, pp. 379–80]; "Sociological Theory of Culture," *ST*, pp. 274–6 [*SD*, pp. 306–8]. In "Competition," he described these two spheres as being "co-determinant" (*mitkonstituierend*). *ESK*, p. 192. [*W*, p. 567.] This absence of causal priority was typical of his methodology, as is evidenced by his preference for "indi-

rect" terminology such as "connect" (*verbinden, verknüpfen*), "penetrate" (*hineinragen, eindringen, durchdringen*), "intertwine" (*verflechten, verweben*), "correspond" (*entsprechen*), and "embed" (*einbetten*).

44 My discussion of the sociology of knowledge here is little more than a sketch. For an in-depth treatment of this discipline in the light of Mannheim's work, see Simonds, *Mannheim's Sociology*.

45 "Problem of Sociology of Knowledge," *ESK*, pp. 186–7 [*W*, pp. 88–91]; *IUE*, pp. 306–9 [*IUG*, pp. 263–5]; *Konservatismus*, part 1. Mannheim defended this method in a joint seminar with Alfred Weber in 1929. "Protokoll der Sitzung der vereinigten Seminare von Prof. A. Weber und Dr. Mannheim, den 21. Febr. 29," typescript (1929), pp. 5–6.

46 For a similar interpretation, see Neusüss, *Utopisches Bewusstsein*, pp. 88–91.

47 Nor was he the only one. Marianne Weber wrote that her circle to which Mannheim belonged, took up "socialistic culture" as one of its topics. *Lebenserinnerungen* (Bremen, 1948), pp. 193–211, especially p. 204.

48 "Konservative Denken," *W*, p. 408. The English version of this passage, which was not only translated but also rewritten, is in *ESSP*, p. 74.

49 "Conservative Thought," *ESSP*, pp. 94–5, 102. [*W*, pp. 411–13, 424.] He wrote: "Political conservatism is, therefore, an objective-spiritual context as opposed to the 'subjectivity' of the isolated individual [in whom the universal trait of traditionalism could be found]. It is not objective in the sense of eternally and universally valid. No a priori deductions can be made from the 'principles' of conservatism, nor does it exist apart from the individuals who realize it in practice and embody it in their actions. It is not an immanent principle with a given law of development which the individual members of the movement merely unfold – possibly in unconscious fashion – without adding anything of their own. In one word, conservatism is not an objective entity in any rightly or wrongly understood Platonist sense of the pre-existence of ideas but, as compared with the hic et nunc lived experience of the particular individual it has a very definite objectivity." Ibid., p. 96.* [P. 414.] This limited objectivity was the same as that he ascribed to conjunctive knowledge in "Sociological Theory of Culture," *ST*, p. 241. [*SD*, p. 269.]

50 "Conservative Thought," *ESSP*, pp. 95–9. [*W*, pp. 411–17.]

51 Ibid., pp. 100–1. [Pp. 421–2.] In place of "world aspiration," he used a synonym, "basic intention" (*Grundintention*). That these were synonyms was made clear in part 1 of *Konservatismus*.

52 Ibid., p. 101, especially note 2. [P. 422, n. 13.]

53 The other types were also from "Competition." *Ideology and Utopia* was already in press when this work was delivered before an academic audience in late 1928. I have included "Competition" in this transitional period because of its primarily analytic nature.

54 "Competition," *ESK*, pp. 208–9.* [*W*, p. 588.]

55 Mannheim allowed for more than two poles, adding socialism to conservatism and liberalism in this essay. He had introduced this triad as early as "Sociological Theory of Culture." In *Ideology and Utopia*, they would be joined by fascism and bureaucratic conservatism.

56 Mannheim wrote: "It can be seen that a position of thought and will, or any type of world interpretation, does not suddenly come from nowhere, but arises from a selection from the sphere of views and aspirations of the competing groups." Ibid., pp. 211–12.* [P. 592.]

57 "Competition," *ESK*, p. 195. [*W*, pp. 571–2.]

58 Ibid., p. 214.* [P. 595.]

59 He wrote: "From the point of view of the social sciences, every historical, *weltanschaulich*, sociological piece of knowledge (even should it prove to be Absolute Truth itself) is clearly rooted in and carried by the drive for power and validity of particular social groups who want to make their interpretation of the world the universal one. . . . This is not merely a matter of the so-called 'public opinion' which is commonly recognized as a superficial phenomenon of collective psychology, but of the inventory of our set of fundamental meanings in terms of which we experience the outside world as well as our inner responses." Ibid., pp. 196–7.* [Pp. 573–4.]

60 "Generations," *ESK*, pp. 278, 290, 312. [*W*, pp. 511–12, 527, 555.]

61 Ibid., pp. 288–90. [Pp. 524–6.]

62 Ibid., p. 303. [P. 543.]

63 In *Ideology and Utopia*, Mannheim also divided perception of historical change into two types. "administration," which was routinized, and "politics," where change resisted routinization.

64 "Generations," *ESK*, pp. 284–86. [*W*, pp. 518–21.]

65 Ibid., pp. 313–15. [Pp. 557–9.]

66 Ibid., pp. 304–5. [Pp. 544–5.] In keeping with the basic structure of his work, Mannheim saw these sociological-dynamic concepts as transcending the mechanistic approach of positivism and the organic approach of the romantic-historical school. Ibid., p. 276, [P. 509.] He presented a similar picture concerning the problem of competition. "Competition," *ESK*, pp. 192–3, 195–7. [*W*, pp. 567, 571–4.]

67 "Generations," *ESK*, p. 314. [*W*, p. 557.]

68 Ibid., p. 316. [Pp. 559–60.]

69 Wohl, *Generation of 1914*, pp. 82–3.

70 In this and the succeeding chapters, I am using this term in the sense of the earlier chapters and not in the special sense defined by Mannheim in "Conservative Thought."

71 "Sociological Theory of Culture," *ST*, p. 266.* [*SD*, p. 297.]

72 Mannheim believed that in the *Bildungskultur* the intellectual could even put himself at the service of another group's aspiration. Ibid., p. 268. [P. 300.]

73 Ibid., p. 269. [P. 301.]

74 "Generations," *ESK*, p. 317 [*W*, p. 561]; "Conservative Thought," *ESSP*, p. 125 [*W*, p. 454].

75 "Conservative Thought," *ESSP*, p. 121. [*W*, p. 449.]

76 Ibid., pp. 127–8.* [Pp. 457–8.] Also see Heeren, "Karl Mannheim and the Intellectual Elite," p. 3.

77 "Conservative Thought," *ESSP*, pp. 125–6. [*W*, pp. 454–5.]

78 Ibid., pp. 138–43. [Pp. 472–9.]

79 Ibid., pp. 145–50. [Pp. 481–8.]

80 Mannheim did indicate that Hegel typified still another stage, but the manuscript broke off abruptly when it came time to discuss that stage. This failure to
deal extensively with Hegel, despite the promise to do so, reflected Mannheim's ambivalence toward him.

81 Mannheim noted their membership in the same circles, especially the *Christ-
lich-deutsche Tischgesellschaft.*

82 "Conservative Thought," *ESSP,* pp. 155–7. [*W,* pp. 495–7.]

83 Here my interpretation differs markedly from that of Kettler, Meja, and
Stehr. They believe that the switch I see completed only with the appearance
of *Ideology and Utopia* actually took place in "Sociological Theory of Culture."
Mannheim's interest in conservatism appears to them, therefore, as a retreat.
(One reason they suggest for this was that he was applying for a position at the
University of Heidelberg and for German citizenship at this time and thus felt
the need to muffle the more radical aspects of his writing.) I, on the other
hand, see *Konservatismus* as a movement toward the political center of construction rather than as a retreat from it. This movement was more muted in
his published writings, due to the uncertainty about whether he should abandon his cultural orientation. This uncertainty could also indicate why he abandoned his plans to discuss Hegel's philosophy.

84 In "Generations," Mannheim wrote that this free-floating quality, which allowed switches in commitment, could be misleading. Those interpreters who
focused solely on the intellectuals might mistake their vacillations for a "wave-
like" change in the *Zeitgeist* (e.g., from the romantic era to the liberal era),
when in fact both poles remained, with varying powers of attraction. The
impetus for change was not that of the intellectuals but rather of the sociopolitical groups whose aspirations made up the poles. *ESK,* p. 317. [*W,* p.
562.] This represented a retreat from the role of intellectuals in the Free
School lecture – these thinkers were not leaders but merely articulators of
others' aspirations.

85 "Competition," *ESK,* p. 221.* [*W,* pp. 603–4.]

86 Ibid., p. 226.* [*P.* 610.]

87 Ibid., pp. 226–8. [Pp. 610–12.] For a criticism of Mannheim on this point, see
Alexander von Schelting, *Max Webers Wissenschaftslehre* (Tübingen, 1934), pp.
119–20.

88 At the end of his life, Mannheim admitted that he had "not succeeded yet
fully" in creating a new epistemology. See Wolff, "Sociology of Knowledge," p.
572.

89 Weber, "Geist und Politik," in *Ideen,* pp. 122–32.

90 Weber wrote: "You have spoken of positions of power, of aspirations that
result from them, of a public interpretation of existence which is combined
with these positions of power and aspirations, but not of other factors in this
context. What is that other than another statement of the materialistic conception of history delivered brilliantly with an extraordinary subtlety? Basically it
is nothing else." *Verhandlungen des Sechsten Deutschen Soziologentages,* p. 92. Also
see Siegfried Marck, "Zum Problem des 'seinsverbundenen Denkens,'" *Archiv*

für systematische Philosophie und Soziologie, 2d series, vol. 33 (1929), pp. 240–1; Neusüss, *Utopisches Bewusstsein,* p. 45.

91 He conceded to Mannheim the following: (1) that competition was a general sociological, and not simply an economic, category; (2) that it could be documented in the sphere of existentially connected thought; (3) that here it played a codetermining role; (4) that Mannheim's four types were fruitful; (5) that the contemporary intellectual situation was correctly characterized; and (6) that metaphysically anchored concepts, knowledge, and values were all existentially connected. *Verhandlungen,* pp. 88–90.

92 This was grasped by Norbert Elias, who stated that most of the contributions to the discussions were not delivered with the intensity of a dialogue but were simply a series of monologues. The exception was Alfred Weber's speech, "which, because it was in a way hostile, had an intensity that corresponded to that developed for us by Dr. Mannheim. The thoughts of Mannheim's presentation were, indeed, . . . in a most decided way revolutionary, not in the sense of a socialistic or social, but of a spiritual revolution. These thoughts are the expression for a convulsion of that spiritual posture which till now has been dominant." Ibid., p. 110.

93 See especially the speech by Lederer. Ibid., pp. 106–7.

94 Ibid., pp. 121, 123–4.

95 Mannheim stated: "Have not the best leaders of the nation censured as an error that people all too willingly shift the problem of politics into the purely spiritual sphere and always relinquish a mastery there where the opportunity to master, to change is present, and content themselves with a 'deeper meaning.' The world wants to be understood and made, and the more it concerns those spheres of endeavor where making is indispensable, the more dangerous it is to resign oneself to understanding alone." Ibid., p. 122.

96 Ironically, the chapter on utopia in this book was dedicated to Alfred Weber and originally was to be part of a *Festschrift* for him on the occasion of his sixtieth birthday. See Emil Lederer et al., *Soziologische Studien; Zur Politik, Wirtschaft und Kultur der Gegenwart* (Potsdam, 1930), p. 304.

4. The political synthesis (1929)

1 See Kurt Wolff's introduction to *FKM,* p. lxi. The present German version of the book contains the original German material plus a translation of the added English material, so that its format is essentially that of the 1936 edition.

2 The correspondence between Mannheim and Louis Wirth, who edited the English translation, sheds a great deal of light on the changes. Wirth and Edward Shils translated the original three essays, trying to be as true as possible to their intent. Wirth also suggested adding Mannheim's 1931 encyclopedia article on the sociology of knowledge, and Mannheim agreed. In the middle of 1935, Mannheim indicated that he wanted not only to make changes in the translation but also to add an introduction that would place the work in context. He felt that Wirth's version would be fine if the book were to

be published only in the United States; but because it was also to be published in England, he was afraid that intellectuals there would dismiss it as an overly abstract product of an inaccessible world. Wirth resisted these changes but eventually gave in. The changes in the English edition, then, were made not only with Mannheim's consent, but to a large extent at his insistence. See the Mannheim–Wirth Correspondence from July 26, 1933, to March 25, 1936. A good description of this exchange can be found in Kettler, Meja, and Stehr, *Karl Mannheim*, pp. 111–13.

3 "The Problem of Theory and Praxis" is the subtitle of the essay. Mannheim made the claim that it was an essay about ideology in *IUG*, p. 50. Most of the introduction also dealt with the development of the theory of ideology and its relation to the sociology of knowledge. Siegfried Landshut wrote: "The phenomenon of ideology is the fundamental phenomenon on which the possibility of such a sociology of knowledge is based." *Kritik der Soziologie* (Munich and Leipzig, 1929), p. 88.

4 This is not simply a problem with those who read the 1936 edition. In the introduction of a collection of essays from the 1920s entitled "The Theory of Ideology and the Sociology of Knowledge," Hans-Joachim Lieber writes: "The central importance of Karl Mannheim for the discussion of the problem of ideology in the 1920's is shown by the fact that after the appearance of his book *Ideology and Utopia*, there was really no discussion of the problem which could not at the same time be taken as a review of the book." Lieber (ed.), *Ideologienlehre und Wissenssoziologie*, p. 41. Neusüss, in *Utopisches Bewusstsein*, focuses on "utopia" but turns it into a sociological rather than a political concept. See especially p. 130. One writer who saw that "ideology" was subordinate to "utopia" was Hans Freyer, *Soziologie als Wirklichkeitswissenschaft* (Leipzig and Berline, 1930), pp. 298–9. This was probably because Mannheim had drawn on an earlier article by Freyer for his concept of utopia. *IUE*, p. 218. [*IUG*, p. 190.]

5 George Lichtheim, "The Concept of Ideology," in George N. Nadel (ed.), *Studies in the Philosophy of History* (New York, 1965), pp. 170–6. The same holds true for Kettler, Meja, and Stehr in *Karl Mannheim*. They certainly recognize that Weber was important for Mannheim, yet give primacy to *History and Class Consciousness* in their discussion of *Ideology and Utopia*. The connection between *History and Class Consciousness* and *Ideology and Utopia* was made in the same year that the latter was published by Julius Kraft; Kraft, "Soziologie oder Soziologismus? Zu Mannheims 'Ideologie und Utopie,'" *Zeitschrift für Völkerpsychologie*, vol. 5 (1929), p. 409.

6 This is not to say that Lukács's work had no effect on Mannheim's. See the following pages of *History and Class Consciousness*, trans. Rodney Livingstone (London, 1971), for concepts that later appeared, often in altered form, in *Ideology and Utopia:* relationism (p. 189), the dialectic (2–5, 190, 249); imputation (51); emphasis on the group over the individual (34); a totality uniting subject and object, theory and practice (27, 155); the struggle to determine the public interpretation of reality (228); the need to rationally understand the political sphere (73–6); the importance of the political party (41–2, 71,

318); the five types of existentially transcendent consciousnesses (48–9, 77, 110–13, 157–8, 172, 191–2, 203); and the relationship of history and class consciousness (180–6).

7 For an analysis of Weber's political concerns, see David Beetham, *Max Weber and the Theory of Modern Politics* (London, 1974).

8 M. Weber, "Politics as a Vocation," pp. 79–80. ["Politik als Beruf," *Gesammelte Politische Schriften*, 3d ed. (Tübingen, 1971), pp. 507–8.]

9 Wolfgang Mommsen, *The Age of Bureaucracy* (New York, 1974), pp. 101–2.

10 M. Weber, "Politics as a Vocation," pp. 109–10. ["Politik," pp. 538–40.]

11 Ibid., pp. 120–1. [Pp. 551–2.] Gerth and Mills's translation, although not literal, is accurate, for the politician following this ethic placed a total priority on valuative ends over means.

12 Ibid., pp. 115, 122. [Pp. 545, 553.] Max Weber made the same point in "Science as a Vocation," p. 155.

13 Ibid., p. 115. [P. 545.]

14 Elsewhere in the speech, he described political activity as partisanship (taking up a cause), struggle for the cause, and suffering for the cause. Ibid., p. 95. [P. 524.]

15 See Marianne Weber, *Max Weber: A Biography* (New York, 1975), pp. 631, 636–7.

16 Meinecke, *Schaffender Spiegel*, pp. 223–4.

17 M. Weber, "Politics as a Vocation," p. 127. ["Politik," p. 559.]

18 Meinecke, *Schaffender Spiegel*, p. 224.

19 M. Weber, "Science as a Vocation," pp. 143–51. Weber did say that scientists had to form an intellectual aristocracy (p. 134), but here he was talking about intellectual ability rather than their hierarchical status. He rejected his brother Alfred's notion of the intellectuals as "spiritual leaders."

20 Wolfgang Schluchter, "Value-Neutrality and the Ethic of Responsibility," in Schluchter and Guenther Roth, *Max Weber's Vision of History* (Berkeley and Los Angeles, 1979), p. 94.

21 M. Weber, "Science as a Vocation," p. 151.

22 Ibid., p. 152.

23 Ibid.

24 Lukács, *History and Class Consciousness*, p. xlvi.* [*Geschichte und Klassenbewusstsein* (Berlin, 1923), p. 11.]

25 This was why Mannheim grouped Lukács and Troeltsch together in "Historicism."

26 Lukács, *History and Class Consciousness*, p. 28. [*Geschichte*, p. 40.]

27 Ibid., pp. 2–3. [Pp. 14–15.]

28 Ibid., pp. 64, 204–5. [Pp. 76, 223–5.] Lukács wrote: "The closer this [dialectical] process comes to its goal the more urgent it becomes for the proletariat to understand its own historical mission and the more vigorously and directly proletarian class consciousness will determine each of its actions. The blind power of the forces at work will only advance 'automatically' to their goal of self-transcendence as long as that goal is not within reach. When the moment of transition to the 'realm of freedom' is objectively given, this

will become apparent just because the blind forces really will hurtle blindly towards the abyss, and only the conscious will of the proletariat will be able to save mankind from the impending catastrophe. In other words, when the final economic crisis of capitalism develops, the fate of the revolution (and with it the fate of mankind) will depend on the ideological maturity of the proletariat, i.e. on its class consciousness." Ibid., pp. 69—70.* [P. 82.]

29 M. Weber, "Politics as a Vocation," p. 125. ["Politik," p. 557.]

30 *IUE*, pp. 192, 205—6. [*IUG*, pp. 169, 179—80.] As early as 1924, Mannheim had seen "utopia" as the anticipation of a world aspiration toward which tension was directed, as a prescientific developmental ideal; however, he had not given it a specific political connotation. See "Sociological Theory of Culture," *ST*, pp. 246—7. [*SD*, pp. 274—5.] In the English edition, *"Wollen"* has been translated as "interests" rather than "will" or "aspiration." This has helped to neutralize the advocatory position of the original work.

31 *IUE*, pp. 194—6. [*IUG*, pp. 171—3.] For example, let us take the American antiwar movement of the 1960s. If that movement made no impact on society, if it did not stimulate a general antimilitarism in the country, then it was ideological. Also, if it inspired a successful backlash that called for more patriotism and greater wars, or if people wanted to end the Vietnam War but not to change any of the institutions that had led to the war, then the antiwar movement was ideological. However, if the movement did change American institutions in the direction of antimilitarism, even if not to the degree it would have liked, then it was utopian.

32 Ibid., pp. 69—71. [Pp. 63—6.]

33 See, for example, Ernst Lewalter, "Wissenssoziologie und Marxismus," *Archiv für Sozialwissenschaft und Sozialpolitik*, vol. 64 (1930), pp. 63—121; R. H. Cox, "Mannheim's Concept of Ideology," *Revue européenne des sciences sociales*, no. 46 (1979), pp. 209—23.

34 *IUE*, pp. 69, 208—9. [*IUG*, pp. 64, 182.] Continuing with my example, one could imagine some members of the antiwar forces who shared certain potentially utopian proposals with the rest of the group but did not share the group's utopian consciousness. Such a person could be a businessperson who opposed the Vietnam War (but not all wars) because of its disastrous effect on his share of the American economy but who did not believe in the social and institutional change that the utopian consciousness demanded. A study of his or her statements would add more to an understanding of the ideological position of the business community than to that of the potentially utopian consciousness of the antiwar group.

35 Ibid., pp. 113—14.* [P. 99.] Mannheim cited Weber here, especially his division of the routinized sphere into traditional and legal-rational components.

36 Ibid., p. 115. [P. 100.] Mannheim did write that economic competition played an important part in this sphere; however, it was largely ignored in *Ideology and Utopia*.

37 Ibid., p. 116.* [Pp. 100—1.]

38 Ibid., p. 212. [P. 185.]

39 Ibid., pp. 147, 195—6. [Pp. 128, 172—3.]

40 There were three major sets of types in the book: (1) three stages of development of the philosophy of consciousness in the introduction, pp. 65–9 [pp.
61–4]; (2) five types of political-historical thinking viewed ideologically in the
essay on political science, pp. 118–46 [pp. 102–28]; and (3) four types of
utopian consciousness in the essay on utopia, pp. 211–47 [pp. 184–213]. For
different interpretations, see Neusüss, *Utopisches Bewusstsein*, pp. 151–82,
and Jacques Maquet, *The Sociology of Knowledge*, trans. John F. Locke (Boston,
1951), p. 271.

41 Mannheim wrote of the bureaucratic conservative: "He takes it for granted
that the specific order prescribed by concrete law is equivalent to order in
general. . . . When faced with the play of hitherto unbound forces, as, for
example, the eruption of collective energies in a revolution, [he] can conceive
of them only as momentary disturbances. . . . Revolution is an irregularity
within the order of rules, but not the life-expression of the social forces which
stand behind such orders and which create, preserve or transform them."
IUE, pp. 118–19.* [*IUG*, p. 103.]

42 For this reason, Mannheim omitted it from the list of utopian consciousnesses. The description of this type had changed from its first appearance, as
the position of Gustav Hugo in *Konservatismus*. In *Ideology and Utopia*, the
characteristic of disillusioning realism was no longer attributed to the bureaucrat, who was characterized more by neutrality than by defensiveness.
Hugo had tried to disarm the political conflict; the bureaucrat in *Ideology and
Utopia* tried to ignore it.

43 *IUE*, p. 213. [*IUG*, p. 186.]

44 Ibid., p. 194. [Pp. 170–1.]

45 Ibid., p. 212. [P. 185.]

46 Ibid., pp. 211–12.* [Pp. 184–5.] Also see p. 193 [p. 170].

47 Thus, Karl Wittfogel was wrong in writing that Mannheim offered no class
analysis of fascism. "Wissen und Gesellschaft," *Unter dem Banner des Marxismus*, vol. 5 (1931), p. 101.

48 Mannheim described the ethic of responsibility as follows: "Its chief imper-
atives are, first, that conduct should not only be in accord with conviction, but
should take into consideration the possible consequences of the action inso-
far as they are calculable, and second, . . . that conviction itself should be
subjected to critical self-examination in order to eliminate all the blindly and
compulsively operating determinants." *IUE*, p. 191. [*IUG*, p. 167.]

49 Mannheim insisted on the importance of the concept of time for utopias.
Ibid., pp. 209–10. [P. 183.] Also see Helmut Schoeck, "Die Zeitlichkeit bei
Karl Mannheim," *Archiv für Rechts- und Sozialphilosophie*, vol. 38 (1949), pp.
372–3.

50 *IUE*, pp. 219–21. [*IUG*, pp. 191–2.]

51 Ibid., pp. 65–6. [Pp. 61–2.]

52 Ibid., p. 234. [P. 203.]

53 Ibid., p. 231. [P. 200.]

54 Ibid., pp. 66–7, 120. [Pp. 62–3, 104.] This was the position of Savigny in
Konservatismus, but here the cultural element was deemphasized.

55 Ibid., pp. 122–3, 222. [Pp. 106–7, 193.]
56 Ibid., pp. 234–5. [P. 203.]
57 Ibid., pp. 128–30, 239–47. [Pp. 111–13, 207–13.]
58 Ibid., pp. 246–7.* [P. 212.]
59 Ibid., p. 250.* [Pp. 215–16.]
60 Ibid., p. 68. [P. 63.]
61 Ibid., pp. 56–62. [Pp. 53–8.]
62 Ibid., pp. 64–70. [Pp. 60–4.]
63 Ibid., p. 75. [P. 69.] This was a continuation of the portrayal of Weber as the representative of disillusioning realism in *Konservatismus*.
64 Ibid., pp. 74–8. [Pp. 68–71.]
65 Ibid., p. 263.* [P. 225.]
66 Both are usually translated as "existentially determined" or "situationally determined." In an earlier version of my work (1974), I noted the difference between the two terms but felt that Mannheim's use was basically chronological, with *"seinsgebunden"* being dropped in favor of the more indirect *"seinsverbunden."* This same position was taken independently by Volker Meja, "The Sociology of Knowledge and the Critique of Ideology," *Cultural Hermeneutics*, vol. 3 (1975), p. 67. Simonds pointed out that a simple chronological interpretation was incorrect and the the two terms had been used together in the same sentence. Simonds, *Mannheim's Sociology*, p. 27. (Also see *IUG*, p. 259.) However, he does not offer an explanation for the use of the two terms that is satisfactory to me. The same holds true for Meja's position, which has been updated in light of Simonds's observations in Kettler, Meja, and Stehr, "Mannheim and Conservatism." The terms are also equated by German scholars. See, for example, Schoeck, "Zeitlichkeit," and Gunther Stern "Ueber die sog. 'Seinsverbundenheit' des Bewusstseins," *Archiv für Sozialwissenschaft und Sozialpolitik*, vol. 64 (1930), pp. 492–509.
67 By "primarily" I do not mean "exclusively." Mannheim's use of the terms did not adhere rigidly to this pattern. This is especially true for "positionally bound."
68 The terms *"seinsgebunden"* and *"seinsverbunden,"* or similar versions of them, appeared earlier in the unpublished works, "Sociological Theory of Culture" and *Konservatismus*, although the distinction there was not as clear because of the primarily nonpolitical nature of these works. Still, the usage was fairly consistent with my interpretation. For example, in "Sociological Theory of Culture," he described the "social bondedness" (*soziale Gebundenheit*) of methodology, i.e., how different methodological approaches were "bound" to certain social strata, which made them one-sided. *ST*, pp. 177,* 272.* [*SD*, pp. 196, 304.] However, he described the type of knowledge that he saw synthesizing these limited approaches as "existentially connected" (*existenzverbunden*). Ibid., p. 181.* [P. 200.] In *Konservatismus* (where *seinsgebunden* and *seinsverbunden* were first used with any frequency), the difference between the two was somewhat muted by the view that conservatism, as a single world aspiration, was both existentially bound and existentially connected. Nevertheless, the difference was there. He described historical thought in gener-

al as existentially connected, whereas existential bondedness was usually reserved for discussions of conservatism specifically. When Savigny opposed
his positive affirmation to that of natural law, he dismissed the latter as too
abstract. His view, on the other hand, was existentially connected, i.e., connected to the sphere of existence in general and hence better suited to be a
universal view. Möser, with his restricted view, did not make such universal
claims, but rather spoke only for a certain rank. This willingness to accept
only a corner of the present meant that his thought was not only existentially
connected, but also communally bound (*gemeinschaftsgebunden*).

69 Thus, when Ernst Grünwald used the phrase *"als seinsverbunden enthüllt"*
(*Soziologie des Wissens*, p. 190), I believe he was incorrect, for thought could
only be "unmasked" as existentially bound, not connected.

70 *IUE*, pp. 78–81, 93. [*IUG*, pp. 71–3, 82.]

71 Ibid., p. 106.* [Pp. 92–3.]

72 The political character of relational knowledge can be seen in Mannheim's
account of the relationship of individual and group consciousness, a very
misunderstood element of his thought. He did not write that all individual
ideas sprang from the group. In fact, he was not overly concerned with the
question: Where do ideas come from? That question was epistemological; his
concerns were political, and his political question was: How is existence
changed and what is the relationship of ideas to that change? He believed
that only groups could change reality politically and, therefore, ideas that
contributed to this change had to be group ideas, had to be connected to the
political position of the group. All utopias were group products. As an individual, one might have a variety of ideas, aspirations, etc., but those were
significant politically only when they were in accord with group consciousness. Those ideas of an individual that could not be imputed to the
position of a group were politically superfluous. This approach begged the
question of whether the ideas originated in the mind of an individual or in a
group mind, the whole question of causality in the relationship between ideas
and existence, for these were epistemological not political questions.

73 *IUE*, p. 95.* [*IUG*, pp. 83–4.]

74 Ibid., p. 260. [P. 223.]

75 Ibid., p. 194. [P. 171.]

76 Mannheim wrote in 1931: "The impetus to research in the sociology of
knowledge may be guided so that it will not absolutize the concept of existential connectedness; rather that precisely the discovery of the *existential connectedness* of the views at hand will be seen as the first step to the solution of the
problem of *existential bondedness* itself." Ibid., p. 301.* [P. 259.]

77 This term is often translated as "socially unattached intelligentsia." I have
chosen the more literal translation because I see Mannheim contrasting the
term to "existentially bound" rather than to "existentially connected."

78 Merton, "Karl Mannheim" p. 507. Also see Hans Speier, "Soziologie oder
Ideologie," *Die Gesellschaft*, vol. 7, pt. 1 (1930), p. 367. Even Mannheim's
friend, Paul Tillich, accused him of this. "Ideologie und Utopie," *Die
Gesellschaft*, vol. 6, pt. 2 (1929), pp. 352–3.

79 Curtius wrote a review of *Ideology and Utopia* entitled "Soziologie – und ihre Grenzen," *Neue Schweizer Rundschau*, vol. 22 (1929), pp. 727–36. His attack was incorporated into a book, *Deutscher Geist in Gefahr* (Stuttgart and Berlin, 1932).

80 Curtius, *Deutscher Geist*, pp. 16–46.

81 Ibid., pp. 77–8.

82 Ibid., pp. 80–1; Curtius, "Soziologie," pp. 728, 732.

83 Curtius, *Deutscher Geist*, p. 96; Curtius, "Soziologie," p. 733.

84 Curtius, *Deutscher Geist*, pp. 98–121; Curtius, "Soziologie," p. 734. Curtius believed that the proper approach to philosophy could be found in the old humanism of classical Germany before the materialistic humanism of the nineteenth century had taken hold. This discipline emphasized the rational, religious, and traditional aspects of philosophy and, therefore, was the true principle of *Bildung*. Germany had to learn from Goethe a "living preservation of timeless spiritual values."

85 Fogarasi, "Die Soziologie der Intelligenz und die Intelligenz der Soziologie," *Unter dem Banner des Marxismus*, vol. 4 (1930), pp. 356–75. (This article is reprinted in Lieber (ed.), *Ideologienlehre und Wissenssoziologie*.) Also see Fogarasi, "Der reactionäre Idealismus – Die Philosophie des Sozialfascismus," *Unter dem Banner des Marxismus*, vol. 5 (1931), pp. 214–31.

86 Fogarasi, "Soziologie der Intelligenz." pp. 367–70, 373–5.

87 Ibid., p. 366.

88 Fogarasi, "Reactionäre Idealismus, " p. 217.

89 Both men identified Mannheim's position with that of Max Weber. Curtius, "Soziologie," pp. 735–6; Fogarasi, "Soziologie der Intelligenz," p. 372.

90 Curtius, "Soziologie," p. 736; Fogarasi, "Soziologie der Intelligenz," pp. 373–4.

91 *IUE*, p. 159. [*IUG*, p. 139.]

92 Ibid., pp. 153–6. [Pp. 134–6.] This theory represented a further development of the concept of the intelligentsia first found in "Conservative Thought." There he also postulated a socially free-floating intelligentsia, but he believed that they had to align themselves with existing social groups; they could not have a social identity of their own. This was close to the position taken by Lukács. Instead of viewing the intelligentsia as a social group made up of heterogeneous parts, he believed that each of these "parts" belonged to a different social group. Even though he had developed his concept of intellectual commitment as an alternative standard of social classification to Marxian economic interest, he had not worked out this alternative completely. However, in *Ideology and Utopia* he did, and he came to the conclusion that the intelligentsia had a different commitment from that of other social groups and could consequently be granted a social existence of their own.

93 Jenö Kurucz misses the point when he writes that Mannheim believed the intelligentisia to be free (unconnected) from every philosophical commitment. Kurucz, "Mannheims Werk in sozialphilosophischer Sicht," *Archiv für Rechts- und Sozialphilosophie* (1963), pp. 88–9. Rather, the intelligentsia were free (unbound) because they were connected to every political commitment.

94 *IUE*, p. 159. [*IUG*, p. 139.]
95 Ibid., p. 259.* [P. 222.]
96 Ibid., pp. 259–60. [Pp. 222–3.]
97 Ibid., p. 259. [P. 222.]
98 The description of the free-floating intelligentsia was undoubtedly written after the description of this fourth group and should be considered an extension of the latter, in spite of the order of the essays in *Ideology and Utopia.*
99 *IUE*, p. 172.* [*IUG*, p. 150.]
100 Ibid., p. 170.* [P. 149.]
101 Ibid., p. 172. [P. 150.]
102 Ibid., p. 163.* [P. 142.] Compare this with the quotation by Weber above in this chapter, referred to in note 21 above.
103 Ibid., p. 169. [P. 148.] Mannheim would elaborate on this in his essays of the early 1930s, published posthumously as *ESC.*
104 Ibid., pp. 176–7.* [P. 154.]
105 Ibid., pp. 163, 189. [Pp. 142, 165.]
106 Ibid., p. 262.* [P. 224.]
107 Here I assume that Lukács agreed with Fogarasi that Marxism was the science of the proletariat. Fogarasi, "Reactionäre Idealismus," p. 217.
108 Lukács could not accept this and claimed that there was no difference between relativism and Mannheim's relationism. Lukács, *Die Zerstörung der Vernunft* (Berlin, 1955), p. 501. Also see Simonds, *Mannheim's Sociology*, p. 11.
109 *IUE*, p. 163. [*IUG*, p. 142.]
110 Ibid., p. 191. [P. 167.]
111 For a discussion of this intention, see the Introduction of Kettler, Meja, and Stehr to *Konservatismus*, as well as their "Mannheim and Conservatism." Mannheim proposed a book of three essays: "Historicism" (Troeltsch), "Problem of Sociology of Knowledge" (Scheler), and an essay on Weber. The project fell through when he refused the publisher's request to rework the first two essays.
112 See Bill Kinser and Neil Kleinman, *The Dream That Was No More a Dream* (New York, 1969).

5. Transition (1930–1936)

1 This is certainly the position of Gunter Remmling in his full-length studies of Mannheim's career. Boris, in the only other lengthy work on Mannheim's English period, accepts Remmling's division of the German and English periods, although he does not accept the divisions within the latter period. *Krise und Planung*, pp. 1, 281. Shorter attempts to connect the two periods, but with interpretations quite different from mine, are Kettler, "Political Theory, Ideology, Sociology: The Question of Karl Mannheim," *Cultural Hermeneutics*, vol. 3 (1975), pp. 69–80, and ch. 3 of Kettler, Meja, and Stehr, *Karl Mannheim.*
2 Remmling writes that Mannheim was also made director of the sociological seminar at the University. *Sociology of Mannheim*, p. 66.
3 Coser, *Masters*, p. 446. Also see Hannah Tillich, *From Time to Time* (New York, 1973), p. 142.

4 *International Institute of Social Research: A Short Description of Its History and Aims* (New York, 1934), p. 3. The institute sought to carry out its program in four main areas: (1) contributions to the development of a theory of change, (2) cooperation of scholars of different departments in order to investigate special sociological problems, (3) studies in the field of economic planning, and (4) publication of a journal of social theory and research. Ibid., pp. 8–11. Max Horkheimer, in his inaugural address as head of the institute, stressed the importance of an interdisciplinary approach for the development of a comprehensive social philosophy. Horkheimer, *Sozialphilosophische Studien,* ed. Werner Brede (Frankfurt/Main, 1932), p. 41. In his later writings, Mannheim was to stress the importance of all these points.

5 Martin Jay, *The Dialectical Imagination* (Boston, 1973), pp. 21, 24, 29, 63, 294. The above-cited *Short Description* lists Mannheim as a participant in a seminar on social history and the history of ideas, p. 12.

6 Conversation with Adolph Lowe (Adolf Löwe) on April 20, 1971. Also see Tillich, *Time to Time,* p. 143; Remmling, *Sociology of Mannheim,* p. 66. Horkheimer criticized *Ideology and Utopia* as a retreat from Marxism back to an earlier Idealism. See *Sozialphilosophische Studien,* p. 32. Herbert Marcuse, who was soon to become a member of the institute, was less critical in "Zur Wahrheitsproblematik der soziologische Methode," *Die Gesellschaft,* vol. 6, pt. 2 (1929), pp. 256–369. Also see Martin Jay, "The Frankfurt School's Critique of Karl Mannheim and the Sociology of Knowledge," *Telos,* no. 20 (1974), pp. 72–89.

7 Conversation with Lowe; Remmling, *Sociology of Mannheim,* p. 66. In a letter to Oscar Jászi's son, Gyuri, who wanted to study in Germany, Mannheim described the academic setting of Frankfurt as a rather intensive, but undogmatic, *"Arbeitsgemeinschaft."* This was in contrast to Berlin, where the atmosphere was much more political. The most significant aspect of this letter was that it was written on January 16, 1933, only two weeks before the Nazi seizure of power began. This letter is located in the Oscar Jászi Collection at Columbia University.

8 Emory Bogardus wrote that Mannheim had to stand silently by while his classes were disrupted by Nazi and anti-Nazi demonstrations. "Mannheim and Social Reconstruction," *Sociology and Social Research,* vol. 32 (1947), p. 548. Tillich reports how helpless the Frankfurt intellectuals felt with the Nazi violence going on around them. *Time to Time,* pp. 149–53. Also see Simonds, *Mannheim's Sociology,* p. 6.

9 Conversation with Jean Floud, April 8, 1971. This difficulty is reflected in his letters to Wirth, which switched to English only when the transitional period had concluded.

10 In 1933, the English began a program to find places in English universities for those academicians who were forced to leave Germany. Most of the emergency positions were at the University of London. Mannheim was the first of the refugees to be placed. For a general description of the process, see Norman Bentwich, *The Rescue and Achievement of Refugee Scholars* (The Hague, 1953), especially pp. 4–40. Mannheim had been actively trying to secure a position in

the United States using Jászi and Wirth as his sponsors. However, he decided to accept the offer from England because, as he wrote to Wirth, Harold Laski had convinced him that he would have a pioneering role in the establishment of sociology in England. See the letter to Wirth of July 26, 1933. Also see Kettler, Meja, and Stehr, *Karl Mannheim*, ch. 3 pp. 108–9.

11 Conversations with Lowe and Floud. It became clear that Mannheim would never receive a professorship at the LSE, due in part to the conflict with Ginsberg. Aside from the question of personality conflict, part of the problem can be seen in an article Ginsberg wrote on German sociology in 1933, where he argued against abstract sociological discussions of matters such as methodology and cited *Ideology and Utopia* as an example of more concrete scholarship. "Recent Tendencies in Sociology," *Economica*, no. 39 (1933), pp. 22, 39. However, Mannheim's work, for reasons we shall see later in this chapter, was becoming more abstract, leading to Ginsberg's disillusionment. See the discussion by Kettler, Meja, and Stehr in *Karl Mannheim*, pp. 118–24.

12 Young made this statement in 1941 over Mannheim's proposed editorship of a study on the workings of democracy. Mannheim's proposal and the responses to it can be found in the papers of Lord A. D. Lindsay, located in the University Archives at the University of Keele, England.

13 Conversation with Floud; Edward Shils, "Karl Mannheim," *International Encyclopedia of the Social Sciences* (New York, 1968), vol. 9, p. 561. A fourth factor contributing to Mannheim's insecurity was his living conditions upon arriving in London. He and his wife lived in a second-rate hotel in Bloomsbury in what has been termed "refugee conditions." It must be pointed out that Mannheim was not alone in these conditions – many academic refugees occupied similar living quarters – and that the times were hard for the English as well. Lowe, a fellow refugee, reports that he and Mannheim in no way felt that they were being mistreated. The purpose here is not to paint a picture of extreme hardship but to point out that Mannheim's material living conditions in no way offset the uncertain intellectual atmosphere and could have aggravated it.

14 Mannheim made this point in "Function of the Refugee," pp. 5–6.

15 In Frankfurt, Mannheim published "Economic Ambition," (1930) and *Gegenwartsaufgaben* (1932), both programmatic speeches to academics; "Wissenssoziologie" (1931), the encyclopedia article summarizing the discipline; "American Sociology," (1932), a book review that contrasted Anglo-American and German sociology; and "The Spiritual Crisis in Light of Sociology" (1932), a newspaper article. Three essays from Frankfurt were modified in England and published posthumously as *ESC*. (See Wolff's Introduction to *FKM*, pp. lxxxvii–lxxxviii.) In England, he published three short essays, "German Sociology," (1934), "The Place of Sociology" (1936), and "The Sociological Nature of Human Valuations" (1936); the Introduction to *IUE* (1936); and, most importantly, *MG* (1934), which was written in German. In addition, a reconstruction of a series of lectures has been published posthumously as *Systematic Sociology*. Of all the nonposthumously published works during this transitional period, only "Economic Ambition" and the third essay of *MG* have the length and style of the earlier German material.

231

16 Those works that restated the nature and methodology of the sociology of knowledge could be considered a subtheme to the basic discussion of the place of sociology.

17 *MS*, p. 53.* [*MG*, pp. 28–9.] Although I will use Mannheim's term "irrationality," "nonrationality" might actually be preferable because a sense of direction and meaning was implied. See Chapter 2 and note 67 to that chapter.

18 Like the earlier themes, these were not simply temporal. Substantial irrationality continued to exist, Mannheim believed, but did not play the dominant role it once had.

19 By definition, substantial irrationality could not be directly related to a stage of thought. This incongruity points out the structural nature of the relationships I am drawing. As in earlier chapters, I am not claiming an identity of contents.

20 *MS*, p. 150. [*MG*, pp 95–6.]

21 Ibid., pp. 67–8. [Pp. 45–7.]

22 Ibid., p. 53. [Pp. 29–30.]

23 Substantial rationality was concerned with the relationship between the knowing subject and the object (the rest of society), whereas functional rationality was concerned only with gaining knowledge about the object. For functional rationality, the subject was interchangeable; it was concerned with a technique usable by anyone and not with placing a certain subject in a certain environment.

24 *MS*, pp. 151–3. [*MG*, pp. 97–9.]

25 Mannheim wrote: "This highly abstract method of thought is the highest refinement of an approach which seeks to realize both practically and theoretically only isolated individual objects, isolated causal sequences, isolated individual sequences of wishes, but which does not yet dare to concern itself with the concrete structure into which this individual object is to be integrated." Ibid., p. 169.* [P. 120.]

26 Ibid., pp. 68–9. [Pp. 47–8.]

27 Ibid., p. 58.* [P. 35.]

28 "Problem of Sociology of Knowledge," *ESK*, p. 175.* [*W*, p. 362.] Also see "Economic Ambition," *ESK*, p. 233. [*W*, p. 629.]

29 *MS*, p. 152. [*MG*, p. 98.]

30 Ibid., pp. 191–3. [Pp. 149–51.] In his interpretation of Mannheim's theory of planning, Karl Popper mistakenly equates understanding society as a whole with changing the whole of society. Popper's attack on Mannheim must be viewed in terms of his initial misinterpretation. Popper, *Poverty of Historicism*, pp. 67-70. Also see Boris, *Krise und Planung*, pp. 195–201.

31 *MS*, p. 70.* [*MG*, p. 49.]

32 *EŚC*, p. 116.

33 *MS*, pp. 81–2. [*MG*, pp. 60–1.]

34 Ibid., p. 81. [Pp. 59, 2–5.]

35 The means by which the elite was selected was bureaucratic and monopolistic, i.e., within the guidelines of the regulating institutions, and favored those "who have a flair for meeting every situation in terms of prescriptions pre-

viously laid down." *ESC*, p. 202. At this stage, such prescriptions were more traditional than legal-bureaucratic.

36 *MS*, pp. 96–7. [*MG*, pp. 73–4.] Mannheim seems to have had in mind the "cultivated" rank in Germany, the *Bildungsbürgertum*, which provided an audience for its institutional, socially active core.

37 Ibid., pp. 68–9. [Pp. 46–7.]

38 *ESC*, pp. 187–8, 216.

39 *MS*, pp. 39–44. [*MG*, pp. 11–18.]

40 Ibid., p. 97 [p. 74]; *ESC*, p. 117.

41 *ESC*, pp. 195–6; *MS*, pp. 63, 85. [*MG*, pp. 41, 63.] It should be noted that Mannheim did not use the term "masses" to refer to a particular group, as Ortega did, but rather to a social-psychological condition. Later, he wrote: "By identifying the increasing numbers in society with the mass these thinkers [e.g., Ortega] prevent a conscientious distinction between the different possibilities of the different forms of group integration. Not every grouping of the many is a mass or crowd. It is important to notice at this point that groups with definite functions and inner articulation do not lower but raise the mental level of their members, whereas the disintegration of personality generally corresponds to disintegrations in society." *D*, p. 92.

42 *MS*, pp. 42–50, 59, 67. [*MG*, pp. 16–25, 36, 45.]

43 Ibid., p. 97. [Pp. 74–5.] Mannheim gave as an example workers' theater plays put on for trade unions and similar "unities."

44 *MG*, p. 2. Also see *MS*, pp. 80–1. [*MG*, pp. 58–9.]

45 *MS*, pp. 45–6, 62–3, 108. [*MG*, pp. 20–1, 40–1, 85–6.]

46 Here, Mannheim's characterization of fascism changed from that of pure irrational will to that of functionally rational manipulation. This meant a switch from the unregulated sphere to the regulated sphere, from being an extreme agent of change to being simply a parasitical exploiter of chaos. Such a switch reflected Mannheim's reaction to the victory of Nazism.

47 Mannheim did classify planning as "political" in *MS* and did contrast it with administration (p. 193 [pp. 151–2]). However, "political" here was almost synonymous with "historical" and did not involve the unregulated competition of parties. He wrote: "Planning is an act of reconstruction of a historically developed society into a unity which is regulated more and more perfectly by mankind."

48 Ibid., p. 152.* [P. 98.] He also wrote: "In the free realm of events, where unregulated selection based on conflict prevails, thinking which is too far ahead of the immediate situation may be dangerous. . . . The increasing density of events makes the possibility of a natural balance through competition or through mutual adaptation more and more hopeless." Ibid., pp. 156–7.* [Pp. 103–5.]

49 Ibid., pp. 153–4.* [Pp. 99–100.]

50 The different versions of this schema are located in *Gegenwartsaufgaben*, pp. 6–27; "Place of Sociology," *ESSP*, pp. 204–8; *ESC*, pp. 55–9; *Systematic Sociology*, pp. 1–4.

51 *Gegenwartsaufgaben*, p. 6. Mannheim said of "systematic and general so-

ciology:" "It is called general sociology because the general forms and tendencies, as they may be found in every society, primitive as well as modern, are described in it. It is called systematic sociology because it does not deal with these factors of the living together of man in a haphazard way but in a systematic order, following the line from the simplest to the most complex." *Systematic Sociology*, p. 2. One should note the change in terminology here. In "Cultural-Sociological Knowledge," "general" referred to an inductive, positivistic methodology, one of three belonging to "sociology." In *Gegenwartsaufgaben*, "general" meant what "sociology" had previously meant and the inductive methodology was now called "the ahistorical, axiomatic approach." In the English writings, the adjective "systematic" was added to "general" and the three-part methodology was dropped.

52 "Sociological Nature of Valuations," *ESSP*, pp. 238–41; *Systematic Sociology*, p. 16. In the English writings, he ignored the historical psychology of Dilthey (which had been his concern in the early German writings) for more abstract psychological theories of human nature such as behaviorism and psychoanalysis.

53 See *Gegenwartsaufgaben*, p. 11.

54 Mannheim cited Max Weber's *Economy and Society* as an example of comparative sociology. *ESC*, p. 56.

55 *Gegenwartsaufgaben*, pp. 14–21, especially p. 20.

56 Mannheim wrote that the sociology of knowledge was an "organ of critical self-control, [and] has already succeeded in detecting and subjecting to control important groups of sources of error." "American Sociology," *ESSP*, pp. 192–3.

57 *ESC*, p. 237. Mannheim believed that Anglo-American sociology showed what could happen when there was no synthesizing factor in the social sciences. English and American sociologists, he said, were interested only in solving specific problems that could be separated from the social fabric as a whole. By dividing up society in this way, they were able to guarantee an exactness of terms within their limited scope of investigation. What seemed to make a problem worth studying in America was the fact that it could be quantified and measured, an attitude he termed the "exactitude complex." He believed that the missing ingredient in American and English sociology was sufficient theory, which provided a synthesis of the whole. "American Sociology," *ESSP*, p. 186–92.

58 *Gegenwartsaufgaben*, pp. 53–6. Mannheim did grant ontology priority over other disciplines, but this was done in passing, while rejecting philosophy's claim to absolute sovereignty (p. 55). Also see *IUE*, p. 294, [*IUG*, p. 252.]

59 "Ankündigung" to *Schriften zur Philosophie und Soziologie*, whose editorship Mannheim was assuming. In this announcement and in other writings of the early years of the second transitional period, he made efforts to convince men like Curtius, who attacked sociology, of the need for philosophers and sociologists to examine how they could work together. Philosophers certainly need not fear sociology, which, he wrote to Eduard Spranger, did not study forces with no meaning, but rather studied powers that were tied to meaning.

Letter to Spranger, April 12, 1929 (Deutsche Bundesarchiv, Koblenz). Also see "Problems of Sociology in Germany," *FKM*, pp. 269–70. [*W*, pp. 622–4.] By 1932, this conciliatory tone, although still present, was less evident.

60 *Gegenwartsaufgaben*, pp. 44–51; *ESC*, pp. 230–9.

61 "Die geistige Krise im Lichte der Soziologie," *Stuttgarter Neues Tageblatt* (Dec. 31, 1932).

62 *Gegenwartsaufgaben*, p. 50.

63 "Place of Sociology," *ESSP*, p. 208. Also see *ESC*, p. 239.

64 *MS*, p. 177. [*MG*, p. 130.]

65 John Stuart Mill, *A System of Logic, Ratiocinative and Inductive*, 9th ed. (London, 1875), vol. 2, pp. 458–9.

66 Mill appears to have used the concept of "primary" in much the same sense that Mannheim did in his dissertation on epistemology.

67 Mill, *System of Logic*, vol. 2, p. 461.

68 Morris Ginsberg, *Sociology* (London, 1937), pp. 19–24. Mannheim was probably introduced to Mill's theory by Ginsberg.

69 *MS*, p. 178. [*MG*, pp. 131–2.]

70 Ginsberg, *Sociology*, p. 24.

71 *MS*, p. 183. [*MG*, pp. 138–9.]

72 Ibid., p. 184. [P. 140.]

73 Ibid., pp. 178–80. [Pp. 131–4.]

74 Ibid., pp. 186–7. [Pp. 143–4.] Here Mannheim was referring to orthodox Marxism. This was basically the same argument that appeared in his German writings, when he accused Marxists of having a limited perspective.

75 Ibid., p. 187. [P. 144.]

76 Ibid., pp. 213–17. [Pp. 179–84.] Also see *Systematic Sociology*, p. 16. Mannheim denied that all behaviorism was fascistic, but rather he said that fascism used behavioristic techniques for its political success.

77 *MS*, pp. 217–20. [*MG*, pp. 184–8.] Also see *Systematic Sociology*, pp. 17–26, and Boris, *Krise und Planung*, pp. 49–51.

78 Mannheim also discussed a third theory, pragmatism, which while "aware of that organic process by which every act of thought is essentially a part of conduct and reject[ing] the older artificial distinction between action and pure theory," suffered the limitation of being concerned only with the everyday practical activity of the individual rather than with society as a whole. Pragmatism dealt with the individual only "at the level of chance discovery – a state of affairs in which the practical, immediate, and often unconscious acts of adaptation are primary." It was a perfectly acceptable theory in a very simplistic and direct society, but not in more complex industrial society. *MS*, pp. 206–7. [*MG*, pp. 170–2.]

79 Ibid., pp. 220–2.* [Pp. 188–9.]

80 See "Economic Ambition," *ESK*, p. 265 [*W*, p. 674], as well as the Stuttgart newspaper article cited in note 61 above.

81 *MS*, p. 75. [*MG*, p. 56.]

82 Sometimes Mannheim's terminology confuses the issue. For example, he took the term "horde solidarity" from Durkheim and with it used the latter's term

"mechanical solidarity." This latter term implied the opposite of the organic phenomenon Mannheim was describing.

83 In addition to the basic trichotomy, Mannheim also retained the more complex version of it from "Competition."

84 See *Gegenwartsaufgaben*, p. 39; *MG*, p. vii; *IUE*, pp. 36–8. In correspondence of this period, he used the term "dialectics" in an almost pejorative sense, implying a political approach without factual controls. See his letter to Spranger, April 12, 1929 (Deutsche Bundesarchiv, Koblenz), and his letter to Gyuri Jászi, Jan. 16, 1933 (Oscar Jászi Papers, Columbia University).

85 As John Heeren notes, this meant a demotion of the intelligentsia from its role in *Ideology and Utopia*. Heeren, "Mannheim and the Intellectual Elite," pp. 8–11. Another group prominent in *Ideology and Utopia* but given little attention in these transitional writings was the socialists, the leading political party.

86 For example, see Adorno, *Prisms*, pp. 38, 43, 46, and Herbert Marcuse's review of *MG* in *Zeitschrift für Sozialforschung*, vol. 4 (1935), p. 271.

87 For example, the trichotomy of thought and morality presented in *MS* was structurally similar to that of political world aspirations in *Ideology and Utopia*; however, the views of the specific types of liberalism, conservatism, and socialism were abstracted into types applied to all people.

88 *MS*, p. 3.

89 Ibid., p. 213.* [*MG*, p. 178.]

90 Ibid., pp. 199–200. [P. 163.]

6. The synthesis of democratic planning (1938–1947)

1 This periodization is arbitrary on my part. In fact, two articles from 1937, ch. 3 of *MS* and "Diagnosis of Our Time," *FKM*, pp. 350–66 ["Zur Diagnose unserer Zeit," *Mass und Wert*, vol. 1 (1937), pp. 100–21], are included in this period. The periodization is supported by Mannheim's letters to Louis Wirth. In his letter of Aug. 13, 1938, he was very pessimistic. He complained about Ginsberg's fear of any new forms of knowledge and stated that a synthesis of American empiricism and certain German approaches would be very fruitful. (This perhaps could be seen as a hint that he would like to come to America. Jászi's letter of April 23, 1936, indicates that Mannheim had been inquiring about employment in the United States.) In Mannheim's letter of April 6, 1939, we see a new optimism. He wrote that the English were changing rapidly and that he now had a "mission." Also see Kettler, Meja, and Stehr, *Karl Mannheim*, pp. 129–30. The most important works are *D; FPD;* the 1940 additions *MS;* "Planned Society and Human Personality," *ESSP*, pp, 255–310; and *Sociology of Education* (with W. A. C. Stewart). Kettler, Meja, and Stehr have raised questions about using works such as *Education* and *FPD*, which were edited and published posthumously. Because Stewart's organization and supplementation of Mannheim's lecture notes in *Education* was so great, he felt obliged to list himself as a coauthor of the book. In spite of the need to assume caution in citing and quoting from the book, it does develop many of the ideas just briefly mentioned in Mannheim's others

works. I believe that somewhat less caution is required in the case of *FPD*. Mannheim's wife Julia certainly felt that the work was true to his views, so much so that she wanted the names of the editors left off the book. Letter to Lindsay, Feb. 24, 1951, located in the Lindsay Papers at Keele.

2 This discussion is based primarily on Noreen Branson and Margot Heinemann, *Britain in the Nineteen Thirties* (London, 1971), and David Thomson, *England in the Twentieth Century* (Baltimore, 1965).

3 Harold Macmillan wrote: "It had become evident that the structure of capitalist society in its old form had broken down. . . . The whole system had to be reassessed. Perhaps it could not survive at all; it certainly could not survive without radical change." Quoted in Branson and Heinemann, *Britain in Thirties*, p. 6.

4 Most of my information about this group comes from Dmitri Mirsky, *The Intelligentsia of Great Britain* (London, 1935), and Stuart Samuels, "English Intellectuals and Politics in the 1930's," in Philip Rieff (ed.), *On Intellectuals* (Garden City, N.Y., 1970), pp. 213–68.

5 William H. Beveridge, "The London School of Economics and the University of London," in Margaret Cole (ed.), *The Webbs and Their Work* (London, 1949), pp. 44–5; John M. Gaus, *Great Britain: A Study in Civic Loyalty* (Chicago, 1929), p. 188. Lord Beveridge, the director of the LSE until 1937, did not share the enthusiasm of the more radical teachers like Harold Laski for political involvement. At one point, he asked Laski to curtail his political activities because they were arousing public opinion that Beveridge felt was detrimental to the LSE. Beveridge admitted that his "swan song" in 1937, in which he called for more political detachment and more emphasis on observation at the expense of theory, did not go over very well among a large part of the audience. Beveridge, *The London School of Economics and Its Problems, 1919–1937* (London, 1960), pp. 36, 56; Beveridge, *Power and Influence* (New York, 1955), pp. 252–4.

6 The Conservative Stanley Baldwin assessed his party's victory in October 1931, thusly: "The electors have declared in no uncertain voice that the insidious doctrines of class warfare cannot make headway against the general desire for national cooperation at a time of national emergency." Quoted in Branson and Heinemann, *Britain in Thirties*, pp. 18–19.

7 Thomson, *England*, p. 181.

8 See Arthur Marwick, *The Home Front* (London, 1976), pp. 10–12.

9 Thomson, *England*, p. 206.

10 Quoted in Maurice Bruce, *The Coming of the Welfare State* (London, 1965), p. 273.

11 See Ibid., pp. 291–3; Thomson, *England*, pp. 205–7; W. Friedmann, *Law and Social Change in Contemporary Britain* (London, 1951), pp. 278–80; Karl de Schweinitz, *England's Road to Social Security* (New York, 1961), pp. 227–46.

12 My information comes primarily from Roger Kojecky, *T. S. Eliot's Social Criticism* (New York, 1972), pp. 163–97, 237–8, and Alec R. Vidler, *Scenes from a Clerical Life* (London, 1977), pp. 116–23. Other members of the Moot were: J. H. Oldham, Eric Fenn, H. A. Hodges, Eleanora Iredale, Adolf Löwe,

Walter Moberly, Walter Oakeshott, Gilbert Shaw, John Baillie, Kathleen
Bliss, and Hector Hetherington.

13 Eliot said: "It was a forum in which men from different disciplines and often
very different outlooks on social questions met together. . . . The existence of
tensions between outlooks, of discussion, of vitality and variety, were themselves a valuable harvest." Quoted in Kojecky, *Eliot's Social Criticism*, p. 197.

14 Vidler, *Scenes*, p. 119; Kojecky, *Eliot's Social Criticism*, p. 197. Kettler, Meja,
and Stehr have noted that the Moot was nowhere as important to the other
members as it was to Mannheim. Thus his centrality for the activities of the
group did not mean centrality for its members' activities in general.

15 F. A. Lea, *The Life of John Middleton Murry* (London, 1959), p. 251. Eliot
expressed similar sentiments in reviewing *MS*. See Eliot, "Man and Society,"
Spectator, vol. 164, no. 5841 (June 7, 1940), p. 782. Mannheim himself
stressed the importance of his experience in *MS*, p. 4.

16 Vidler, *Scenes*, p. 123. Eliot wrote in *The Times* on Mannheim's death of "the
remarkable influence which Mannheim had come to exercise, within the
short period of his residence in this country, upon men of his own generation, not all engaged in the same studies, who had the benefit of his acquain-
tance. In informal discussion among a small group, he gained an ascendancy
which he never sought, but which was, on the contrary, imposed upon him by
the eagerness of others to listen to what he had to say." Quoted in Kojecky,
Eliot's Social Criticism, pp. 196–7. Lord A. D. Lindsay, who although not a
member of the Moot had close ties to its members, wished for a short book
entitled "The Wisdom of Mannheim." See his review of *FPD* in *British Journal
of Sociology*, vol. 3 (1952), p. 86.

17 Mannheim continued to teach at the LSE, but in a marginal position. In a
letter to Wirth (Sept. 17, 1939), he wrote that, due to wartime economies at
the LSE, its director had advised him to explore the possibility of employment in the United States. Also see Kettler, Meja, and Stehr, *Karl Mannheim*, p. 130. In some unpublished notes entitled "The Place of the Study of
Modern Society in a Militant Democracy: Some Practical Suggestions," written in the early 1940s and submitted to Lindsay, Mannheim advocated the
creation of a new academic faculty to deal exclusively with the problems of
modern society. He stated that, if such a faculty were established at the LSE, it
should be independent from the Department of Sociology. This document is
in the Lindsay Papers at Keele.

18 Friends, critics, and detractors agreed that Mannheim's popularity was at its
height at the time of his death. This popularity was lamented by people like
G. F. Bantock, "The Cultural Implications of Planning and Popularization,"
Scrutiny, vol. 14 (1947), pp. 171–2, and Karl Popper, *Poverty of Historicism*, p.
80; it was welcomed by men like Adolf Löwe and A. D. Lindsay. In an
obituary delivered over the BBC, Lindsay said that a "surprising number" of
influential people wrote and consulted Mannheim. "In the years he spent in
this country he exerted a remarkable influence. He converted some of our
leading educationalists to a belief in the importance of sociology in education." (In Lindsay Papers at Keele.) Jean Floud and W. A. C. Stewart, the

former a critic of Mannheim, the latter a supporter, agree that his popularity was a passing thing and that his influence disappeared rather quickly after his death. Above-cited conversation with Floud; Stewart, "Karl Mannheim and the Sociology of Education," *British Journal of Educational Studies,* vol. 1 (1953), pp. 99, 106; Stewart, *Karl Mannheim,* p. 35.

19 The following are examples of Mannheim's faith in reaching the masses: (a) In the Keele collection are transcripts from two sets of BBC lectures that Mannheim gave, one to high school students and one to the postwar German public; (b) Coser notes that none of Mannheim's later English articles appeared in the type of academic journal in which his German writings appeared (*Masters,* p. 462); (c) at the time of his death, he was seriously considering a position with UNESCO, and he was asked to help organize the University of Canberra in Australia; (d) the personal assistant of Lord Beveridge attended the Moot meeting of January 1943, indicating possible political influence (Kojecky, *Eliot's Social Criticism,* p. 184). It must be remembered that here I am interested in Mannheim's perspective and aspirations and not in the realities of the situation.

20 Letter of Nov. 19, 1940, in Lindsay Papers at Keele.

21 "Topic for the Next Meeting of the Moot." This paper was prepared for the meeting of Jan. 10, 1941, and is located in the Mannheim Papers at Keele. In it he addressed an idea previously taken up by the Moot – the "Order." The Moot saw such an entity as a democratic alternative to the "orders" of the totalitarian regimes, which operated outside traditional institutions and were able to deal with the processes of change. In his paper, Mannheim described the "Order" as a "fellowship of pioneering minds" whose task it was to stimulate new ways of thinking to meet the needs of the changing times. Its task was to penetrate the life of closed groups (i.e., clubs, common rooms, political parties) and infuse them with new energies from the more activistic elements of society (i.e., the youth). What the "Order" was not to do was impose any kind of rigid structure either upon itself or upon traditional institutions. It was to operate within established democratic institutions. He did not assign it the synthetic positions of either the Budapest intelligentsia or the free-floating intelligentsia from *Ideology and Utopia.* For a different view of this concept, see Kettler, Meja, and Stehr, *Karl Mannheim,* pp. 138–43.

22 *MS,* p. 5.

23 Löwe, *The Price of Liberty* (London, 1937).

24 Ibid., p. 26.

25 See *FPD,* pp. 99–100, 220; *MS,* p. 5. Also see his earlier "German Sociology," *ESSP,* pp. 226–7. His assertion that Britain was the last representative of European culture came at the Moot meeting of Nov. 20, 1944. (In Mannheim Papers at Keele.)

26 *FPD,* p. 29; *D,* p. 26.

27 Remmling made a similar observation, but with different conclusions. See *Wissenssoziologie,* p. 175, and *Sociology of Mannheim,* pp. 104–5.

28 *D,* p. 7.

29 Ibid., p. 25.

30 *MS*, p. 352; "Planned Society and Personality," *ESSP*, p. 308.

31 *D*, p. 69.

32 *FPD*, pp. 199–206. He wrote: "Integrative behavior is more than compromise. It means that people, though fully aware of the fact that differences of constitution and social position, of drives and interests, shape their experience and attitude to life in different ways, yet transmute their different approaches for the purpose of co-operating in a common way of life. Such transmutation is a creative form of integration: out of the process of common living and co-operative pursuits, a new purpose emerges which the partners come to cherish even more than their original aims. From the very outset this kind of integration offers scope for the dissenter or the man of initiative whose contribution, which may differ from ours, is to be absorbed, not excluded" (p. 203).

33 Ibid., pp. 192, 280.

34 Ibid., p. 36; *MS*, p. 342. Mannheim wrote: "Planned democratic society needs a new type of party system, in which the right to criticize is as strongly developed as the duty to be responsible to the whole. This means that the liberal education for intelligent partisanship, which is mainly defending the interests of your faction and party and leaves the final integration to a large extent to the mutual harmony of interests, must gradually be replaced by a new education for responsible criticism, wherein consciousness of the whole is at least as important as awareness of your own interests." *D*, p. 102. He seems to have favored a two-party system. See *FPD*, pp. 161–7. It should be noted that he used the term "interest," rather than "will" or "aspiration," in conjunction with parties. This helps to explain why *"Wollen"* was translated as "interests" in *IUE*.

35 See especially *D*, pp. 31–53. Also, "Topics for the Next Meeting of the Moot." This position is similar to that presented in the earlier "Science and Youth" (1922).

36 Among the concrete suggestions he offered were the breakdown of the old segregationist attitudes in the public schools and the creation of a national youth movement.

37 This point was emphasized by Adolph Lowe in the above-cited conversation; see Chapter 5, note 6.

38 Eliot, *The Idea of a Christian Society* (New York, 1940), p. 10. Also see J. H. Oldham, *Church, Community and State* (London, 1935), p. 15, and John Middleton Murry, *The Price of Leadership* (London, 1939), pp. 78–9.

39 Eliot, *Idea*, p. 43; Eliot, *Notes toward the Definition of Culture* (New York, 1949), pp. 26–32. Christopher Dawson wrote: "Culture is the form of society. The society without culture is a formless society – a crowd or a collection of individuals brought together by the needs of the moment – while the stronger a culture is, the more completely does it inform and transform the diverse human material of which it is composed. What then is the relation of culture to religion? It is clear that a common way of life involves a common view of life, common standards of value, and consequently a culture is a spiritual community which owes its unity to common beliefs and common ways of

thought far more than to say uniformity of physical type. . . . Religion has been the great unifying force in culture. It has been the guardian of tradition, the preserver of moral law, the educator and teacher of wisdom." *Religion and Culture* (London, 1948), pp. 48–50.

40 Murry, *Price,* pp. 186–7. Oldham was the most direct in identifying Christianity with community: "The Christian Church is committed by its central afffirmations to the belief that the life of man finds its meaning and fulfillment in a community of persons. . . . God adopts us as sons and admits us to a life of communion and personal intercourse with Himself. His Word to us is a word which binds us to our fellow men and unites us with them in a community where love rules. . . . The Christian belief in the supremacy of the personal is the antithesis of the individualism of the humanistic cult of personality. . . . Persons can be persons only in mutuality. Persons and community are correlative terms. Neither can exist without the other." *Church,* pp. 36–8.

41 Murry, *Price,* pp. 186–8.

42 See Dawson, *Religion,* p. 57; Vidler, *Essays in Liberality* (London, 1957), p. 24.

43 Vidler, *Liberality,* pp. 115–22.

44 See, for example, Walter Moberly, *The Universities and Cultural Leadership* (London, 1951), pp. 21–8.

45 Murry emphasized the connection between Christianity and toleration and individual responsibility in *The Free Society* (London, 1948), pp. 121, 125, 133, 145. In one of the "Moot Papers" among Lord Lindsay's papers at Keele, there is an interesting exchange between Eliot and Mannheim in which both agreed that culture had to be democratized, although Eliot expressed more reservations. Also see Kojecky, *Eliot's Social Criticism,* p. 196.

46 Mannheim wrote: "In the past religion fulfilled these functions of interpretation and integration. In the old days religion was a stabilizer; today we turn to it again for assistance in the transition. That means that our religious leaders must keep up with the changing order, building their world outlook and policy upon deeper insight and intellectual comprehension. In view of our need for balance, their interpretation must not be so extremist as to destroy the psychological equilibrium and feeling of security during the transition." *FPD,* p. 313. For a statement on how religion was especially suited for this purpose in England, see *D,* p. 101.

47 Mannheim admitted that there could be various interpretations of the Christian paradigmatic experience, for example, original sin, "the liberating and creative power of love," or "the deeper meaning of suffering." His answer to the question of the relationship of conflicting interpretations of the paradigmatic experience was the same appeal to toleration that characterized his description of the integrative democratic personality. He wrote: "The fact of there being only one Truth does not mean that any group believing itself to be in possession of that truth has the right or even the obligation to extirpate believers in some other creed. If there is indeed only one Truth, it is bound to be more comprehensive than any one human being or any one party could grasp. It is worth listening to everyone, because you can never tell through what individual or what group the voice of God may speak. This is the only

241

way of religious unification and integration compatible with a dynamically planned society on the ideal of planned freedom." *FPD*, p. 288.

48 *D*, pp. 134–6.

49 Ibid., p. 135.

50 Ibid., pp. 117–8.

51 Mannheim wrote: "In periods of change in the past it was the function of religions and of the Church to interpret the transition; to let the members of the community know man's fate, his place in the world, and what man should live by. Today, such collective guidance will have to embody the sociological approach, in order that we may understand social change and its causes." *FPD*, p. 312.

52 *D*, pp. 114, 136; *FPD*, pp. 19–20.

53 See *FPD*, pp. 302–3.

54 *D*, p. 139.

55 *FPD*, p. 244.

56 *MS*, p. 288.

57 Ibid., p. 377; *FPD*, pp. 242, 311; *D*, p. 78.

58 *FPD*, pp. 212, 311.

59 Ibid., p. 201.

60 *D*, p. 52.

61 Mannheim wrote: "In the past mere habit-making and unconscious solidarity might have sufficed, . . . but in a modern democracy solidarity with one's country is only possible if the citizen is capable of judging the issues on which he is called to make decisions; and this power of discrimination in its turn depends upon the thorough understanding of social relations." "Sociology for the Educator," in D. M. E. Dymes (ed.), *Sociology and Education*, p. 5. Also see *FPD*, p. 61.

62 *FPD*, p. 64.

63 In *FPD*, Mannheim wrote: "The author's philosophy has always been guided by the idea of *Seinsverbundenheit*, i.e., by the idea that mental phenomena are related to the environment, the situation and the field, and do not exist in an abstract heaven. . . . The teacher as well as the pupil must have his eyes open to awareness of the milieu in which conscience can actually emerge and achieve power over the individual and others" (p. 216).

64 The terms "communal" and "functional" come from *FPD*, p. 56. In *MS*, he used the terms "communities" and "associations" and cited Tönnies's work (p. 289).

65 *FPD*, p. 58; *MS*, p. 290.

66 *FPD*, p. 57.

67 In *FPD*, p. 109, Mannheim listed four stages in the development of the modern frame group that corresponded to those of *MS* discussed in the previous chapter.

68 *FPD*, p. 57; *MS*, pp. 293–5.

69 Mannheim wrote: "We may call a person 'emancipated' who does not think in terms of 'my country – right or wrong,' who is not a chauvinist expecting his parish church to be the most magnificent in the world. He achieves

emancipation by partial uprooting, by selecting for personal identification only certain traditions and values of his community. In doing so he does not shut out the character-forming influences of community participation, nor does he sacrifice his right to independent thought and personal development." *FPD*, p. 63.

70 Ibid., pp. 45–6.

71 Ibid., p. 6; *D*, p. 1; *MS*, p. 271.

72 *FPD*, pp. 46–7; *MS*, pp. 274–5.

73 Of course, individual forms of social technology could be judged in a substantially rational way as either inconsistent with the basic consensus or outmoded, to be replaced by other forms. But such decisions did not concern the innate "goodness" of the technology.

74 *D*, pp. 2–3; *FPD*, pp. 6–8; *MS*, p. 271; "Diagnosis," *FKM*, pp. 354–5, 366. [*Mass und Wert*, pp. 106, 121.]

75 In addition to *Education*, there are a number of items, including the notes on which that book was based, among the Keele Papers that document Mannheim's great interest in education.

76 H. C. Dent, *Education in Transition* (New York, 1944), p. 78.

77 Ibid., pp. 1–14, 233.

78 Leavis wrote: "Schools and colleges are, or should be, . . . trying to preserve and develop a continuity of consciousness and a mature directing sense of value . . . informed by a traditional wisdom. . . . The universities are recognized symbols of . . . cultural tradition still conceived as a directing force, representing a wisdom older than modern civilization and having an authority that should check and control the blind drive onward of material and mechanical development, with its human consequences." Quoted in Kneller, *Higher Learning in Britain* (Berkeley and Los Angeles, 1955), p. 110.

79 Quoted in ibid., p. 118.

80 Fred Clarke, *Education and Social Change* (London, 1940), pp. 26, 65; Clarke, *The Study of Education in England* (London, 1943), p. 54.

81 Clarke, *Study of Education*, pp. 3–14. He, like Mannheim, also realized the dangers of becoming too centralized.

82 Clarke, *Education and Change*, p. 4. Also see Adolf Löwe, *The Universities in Transformation* (London, 1940), especially pp. 11–19.

83 Clarke, *Education and Change*, pp. 30, 61–7.

84 Kettler, Meja, and Stehr have used a talk by Clarke in 1943 as evidence that he had moved away from Mannheim (who also spoke at the conference) by rejecting sociology in favor of history in the school curriculum. See their *Karl Mannheim*, pp. 156–7. I disagree with this contention. First, it is inconsistent with Clarke's other writings at the time and with the fact that he was instrumental in Mannheim's appointment to a chair at the Institute of Education in 1946. Second, the speech itself, when placed in context, did not contradict Mannheim's position. Clarke began by saying that the "training of the citizen in sound social judgement has now become for us a matter of life or death," a statement with which Mannheim agreed. He then discussed some fallacies of sociology and the importance of history. He was not against sociology but felt

that it had to be subordinate to the study of history, particularly in the education of younger children. He believed that history built a commitment to a general consensus, a sense of participation in the national community of values, and a healthy skepticism toward abstraction. To substitute an abstract sociology for this kind of discipline (which included historical legends as well as more factual history) would be to deprive children of this basic foundation. See Clarke, "History Teaching and Sociology," in Dymes (ed.), *Sociology and Education*, pp. 81–95. None of this contradicted the position of Mannheim, who emphasized the need for a commitment to a consensus of values. In England, as in Germany, Mannheim saw sociology as a clarifying discipline, one that provided perspective but could not create values itself. This was why he placed so much emphasis on spontaneous collectivism and paradigmatic Christianity.

85 Mannheim wrote that communal education permeated the entire traditional society and was largely unconscious. Learning was not a conscious process that had to take place in a formalized institution. In fact, learning was not a separate problem in itself. "Education was simply one of the unconscious techniques for assisting the infant to grow up into a given social order." *Education*, p. 159; *D*, p. 62.
86 *Education*, pp. 18, 159; *D*, pp. 57, 65–7.
87 *D*, pp. 54–6.
88 Ibid., p. 76.
89 See, for example, *D*, pp. 59–60, 74; *FPD*, pp. 105, 259; "Sociology for Educator," pp. 4–9.
90 The publication of *Education* has helped to erase the mistaken view that Mannheim was not interested in this problem. See, for example, Jean Floud and A. H. Halsey, "The Sociology of Education," *Current Sociology*, vol. 7 (1958), pp. 168–78.
91 *Education*, p. 82.
92 Ibid., pp. 28–32.
93 Ibid., pp. 117–30.
94 Ibid., p. 130; *D*, p. 54; *FPD*, pp. 253–5. This concern for adult education went back to his Budapest days.
95 *Education*, pp. 19, 129–30, 135–6; "Planned Society and Personality," *ESSP*, p. 276; *FPD*, pp. 247–8.
96 *MS*, p. 295.
97 Ibid., pp. 306–9. Other social mechanisms cited by Mannheim were the division of labor, the distribution of power, cooperation, and methods of creating social hierarchy.
98 Ibid., pp. 295–8.
99 Ibid., pp. 299–306.
100 Ibid., p. 306.
101 In his last work, *FPD*, Mannheim did not make the distinction between mechanisms, field structures, and situations. Instead, he simply referred to mechanisms (pp. 191–2).
102 *FPD*, pp. 191–7, 234–5; "Planned Society and Personality," *ESSP*, p. 286.

103 *FPD*, p. 235.
104 *MS*, pp. 295–9; *FPD*, pp. 21, 79–80, 119–27.
105 *MS*, pp. 301–3.
106 *FPD*, p. 173.
107 Ibid., pp. 29, 176; *D*, pp. 4–5; *MS*, p. 262; "Diagnosis," *FKM*, pp. 362–3. [*Mass und Wert*, p. 117.]
108 *MS*, pp. 262–3.
109 "Planned Society and Personality," *ESSP*, p. 307.
110 *MS*, p. 263; "Diagnosis," *FKM*, p. 363. [*Mass und Wert*, p. 117.]
111 *FPD*, pp. 149–69; *MS*, pp. 327–44; *D*, p. 49.
112 *FPD*, p. 169.
113 *British Journal of Sociology*, vol. 3 (1952), p. 86.
114 See Remmling, *Sociology of Mannheim*, pp. 109, 124; Coser, *Masters*, p. 441; Wilhelm Röpke, *Die Gesellschaftskrise der Gegenwart* (Zürich, 1942), pp. 256–7; Floud, "Karl Mannheim," *New Society*, no. 222 (Dec. 29, 1966), p. 971.
115 See Eric Hoyle, "The Elite Concept in Karl Mannheim's Sociology of Education," *Sociological Review*, vol. 12 (1964), pp. 55–71.
116 Kojecky, *Eliot's Social Criticism*, p. 170.
117 This position can be seen in notes for a series of BBC talks, "Talks for Sixth Forms: What Is Sociology?," located in his papers at Keele.
118 *D*, p. 43. Also see *D*, p. 27, and *FPD*, p. 140.
119 "The Meaning of Popularization in a Mass Society," *Christian Newsletter*, no. 227 (Feb. 7, 1945), p. 8.
120 Ibid., p. 10.
121 Floud, "Mannheim," in Judges (ed.), *Function of Teaching*, p. 61.
122 Conversely, much of the contemporary criticism leveled against Mannheim in England contained the argument that he was introducing Germanic speculation into the country. When Montgomery Belgion made this charge in a particularly chauvinistic manner, he was criticized for his xenophobia but not for his view that Mannheim was a speculator and that "all sociology is largely tosh." It was left to Mannheim to defend his position in "Function of Refugee." See Belgion et al., "The Germanization of Britain," *New English Weekly*, vol. 26, no. 18 (Feb. 15, 1945), pp. 137–8; no. 20 (March 1), pp. 155–6; no. 21 (March 8), pp. 167–8; no. 22 (March 15), p. 176; no. (March 22), p. 184; no. 24 (March 29), p. 192; and also vol. 27, no. 1 (April 19), pp. 5–6; no. 3 (May 3), pp. 27–8.
123 This approach can be seen in some of the documents from the Keele Collection. See "Studies in Democracy; A Research Plan" (1942), which can be found in the Lindsay Papers, and "A Syllabus on Power" (1942). The latter, along with other English material and English translations of some of the Hungarian material, can be found in L. Charles Cooper, "The Hindu Prince: A Sociological Biography of Karl Mannheim," vol. 2, appendices. Unpublished Typescript. These documents outline topics to be studied rather than offer any kind of definitive answers.
124 Lindsay wrote: "Mannheim always resisted very strongly the suggestion that legislation, like moral action, was partly a leap in the dark. One always felt

that he had a sociological faith that all these blanks of ignorance about society could be overcome." Review of *FPD*, p. 86.

125 Floud, "Mannheim," *New Society*, p. 969.
126 Friedmann, *Retracking America*, pp. 43–4.
127 *FPD*, pp. 34, 118; *D*, pp. 6, 70.
128 Hoyle, in presenting Mannheim as an elitist, denies this point and quotes A. V. Judges: "Karl Mannheim used to teach that one of the endeavors of a governing elite must, in the nature of things, be to stifle ideas among the masses and to depress their intellectual level." Hoyle, unlike Judges, does not seem to realize that Mannheim's description of this condition did not mean his advocacy of it. Instead, Mannheim prescribed democratic education and popularization to counteract this tendency he diagnosed in the elite. See Judges, "Education in a Changing Society," *Yearbook of Education* (1950), p. 185.
129 *FPD*, p. 202.
130 Ibid., p. 312.
131 From the typescript copy of a review of Eliot's *Notes towards the Definition of Culture* located in the Lindsay Papers at Keele.
132 Peter Laslett, "Karl Mannheim in 1939: A Student's Recollection," *Revue européenne des sciences sociales*, no. 46 (1979), p. 223.

Conclusion: Mannheim's legacy

1 *MS*, p. 5.
2 Letter to Mannheim, Dec. 19, 1936. Jászi Papers, Columbia University.
3 Letter to Jászi, Nov. 8, 1936. Jászi Papers, Columbia University.
4 *D*, p. 108.
5 *FPD*, p. xvii.

Bibliography

In light of the bibliographical information that often accompanies works by and about Mannheim, I have limited notation here to works cited in my notes.

Works by Mannheim

To aid my presentation of the development of Mannheim's thought, I have listed his works, including those within the same year, in their order of appearance.

1910–16   "Karl Mannheim's Letters to Lukács, 1910–1916," Ed. Eva Gábor. *New Hungarian Quarterly*, vol. 16, no. 57 (1975), pp. 93–105.

1916   Review of Arthur Liebert's *Das Problem der Geltung*. In *Athenaeum*, vol. 2 (1916), pp. 489–93.

1917   "A háboru bölcseletéhez." *Huszadik Század*, vol. 36 (1917), pp. 416–18.

1917   Review of Ernest Cassirer's *Freiheit und Form: Studien zur deutschen Geistesgeschichte*. In *Athenaeum*, vol. 3 (1917), pp. 409–13.

1918   *Lélek és kultura*. [Trans. as "Seele und Kultur" in *W*, pp. 66–84.]

1918   Review of Ernst Bloch's *Geist der Utopie*. In *Athenaeum*, vol. 4 (1918), pp. 207–11.

1918   "Az ismeretelmélet szerkezeti elemzése." *Athenaeum*, vol. 4 (1918), pp. 233–47, 315–30.

1918   "Georg Simmel, mint filozófus." *Huszadik Század*, vol. 38 (1918), pp. 194–6.

1920   "Die Dame aus Biarritz; ein Spiel in vier Szenen." Typescript. 1920. Magyar Tudományos Akadémia Kézirattára, Budapest.

1920   Review of Georg Lukács's *Die Theorie des Romans*. In *W*, pp. 85–90. [Trans. as "A review of Georg Lukács's *Theory of the Novel*," in *FKM*, pp. 3–7.]

1921   "Heidelbergi levél." *Tüz*, no. 15 (Nov.–Dec. 1921), pp. 91–5.

1921–22   "Beiträge zur Theorie der Weltanschauungs-Interpretation." In *W*, pp. 91–154. [Trans. as "On the Interpretation of '*Weltanschauung*.'" In *ESK*, pp. 33–83.]

1922   "Heidelbergi levelek." *Tüz*, no. 15 (April–May 1922), pp. 91–5.

1922   "Die Strukturanalyse der Erkenntnistheorie." In *W*, pp. 166–245.

[Trans. as "Structural Analysis of Epistemology." In *ESSP*, pp. 15–73.]

1922   "Zum Problem einer Klassifikation der Wissenschaften." In *W*, pp. 155–65.

1922   "Ueber die Eigenart kultursoziologischer Erkenntnis." In *SD*, pp. 33–154. [Trans. as "The Distinctive Character of Cultural-Sociological Knowledge." In *ST*, pp. 31–139.]

1922   "Wissenschaft und Jugend." *Frankfurter Zeitung*, evening Ed., higher education section, Nov. 30, 1922.

1924   "Levelek az emigrációból." *Diogenes*, nos. 1–2 (1924), pp. 13–15, 20–3.

1924   "Historismus." In *W*, pp. 246–307. [Trans. as "Historicism." In *ESK*, pp. 84–133.]

1924   "Eine soziologische Theorie der Kultur und ihre Erkennbarkeit (Konjunktives und kommunikatives Denken)." In *SD*, pp. 155–322. [Trans. as "A Sociological Theory of Culture and Its Knowability (Conjunctive and Communicative Thinking)." In *ST*, pp. 141–288.]

1925   *Konservatismus; Ein Beitrag zur Soziologie des Wissens*. Ed. David Kettler, Volker Meja, and Nico Stehr. Frankfurt am Main, 1984.

1925   "Das Problem einer Soziologie des Wissens." In *W*, pp. 308–87. [Trans. as "The Problem of a Sociology of Knowledge." In *ESK*, pp. 134–90.]

1926   "Ideologische und soziologische Interpretation der geistigen Gebilde." In *W*, pp. 388–407. [Trans. as "The Ideological and the Sociological Interpretation of Intellectual Phenomena." In *FKM*, pp. 116–31.]

1927   "Das konservative Denken." In *W*, pp. 408–508. [Trans. as "Conservative Thought." In *ESSP*, pp. 74–164.]

1928   "Das Problem der Generationen." In *W*, pp. 509–65. [Trans. as "The Problem of Generations." In *ESK*, pp. 276–322.]

1929   "Die Bedeutung der Konkurrenz im Gebiete des Geistigen." In *W*, pp. 566–613. [Trans. as "Competition as a Cultural Phenomenon." In *ESK*, pp. 191–229.]

1929   *Ideologie und Utopie*. 5th ed. Frankfurt am Main, 1969. [For trans., see 1936, *Ideology and Utopia.]*

1929   "Ankündigung" ["Announcement"]. To *Schriften zur Philosophie und Soziologie*.

1929   "Zur Problematik der Soziologie in Deutschland." In *W*, pp. 614–24. [Trans. as "Problems of Sociology in Germany," In *FKM*, pp. 262–70.]

1929   Letter to Eduard Spranger. April 12, 1929. Deutsche Bundesarchiv, Koblenz.

1930   "Ueber das Wesen und die Bedeutung des wirtschaftlichen Erfolgstrebens; Ein Beitrag zur Wirtschaftssoziologie." In *W*, pp. 625–87. [Trans. as "On the Nature of Economic Ambition and Its Significance for the Social Education of Man." In *ESK*, pp. 230–75.]

Bibliography

1930–42	Correspondence with Louis Wirth. Nov. 17, 1930–April 19, 1942. University of Chicago Library, Chicago.
1930–35	*Essays on the Sociology of Culture.* Ed. Ernest Mannheim and Paul Kecskemeti. London, 1956.
1931	"Wissenssoziologie." In *IUG*, pp. 227–67. [Trans. in *IUE*, pp. 264–311.]
1932	*Die Gegenwartsaufgaben der Soziologie: Ihre Lehrgestalt.* Tübingen, 1932.
1932	"American Sociology." In *ESSP*, pp. 185–94.
1932	"Die geistige Krise im Lichte der Soziologie." *Stuttgarter Neues Tageblatt,* Dec. 31, 1932.
1933–36	Correspondence with Oscar Jászi. Jan. 16, 1933–Nov. 8, 1936. Jászi Papers. Columbia University, New York.
1934	"German Sociology (1918–1933)." In *ESSP*, pp. 209–28.
1934–35	*Systematic Sociology: An Introduction to the Study of Society.* Ed. W. A. C. Stewart and J. Erös. New York, n.d.
1934–46	Unpublished papers in the Archives at the University of Keele, England.
1935	*Mensch und Gesellschaft im Zeitalter des Umbaus.* Leiden, 1935. [For trans., see 1940, *Man and Society in an Age of Reconstruction.*]
1936	"The Place of Sociology." In *ESSP*, pp. 195–208.
1936	"A Few Concrete Examples Concerning the Sociological Nature of Human Valuations." In *ESSP*, pp. 231–42.
1936	*Ideology and Utopia: An Introduction to the Sociology of Knowledge.* Trans. Louis Wirth and Edward Shils. New York, n.d.
1937	"Zur Diagnose unserer Zeit." *Mass und Wert,* vol. 1 (1937), pp. 100–21. [Trans. as "On the Diagnosis of Our Time." In *FKM*, pp. 350–66.]
1938	"Planned Society and the Problem of Human Personality: A Sociological Analysis." In *ESSP*, pp. 253–310.
1938	Letter to Alfred Weber. July 25, 1938. Deutsche Bundesarchiv, Koblenz.
1940	*Man and Society in an Age of Reconstruction.* Trans. Edward Shils. New York, n.d.
1940	"On War-Conditioned Changes in our Psychic Economy." In *ESSP*, pp. 243–51.
1940–46	*An Introduction to the Sociology of Education.* With W. A. C. Stewart. London, 1962.
1943	*Diagnosis of Our Time: Wartime Essays of a Sociologist.* London, 1943.
1944	"Democratic Planning and the New Science of Society." In J. R. M. Brumwell (ed.), *This Changing World,* pp. 71–82. London, 1944.
1945	"The Meaning of Popularization in a Mass Society." *Christian Newsletter,* no. 227 (Feb. 7, 1945), pp. 7–12.
1945	"The Function of the Refugee." *New English Weekly,* vol. 27 (April 19, 1945), pp. 5–6.
1947	*Freedom, Power and Democratic Planning.* Ed. Ernest K. Bramstedt and Hans Gerth. London, 1951.

Other works

Adorno, Theodor. *Prisms.* Trans. Samuel and Shierry Weber. London, 1967.
Arato, Andrew, and Paul Breines. *The Young Lukács and the Origins of Western Marxism.* New York, 1979.
Bantock, G. H. "The Cultural Implications of Planning and Popularization." *Scrutiny,* vol. 14 (1947), pp. 171–84.
Baum, Gregory. *Truth Beyond Relativism: Karl Mannheim's Sociology of Knowledge.* Milwaukee, 1977.
Beetham, David. *Max Weber and the Theory of Modern Politics.* London, 1974.
Belgion, Montgomery, et al. "The Germanization of Britain." *New English Weekly,* vol. 26, no. 18 (Feb. 15, 1945), pp. 137–8; no. 20 (March 1), pp. 155–6; no. 21 (March 8), pp. 167–8; no. 22 (March 15), p. 176; no. 23 (March 22), p. 184; no. 24 (March 29), p. 192. Also vol. 27, no. 1 (April 19), pp. 5–6, 12; no. 3 (May 3), pp. 27–8.
Below, Georg von. *Deutsche Geschichtschreibung von den Befreiungskriegen bis zu unseren Tagen.* Leipzig, 1916.
Soziologie als Lehrfach. Munich and Leipzig, 1920.
"Zur Beurteilung Heinrich Leos." *Archiv für Kulturgeschichte,* vol. 9 (1911), pp. 199–210.
Bentwich, Norman. *The Rescue and Achievement of Refugee Scholars.* The Hague, 1953.
Beveridge, William H. *The London School of Economics and Its Problems, 1919–1937.* London, 1960.
"The London School of Economics and the University of London," in Margaret Cole (ed.), *The Webbs and Their Work,* pp. 41–53. London, 1949.
Power and Influence. New York, 1955.
Bogardus, Emory. "Mannheim and Social Reconstruction." *Sociology and Social Research,* vol. 32 (1947), pp. 548–57.
Boris, Dieter. *Krise und Planung: Die politische Soziologie im Spätwerk Karl Mannheims.* Stuttgart, 1971.
Bramstedt, Ernest K. *Aristocracy and the Middle Classes in Germany.* Chicago, 1964.
Branson, Noreen, and Margot Heinemann. *Britain in the Nineteen Thirties.* London, 1971.
Brecht, Arnold. *The Political Education of Arnold Brecht.* Princeton, 1970.
Brinkmann, Carl. *Versuch einer Gesellschaftswissenschaft.* Munich and Leipzig, 1919.
Bruce, Maurice. *The Coming of the Welfare State.* London, 1965.
Clapham, J. H. *The Economic Development of France and Germany, 1815–1914.* Cambridge, 1966.
Clarke, Fred. *Education and Social Change.* London, 1940.
"History Teaching and Sociology." in D. M. E. Dymes (ed.), *Sociology and Education,* pp. 81–95. Malvern, 1944.
The Study of Education in England. London, 1943.
Congdon, Lee. "Beyond the 'Hungarian Wasteland:' A Study in the Ideology of National Regeneration, 1900–1919." Ph.D. dissertation. Dekalb, Ill., 1973.

Bibliography

"Karl Mannheim as Philosopher." *Journal of European Studies*, vol. 7 (1977), pp. 1–18.

"The Unexpected Revolutionary: Lukács's Road to Marx." *Survey*, vol. 20 (1974), pp. 176–205.

The Young Lukács. Chapel Hill, N.C., 1983.

Cooper, L. Charles. "The Hindu Prince: A Sociological Biography of Karl Mannheim." Vol. 2, appendices. Unpublished typescript.

Coser, Lewis. *Masters of Sociological Thought.* New York, 1971.

(ed.). *Georg Simmel.* Englewood Cliffs, N. J., 1965.

Cox, R. H. "Mannheim's Concept of Ideology." *Revue européenne des sciences sociales*, no. 46 (1979), pp. 209–23.

Curtis, James E., and John W. Petras (eds). *The Sociology of Knowledge: A Reader.* New York, 1970.

Curtius, Ernst Robert. *Deutscher Geist in Gefahr.* Stuttgart and Berlin, 1932.

"Soziologie – und ihre Grenzen." *Neue Schweizer Rundschau*, vol. 22 (1929), pp. 727–36.

Dahm, Karl Wilhelm. *Pfarrer und Politik.* Köln and Opladen, 1965.

Dahrendorf, Ralf. *Society and Democracy in Germany.* Garden City, N.Y., 1969.

Dawson, Christopher. *Religion and Culture.* London, 1948.

Deak, Istvan. *Weimar Germany's Left-Wing Intellectuals.* Berkeley and Los Angeles, 1968.

Dent, H. C. *Education in Transition.* New York, 1944.

Dilthey, Wilhelm. *Einleitung in die Geisteswissenschaften.* Vol. 1 of *Gesammelte Schriften.* Stuttgart, 1966.

Eisenstadt, S. N. "Intellectuals and Tradition." *Daedalus*, vol. 101 (1972), pp. 1–19.

Eliot, T. S. *The Idea of a Christian Society.* New York, 1940.

"Man and Society." *Spectator*, vol. 164, no. 5841 (June 7, 1940), p. 782.

Notes towards the Definition of Culture. New York, 1949.

Eppstein, Paul. "Die Fragestellung nach der Wirklichkeit im historischen Materialismus." *Archiv für Sozialwissenschaft und Sozialpolitik*, vol. 60 (1928), pp. 449–507.

Epstein, Klaus. *The Genesis of German Conservatism.* Princeton, N.J., 1966.

Floud, Jean. "Karl Mannheim." In A. V. Judges (ed.), *The Function of Teaching*, pp. 40–66. London, 1959.

"Karl Mannheim." *New Society*, no. 222 (Dec. 29, 1966), pp. 969–71.

and A. H. Halsey. "The Sociology of Education." *Current Sociology*, vol. 7 (1958), pp. 165–93.

Fogarasi, Adelbert. "Der reactionäre Idealismus – Die Philosophie des Sozialfaschismus." *Unter dem Banner des Marxismus*, vol. 5 (1931), pp. 214–31.

"Die Soziologie der Intelligenz und die Intelligenz der Soziologie." *Unter dem Banner des Marxismus*, vol. 4 (1930), pp. 356–75.

Freyer, Hans. *Soziologie als Wirklichkeitswissenschaft.* Leipzig and Berlin, 1930.

Friedmann, John. *Retracking America: A Theory of Transactive Planning.* Garden City, N.Y., 1973.

251

Bibliography

Friedmann, W. *Law and Social Change in Contemporary Britain.* London, 1951.

Gábor, Eva. "Mannheim in Hungary and in Weimar Germany." *International Society for the Sociology of Knowledge Newsletter,* vol. 9 (1983), pp. 7–14.

Gaus, John M. *Great Britain: A Study of Civic Loyalty.* Chicago, 1929.

Geiger, Theodor. *Die soziale Schichtung des deutschen Volkes.* Darmstadt, 1967.

Ginsberg, Morris. "Recent Tendencies in Sociology." *Economica,* no. 39 (1933), pp. 22–39.

Sociology. London, 1937.

Der Grosse Brockhaus. 15th ed. Leipzig, 1928–35.

Grünwald, Ernst. *Das Problem der Soziologie des Wissens.* Vienna and Leipzig, 1934.

Hauser, Arnold, and Georg Lukács. "On Youth, Art and Philosophy; A 1969 Radio Meeting." *New Hungarian Quarterly,* vol. 16, no. 58 (1975), pp. 96–105.

Heeren, John. "Karl Mannheim and the Intellectual Elite." *British Journal of Sociology,* vol,. 22 (1971), pp. 1–15.

Henning, Hansjoachim. *Das westdeutsche Bürgertum in der Epoche der Hochindustrialisierung, 1960–1914.* Wiesbaden, 1972.

Hinshaw, Virgil G., Jr. "The Epistemological Relevance of Mannheim's Sociology of Knowledge." In Gunter W. Remmling (ed.), *Towards the Sociology of Knowledge,* pp. 229–44. London, 1973.

Holborn, Hajo. *Germany and Europe.* Garden City, N.Y., 1971.

Honigsheim, Paul. "Der Max-Weber-Kreis in Heidelberg." *Kölner Vierteljahrshefte für Soziologie,* vol. 5 (1926), pp. 270–87.

Horkheimer, Max. *Sozialphilosophische Studien; Aufsätze, Reden und Vorträge, 1930–1972.* Ed. Werner Brede. Frankfurt am Main, 1972.

Horváth, Zoltán. *Die Jahrhundertwende in Ungarn.* Trans. Geza Engl. Neuwied, 1966.

Hoyle, Eric, "The Elite Concept in Karl Mannheim's Sociology of Education." *Sociological Review,* vol. 12 (1964), pp. 55–71.

Hughes, H. Stuart. *Consciousness and Society.* New York, 1961.

Iggers, Georg G. *The German Conception of History.* Middletown, Conn., 1968.

International Institute of Social Research: A Short Description of Its History and Aims. New York, 1934.

Jaeggi, Urs. *Die gesellschaftliche Elite.* Berne, 1960.

Jászi, Oscar. Review of Mannheim's *Lélek és Kultura.* In *Huszadik Század,* vol. 37 (1918), p. 192.

Revolution and Counter-Revolution in Hungary. Trans. E. W. Dicks. London, 1924.

Jay, Martin. *The Dialectical Imagination.* Boston, 1973.

"The Frankfurt School's Critique of Karl Mannheim and the Sociology of Knowledge." *Telos,* no. 20 (1970), pp. 72–89.

Johnston, William. *The Austrian Mind.* Berkeley and Los Angeles, 1972.

Joravsky, David. *Soviet Marxism and Natural Science, 1917–1932.* London, 1961.

Judges, A. V. "Education in a Changing Society." *Yearbook of Education,* 1950, pp. 184–99.

Kautsky, Karl, *The Social Revolution.* Trans. A. M. and May Wood Simons. Chicago, 1916.

Bibliography

Kettler, David. "Culture and Revolution: Lukács in the Hungarian Revolutions of 1918/1919." *Telos*, no. 10 (1971), pp. 35–92.

Marxismus und Kultur. Trans. Erich Weck and Tobias Rülcker. Neuwied, 1967.

"Political Theory, Ideology, Sociology: The Question of Karl Mannheim." *Cultural Hermeneutics*, vol. 3 (1975), pp. 69–80.

"Sociology of Knowledge and Moral Philosophy." *Political Science Quarterly*, vol. 82 (1967), pp. 399–426.

Kettler, David, Volker Meja, and Nico Stehr. *Karl Mannheim*. London and Chichester, 1984.

Kettler, David, Volker Meja, and Nico Stehr. "Karl Mannheim and Conservatism: The Ancestry of Historical Thinking." *American Sociological Review*, vol, 49 (1984), pp. 71–85.

Kinser, Bill, and Neil Kleinman. *The Dream That Was No More a Dream*. New York, 1969.

Klemperer, Klemens von. *Germany's New Conservatism*. Princeton, N.J., 1968.

Kneller, George F. *Higher Learning in Britain*. Berkeley and Los Angeles, 1955.

König, René. "Die Begriffe Gemeinschaft und Gesellschaft bei Ferdinand Tönnies." *Kölner Zeitschrift für Soziologie und Sozialpsychologie*, vol. 7 (1955), pp. 348–420.

"Zur Soziologie der zwanziger Jahre." In Leonard Reinisch (ed.), *Die Zeit ohne Eigenschaften*, pp. 82–118. Stuttgart, 1961.

Kojecky, Roger. *T. S. Eliot's Social Criticism*. New York, 1972.

Kraft, Julius. "Soziologie oder Soziologismus? Zu Mannheims 'Ideolgie und Utopie.'" *Zeitschrift für Völkerpsychologie*, vol. 5 (1929), pp. 406–17.

Krill, Hans-Heinz. *Die Rankerenaissance: Max Lenz und Erich Marcks*. Berlin, 1962.

Kurucz, Jenö. "Mannheims Werk in sozialphilosophischer Sicht." *Archiv für Rechts- und Sozialphilosophie*, 1963, pp. 85–95.

Struktur und Frunktion der Intelligenz während der Weimarer Republik. Köln, 1967.

Landshut, Siegfried. *Kritik der Soziologie*. Munich and Leipzig, 1929.

Lang, Julia. Review of Mannheim's *Lélek és Kultura*. In *Athenaeum*, vol. 4 (1918), pp. 159–60.

Laslett, Peter. "Karl Mannheim in 1939: A Student's Recollection." *Revue européenne des sciences sociales*, no. 46 (1979), pp. 223–6.

Lea, F. A. *The Life of John Middleton Murry*. London, 1959.

Lederer, Emil, et al. *Soziologische Studien; Zur Politik, Wirtschaft und Kultur der Gegenwart*. Potsdam, 1930.

Lenk, Kurt (ed.). *Ideologie: Ideologiekritik und Wissenssoziologie*. Neuwied, 1967.

Marx in der Wissenssoziologie. Neuwied, 1972.

Lewalter, Ernst. "Wissenssoziologie und Marxismus." *Archiv für Sozialwissenschaft und Sozialpolitik*, vol. 64 (1930), pp. 63–121.

Lichtheim, George. "The Concept of Ideology." In George H. Nadel (ed.), *Studies in the Philosophy of History*, pp. 148–79. New York, 1965.

Lieber, Hans-Joachim (ed.). *Ideologie, Wissenschaft, Gesellschaft; Neuere Beiträge zur Diskussion*. Darmstadt, 1976.

(ed.). *Ideologienlehre und Wissenssoziologie*. Darmstadt, 1974.

Lilge, Frederic. *The Abuse of Learning*. New York, 1948.

Bibliography

Lindsay, A. D. Review of Mannheim's *Freedom, Power and Democratic Planning*. In *British Journal of Sociology*, vol. 3 (1952), pp. 85–6.

Unpublished papers in the Archives at the University of Keele, England.

Loader, Colin. "German Historicism and Its Crisis." *Journal of Modern History*, vol. 48 (1976), on-demand supplement, pp. 85–119.

Löwe, Adolf. *The Price of Liberty*. London, 1937.

The Universities in Transformation. London, 1940.

Lukács, Georg. *Geschichte und Klassenbewusstsein*. Berlin, 1923.

History and Class Consciousness. Trans. Rodney Livingstone. London, 1971.

Marxism and Human Liberation. Trans. E. San Juan, Jr. New York, 1973.

Theory of the Novel. Trans. Anna Bostock. London, 1971.

Die Zerstörung der Vernunft. Berlin, 1955.

"Zum Wesen und zur Methode der Kultursoziologie." *Archiv für Sozialwissenschaft und Sozialpolitik*, vol. 39 (1915), pp. 216–22.

"Zur Soziologie des modernen Dramas." *Archiv für Sozialwissenschaft und Sozialpolitik*, vol. 38 (1911), pp. 303–45.

Man, Hendrik de. *The Psychology of Socialism*. Trans. Eden and Cedar Paul. London.

Mandelbaum, Maurice. *The Problem of Historical Knowledge*. New York, 1938.

Maquet, Jacques. *The Sociology of Knowledge*. Trans. John F. Locke. Boston, 1951.

Marck, Siegfried. "Zum Problem des 'seinsverbundenen Denkens.'" *Archiv für systematische Philosophie und Soziologie*, vol. 33 (1929), pp. 238–52.

Marcuse, Herbert. Review of Mannheim's *Mensch und Gesellschaft im Zeitalter des Umbaus*. In *Zeitschrift für Sozialforschung*, vol. 4 (1935), pp. 269–71.

"Zur Wahrheitsproblematik der soziologischen Methode." *Die Gesellschaft*, vol. 6, no. 2 (1929), pp. 356–69.

Marwick, Arthur. *The Home Front*. London, 1976.

McCagg, William O., Jr. *Jewish Nobles and Geniuses in Modern Hungary*. Boulder, 1972.

Meinecke, Friedrich. *Schaffender Spiegel*. Stuttgart, 1948.

Meja, Volker. "The Sociology of Knowledge and the Critique of Ideology." *Culture Hermeneutics*, vol. 3 (1975), pp. 57–68

Merton, Robert. *Social Theory and Social Structure*. Rev. ed. Glencoe, Ill., 1962.

Mészáros, István. *Lukács' Concept of Dialectic*. London, 1972.

Mill, John Stuart. *A System of Logic, Ratiocinative and Inductive*. 9th ed. London, 1875.

Mirsky, Dmitri. *The Intelligentsia of Great Britain*. London, 1935.

Mitzman, Arthur. "Tönnies and German Society, 1887–1914." *Journal of the History of Ideas*, vol. 32 (1971), pp. 507–24.

Moberly, Walter. *The Universities and Cultural Leadership*. London, 1951.

Mommsen, Wolfgang. *The Age of Bureaucracy*. New York, 1974.

Morrish, Ivor. "Die Soziologie der Erziehung." In Bernd Götz and Jochem Kaltschmid (eds.), *Erziehungswissenschaft und Soziologie*, pp. 200–215. Darmstadt, 1977.

Murry, John Middleton. *The Free Society*. London, 1948.

The Price of Leadership. London, 1939.

Bibliography

Neusüss, Arnhelm. *Die Theorien des utopischen Bewusstseins und der "freischwebenden Intelligenz" in der Wissenssoziologie Karl Mannheims.* Marburg, 1966.

O'Boyle, Leonore. "Klassiche Bildung und soziale Struktur in Deutschland zwischen 1800 und 1848." *Historische Zeitschrift,* vol. 207 (1968), pp. 584–608.

Oldham, J. H. *Church, Community and State.* London, 1935.

Popper, Karl. *The Poverty of Historicism.* New York, 1961.

"Protokoll der Sitzung der vereinigten Seminare von Prof. A. Weber und Dr. Mannheim, den 21. Febr. 29." Typescript. Heidelberg, 1929.

Remmling, Gunter W. *The Sociology of Karl Mannheim.* London, 1975.

Wissenssoziologie und Gesellschaftsplanung; Das Werk Karl Mannheim. Dortmund, 1968.

Rickert, Heinrich. *Science and History.* Ed. Arthur Goddard. Trans. George Reisman. Princeton, N.J., 1962.

Ringer, Fritz. *The Decline of the German Mandarins.* Cambridge, Mass., 1969.

Röpke, Wilhelm. *Die Gesellschaftskrise der Gegenwart.* Zürich, 1942.

Rothacker, Erich. *Logik und Systematik der Geisteswissenschaften.* Darmstadt, 1970.

Samuels, Stuart. "English Intellectuals and Politics in the 1930's." In Philip Rieff (ed.), *On Intellectuals,* pp. 213–68. Garden City, N.Y., 1970.

Sauer, Wolfgang. "Weimar Culture: Experiments in Modernism." *Social Research,* vol. 39 (1972), pp. 254–84.

Scheler, Max. *Philosophische Weltanschauung.* Bern and Munich, 1968.

Die Wissenformen und die Gesellschaft. Bern, 1960.

Schelsky, Helmut. *Einsamkeit und Freiheit: Idee und Gestalt der deutschen Universität und ihrer Reformen.* 2d ed. Düsseldorf, 1971.

Schelting, Alexander von. *Max Webers Wissenschaftslehre.* Tübingen, 1934.

Schluchter, Wolfgang, and Guenther Roth. *Max Weber's Vision of History.* Berkeley and Los Angeles, 1979.

Schoeck, Helmut. "Der sozialökonomische Aspekt in der Wissenssoziologie Karl Mannheims." *Zeitschrift für die gesamte Staatswissenschaft,* vol. 106 (1950), pp. 34–45.

Die Soziologie und die Gesellschaften. 2d ed. Munich, 1964.

"Die Zeitlichkeit bei Karl Mannheim." *Archiv für Rechts- und Sozialphilosophie,* vol. 38 (1949), pp. 371–82.

Schweinitz, Karl de. *England's Road to Social Security.* New York, 1961.

Shils, Edward. "*Ideology and Utopia,* by Karl Mannheim." *Daedalus,* vol. 103 (1974), pp. 83–9.

"Karl Mannheim." *International Encyclopedia of Social Sciences,* vol. 9, pp. 557–62. New York, 1968.

Shklar, Judith. "The Political Theory of Utopia: From Melancholy to Nostalgia." *Daedalus,* vol. 94 (1965), pp. 361–87.

Simmel, Georg. *The Conflict in Modern Culture and other Essays.* Trans. K. Peter Etzkorn. New York, 1968.

The Sociology of Georg Simmel. Trans. and ed. Kurt H. Wolff. New York, 1967.

Simonds, A. P. *Karl Mannheim's Sociology of Knowledge.* Oxford, 1978.

"Mannheim's Sociology of Knowledge as a Hermeneutic Method." *Cultural Hermeneutics,* vol. 3 (1975), pp. 81–104.

Sombart, Werner, *Händler und Helden*. Munich, 1915.

Sontheimer, Kurt. *Antidemocratisches Denken in der Weimarer Republik*. Munich, 1968.

Speier, Hans. "Soziologie oder Ideologie." *Die Gesellschaft*, vol. 7, no. 2 (1930), pp. 357–72.

Spitzer, Alan B. "The Historical Problem of Generations." *American Historical Review*, vol. 78 (1973), pp. 1354–85.

Spranger, Eduard. "Allgemeine Kulturgeschichte und Methodenlehre: Eröffnungsbericht." *Archiv für Kulturgeschichte*, vol. 9 (1911), pp. 363–381.

Die deutsche Bildungsideal der Gegenwart in Geschichtsphilosophischer Beleuctung. Leipzig, 1928.

Steinberg, Sigfrid (ed.). *Die Geschichtswissenschaft der Gegenwart in Selbstdarstellungen*. Leipzig. 1925–26.

Stern, Fritz. "The Political Consequences of the Unpolitical German." In *History 3*, pp. 104–34. New York, 1960.

The Politics of Cultural Despair. Garden City, N.Y., 1965.

Stern, Gunther. "Ueber die sog. 'Seinsverbundenheit' des Bewusstseins." *Archiv für Sozialwissenschaft und Sozialpolitik*, vol. 64 (1930), pp. 492–509.

Stewart, W. A. C. "Karl Mannheim and the Sociology of Education." *British Journal of Educational Studies*, vol. 1 (1953), pp. 99–113.

Karl Mannheim and Social Thought. London, 1967.

Thomson, David. *England in the Twentieth Century*. Baltimore, 1965.

Tillich, Hannah. *From Time to Time*. New York, 1973

Tillich, Paul. "Ideologie und Utopie." *Die Gesellschaft*, vol. 6, pt. 2 (1929), pp. 348–55.

Tökei, Ferenc. "Lukács and Hungarian Culture," *New Hungarian Quarterly*, vol. 13, no. 47 (1972), pp. 108–22.

Tökes, Rudolf F. *Béla Kun and the Hungarian Soviet Republic*. New York, 1967.

Tönnies, Ferdinand. *Community and Society*. Trans. Charles P. Loomis. New York, 1963.

Gemeinschaft und Gesellschaft. Leipzig, 1887.

Troeltsch, Ernst. *Der Historismus und seine Probleme*. Vol. 3 of *Gesammelte Schriften*. Tübingen, 1922.

Verhandlungen des Sechsten Deutschen Soziologentages vom 17. bis 19. September 1928 in Zürich. Tübingen, 1929.

Vidler, Alec R. *Essays in Liberality*. London, 1957.

Scenes from a Clerical Life. London, 1977.

Vondung, Klaus (ed.). *Das wilhelminische Bildungsbürgertum: Zur Sozialgeschichte seiner Ideen*. Göttingen, 1976.

Weber, Alfred. *Ideen zur Staats- und Kultursoziologie*. Karlsruhe, 1927.

Die Not der geistigen Arbeiter. Munich and Leipzig, 1923.

"Prinzipells zur Kultursoziologie: Gesellschaftsprozess, Zivilisationsprocess und Kulturbewegung." *Archiv für Sozialwissenschaft und Sozialpolitik*, vol. 47 (1920–21), pp. 1–49.

Weber, Marianne. *Lebenserinnerungen*. Bremen, 1948.

Max Weber: A Biography. Trans. and ed. Harry Zohn. New York, 1975.

Bibliography

Weber, Max. *Economy and Society.* Ed. Guenther Roth and Claus Wittich. Trans. Ephraim Fischoff et al. Berkeley and Los Angeles, 1978.

From Max Weber. Ed. and trans. H. H. Gerth and C. Wright Mills. New York, 1958.

Gesammelte Aufsätze zur Wissenschaftslehre. 3d ed. Tübingen, 1968.

Gesammelte Politische Schriften. 3rd ed. Tübingen, 1971.

White, Hayden. *Metahistory: The Historical Imagination in the Nineteenth Century.* Baltimore, 1973.

Williams, Raymond. *Marxism and Literature.* Oxford, 1977.

Windelband, Wilhelm. *Präludien.* Tübingen, 1924.

Wittfogel, Karl. "Wissen und Gesellschaft." *Unter dem Banner des Marxismus,* vol. 5 (1931), pp. 83–102.

Wohl, Robert. *The Generation of 1914.* Cambridge, Mass., 1979.

Wolff, Kurt H. "The Sociology of Knowledge and Sociological Theory." In Llewellyn Gross (ed.), *Symposium on Sociological Theory,* pp. 567–602. New York, 1959.

Zeitlin, Irving M. *Ideology and the Development of Sociological Theory.* Englewood Cliffs, N.J., 1968.

Zitta, Victor. *Georg Lukács's Marxism: Alienation, Dialectics, Revolution.* The Hague, 1964.

Index

academics, German, 17–26, 37, 179
adequacy, standard of, 48
administration, 96, 102–3, 104, 122, 124, 219
Ady, Endre, 203
Alexander, Bernát, 195
alienation, 30–1, 35, 74
analysis, and valuation, 5, 58, 66, 93, 112, 183–4
Aquinas, Thomas, 70
art, 39–40
art aspiration, 82, 207, 210
aspiration, *see* art aspiration, will, world aspiration

Becher, Erich, 205
behaviorism, 143
Belgion, Montgomery, 245
Below, Georg von, 200
Bernal, J. D., 164
Beveridge, William, 150–1, 237, 239
Bildung, 16, 18–9, 25, 26, 28, 84, 116, 128, 139, 140, 147, 149, 159, 171, 185, 187, 197, 228
Bildungsbürgertum, 16–7, 26, 197, 200–1, 233
Bildungskultur, 84–5, 90–1, 92, 219
Bloch, Ernst, 203
Boris, Dieter, 229
bureaucratic conservatism, 88, 104–5, 106, 108–9, 225

capitalism, 70, 109, 170
center of construction, 4–5, 57, 59, 66, 83, 85, 137, 144, 182–3, 186
chiliasm, 104–5, 106, 108–9, 124, 136
Christianity, 154, 156–9, 241
clarification, 89, 99, 101, 167, 211
Clarke, Fred, 151, 164–5, 243–4
class, 75, 77, 81–2, 83, 119, 117, 213
"Classification of the Sciences," 48
collective mental image, 73
commitment, 75, 119, 155
competition, 70, 79, 136, 169–70
"Competition," 67, 80–2, 83, 91, 92, 132, 135, 155, 218
Comte, Auguste, 5, 23, 173, 176, 185, 210

conduct, types of, 132
consciousness: class, 100, 110, 121, 160, 224; utopian, 102, 104
consensus, 69, 161
conservatism, 78–80, 86–90, 106–11, 218, 226
Conservatism, 67, 75–9, 87–90, 123, 220
"Conservative Thought," 67, 78, 85, 90, 184
constellation, 6, 185–6
context of lived experience, 40, 48–9, 52, 58, 73, 105, 209
continuum of everyday experience, 131–2, 174
coordination, 171
Coser, Lewis, 125, 239
cultural community, 69–70
cultural fields, types of, 55–8
cultural hegemony, 196
cultural product, 30–31, 41, 46, 73
"Cultural-Sociological Knowledge," 41, 48–53, 56, 58, 59, 60, 61, 66, 67, 69, 70, 73, 74, 82, 137, 140, 215
culture, 28–9, 30–3, 36, 45, 89, 185; objective, 30–1; subjective, 31, 34, 35
Curtius, Ernst Robert, 116–18, 120, 228, 234

Dahrendorf, Ralf, 15
Dawson, Christopher, 151, 240
democracy, 154, 158–9, 160
Dent, H. C., 163
depth of penetration, 59, 61
Descartes, René, 70
dialectic, 74, 236
dialectical transcendence, 99, 100, 101, 118
Dilthey, Wilhelm, 49, 199, 207, 217, 234
disillusioning realism, 88, 94, 122, 225, 226
displacement, 50, 204
Durkheim, Emile, 235–6
dynamic hierarchy, 4, 182
dynamic totality, 3, 178–9

education, 162–8, 189
Elias, Norbert, 221

258

Eliot, T. S., 151, 156–7, 173, 238, 241
elites, 132, 152, 153, 173–4
Enlightenment, 53, 55, 78, 86, 88, 107
entelechy, 82–3
epistemology, 41–4, 91, 220
"Epistemology," 41, 42–4, 45, 47–8, 52, 55, 61, 74, 91
Eppstein, Paul, 215
esoteric stream of transmission, 131–2, 174
essayistic-experimental attitude, 2, 184–5
ethic: of fatalism, 97, 104, 106, 111, 124; of responsibility, 97, 104, 106, 108, 116, 119, 121, 122, 162, 176, 188, 225; of ultimate ends (conviction), 97, 104, 106, 119, 124
existence, 62, 105; public interpretation of, 80, 86, 92; relation to meaning, 30, 40, 41, 42, 53, 71, 72, 74, 144, 204
existential bondedness, 34, 112–3, 115, 118, 161, 226–7
existential congruence, 115
existential connectedness, 112–3, 115, 118, 161, 226–7, 242
existential transcendence, 105, 113, 115, 119
experiential realm, 68–70, 73, 80, 105
explanation, 40–1

fascism, 105–6, 143, 223
field structure, 168, 169, 170, 171
Floud, Jean, 174, 238
Fogarasi, Adelbert, 117–8, 120, 229
formation, 44–5, 58
Free School lecture, 29–33, 34, 35, 37, 38, 45, 47, 50, 53, 70, 71, 73, 74, 86, 105, 111, 128, 138, 139, 153, 186, 189
Free School of the Human Sciences, 13, 27, 32–3, 63
Free School of the Social Sciences, 12
Freedom, Power and Democratic Planning, 173
Freyer, Hans, 222
Friedmann, John, 175

Galileo Club, 12, 196
Gemeinschaft, 20–1, 23, 30, 32, 51, 68, 69, 74, 101, 103, 116, 119, 132, 135, 161, 185, 198, 199, 210
generation, 38, 81–3
generational unity, 83
"Generations," 67, 81–3, 85, 90, 156
George, Stefan, 36–7, 54, 203
Gesellschaft, 20–1, 23, 32, 68, 77, 102, 103, 130, 133, 155, 161, 162, 185
Ginsberg, Morris, 127, 141, 231, 236
groups, communal and functional, 162, 242
Grünwald, Ernst, 227

Heeren, John, 236
Hegel, G. W. F., 57, 59, 107, 209, 220
historicism, 53–62, 88, 90, 147, 198, 211, 214; dynamic, 57–61, 65, 213; monadic, 18, 25, 26, 39, 99, 100, 162, 179, 180, 185; traditional, 32, 112, 219
"Historicism," 5, 30, 53–62, 66, 68, 85, 112–13, 114, 123, 186, 187
History and Class Consciousness, 64–5, 77, 96, 109, 123, 222
history, theory of, 103–4
Horkheimer, Max, 230
Horthy, Nicolas, 14–15, 196
Hoyle, Eric, 246
Hugo, Gustav, 76, 87–90, 225
Husserl, Edmund, 57

ideal type, 179–80
"Ideological and Sociological Interpretation," 67, 215
ideology, 40, 71, 95, 113, 115, 117, 138, 222; general, total conception of, 111; particular conception of, 110; special, total conception of, 111; total conception of, 102, 110
Ideology and Utopia, 5, 34, 43–4, 54, 66, 78, 83, 89, 91, 95–124, 131, 132, 135–7, 138, 144, 146, 147, 154, 161, 172, 180, 183, 184, 186–7
imputation, 49, 74, 76, 180
Institute for Social Research, 125–6, 230
Institute of Education, 151, 163
intellectuals, 36, 84–5, 86; expressionist, 17, 24; four types of, 119–20; of Frankfurt, 126, 150; free-floating, 89, 90
intelligentsia: of Budapest, 10–5, 26–7, 32, 38, 63, 122, 178–9, 181, 185, 239; free-floating, 34, 85, 115–19, 120, 161, 228, 229, 236, 239
interest, 75, 217, 224, 240
interpretation, 50, 68–9, 144; documentary, 45–7, 207; types of, 40–1
irrationality, substantial, 128–9, 232

Jászi, Oscar, 11–14, 188, 194
Jay, Martin, 125
Judges, A. V., 246

Kant, Immanuel, 43, 209
Kautsky, Karl, 200
Kecskemeti, Paul, 205
Kettler, David, 62, 220, 222, 236, 243
key position, 136, 142–3, 144, 170
Kneller, George, 164
knowledge: for achievement, 72; for *Bildung*, 72, 85; communicative, 67–8; conjunctive, 67–8, 85, 218; for salvation, 71–2

259

König, René, 199
Kurucz, Jenö, 228

"The Lady from Biarritz," 33–5
Landshut, Siegfried, 222
Laski, Harold, 231, 237
Laslett, Peter, 177
Leavis, F. R., 164, 243
Lederer, Emil, 201
Letters: from exile, 54, 196; "Letters to Lukács," 28–9, 39, 40, 185
Lezsnai, Anna, 14, 194, 195
liberalism, 80, 87, 106–11
Lichtheim, Georg, 96
Lieber, Hans-Joachim, 222
Liebert, Arthur, 205–6
Lindsay, A. D., 152, 173, 177, 238, 245–6
logic, 43, 205, 206
London School of Economics, 127, 149, 237, 238
Löwe, Adolf (Adolph Lowe), 151, 152–3, 231
Lukács, Georg, 12–4, 27, 28–9, 35, 36, 37, 64–5, 77, 94, 96, 99–101, 109, 115, 121, 123, 180, 194, 195, 204, 208, 214, 222, 223, 229

McCagg, William, 194, 197
Man, Hendrik de, 199–200
Man and Society, 128, 130, 135–7, 143, 144, 146, 147, 183, 186, 188
manipulation, 144, 147–8, 163
Mannheim, Julia (Lang), 138, 195, 237
Marxism, 23, 24, 35, 71, 75, 81–2, 92–3, 109, 111, 119–20, 127, 160, 164, 197, 199–200, 209, 210
massification, 134, 136, 173, 183, 187, 233
meaning, 31, 198; documentary, 45–7, 58; expressive, 44–5, 46, 58, 207, 211; objective, 44–5, 207; relation to existence, 30, 40, 41, 42, 46, 53, 71, 72, 74, 144, 204; three levels of, 44–7
Meinecke, Friedrich, 19, 25, 97–8
Meja, Volker, 220, 222, 226, 236, 243
Merton, Robert, 192
Mézáros, István, 12
Mill, John Stuart, 140–1
Mommsen, Wolfgang, 96
Moot, 149, 151, 152, 156–8, 177, 237–8, 239
morality, stages of, 128–31
Möser, Justus, 76, 86–90, 227
Müller, Adam, 76, 87–90
Murry, John Middleton, 151, 157
mysticism, 31, 35, 37, 97, 105, 124, 203

National Socialism (Nazism), 123, 124, 125, 126, 135, 145, 146, 156, 187, 230, 233

Nyugat, 12, 194

Oldham, J. H., 151, 241
ontology, 43, 206
"Order," 239

Parliament, 172–3
Paulsen, Friedrich, 197
perspectivism, 6–7, 59, 68, 178, 179, 212, 215
philosophy, 29, 40, 50, 53, 72, 116, 139, 213, 234; cultural, 44, 123; of history, 52, 57, 59, 60, 72, 210
Pinder, Wilhelm, 82–3
planning, 128, 130–1, 144, 148, 149, 168; democratic, 153, 173, 189
pluralism, 25, 32–3, 74, 79, 81, 91, 99, 103, 111, 112, 123, 213
political party, 80, 83, 103, 117, 119, 122, 123, 135, 145, 155
political science, 44, 119, 120–1, 122, 144
politics, 66, 67, 77, 79, 89, 92–4, 95, 102, 103, 123, 187, 219, 233
"Politics as a Vocation," 25–6, 96, 100, 102
Popper, Karl, 232
popularization, 173–4
positional bondedness, 34, 59–60, 112–3, 226
positive affirmation, 54, 88
positivism, 71, 219
power, 162–3
pragmatism, 235
Present Tasks, 138–9, 145
principia media, 140–3, 144, 147
"Problem of Sociology of Knowledge," 66, 71–2, 74–6, 80, 112
psychoanalysis, 143
psychology, 40, 43, 49, 137–8, 141, 206, 234
public: disintegrated, 134, 146, 187; organic, 132, 146; types of, 132–5

rationality: functional, 128–9, 232; substantial, 128–9, 162, 232
rationalization, 103
refugee, 7–8, 15, 27, 63–4, 126–7, 146, 179, 180, 181, 196
relationism, 59, 91, 113–5, 121, 215
relativism, 47, 57, 112, 113, 116, 117, 155
Remmling, Gunther, 229
Riegl, Alois, 82, 207, 210
Ringer, Fritz, 17
Romanticism, 53, 86–7, 88, 90

Sauer, Wolfgang, 17
Savigny, Friedrich von, 76, 87–90, 225, 227
Scheler, Max, 71–2, 81, 85, 216–7, 229

260

Schluchter, Wolfgang, 98
Schmoller, Gustav, 24
science, 98, 101; cultural (human), 21–2,
    29, 39–40, 67; division of, 21–3, 39–40,
    67; natural, 21–3, 29, 39–40, 67; philo-
    sophical, 21–2, 29, 40; specialized, 21–2,
    29, 55
"Science and Youth," 37–8
"Science as a Vocation," 25, 96, 98, 120
selection, 81, 91, 137, 144
self-relativization, 62, 70
Shils, Edward, 221
Simmel, Georg, 7, 12, 13, 32, 62–3, 94,
    181, 195, 209
Simonds, A. P., 1, 193, 226
situation, 168, 169, 171
social mechanism, 168, 169, 170
social stratum, 76–7
social technique, 163, 169
socialism, 106, 109–11, 236
society, 132–4
Society for the Social Sciences, 12, 14
"Sociological Theory of Culture," 53–4,
    61–2, 66, 67–71, 73, 77, 79, 84, 88, 90–
    1, 92, 123, 214
sociology, 39, 40, 46, 49–53, 59–60, 66,
    71, 72, 116, 125, 128, 145, 159, 166–7,
    174, 200, 233–4; of culture, 49–53, 67,
    69, 78, 140, 144, 209, 210, 211; of
    knowledge, 41, 65, 67–77, 80, 82, 93,
    111, 112, 117, 123, 138, 148, 166, 183,
    184, 216–17, 218; types of, 50–3, 137–
    40
Sombart, Werner, 24, 207
soul, 30–1, 37, 45, 49, 73
"Spiritual Crisis in Light of Sociology," 139
spiritual stratum, 76–7
Spranger, Eduard, 19, 234
Stehr, Nico, 220, 222, 236, 243
Stewart, W. A. C., 238–9
stranger, 7–8, 62–3, 181
strategy, 130
struggle for primacy, 43–4, 47
style of thought, 76
subject, 46, 57; relation to object, 42; tran-
    scendental-logical, 41, 44, 55, 74
subordination (overcoming), 92, 99, 100,
    101, 118
synthesis, 6, 32–3, 61–2, 64, 81, 91, 92, 93,
    108, 110, 119, 146, 154, 161, 181, 185,
    211
system, epistemological, 41–3
systematization, 41–3, 45–6, 205, 212
Szellem, 195

Theory of the Novel, review of, 39, 187
Thomson, David, 150
thought, stages of, 128–31
Tillich, Paul, 152
Tönnies, Ferdinand, 20–1, 23, 30, 32, 70,
    77, 101, 102, 130, 135, 161, 195, 199,
    202, 209, 215, 242
traditionalism, 78, 103, 108, 218
Troeltsch, Ernst, 18, 27, 39, 63–5, 66, 92,
    99, 214, 223, 229

understanding, 68, 211
unmasking, 34–5, 71, 100–1, 138, 160,
    227
utopia, 58, 87, 95, 113, 114, 115, 119, 124,
    212, 222, 224, 227

valuation, 43, 59, 67, 113, 114, 115, 144,
    186; and analysis, 5, 58, 66, 112, 183–4
Volksgeist, 17, 88–9, 108, 211
Vondung, Klaus, 16

Webb, Sidney and Beatrice, 149
Weber, Alfred, 15, 27, 28, 38, 39, 54, 83,
    85, 92–3, 94, 156, 196, 200, 201, 215,
    216, 220–1, 223
Weber, Marianne, 218
Weber, Max, 5, 12, 25–7, 37–8, 54, 80, 88,
    94, 96–101, 102, 106, 111, 116, 119,
    120, 121–3, 124, 179, 180, 187, 201,
    207, 209, 210, 222, 223, 226, 229
Weimar Republic, 24–5, 92, 95, 123, 142,
    154, 156, 200
"*Weltanschauung*," 41, 44–9, 52, 58, 77
Weltanschauungspartei, 26, 80, 96
Wilhelm II, 24
will, 101, 102, 104, 111, 119, 121, 124,
    135, 144, 172, 186, 187, 207, 224, 240
Williams, Raymond, 196
Windelband, Wilhelm, 22, 199
Wirth, Louis, 221–2
Wittfogel, Karl, 225
Wohl, Robert, 83
Wolff, Kurt, 95
work, 30–1, 73
world aspiration, 76–7, 82, 102, 217, 218,
    224
world view, 30, 45–6, 49, 73, 75–6, 79,
    208

Young, G. M., 127, 231
youth, 37–8, 83–4, 92, 156

Zalai, Béla, 195

261